THE HISTORY & T
ASHBOURN, THE VAL
AND THE ADJACE

ASHBOURN

FROM THE DERBY ROAD.

Drawn & Printed by Rayner, Derby

Published by Dawson & Hobson, Ashbourn.

THE
HISTORY & TOPOGRAPHY
OF
ASHBOURN,
The Valley of the Dove,
AND
THE ADJACENT VILLAGES;
With Illustrations.

Dovedale.

THE

HISTORY AND TOPOGRAPHY

OF

ASHBOURN,

THE VALLEY OF THE DOVE,

AND THE

ADJACENT VILLAGES;

WITH BIOGRAPHICAL SKETCHES OF EMINENT NATIVES, &c.

Illustrated

BY NUMEROUS ORIGINAL DRAWINGS ON STONE, AND WOOD CUTS.

MOORLAND REPRINTS

First published 1839
This edition published 1978

ISBN 0 903485 49 4

British Library Cataloguing in Publication Data
The history and topography of Ashbourn,
  the Valley of the Dove, and the adjacent
  villages.
  1. Ashbourne region, Derbyshire – History
  942.5'13   DA690.A797

Printed in Great Britain by:
Redwood Burn Limited, Trowbridge & Esher

for the Publishers:
Moorland Publishing Company,
The Market Place, Hartington, Buxton,
Derbys, SK17 0AL, England

PREFACE.

THE following pages are the results of an attempt to illustrate in a popular manner the history and topography of that highly beautiful and diversified tract of country, THE VALLEY OF THE DOVE; of which, from its locality, the town of ASHBOURN may be said to form the central point. The first seven chapters of the work are confined principally to the general, parochial, and family history of that town; including also biographical sketches of its eminent natives or residents, from sources in some instances original, and in others scarce, or perhaps inaccessible to the general reader; and such of its historical, antiquarian, and literary reminiscences as were deemed worthy of preservation. The eighth chapter is devoted to a similar illustration of various hamlets, villages, and sites, immediately contiguous to the town; the ninth and following divisions, of those on the banks of the Dove, (traced downwards from her source), and one or two of her tributary streams.

To account for any incongruity of plan which may appear, it is proper to remark, that the latter chapters of the work form an extension of or addition to the original design. In the course of publication in a periodical form, the compilers received a degree of support, as encouraging as it was (in extent, at least) unexpected, from persons residing at a wide distance from the locality. To such readers, lengthened parochial details, connected with an isolated district, (which, had the prospectus been adhered to, must have occupied a very considerable space,) would of necessity prove tedious and barren of interest. That the work might sustain its popular character, and not disappoint their fair expectations, it was resolved to abridge much of that mere local information. A further inducement to the adoption of this plan was the desire to insure some remuneration for a large expenditure of labour and capital, (incidental to topographical works on the smallest scale,) which the support of the single district more directly interested, however cheerfully tendered, has in the vast majority of instances failed to secure.

Hence it was resolved to follow out in these historical and topographical sketches, the entire Valley of the Dove,—a field which, in addition to its claims in a picturesque point of view, presents some antiquarian remains, and other objects for illustration, possessing interest as well to the general reader, as to the local resident who has taste to appreciate what is beautiful, or to search out and inquire into the curious usages of olden times. And, after all, it is humbly believed, that the reader of the latter class will find in these pages an amount of really important information, bearing upon his own particular locality, as ample as any previous topographical work will afford.

How far the compilers have succeeded in the attempt to blend what is curious with that which is really useful, their subscribers and the public must determine. Imperfections of execution, and omissions, for some of which, however, they cannot be held responsible, will doubtless appear; perfect accuracy, too, in a work involving so many dates and circumstances, is not perhaps always attained, but the very favourable manner in which, from their very commencement, these papers have been noticed by the public press, leads the compilers to believe that their strenuous exertions to render them as a whole worthy of general acceptation, have not been unavailing.

One portion of this work, from the attention it has excited, seems to require a passing allusion,—that is, the memoir of Mr. Richard Cadman Etches. Had the career of that enterprising individual been less extraordinary, and his services to this country less important, it would have been needless for the compilers to assert, that they believe every tittle of this narrative to be literally and strictly correct; that no fact is exaggerated, and that the testimony of his contemporaries will confirm a statement derived from clear and incontrovertible documentary evidence.

It should be stated that the descriptions of the scenery of the Dove and of the country bordering upon it, as well as of those other objects most prominently deserving of notice, are for the most part the notes of an actual survey, undertaken during the summer of the last and the spring of the present year.

The compilers, in conclusion, would offer their best thanks to their numerous subscribers, and particularly to those among them who have aided their labours by the communication of articles of intelligence.

Ashbourn, June 20th, 1839.

CONTENTS.

ILLUSTRATIONS.

THE

HISTORY OF ASHBOURN,

AND OF

THE ADJACENT VILLAGES, &c.

THE
HISTORY OF ASHBOURN.

CHAPTER I.

Introductory Remarks.—First Historical Notice of the Town of Ashbourn.—
Notices of its Early Possessors from the time of William the Conqueror, down
to the 14th Year of the Reign of Edward IV.

FOR the most part the history of a town is written in
consequence of important, exciting, or instructive events
that have had birth within its walls. Notwithstanding, the
history of a town may be both entertaining and useful,
although it has not been the stage on which splendid actions
have been performed. A town may be so situated, as never
itself to have been the scene of such great deeds as to have
acquired for it a Roman or a Punic celebrity, and yet be the
point from which the historian may, with perfect judgment,
choose to view remarkable events that have occurred in its
vicinity. It may be a town, connected, on account of the
local jurisdiction centered in it, with villages and sites
whose traditions are interwoven with facts and circumstances
that claim the attention of the historian, and consequently
of each and every one of the enlightened or curious portion
of mankind. It may be a town so peculiarly and happily
situated, having its locality so beautifully and bounteously

1

favoured by nature, and which locality has been therefore
chosen for the congregated residences of men; and it also
may be so far the centre of many lovely spots, whose fertile
soil, productions, and delightful scenery, make it, as it were,
the minor metropolis of the villages and hamlets which lie
clustered around it, that the historian fixes upon it, not as
a subject for gorgeous description or highly-wrought recital,
but as one that affords scope for the relation of matters and
the painting of objects which come home to all men's
bosoms, but which interest more particularly, the affections
of those who have either been born in it, or in its neighbourhood, or whom circumstances have caused to become
temporary or permanent residents in it or its vicinity.

The town of Ashbourn possesses these supposed peculiarities and advantages; and for that reason it has been
deemed worthy of historical notice.

The period at which the first foundation of Ashbourn
took place, is not pointed out either by oral or written
tradition. It is buried in impenetrable obscurity. The first
mention of the town is to be found in Domesday-Book, and
its name in that celebrated survey is written *Esseburne.**

---

* Domesday Book, if not the most ancient, is yet the most venerable monument of Great Britain. It contains an account of all the lands in England,
except the four northern counties, Northumberland, Cumberland, Westmoreland,
and Durham, and part of Lancashire; and describes the quantity and particular nature of them, whether meadow, pasture, arable, wood, or waste land.
It mentions the rent and taxation, and records the several possessors of land,
their number and distinct degrees. King Alfred, about the year 900, compiled
a record of the like nature, of which this is in some measure a copy. The
reason assigned for the survey was, that every man should be satisfied with his
own right, and not usurp with impunity what belonged to another. By it, also,
the King (Wm. I.) would acquire an exact knowledge of the property of the
crown, by the forfeitures of the lands of the English nobility who fell at the
battle of Hastings; and he was thus enabled to remunerate his Norman followers, by the grants of their confiscated estates. When it has been necessary
to distinguish whether lands were held in ancient demesne, or in what other
manner, recourse has always been had to Domesday-Book, and to that only
to determine the question. The record is written on vellum, and is comprised
in two volumes. It is now deposited in the Chapter-House, Westminster.—
Grose's Antiquities.

As in the reign of Edward the Confessor, nothing can be traced to prove who was the particular possessor of the town and manor of Ashbourn, it must be supposed that they belonged to that prince; and, in consequence, William the Conqueror, who claimed the crown of England, which was bequeathed to him by the former monarch, took possession of Ashbourn, considering it a royal demesne. It is mentioned as being such in Domesday-Book, which was compiled about the year 1080, (fourteen years after the accession of William,) and as it did not come into the possession of William Ferrers until the 11th of July, in the first year of the reign of King John, (1199) it remained to a certainty, and without interruption, a royal demesne, for upwards of the space of 133 years. Indeed it seems very probable that under the Saxon domination, it always formed part of the royal demesnes.

It will be a curious thing to trace, as far as correct public and documentary information will permit, the different services performed by the several individuals who obtained, by royal charter, possession of the town and manor

---

The following is a translation of the passage in Domesday-Book which refers to Ashbourn:

"*In Esseburne there are three carucates of land to be taxed. Land to three ploughs. It is waste, yet it pays twenty shillings. There is a priest and a church, with one carucate of land to be taxed; and he has there two villanes and two bordars, having half a plough. Himself has one plough, and one vassal who pays sixteen-pence; and twenty acres of meadow. These five manors, Derelei, Metesford, Werchesuorde, Esseburne, and Peureuuic, with their berewicks, paid in King Edward's time, thirty-two pounds, and six sextaries and a half of honey, now forty pounds of pure silver.*"

[A *villane* held a small portion of land under his lord, and was bound to certain services in return; a *bordar* was a cottager; and the term *berewick* signified a village or hamlet.]

The writer conjectures, that the term *Esseburne* simply means *ash-brook*. It is a very common thing throughout England, and particularly in Derbyshire and Staffordshire, to have the first syllable of the names of towns and villages formed from the appellation of the things for which the vicinity of the brooks or *bourns* on which they were first built were at the time remarkable. *Farey* remarks that some parts of Derbyshire are particularly favourable to the growth of the ash, and that several places seem to have derived the prefix of their names from it.

of Ashbourn. In doing so, it will of course be demon-
strated, for what good or evil deeds, supposed or real, those
demesnes were granted to, or wrested from the different
possessors.

During the early disputes between the baronial power
and the kingly, the possession of Ashbourn often changed
hands. The gift of the town and castle of Tutbury was
chiefly conferred by the crown as a recompense for eminent
services. The lords of what is called *The Honor of Tutbury*
were, in consequence of such right, lords of the manor and
town of Ashbourn, and it will not be incorrect to infer that
they ranked amongst the most distinguished, the most
powerful, and the most wealthy noblemen in the land. The
history of those individuals is therefore intimately linked
with that of Ashbourn; and, in consequence of that
connexion, it has been judged necessary to make brief
allusion to the events in which they were concerned.

In the well-known document, called "The Roll of Battell
Abbeie," which contains a list of the names of the noblemen
and gentlemen who fought under the Duke of Normandy,
at the battle of Hastings, is to be found that of Henry de
Ferraris or Ferrers. When, by chance of battle, the Duke
became the first of the Norman line that reigned in
England, Henry de Ferrers was an especial favourite with
that monarch, and the town and castle of Tutbury were
granted to him. The motives that induced the king to hold
this nobleman in such high estimation, proceeded from the
experience of his great political knowledge and integrity.
He was appointed under royal commission, to superintend the general survey of the kingdom, the result of which
is to be found in Domesday-Book. It appears from this
survey, that besides Tutbury, he possessed seven lordships
in Staffordshire, thirty-five in Leicestershire, six in Warwickshire, three in Nottinghamshire, and *ninety-five* in
Derbyshire. He left at his death but one son, named
Robert, his two other sons having died during the life-time
of their father. This Robert, in consequence of the personal

valour he displayed in repelling the invasion of David, King of Scotland, was created an earl by King Stephen. Robert de Ferrers led under him in this campaign, a body of soldiers chiefly raised in Derbyshire, and he had recourse to the following plan in order to animate his troops. He promised a considerable grant of land in Needwood Forest to the man who should most distinguish himself by daring deeds of arms. The contending armies met near Northallerton, and the encouragement held out produced the desired effect, for the Scotch, though they made an obstinate resistance, were routed with great loss. The Derbyshire men greatly distinguished themselves throughout the battle, and one of them, named Ralph, claimed and obtained the promised grant of land. This earl was succeeded by a son of the same name, who did not distinguish himself by any remarkable action. He was succeeded by his son William, who rebelled against Henry II. and participated in the treason of the unnatural sons of that great but unhappy monarch.

These were the immediate ancestors of William, Earl Ferrers, created in consequence of his loyalty and great services, Earl of Derby, by King John, in the first year of that monarch's reign. This title was bestowed by a special charter, at Northampton; and it is said that on this occasion the King himself girded him with a sword. He obtained a grant of every third penny out of the pleas that came before the sheriff of the county of Derby. He also received many other royal grants, and among them, on the 11th of July in the same year, (1199) the grant in fee-farm to himself and his heirs, of the manors of Wirksworth and Ashbourn, together with the whole Wapentake, on condition that he paid to the Exchequer £70 at Michaelmas and Easter, by even portions. In the fifth year of the same reign, he obtained a grant of the *inheritance* of these manors, with the Wapentake, for which grant he paid 500 marks. He received many other valuable estates from King John, and when the Pope had deposed that weak and vicious

Prince, the Earl proved to him his fidelity, and showed at the same time, the great influence of his own character, by becoming surety that John should adhere to those degrading conditions to which the Pope had obliged him to submit. He was also of great service to Henry the Third, and was fixed upon as one of the arbitrators between that monarch and his disaffected barons. He died in the year 1247, at an advanced age.

He was succeeded by his son William, who was chiefly remarkable for the prudence with which he managed his vast estates. He died in the year 1254.

The last of this family that possessed the town and manor of Ashbourn, was Robert, eldest son of the late Earl. Unfortunately for himself, he was but a youth at the time of his father's death. The early loss of a wise and virtuous parent, proved to him, as it must do to all children, the severest of misfortunes. Naturally fickle and perverse, his disposition, uncurbed by parental authority, at length became outrageous. No sooner had he obtained his majority, than he threw off the shackles of restraint, openly rebelled against the king, and yet was not prudent enough to act in concert with the other powerful barons who opposed their sovereign. His extensive estates furnished him with many followers; and the first use he made of their services was, to enter Worcester, which city he pillaged, destroyed the unoffending Jews that dwelt there, plundered both the private and religious houses, and did much damage to the crown lands in the neighbourhood. The King, to punish the Earl for this outrage upon the royal property, sent his son Edward with a large army against him. The castle of Tutbury was demolished; the lands around it laid waste with fire and sword, and the peaceful occupiers of them thus suffered for offences of which they were guiltless. The Earl, notwithstanding, continued to make war against the King. When the King, by the bravery of Prince Edward, was rescued, from the hands of the Barons, and his authority comparatively restored, he resolved to punish the Earl of Derby. The Earl was charged with high crimes and misdemeanors, and a day was fixed for his trial; but anticipating his conviction as certain, he acknowledged his guilt, and appealed to the King's mercy. He received at the monarch's hands more clemency and generosity than he merited. On the following mild conditions he obtained his pardon, viz: that he should present the King with a cup of gold, set with precious stones, and pay a fine of 1,500 marks; with an express understanding, however, that if ever he rebelled again, he should be totally disinherited. In the very face of these solemn engagements with the King, the Earl of Derby once more rebelled, and having raised an army in the northern parts of Derbyshire, he took forcible possession of Chesterfield. His treason and treachery did not long remain unpunished; for Henry, the eldest son of the King of Almaine, attacked him there on the 24th of May, 1266, and completely routed his forces. It was with difficulty that he escaped from the field of battle to the church, in which he concealed himself under some bags of wool. One solitary individual perceived him in his retreat: this was a young female, whose lover had been compelled to fight for the Earl, and had fallen in the battle. Looking upon this perfidious nobleman as the sole cause of her misfortunes, she pointed out to his enemies the place of his concealment. He was immediately dragged from it, and conveyed, under a strong escort, to London, where he was thrown into prison. The same year he was attainted, and his confiscated lands were given to Edmund, the son of Henry the Third, by two grants from that King, bearing date the 28th of June, and 5th of August, 1266. It will be perceived, from the foregoing historical data, that the town and manor of Ashbourn remained in possession of the family of Ferrers, from the 11th of July, 1199, to the 28th of June, 1266, a period of about 67 years.*

---

*Among the arms of the first possessors of the town and manor of Ashbourn, painted on the windows of the church, those of the family of Ferrers are still visible.

2

Edmund of Lancaster, surnamed Crouchback, a scion of royalty, now becomes possessor of the town and manor of Ashbourn.   In his youth he was invested with the title of King of Sicily, the symbol of his authority being a sancti-fied ring, sent him by the Pope; but this investiture was only a pretence of his Holiness, to draw large sums of money from this country.   He was also made Earl of Chester, and had the lands of Simon de Montford, with the Honor of Leicester granted him, on the death of that nobleman at the battle of Evesham.   He accompanied his brother (Edward I.) to the Holy land, and on his return he had a renewal of the grant of the wapentake of Wirksworth, with the manors of Wirksworth and Ashbourn, and again, in the 13th year of the same reign, he received a further confirmation of all the lands of Robert de Ferrers.   In the year 1297, he accompanied the Earl of Lincoln and others, to the siege of Bayonne, where he died.*

---

*It appears, that in the fourth year of the reign of Edward I. an inquiry was made into the state of the Royal Burgs, by certain officers of the Crown. The following document embodies the result of this inquiry, in reference to Ashbourn; and it contains some curious particulars respecting the local govern-ment of the town at this early period :—

" The officers declare, that the masters of the hospital of St. John de Yeveley have tenants under them, from the other side of the water of Esseburne, called Schole Brook, in the Wapentake of Lutchyrch, who sell bread and ale contrary to the assize, and that the said masters receive the bread and ale so sold unjustly, to the great prejudice and injury of the freemen and the Burg of Esseburne, and they know not by what warrant.   They also declare, that the said masters of the hospital appropriate to themselves, and seduce persons from the Royal Burg of Esseburne to be tenants under themselves and under their protection, whence the lord the King loses toll and passage-fees from tenants of this kind.   And also the masters have made for themselves a new stamp and stamp gallon and bushel measures, without such warrant as the inhabitants of the Burg have been accustomed to. And the said masters have an oven for mak-ing saleable bread, to the grievous loss of the aforesaid royal Burg of Esseburne. Also they declare, that from that side of the aforesaid water, there is a certain township called Campdene-street, [Compton] which ought to be as it were a country village : and that men remain in the said township, and sell bread and ale, contrary to the Assize, and without warrant.   And that they put the said bread for sale into their windows, and they use the aforesaid stamp for bread, for bottles, and for bushels, without warrant, to the great loss of our said Lord, the King. They also declare, that Robert de Mapleton has an oven in that part in Campdene-street, and that he had spoken with a certain Robert of Esseburne, who then possessed the said village, concerning a firm agreement; and he conceded to the said Robert of Esseburne, that for the space of one year he might make bread for sale in the aforesaid oven; whence on account of that oven, and the oven of the above-named Masters of the Hospital, the said Burg of the lord the King was greatly injured and aggrieved. And that Thomas, the son and heir of the said Robert de Mapleton, holds the said oven for a yearly sum of money, which sum of money ought to be paid yearly to our Lord, the King, on account of an agreement sanctioned between Robert, Earl Ferrers, and Henry de Esseburne, and this Agreement bears date in the reign of the late Lord King, Henry III. and runs thus—' Of those who possess liberties granted them by our Lord, the King, &c.' [At this time, the Lords of Manors monopolised the privilege of baking their tenants' bread, at the common *fourne*, or oven.]

" They also declare, that Thomas de Mapleton, Richard Hervi, Nicholas de Mercinton, and Henry of Esseburne, Clerk, do not rightly exercise the freedom of the town of Esseburne, as they ought to do, for that they fine the bakers and the brewers in their absence, and not in full court, as was customary to be done; and that they fine them at their own discretion; and that there used to be in the said town only two assessors, and that now there are four, contrary to the liberty of the aforesaid town, and therefore to the grievous loss and detriment of the aforesaid Burg of our Lord the King, who now reigns.

" And further, they declare, that a certain vicar, namely, of the Church of Esseburne, obstructed a path-way near Lovedich, and that Peter de Wyneton, now Rector of the Church, supports him in that injury. They also declare, that a certain Ranulph of Mercinton, obstructed another path leading out of the King's highway from Esseburne to Scholebrook, between the new place and tenement of the said Ranulph : and Roger de Mercinton abets him in the same injury.

" Of military tenures, &c :—They declare that two messuages at the end of the town of Esseburne towards Underwood, were given in charity to the Abbey of Miravalli, [in the county of Warwick] to make for the monks of that place a house of hospitality, by Lord William, the old Earl Ferrers, that nothing is paid, and that the messuages are lying waste.

" Concerning the clergy and other magistrates :—They declare, that Thomas de Gloucheswich was seized and detained in person, and put in chains, on suspicion, and liberated by Henry Oweyn, then bailiff of Lord Edmund, for XLs.

"Persons they fined and liberated in the time of the late King Henry:—They also declare that Laurence, Clerk, and Nicholas of Mercinton, in the time of the late King Henry, by night seized two men and two women of Esseburne, upon suspicion, and took from them a certain quantity of wax and cloth, of the value of XXs. and more, and promised them to get a warrant respecting the wax and cloth, which they have never restored."

The town and manor of Ashbourn, next came into the possession of Thomas, second Earl of Lancaster. The readers of English history will recollect that this was the famous Earl of Lancaster who, not being able to brook the indignities done to the English barons, by Gavestone and the Spencers, minions of Edward the Second, passed his life in a state of open warfare with that weak and effeminate monarch. He was at length taken prisoner, arraigned before a council of the King's officers, tried by court-martial, instead of by his own peers, and was condemned to be hanged, drawn, and beheaded; which execution he suffered near Pontefract, under circumstances of the greatest indignity.

The King, after the death of this Earl, seized upon all his estates, so that Ashbourn once more became a demesne of the Crown. It would appear that it did not remain so long, as all the estates belonging to the late Earl of Lancaster were consigned to the custody of Roger Beler, of Kirkby Belers, in the county of Leicester, who was attached to the King's person. This individual, however, might only be a *locum tenens* for the King. The unhappy Edward the Second in a short time became the captive of Henry de Lancaster, brother to the late Earl; but it being judged that this keeper's treatment of the deposed monarch was too humane, he was delivered into less merciful hands, and by them barbarously murdered at Berkeley.

In the first year of the reign of Edward the Third, (1327) Henry de Lancaster, laid claim to the estates possessed by his late brother; and his claim rested upon the ground that his brother had not been tried by his peers, according to law and Magna Charta. His claim was allowed, and an act of Parliament was passed, which reversed the attainder of Thomas, Earl of Lancaster. Consequently, Tutbury, and the places within its Honor, returned again into the possession of the house of Lancaster.

There are few transactions of the life of this Henry, Earl of Lancaster upon record, which are at all connected with the Honor of Tutbury. It is, however, completely certain that he was lord of the manor of Ashbourn, since, as superior lord of the Honor of Tutbury, he claimed the manor and wapentake of Wirksworth, and a toll upon all cattle and merchandise offered for sale in the town of Ashbourn; and these claims were fully confirmed. He died at Leicester, in the year 1345.*

The son of this Earl of Lancaster was the next owner of the manor of Ashbourn. He was created, during his father's life-time, Earl of Derby; and in consequence of the greater part of his life having been passed in foreign service, there are few circumstances to record respecting his connexion with the Honor of Tutbury. In 1351, he was created a Duke, and was the first English subject, except those of royal blood, who had been invested with that title since the time of the Norman conquest. He was one of the greatest captains of the age. His chivalrous exploits formed a theme of exultation to every Englishman, and produced a paralysing dread in the hearts of all his opponents. He died of the plague, at Leicester, on the 24th of March, 1361. This nobleman left two daughters, Maud and Blanch, between whom his extensive possessions were divided. Blanch received for her portion those estates which had previously formed the earldoms of Derby and Lancaster. She became the consort of the renowned John of Gaunt, and it seems more than probable, that through this alliance, he became lord of the manor of Ashbourn. The Honor of Tutbury certainly belonged to her. At her death John of Gaunt married Constance, Queen of Castile, and that lady resided almost constantly at Tutbury; whence it must be inferred, that by the death of his first wife, Blanch, who inherited the estates of the Earls of Derby, the Duke of Lancaster did not lose possession of those places comprehended within the Honor of Tutbury. When the Duke died, Richard the Second, who was his nephew,

---

*It is stated by several writers, that Roger Mortimer, Earl of March, procured from Edward III. for his son, a grant of Risley, and Ashbourn in the Peak.— If the Earl of March did possess the manor of Ashbourn, it must have been for a short period, during the boyhood of Edward III.

seized upon all his property, and gave orders that the rents
and revenues arising from his estates should be forthwith
paid to himself. It is therefore reasonable to suppose, that
the town and manor of Ashbourn once more became a royal
demesne. On the accession of Henry the Fourth, the
Castle and Honor of Tutbury, and the rest of the Duchy of
Lancaster, were annexed to the crown.*

It is satisfactorily proved, by a document, drawn up in the
second year of the reign of Henry V. called "TheCoucher,"
that the manor of Ashbourn at that time formed part and
parcel of the Honor of Tutbury. An officer, called a 'bailiff'
was then appointed to protect the interests of the Honor in
this town.

The next person to whom the manor of Ashbourn
belonged, was George, Duke of Clarence, chiefly known
by the whimsical choice of the manner in which he
wished to die, when adjudged guilty of high treason against
his brother, Edward IV. That choice was, to be drowned
in a butt of Malvoisie. When Edward IV. had obtained
ascendancy over the weak and unfortunate Henry VI., he
dissevered the Honor of Tutbury from the paternal estates
of the deposed monarch, and granted it, in the fifth year
of his reign, to George, Duke of Clarence, and his heirs:
it was not long, however, before that ambitious and fickle
prince joined the Earl of Warwick in rebellion against
his royal brother, and although a partial reconciliation took
place between them, Edward thought fit to annul the grant
he had before made; and in the thirteenth year of his reign,
he issued a warrant to resume the possession of these estates,
and they were accordingly granted in that year, to Thomas,
Archbishop of Canterbury, and other trustees, to hold for
the King, during his absence in France. The Honor and
Castle of Tutbury have ever since remained part of the
Duchy of Lancaster.†

---

*At some period in this reign, John Mowbray, Duke of Norfolk, is said to have
held the manor.

† See *Sir O. Mosley's History of Tutbury*, from which, and from public and
private documentary information, the preceding facts have been derived.

CHAPTER II.

Continuation of the History of the Early Possessors of Ashbourn.—The Cokayne Family.—Public Events which occurred in the town and Neighbourhood, during the Great Rebellion.—Skirmishes between the Royalists and the Parliamentarians.—Biographical Sketch of Mr. John Hieron, an eminent Nonconformist Minister.

The Manor of Ashbourn, it is supposed, continued to be annexed to the Earldom and Duchy of Lancaster, from the reign of Edward the Fourth, until that of Charles the First. There is, however, no doubt but that, between these periods, the manor came into the possession of the heads of the very ancient family of the Cokaynes. This family flourished in the town as early as the reign of Edward I. They subsequently possessed considerable estates in the town and neighbourhood, and Ashbourn Hall was, for several generations, their principal residence, but at what particular time they held the manorial rights of the town, cannot be clearly proved.

The following were the most distinguished members of this ancient and honourable family.* John Cokayne, who

---

*Sir Aston Cokayne affirms, in one of his poems, that his ancestor, Cokayne, a knight, was allied to the Conqueror, and lived in his reign, at Hemingham Castle, where "lately hung his bow and arrows, his sword and buckler;" and that all this was attested by "Mr. John Cokayne, of Rushton, my lord's cousin-germane, who had an antient evidence to prove it."

was chosen to represent the county of Derby in several parliaments and councils, during the reign of Edward III. His eldest son, Edmund, appears to have been the first of the family that was knighted, and he added considerably to the estates and influence of his family, by marrying Elizabeth, daughter of Richard de Herthill, and heiress to that property. The brother of Sir Edmund was Sir John Cokayne, ancestor of the Cokaynes of Hatley, in Bedfordshire. He was one of the most celebrated of the family, since it appears that he was Recorder of London, and Parliamentary representative of the county of Derby, in the reigns of Richard II. and Henry IV. He was afterwards Chief Baron of the Exchequer, and one of the Justices of the Court of Common Pleas. He steadily adhered to the cause of King Henry IV. and was slain at the battle of Shrewsbury. Thomas Cokayne chiefly resided at Pooley, in Warwickshire : he lived in the reign of Henry VII. and was killed in Polesworth church-yard, in a quarrel with Thomas Burdett, Esq. of Bramcote. His son, Sir Thomas, was present with King Henry VIII. at the sieges of Therovenne and Tournay, and in consequence of his gallant conduct, he was created a banneret in the open field. His grandson, Sir Thomas Cokayne, served under the Earl of Hertford, and was knighted at the taking of Edinburgh, in 1544. He was several times High Sheriff for the counties of Derby and Nottingham, and contributed £50 to the fund that was raised to meet the expences of opposing the Spanish Armada. He died in 1592.*

Sir Aston Cokayne, the most widely-known of the family, was son of Thomas Cokayne,† by Anne, daughter of Sir John Stanhope, of Elvaston. He received his education at Trinity College, Cambridge, and afterwards entered the

---

*He was the author of a short Treatise on Hunting, which is now extremely rare.

†This Thomas Cokayne was born at Mappleton, where the family appear to have had a seat. He resided in London, under the feigned name of Brown, and was buried in the church of St. Giles's in the Fields.

Inns of Court, in London. He married the daughter of
Sir Gilbert Kniveton, of Mercaston. Sir Aston suffered
much during the civil wars in the reign of Charles the First,
on account of his religion, which was that of the Church of
Rome. It seems, that either in consequence of his attachment to the House of Stuart, or, more probably, on account
of his personal extravagance, that his property became
greatly lessened long before his death. He retired to his
estate at Pooley, where he gave himself up to his books and
his boon companions. His literary acquaintances were
numerous, and they comprised the first writers and wits of
the age. In one of his epigrams, he boasts of his intimacy
with Donne, Suckling, Randolph, Drayton, Massinger,
Habbington, Sandys, May, Jonson, and others. This
epigram is addressed to his cousin, the celebrated Charles
Cotton, better known by his treatise on angling, than by
his many other literary productions. The mind of Sir Aston
was evidently very highly cultivated, and his talents were
great; though he did not possess much of that rare capacity
which is understood by the vague appellation of 'genius.'
His studies were chiefly confined to the poetry of his time,
and to that portion of it most deeply marked with cavalier
levity. His poems principally consist of addresses to his
literary contemporaries, and to the heads of families resident
in his own neighbourhood.* Towards the end of his life
his pecuniary matters became extremely embarrassed, for
he was obliged to sell his lordship of Pooley to Humphrey
Jennings, Esq., reserving to himself, however, a small
annuity. In the year 1671, he joined with his son, Thomas
Cokayne, (the last male heir of this branch of the family) in
the sale of his "fair lordship of Ashbourn," to Sir William
Boothby, Bart., of Broadlow Ash: thus giving the finishing

*His works are now become very scarce, and are eagerly sought after. The
copy from which this information has chiefly been derived, forms a part of
the valuable collection of Derbyshire works, in the library of Thomas Bateman,
Esq. of Middleton.

3

stroke to an old and venerable inheritance. Sir Aston then
retired to Derby, where he died in February, 1683, aged 76.

During the unhappy civil dissensions in the reign of the
first Charles, which have been before alluded to, several
skirmishes took place between the contending parties, in
the town and neighbourhood of Ashbourn. Sir John Gell
was commissioned by the Earl of Essex, leader of the
Parliamentary forces, to raise a regiment in support of their
cause.* Of this regiment, Sir John was appointed colonel,
and his brother, Thomas Gell, Esq., lieutenant-colonel.
From the *parliamentarian* accounts† of the transactions in
which the regiment was engaged, it appears, that Sir
Richard Fleetwood, on the side of the royalists, had
fortified his house (Wootton Lodge.) "Here," says the
narrator, "he increased very strong, both in horse and foot,
and did great hurt in plundering the traffique betwixt
Lancashire, Cheshire, and Derby, by robbing and stopping
of carriers, which went weekly from Manchester to London."
Another account says, that "this was one of the strongest
places in the county, exceedingly well provided with all
necessaries." As may naturally be supposed, the neighbouring inhabitants suffered considerably from the depredations thus committed. The fact having been made

---

*When Sir John Gell had declared himself in favour of the parliament, he
assembled his regiment at Chesterfield; upon which the Earls of Devonshire
and Chesterfield, the High Sheriff; Sir John Harpur, Bart. of Calke; Sir John
Fitzherbert, of Norbury; Sir Edward Vernon, and many others of the nobility
and gentry of the county, who were mostly royalists, assembled at Tutbury, to
concert measures for preventing his further progress.   The result of the
conference was a remonstrance against Sir John's proceedings; to which he
replied, that " he was surprised they should so soon become jealous of him, who
was a countryman of their own, and well known to all of them; that his
intentions were honourable; and that his only desire was to clear the country of
thieves and robbers, who preyed upon the public; and to maintain the laws of
the land and the liberties of the subject."—*History of Tutbury.*

Sir John Gell, Bart. was of the Hopton family, and the present Philip Gell,
Esq. is descended from him.

†Sir John Gell's and Sir George Gresley's MSS. Narratives ; These accounts
are chiefly confined to the proceedings of the Parliamentarian forces : consequently, they make but little reference to the successful actions of the royalists.

known to Sir John Gell, he dispatched his lieutenant-colonel, with a force of about four hundred foot, and one troop of horse, against Sir Richard Fleetwood. They laid siege to his house, took it by storm, and carried Sir Richard and his whole party, in number about seventy, prisoners to Derby. These transactions took place in the year 1643.

In the winter of that year, Colonel Gell ordered Major Mollanus, at the head of a party of 250 horse, to proceed to Leek, at which place Sir Thomas Fairfax was expected to join him. Major Mollanus, receiving intelligence, on his route into Staffordshire, that the royalists' forces had fallen upon the Moorlanders, at Hartington, immediately marched to their relief. Before his arrival, however, the royalists had taken all the infantry, in number about 240; but the cavalry had effected their escape. These prisoners were afterwards liberated by Colonel Gell. Resuming his march to Leek, Major Mollanus overtook and attacked the royalists, who were on their way to the same place. He succeeded in routing them: killing five officers, and taking thirty-five prisoners. The parliamentarian forces remained at Leek about fourteen days; Sir Thomas Fairfax not arriving, they then retreated to Derby, and on their way to that town, took twenty-six prisoners at Ashbourn.

In the month of February, 1644, the royalists from Bakewell, and other parts of the county, daily assembled at Ashbourn, in such force as to obstruct all communication between the town and the neighbouring villages; thereby preventing the country people from attending the market. Information of this state of things having been conveyed to Colonel Gell, he dispatched a party of 500 horse, under the command of Major Sanders, with orders to disperse the royalists; which orders were speedily executed. The parliamentarian troops remained in the town for some time, and the royalists formed the design of surprising them; for which purpose they assembled a strong force. Major Sanders, having been apprised of their intention, drew his dragoons into the lanes and hedges in the outskirts of the town, and falling upon the rear of the royalists, he routed them, pursuing them as far as the village of Tissington, where they were completely defeated, with the loss of 170 prisoners, and numbers killed and wounded.

The royalists soon afterwards assembled in great force, in and near Lichfield, Burton, and Ashby-de-la-Zouch, with the design of marching to the relief of Wingfield Manor, then closely besieged by Colonel Gell. That officer immediately sent. Major Sanders, with a party of dragoons, into the neighbourhood of Derby, to intercept them. Having had intimation that a detachment of the royalists, under the command of Colonel Eyre, lay in Boylston church, Major Sanders and his dragoons proceeded thither. Alighting from their horses, they surrounded the church, and captured the whole regiment: " soe taking men, armes, collours, and all, without loss of one man on either side." The Major then attacked the royalists, at Burton-on-Trent, and, after some sharp fighting, succeeded in driving them from the town.   In this affair, the royalists had seventeen killed, and many made prisoners; the latter were marched to Boylston, and, for security, were lodged in the church, with those previously captured.   The whole of these prisoners were then conveyed to Derby.

At an early period of the war, the Castle of Tutbury was garrisoned for the king.   In the year 1644, Colonel Gell formed the determination of stationing some of his own troops in its vicinity, to watch the proceedings of the garrison.   For this purpose, he fortified Barton House,* which was well situated for intercepting the communication between the castle and the northern parts of the counties of Derby and Stafford. From this garrison many attacks were successfully made against the royalists, who also suffered

---

*Barton House is situated in the parish of Barton Blount, about eight miles from Ashbourn. The old hall was a castellated building, surrounded by a moat. The present owner has enlarged and modernized the building.   It stands in a fine open country, surrounded by excellent land, about four miles from Tutbury.
Glover.

considerably by the loss of their supplies. On the 12th of August, 1645, shortly after the fatal battle of Naseby, the unfortunate Charles, with the remnant of his army, consisting of 3,000 men, paid his last visit to his loyal garrison of Tutbury.* The next day he proceeded to Ashbourn, but during his march to this town, he was much harassed by a party of 500 dragoons, from the garrison of Barton House, who attacked the rear of his army. A sharp skirmish took place, and the royalists appear to have had the advantage. After they had lost four or five men, and had twenty wounded, they joined the King at Ashbourn.† The parliamentarian narrative states, that in this encounter, the royalists lost twenty-six men. The King and his army then proceeded on their march to Doncaster. The subsequent events in the life of the unhappy monarch are well known to every reader of history.

In this reign, the town of Ashbourn was favoured with the ministerial labours of Mr. John Hieron, a divine of the most exemplary character, and possessed of extraordinary talent and acquirements. At that period, when it was extremely hazardous for any minister to distinguish himself by unflinching adherence to the strict letter of the gospel, Mr. Hieron, rather than swerve from his already-declared and fixed principles, preferred to suffer a very severe and harassing persecution.

---

*This Castle was one of the last places within the county which held out for the King: the natural strength of its situation, and the well-known bravery of its garrison, rendered it almost impregnable. Incessant fatigue and badness of diet, at length brought disease into the garrison; and this calamity was followed by the arrival of a large army, under Sir William Brereton, who closely invested the castle. The garrison held out for about three weeks, when it surrendered, on the 20th of April 1646. The governor of the castle was Sir Andrew Kniveton, of Bradley, near Ashbourn, and Mercaston, in the county of Derby. He was so impoverished by the civil wars, that he sold the family estates, and the title is now extinct.—*History of Tutbury.*

†It is said, that during his stay in the town, the King attended Divine service at the church. The following is an extract from the church-register of this period:—" 1645, August. King Charles came to the church, and many more, and talked with Mr. Peacock,"[the vicar.]

In order to rescue the memory of this worthy man from
oblivion, it has been deemed necessary to enter, at some
length, into the details of his life.   As some of the events
in which he was concerned, are connected with the civil
commotions just noticed, these details are here introduced.
With the exception of some slight alterations, they are
presented in the language of his original biographer.*

John Hieron was born in the year 1608, at Stapenhill,
of which village his father was vicar.   He received his
education at Repton School, "and here," his biographer
remarks, "he got that foundation of school learning, that
bore a very great superstructure of divinity, history, and
philosophy." He then entered Christ's College, Cambridge.
His first appointment was that of chaplain to Sir H. Leigh,
of Eggington.   About the year 1632, Catharine, Countess
of Chesterfield, a pious lady, of noble extraction, wished to
engage Mr. Hieron to preach a weekly lecture at Bretby.
This additional duty he also accepted.   In the ensuing
year, he removed to Ashbourn; and the following are the
circumstances attendant on his introduction to the town.

'Mr. Joseph Taylor, Lecturer and Master of the Grammar School, being
disabled by sickness, from fulfilling his duties, had engaged Mr. Hieron to
supply his place. Mr. Taylor, wishing to resign the latter situation, set himself to
work, and improved his interest in the company, (consisting of three Governors
and twelve Assistants,) in whom the right of election lay, and engaged ten of
them for Mr. Hieron. But it being noised abroad that the situation would soon
become vacant, one Mr. Cox put in for it, who, though he could not gain the
majority of the Governors and Assistants, yet, through the influence of some
great neighbours, obtained the support of a majority of the heirs of the
founders, who had power to stop the election.   Mr. Taylor having resigned,
twelve out of the fifteen Governors and Assistants chose Mr. Hieron.   But the
heirs of the founders not consenting, the election was not ratified, and so it fell
to the Bishop of the Diocese to choose.   Mr. Hieron, was examined by Basier,
the Bishop's chaplain, who commended him much for his skill in the tongues.
The Bishop readily gave him his title.   But a question now arose, whether
Bishop Merton, being then elect of Durham, could act as Bishop of Lichfield
and Coventry.   Hereupon application was made to Archbishop Abbot, and he
gave Mr. Hieron his title.   Then a new dispute arose, that it was only the
bishop of the Diocese that could give the title; and that therefore it could not

---

*The Life of Mr. John Hieron, by Robert Porter.   London: 1691.

be done until the Bishoprick were filled. When Bishop Wright was installed, each party applied to him; he recommended that both Mr. Hieron and Mr. Cox should be set aside, which was accordingly done; and a Mr. Mountney was then proposed and elected. Mr. Hieron was content; " having the Lecture at the truly honourable the Countess of Chesterfield's, (for which she promised him ten pounds a year, but gave him twelve,") he deeemed that sufficient, and would gladly have resigned at an early stage of the contest.

' After the Lecturer's place was void, by the death of Mr. Taylor, the trustees chose Mr. Hieron as his successor. Mountney proved to be a most immoral character, a great dishonour to the School, and a vexation to the town. Application was made to the Bishop to remove him; but he alleged he could not. The Governors then stopped his salary, and afterwards articled against him in the High Commission; but that way giving them no relief, they were at last forced to sue him at common law. The cause came for trial before Judge Hatton, or his colleague, and Mountney was cast and ejected.'

The malevolent feelings which this contest excited in the minds of Mr. Hieron's opponents, were the cause of his first troubles. In December, 1637, Mr. Hieron and Mr. Lees, of Ashbourn, were summoned to appear before the High Commission, at the Manor of Lambeth, to answer to such articles as should be exhibited against them. The summons was delivered by a ' pursuivant, who had his fees: and Mr. Hieron's share was four pounds. To London they accordingly went, and made their way to Holt, who was *apparitor apparitorum.* He, when treated with sack and paid with gold, shewed them the articles, which contained trivial charges, incapable of proof: against Mr. Lees, it was urged, "*that when he was churchwarden, he had brewed ale in the church !*"* The charges against Mr. Hieron were, that in preaching from that text, "*Fear God, and honour the king*," he had said "*there were some who neither feared God, nor honoured the king, but walked the streets with impudent faces ;*" whereby he meant as they suggested, my lord Bishop and Andrew Kniveton. And that he had used the expression, "*removing mountains*," whereby he meant to cast reflections on Mr. Mountney, the Governors of the

* This charge had no other foundation than a remark of one of the workmen employed in pointing the church steeple, " *that the mortar should be tempered with liquor made of malt !*" '

Grammar School having *removed* him from his situation.'
No prosecutor appearing to prove these ridiculous charges,
Mr. Hieron and Mr. Lees employed a proctor to move, that
since no prosecutor appeared, the Court would dismiss
them. 'He, like a proctor of such a Court, moved that the
Court itself would appoint a prosecutor.' At length,
through the interference of Dr. Bray, the Archbishop's
chaplain, they obtained their discharge.

'When the civil wars broke out, a party of the royalists,
under Sir Francis Wortley, came to Ashbourn. In the
dead of the night, Captains Bard and Dennis broke into
Mr. Hieron's house, and took him from his bed. Captain
Dennis said to Mr. Hieron, "Gentlemen cannot drink the
King's health; but you must reprove them for it." They
then conveyed him to their court of guard, and kept him
there until morning; when, urging him to speak of many
things, they lay at catch for matter to accuse him. Sir
Francis Wortley charged him with preaching against
episcopacy; he answered "Never! but against the exorbi-
tancies of it." His wife's father passed his word for him,
which was at present satisfying. The next day he appeared,
Sir Francis inclined to release him; but would have him
call the parliament "a company of dissemblers:" this he
refused to do. In the upshot they discharged him. He then
desired his horse and saddle might be restored: "Nay,"
saith Sir Francis, "you may be glad you are at liberty
yourself." During his imprisonment, Captain Bard had
been with an honourable person then living in Ashbourn,
Mrs. Cokayne, (half-sister to Philip, Earl of Chesterfield,)
a royalist, of highest elevation, yet a woman of sense, that
knew Mr. Hieron's worth, and bare a fair respect to him.
She represented him in his true character to Captain Bard,
which he credited, and was so convinced, that he came to
Mr. Hieron to excuse himself; and told him that they, (the
royalists) "did not molest him, until they had received some
scores of complaints against him: through which they
thought him to be one that had no fellow: but now he

(Captain Bard) perceived his mistake, and was sorry for what had occurred. He then exerted himself to procure the restoration of Mr. Hieron's horse, which he effected on payment of twenty shillings for him. The Captain was so ingenuous, that after his departure from Ashbourn, he wrote to Mr. Hieron, requesting his forgiveness.' 'Thus,' adds the biographer, ' God brought forth this good man's righteousness, to the shame of his false accusers.'

This lawless outrage, it appears, was instigated by some gentlemen of the town, whom Mr. Hieron had thought proper to rebuke, for the licentiousness of their conduct, in openly 'drinking healths' in the market-place, on the Sabbath-day. In these unsettled times, a general laxity of opinion prevailed in reference to the observance of that day. A book, professedly in defence of Sabbath-day sports, now made its appearance; and the people were not slow to avail themselves of its authority. Bear-baiting, ' shooting at the butts,' and other out-door sports, were openly practised in Ashbourn, as in most country towns; Sunday-trading, had also become general, and even the Bishop of the Diocese had the indiscretion to encourage it in a particular instance. Mr. Hieron, however, who was eminently zealous and faithful in the discharge of his ministerial duties, failed not to reprove him. The facts of the case are thus detailed :—

' Mr. Taylor, (Mr. Hieron's predecessor) preaching on the observance of the Sabbath, took occasion to reprove certain tradesmen of Ashbourn, for selling provisions on the morning of that day. When Bishop Wright afterwards visited the town, some who were loath to forego that bad custom, dealt with him in private about it, and so far gained upon him, that in his charge, or speech he defended the practice; using the following instance:—"Suppose," said he, "a labouring man receives his wages so late on the Saturday night, that before he can get home the shops are closed, and no meat then to be bought; shall not the poor man therefore have a chop of meat to his dinner the next day?" With great noise, the Bishop added, " God forbid!" Mr. Hieron well understood this reflection. Nevertheless, when lecturing on the 4th Commandment, he alluded, in pointed terms, to the Bishop's connivance at the sin of Sabbath-breaking: " Some may say," remarked Mr. Hieron, " that my lord Bishop gives us leave; but suppose that were so, whether is it reasonable to regard what one Bishop might say in a private place, more than what that Bishop

4

and all the Bishops in England had said in Parliament?" And having the
statute of the 3d of Charles, [prohibiting the selling of provisions on the Lord's-
day,] with him in the pulpit, he read it to his congregation, telling them, that
"there were but so many years past since this was enacted by King, Lords,
and Commons; and that this very Bishop on whose authority they so much
relied, was one of the number! (being then Bishop of Bristol.") 'Whether the
tradesmen reformed or not,' says the writer,' I cannot well say, but Mr. Hieron
did his duty with zeal and courage.'

In revenge of his reproofs, Mr. Hieron's enemies represented him as a Roundhead; and consequently the royalists
persecuted him with unrelenting severity. Twice was his
house broken open and robbed by them, and several times
he himself narrowly escaped falling into their hands.—
The perpetual alarm and disquietude to which his family
were subjected through these continued outrages, at length
induced Mr. Hieron to quit the scene of his labours; and he
then took refuge in the town of Derby. Shortly after his
arrival, he was appointed by Sir John Gell, (the Governor
of that town,) to the ministry of Breadsall; here he
continued in peace until the passing of the Act of Uniformity, on the 24th of August, 1662, when he was ejected. He
then removed to Little Eaton, where he remained between
three and four years, 'enjoying peace and quietness, and
doing good according to his opportunities.' 'And now'
adds the writer, 'comes the hurricane of the Oxford Act, to
scatter those whom the Uniformity Act had removed.
Under this statute Mr. Hieron fell; he was not likely to
swear what he could not, durst not, say.' He nevertheless,
continued to preach, though in so doing he exposed himself to much persecution, and to many trials. He resided
successively at Ashby-de-la-Zouch, at Newthorp, in Nottinghamshire, and at Losco, in Derbyshire, at which place
he died, on the 6th of July, 1682, in the 74th year of
his age; having been an ordained minister fifty-two years.
During that time he had preached in ninety-six churches
and chapels in this and the adjoining counties, and at 'little
sanctuaries' innumerable, after his exclusion from the public
exercise of the ministry. The character and endowments

of this laborious and useful minister, are described in the following passage, abridged from his biographer :—

'He was a good man, he was a learned man; he had much of Egypt's gold and treasure, and brought it all to God's tabernacle. He was well read in books and good authors: a very studious man. He was well seen in history, and very frequently in converse made an excellent use thereof. He was a close and wise reprover; able and apt to teach. He was a *mall* of unsound opinions, though he did not delight in preaching controversies. His sermons were no flattering glosses, but true mirrors, to show men the complexion of their souls. He had art enough but he concealed it; he had much learning, but it all served divinity; he had logic and philosophy enough, but he planted no Aristotle's grove by the side of God's Altar. If ever man prophecyed according to the proportion of faith; if ever man compared spiritual things with spiritual; if ever man spake as the Lord's messenger in the Lord's message, he did.'

It may be added, that Mr. Hieron's published works, consisting of Letters, Sermons, and Lectures on Heads of Divinity, are distinguished by all that force of style, and fervour of piety, for which the writings of the most eminent puritan divines are so remarkable.

CHAPTER III.

Rebellion of the Stuarts.—Entry of the Pretender and his Army.—The Boothby
Family.—Notice of Sir Brooke Boothby's Works.—Memoir of Dr. John
Taylor, LL.D.—His intimacy with Dr. Samuel Johnson, &c.

About one hundred years later than the visit of Charles I.
to Ashbourn, one of his descendants, no longer considered
by the party in power a rightful claimant to the throne,
marched through that town, to endeavour to enforce his
father's claims to the crown of England. Charles Edward,
(commonly called the Pretender,) at the time referred to,
was about twenty-five years of age : in person he was tall
and handsome; he possessed, on some occasions, intrepidity,
and was imbued with an ardent love of enterprise. His
manners, though he was brought up amid the gaieties of
foreign courts, were rather reserved, and his intellect was
by no means of comprehensive character. His youth, his
hereditary claims, and the misfortunes of his family, procured him adherents, and even personal admirers; but both
he and his counsellors seem to have wanted talent to
seize the advantages which the state of the nation then
afforded them. That state was one of wide suffering and
discontent, for many of the best constitutional securities of
the people's property and liberty had been sacrificed in
attempts to insure the stability of the new throne. However the people of England, and even the majority of the

lowlanders of Scotland, could not make up their minds to believe that 57 years of exile had cured the hereditary vices of the Stuarts. These vices were founded on the acknowledged bigotry and despotism of the family.

The Chevalier de St. George, son of James II., and the father of Charles Edward, had in his youth given instances of great personal courage. He had the important command of the household troops in the French service, and at the battle of Malplaquet, he led his regiment twelve times to the charge. He made two attempts upon Scotland, but did not succeed in either of them. In the last attempt, which took place in 1719, he was aided by the court of Spain; but England, having shortly afterwards concluded peace with that government, the Chevalier de St. George returned to the Papal States, where he lived in retirement, upon a pension allowed him by the Holy See.

In 1744, an enterprise against this country was encouraged by the Court of France in favour of the Stuarts. Prince Charles Edward was invited from Rome to be placed at the head of it. The British dominions were in a state of great agitation and alarm, and the country was occupied in the means of defence, when the gratifying intelligence arrived, that the principal part of the French fleet had been driven back with great loss, by storm and contrary winds. Charles Edward was however at that period of life when hope is seldom relinquished, when any probable means of obtaining the object aimed at present themselves; and his partisans, who were certainly numerous, both in England and Scotland, encouraged him to indulge the expectation, that as soon as he should set foot on British territory, there would be a general rising in his favour. In the summer of 1745, he found himself able, by the contributions of his adherents, to purchase a quantity of arms, with which he embarked in a small frigate, and landed on one of the little desert islands of the Hebrides. He gained several minor successes, and afterwards the celebrated battle of Preston Pans. He took possession of Edinburgh, and his

father was proclaimed king in the market-place   The
Prince soon obtained possession of nearly all Scotland,
except the fortresses which he wanted artillery to reduce.
At the head of little more than five thousand men, he
resolved to make an expedition into England, and, at
the beginning of November he invested Carlisle, which
immediately surrendered. He then advanced to Penrith,
Preston, and Manchester, where he was joined by two
hundred English Catholics, under Colonel Townley. At
Manchester he was received with illuminations and other
public testimonies of congratulation; but the English were
cautious in joining his standard, and he began to be aware
that his situation was extremely critical. However, he
resolved to advance, and passed through Stockport, Maccles-
field, and Congleton, and would probably have proceeded
onward by Birmingham and Oxford, towards London, had
he not been informed that the Duke of Cumberland, the
King's son, was awaiting him in that direction, ready to
give him battle. He therefore turned off suddenly to the
left, and marched to Ashbourn, where, during his short
stay, he took possession of Ashbourn Hall.*

The following memoranda, from the pen of an eye-witness, contain some interesting particulars relative to the
coming of the rebels to Ashbourn :—

"On Tuesday, the 3rd of December, 1745, at night, the
vanguard of the rebels came from Leek to Ashbourn,

---

*A curious anecdote connected with the Prince's visit to the town, is still in
circulation :—

'A private, passing through the market-place, requested a lad to direct him
to a shop where he might purchase spirits. The lad accordingly pointed out a
spirit-shop, the proprietor of which happened to be standing by at the time.
He, fearing the visit of the Highlander, thought proper to deny the fact, and
accused the lad of lying. The Highlander having ascertained that the person
did keep a spirit-shop, reported the occurrence to his commanding officer. A
court-martial was instituted to inquire into the case, and the spirit-dealer being
adjudged guilty, was sentenced to lose his ears. His wife, a beautiful woman,
was horror-struck at the barbarous sentence. She flew to the Chevalier, and by
her tears and urgent entreaties, succeeded in obtaining her husband's pardon.'

They were in number about 2,000, (horse and foot.)   On Wednesday morning, they proclaimed their Prince at the Market Cross; and then proceeded to Derby. On the same day another body came, (about 8,000, horse and foot.) Their Prince, who was on foot, baited at the "Three Horse Shoes," in Compton; they went to Derby that night.   On the following Friday, the whole body returned to Ashbourn (which put the inhabitants in the utmost confusion.) They stayed all night ; and on Saturday morning, to our great joy, they marched towards Leek.   The Prince and his retinue, quartered at Ashbourn Hall, on their return from Derby. There were many fine men among them, (especially in the vanguard,) which had a very fine appearance. They had with them fifteen field pieces, each about three inches diameter, and about fifty covered carts, containing ammunition, &c.   As the rebels went through, they behaved better than was expected; but as they came back, they were very insolent and impudent."

The *Derby Mercury* of December 12th, 1745, states,— "During their stay in Ashbourn the rebels plundered some gentlemen's houses to a great value. Two of them went to Clifton, near Ashbourn, and demanded a horse of one Humphrey Bown; upon his refusal, they shot him dead upon the spot, and then took to their heels. They also shot an innkeeper at Hanging Bridge, and plundered and robbed all round the country."

The same journal gives a circumstantial account of the conduct and proceedings of the rebel troops, during the time they remained in Derby :—

"Derby, Dec. 12th.   The chief business of late, among all ranks of people here, and in our neighbourhood, has been concerning the progress the rebels have made in England since their first step into it, little imagining they would have advanced so near the metropolis of the kingdom, as the capital of our county ; though for several days before they approached near us, we were not without our fears, and had proper persons constantly out to watch and bring us an account of their motions. His Grace the Duke of Devonshire (who has been indefatigable in his care for the preservation of his county) left Chatsworth about a fortnight ago, with the Marquis of Hartington, his eldest son, and came to the George Inn here, where they continued some days, waiting the event, and to concert the most proper measures for the safety of the public at a time of so much danger.   We had also in town near six hundred men, lately raised by a subscription of the gentlemen of this town and county, besides above one hundred and twenty raised by His Grace, and kept at his own expense ; these were reviewed by His Grace,

&c. on Tuesday, the 3d instant; and went through their exercise to the great satisfaction of all present; His Grace also reviewed two or three other companies then in the field; and we were then all in high spirits, by some tidings just received that the Duke of Cumberland's army was near the rebels, and 'twas expected a battle would ensue the next day. But alas! how soon were we thrown into the utmost confusion, on hearing about an hour after, of the approach of the vanguard of the rebels towards Ashbourn: the hurry also was much increased by the number of soldiers and their immediate orders to march out of town; and nothing but distraction was to be read on every countenance. The best part of the effects and valuables had been secreted some days before, and most of the principal gentlemen and trades-men with their wives and children, were retiring as fast as possible. About four or five o'clock the same evening, all the soldiers were drawn up in the market-place, and stood under arms a considerable time, when they were ordered again to their quarters to refresh themselves: and about seven the same evening Captain Lowe of Hazlewood, marched into the town, at the head of a company of brave men. About ten the drums beat to arms, and being again drawn up, they all marched off by torch-light towards Nottingham, headed by His Grace the Duke of Devonshire, &c. The next morning (Wednesday) about eleven o'clock, two of the rebels' van-guard rode into the town, and at their entrance gave a specimen of what we were to expect from such villains, by seizing a very good horse, belonging to young Mr. Stamford; after which, they rode up to the George, and there inquiring for the magistrates, demanded billets for 9,000 men or more. In a short time after the van-guard rode into the town, consisting of about thirty men, clothed in blue, faced with red, most of 'em had a scarlet waistcoat with gold lace, and being likely men, made a good appearance. They were drawn up in the market-place, and sat on horse-back two or three hours: at the same time the bells were rung, and several bonfires made, to prevent any resentment from 'em, that might ensue on our showing a dislike to their coming among us. About three in the afternoon Lord Elcho, with the life-guards, and many of their chiefs, also arrived on horseback, to the number of about one hundred and fifty, most of them clothed as above; these made a fine show, being the flower of their army. Soon after their main body marched into the town in tolerable order, six or eight abreast, with about eight stand-ards, most of them white flags and a red cross. They had several bag-pipers, who played as they marched along; and appeared in general to answer the description we have long had of them: viz't. most of their main body a parcel of shabby, pitiful looking fellows, mixed up with old men and boys; dress'd in dirty plaids, and as dirty shirts, without breeches, and wore their stockings made of plaid, not much above half way up their legs, and some without shoes, or next to none, and numbers of them so fatigued with their long march, that they really com-manded our pity rather than our fear. Whilst the market-place was filled with them, they ordered their pretended Prince, before he arrived, to be publicly proclaimed, which was accord-ingly done by the common cryer: they then insisted upon the magistrates appearing in their gowns, but being told they had sent them out of the town, were content to have that ceremony excused. Their Prince (as they called him) did not arrive till the dusk of the evening; he walked on foot, being attended by a great body of his men, who conducted him to his lodgings, (the Lord Exeter's) where he had guards placed all round his house. Every house almost by this time was pretty well filled (tho' they kept driving in till ten or eleven at night) and we tho't we should have never seen the last of them. The Duke of Athol had his lodgings at Thomas Gisborne's, esq.; the Duke of Perth at Mr. Rivett's; Lord Elcho, at Mr. Storer's; Lord George Murray at Mr. Heathcote's; Lord Pitsligo, at Mr Meynell's; old Gordon, of Glenbucket, at Mr. Alderman Smith's; Lord Nairn at Mr. John Bingham's; Lady Ogilvie, Mrs. Murray, and some other persons of distinction, at Mr. Francey's: and their other chiefs and great officers were lodged at the best gentlemen's houses. Many common ordinary houses, both public and private, had forty or fifty men each, and some gentlemen near one hundred. At their coming in they were generally treated with bread, cheese, beer, and ale, whilst all hands were aloft, getting their suppers ready; after supper, being weary with their long march, they went to rest, many of them upon straw, and others upon beds. Being refreshed with a night's rest, they were very alert the next day, running about from one shop to another, to buy, or rather steal, tradesmen's goods, viz't. gloves, buckles, powder-flasks, buttons, handkerchiefs, shoes, &c.; and the town being filled with them, looked like some fair in the Highlands: nothing was more common for them if they liked a person's shoes better than their own, to demand them off their feet, and not to give them anything, or however what they pleas'd for 'em. The longer they stayed the more insolent and outrageous they grew, demanding everything by threats, drawn swords, and pistols clapped to the breast of many persons, not only by common men but by their officers; so that several persons were obliged to abscond, to preserve their lives. They appointed prayers to be read about six this evening at the great church, which was accordingly performed by one of their priests. They ordered the cryer to make public proclamation about the town, for all persons that paid any excise, to pay what was due by five o'clock the same evening, on pain of military execution; by which means they collected a considerable sum of money. They also demanded what money the gentlemen had lately subscribed and paid, towards raising men in this town and county, which many gentlemen were obliged to pay. They also made a demand of £100 upon the post-office, and afterwards insisted upon £50, which not being complied with, they took the post-chaise along with them. They broke open closets, chests, boxes, &c. at several gentlemen's houses, took away all the guns, pistols, swords, and all other arms they could find, in every house; pilfered and stole linen, stockings, shoes, and almost everything they laid their hands on. In short, they committed almost all manner of outrages, which, were they to be particularized, would more than fill our paper. We esteem'd them very civil fellows who did not threaten us, but went away quietly, without paying their quarters : and those that did pay it was so small 'twas scarcely worth th' accepting. They beat up for volunteers, offering five shillings advance, and five guineas when they came to London, but met with very little success : only two or three loose fellows enter'd, who serv'd their master but a short time, two being taken the next day, viz't. one Cooke, a journeyman blacksmith, who we hear is in Nottingham jail : the other is one Sparks of this town, who was taken plundering at Squire Meynell's, at Bradley, and brought here last Saturday night : and being examined before our Justices, was the same night committed to jail ; when they were taking him thither, the populace shew'd so just an abhorrence of his actions, that it was thought they would have ty'd him up, before they could have got him into custody. The other is Hewitt, a butcher, who we hear is still with them. These and such fellows, it is thought, were our greatest enemies, by informing the rebels of many particulars concerning the gentlemen in this town and neighbour- hood. Early on Friday morning their drums beat to arms, and their bagpipers played about the town; no one then knowing their route, but most people imagined they would march to Loughborough for London, their advanced guard having secured the pass at Swarkstone bridge. However we were soon undeceived by their precipitate retreat the same road they came, march- ing off about seven o'clock in the morning. The reason for their return back was not known, but thought to proceed from their fear of being surprised by the Duke of Cumberland's army : their chiefs seeming much confused, and all in a great hurry ; many of their men left their shoes, swords, pistols, targets, shot, powder, bullets, and other odd things behind them where they quartered : a plain proof of their confusion. Their pretended; Prince, mounted upon a black horse, (said to be the brave Colonel Gardiner's) left his lodgings about nine o'clock, and riding across the market-place, went through the Rotten-row, then turned down Sadler-Gate towards Ashbourn, preceded and followed by the main body of his army. We were rid of them all (except a few stragglers) by eleven o'clock. Their hussars were a parcel of fierce and desperate ruffians, and were the last body that quitted the town. They rode out to the neighbouring villages, plundering most of the gentlemen's houses for arms and horses, of which they got a great number. The honest farmers hereabout are all great sufferers, many of em having scarce a horse left, and others forced to go with their artillery. We had little or no market last Friday ; nor no divine service at any of the churches last Sunday. But as we are now pretty well settled again, hope we shall soon overcome our late misfortunes, and see all things roll again in their proper channel."

On their arrival at Derby, the rebel chiefs held a council of war, but the only resolution they appear to have formed, was that of levying money on the inhabitants, and they actually pro- c ured a sum little short of £3,000. On the evening of the second day, another council of war was privately held at the head-quarters. Their situation by this time appeared critical, and many of the chiefs assumed a bold and commanding tone. They were overheard to complain "that the English promises of support were delusive; that they were extremely loyal to the House of Stuart, when warmed by a good fire and good liquor : but the warmth of their fire, their liquor, and their loyalty, evaporated together."—*Hutton.*

5

Prince Charles, on his departure from Ashbourn, retreated northwards, through Yorkshire, to Carlisle, which city he entered on the 19th of December; having, in thirteen days, in the middle of winter, and in the vicinity of two considerable armies, effected a retreat of more than one hundred and eighty miles.* He then led his Highland followers across the border, into their native land, where he took several towns, and obtained some important reinforcements. In this condition, he attempted the siege of Stirling Castle, and gained a complete victory over the English general Hawley, who with a strong force, had undertaken to raise the siege. Thus far, the affairs of the enterprising Charles Edward were by no means unprosperous, but his fate was ultimately decided at the sanguinary battle of Culloden, which took place in the month of April, 1746. At one o'clock in the afternoon, the Duke of Cumberland drew up the royal forces in order of battle, and his artillery commenced a most destructive fire upon the enemy. The conflict was severe, but of short duration. The Highlanders made a furious charge, and threw the left wing of the royal army into confusion; at this critical moment, the dragoons fell upon the Highlanders, sword in hand, and speedily put them to flight. The carnage that ensued was terrific; in less than thirty minutes they were totally defeated, and the field was covered with their wounded and slain. The Prince having thus witnessed the destruction of his hopes, fled from the fatal plain. Disguised as a peasant, and without attendants, he wandered for several months among the rocks and wilds of the country; and although the sum

---

*The progress of Prince Charles from the borders of Scotland to the very centre of England, at the head of little more than 7,000 men, and in the face of regular troops, commanded by distinguished generals, is a curious fact; nor is his retreat from Derby to the northern kingdom less worthy of attention.—The very day previous to the entrance of the rebels into Ashbourn, the Duke of Cumberland's army was no further off than Lichfield. It seems that the royal armies were little acquainted with the movements of each other or of the enemy, and that the young Pretender, by turning his march towards Derby, baffled both Marshal Wade and the Duke of Cumberland.—*Glover.*

of £30,000 was offered for his apprehension, he succeeded in eluding the pursuit of his enemies. At length, he embarked on board a privateer, hired for the purpose by his adherents, and landed in safety, at Roseau, in Bretagne.— He died at Rome, in the year, 1788.

It has been shown in the preceding chapter, that in the year 1671, the manor of Ashbourn came into the possession of Sir William Boothby, Bart.; in whose family it has ever since remained.* Sir William was knighted on the field by King Charles II., who renewed gratis, the patent of baronetcy granted to his ancestor, Sir Henry Boothby, by King Charles I., but which patent was prevented passing the great seal, in consequence of the confusion of the times. Sir Brooke Boothby, the sixth Baronet, was distinguished for his varied literary and polite acquirements. In 1792,

---

*The name of *Boothby* can be traced to a very remote era in the history of this country,—as far back as the reign of the Saxon King Egbert, who flourished upwards of a thousand years ago. The name, therefore, is connected with the first establishment of the Saxon Heptarchy. King Egbert caused the Heptarchy to be divided into counties, hundreds, and wapentakes; and it is found that one of the wapentakes of Lincolnshire, is called *Boothby*, a conjectural proof that it then, or originally, belonged to a family of that name. In the county of Lincoln there is also a market-town called *Boothby Paynell*, and a manor-house bearing the same name. These are said, by the ancient historians, Camden and Leland, to have received their names from the Boothby family, who resided there. In the additions to Camden, by Mr. E. Wilson, it is stated that the heir-general of the Boothby family married Paynell, Lord of Bampton, in the county of Devon. The same coat of arms which is now borne by the Boothbys, was lately to be found painted on the windows of the church, and in the ancient hall at that place. The exact lineal succession of a family of so ancient a descent, cannot, with precision, be traced through the earliest generations. However, it is found that Adam de Boothby was Abbot of Peterborough, in 1321. Theobaldus de Boothby was governor of Pontefract castle, which he held a long time against the Lancastrians, during the civil war of the rival Roses.

Sir William married the daughter and co-heiress of Sir William Brooke, nephew and male heir of Henry Brooke, the last Lord Cobham. Charles II. by special patent, 1665, granted that Lady Boothby, Lady Denham, and Lady Whitmore, the daughters of Sir William Brooke, should have place and precedency due to the daughters of Barons.—*Glover.*

he wrote a pamphlet in two parts, entitled, " Observations
on the Appeal (Burke's) from the New to the Old Whigs ;
and on Paine's Rights of Man."   In this pamphlet, Sir
Brooke combats, with much vigour of thought, and sound
argument, the extreme—diversely extreme—doctrines of
Mr. Burke and Paine ; and in so doing, exposes, with well-
merited   severity,   the   destructive   tendency   of Paine's
writings.   The following striking passages in reference to
a constitutional monarchy and an hereditary legislature, are
worthy of preservation:

" We love and venerate our limited monarch, because we believe he preserves
us from a ferocious venal democracy, from a cruel haughty aristocracy, and
from the unlimited tyranny of a master; because we trust that he is at this
moment, possessed of powers to withold (if it were necessary,) the hand of the
constitution from committing the desperate act of suicide recommended in this
' Rights of Man;' from sacrificing our religion and laws, and morals, our
customs and manners, upon the altar of I know not what deaf and dumb idol."

*   *   *   *

" There have always existed, in greater or smaller degrees, two descriptions
of persons alike dangerous and unfriendly to the mixed government of England;
those who desire a republican form, and those who wish to give the King a
control over the laws; and these two parties have at all times been opposed by
the constitutional Whigs, esteeming the constitution such as it is, fully adequate
to civil liberty, and the best adapted to the genius of the nation; and the
attachment of these men to the monarchy is strong and uniform, because
founded on the opinion of public advantage.   As long as the King remains
within the limits of the constitution, he is sure of the respect and support of
these men ; but they will not go a step further; for their attachment is adherence to the constitutional monarch, and not personal devotion to the man.
While he is a King according to the law, they venerate him as the palladium
of their liberties; if he endeavours to become more, they will not only withdraw
their respect and veneration, but their allegiance also; they will, if necessary,
depose the monarch, to preserve the monarchy."

In defending an hereditary legislature, Sir Brooke remarks, " In an hereditary body, consisting of the richer and better sort, the *optimates*, or *primores*, such
as the British House of Lords, the best education that the country affords is
sure to be given to the rising expectant members, and a majority of them will
be nurtured in the principles of honour, if not of virtue : if they are not all men
of genius, they are at least all men of liberal education ; so that with their
common chance for natural endowments, they have the superior advantages of
an education preparatory to their future destination ; as well as the greatest
interest in the preservation of the republic.   And the experience of the fact is
conformable to this view of the subject.   No public assembly has preserved a

higher character for wisdom and integrity, than the House of Peers : the judgment of the *Areopagus* to which it is said the Gods might have appealed, were
not more just and pure, than the decision of this high court of *dernier resort.*"

Sir Brooke Boothby's poetical talents were of no ordinary
character. If his works do not possess in an intense degree
the *vis poetica*, they are extremely, and, upon the whole,
exquisitely polished. In 1796, he published a collection of
sonnets, under the general title of "Sorrows sacred to the
Memory of Penelope." Penelope was the only daughter of
Sir Brooke, and he did all that a tender parent could do
to preserve from oblivion a child, that, from every account,
gave the surest prognostics, that she was one of those
"young Peris of the west" that would

"Not unbeseem the promise of their spring."

In order to perpetuate the memory of this beautiful and
amiable child, he employed, in addition to his own poetical
talents, the abilities of the greatest artists of the day,—
of Sir Joshua Reynolds, as painter, and of Banks, as
sculptor. Fuseli also was employed to increase, by an
allegorical painting, the fame of this lovely girl.

Of Sir Brooke's sonnets the following will perhaps best
show the extent of his poetical acquirements, and the
extraordinary poignancy of his grief. It refers directly
to the object of his sorrows, and the concluding lines
embrace a classical allusion, applied with excellent feeling
and pure taste :

"Death! thy cold hand the brightest flower has chill'd,
That e'er suffused love's cheek with rosy dies;
Quench'd the soft radiance of the loveliest eyes,
And accents tuned to sweetest music still'd;
    The springing buds of hope and pleasure kill'd;
Joy's cheerful measures changed to doleful sighs;
Of fairest form, and fairest mind the ties
For ever rent in twain.—So Heaven has will'd!
    Though in the bloom of health, thy arrow fled,
Sudden as sure; long had prophetic dread
Hung o'er my heart, and all my thoughts depress'd.
    Oft when in flowery wreaths, I saw her dress'd,
A beauteous victim seemed to meet my eyes,
To early fate a destined sacrifice."

On perusing Sir Brooke Boothby's writings, it is apparent that he was a man of very extensive reading, and that he had cultivated with ardour those abilities with which nature had endowed him.   He died at Boulogne-sur-Mer, on the 23d of January, 1824,—the 80th year of his age.*

The present possessor of the manor of Ashbourn is Sir William Boothby, Bart.

Ashbourn was the birth-place and residence of John Taylor, D.D. who has acquired some celebrity as the school-fellow and friend of Dr. Samuel Johnson. In the year, 1740, Dr. Taylor was presented to the valuable living of Market Bosworth, and in 1745, he was installed a prebend of Westminster.† He was many years in the commission of the peace for the counties of Derby and Leicester. He was the author of a 'Letter to Dr. Johnson, on the subject of a Future State;' he also published several Sermons, but from the peculiarity of their style, it is supposed that Johnson had some share in their composition.   Dr. Taylor received several visits from Johnson, and on two occasions he was accompanied by Boswell, who has described, with characteristic minuteness, the habits and conversation of the two friends :‡   He writes—

"On March 26, 1776, there came for us [to Lichfield] an equipage properly suited to a wealthy well-beneficed clergyman : Dr. Taylor's large roomy post-chaise, drawn by four stout plump horses, and driven by two steady jolly postillions, which conveyed us to Ashbourn; where I found my friend's school-fellow living upon an establishment perfectly corresponding with his substantial creditable equipage: his house, garden, pleasure-grounds, table, in short, everything good, and no scantiness appearing. Dr. Taylor had a good estate of his own, and good preferment in the church. He was a diligent justice of the peace, and presided over the town of Ashbourn, to the inhabitants of which I was told he was very liberal: and as a proof of this it was mentioned to me, he had, the preceding winter, distributed £200 among such of them as stood in need of his assistance. He had consequently, a considerable political interest in the county of Derby, which he employed to support the Devonshire family: for though the school-fellow and friend of Johnson, he was a Whig. I could not perceive in his character much congeniality of any sort with that of Johnson, who, however, said to me, 'Sir, he has a very strong understanding.' His size, and figure, and countenance, and manner, were that of a hearty English squire, with the parson super-induced: and I took particular notice of his upper servant, Mr. Peters, a decent, grave man, in purple clothes, and a large white wig, like the butler or *major domo* of a bishop."

At a subsequent visit in 1777, Boswell writes, "Taylor thus described to me his friend Johnson: 'He is a man of a very clear head, great power of words, and a very gay imagination; but there is no disputing with him. He will not hear you, and having a louder voice than you, must roar you down.'"

"On Sunday, Sept. 12, we went to the church of Ashbourn, which is one of the largest and most luminous that I have seen in any town of the same size."

"Johnson and Taylor were so different from each other, that I wondered at their preserving an intimacy. Their having been at school and college together, might in some degree account for this; but Sir Joshua Reynolds has furnished me with a stronger reason: for Johnson mentioned to him that he had been told by Taylor he was to be his heir. I shall not take it upon me to animadvert upon this ; but certain it is that Johnson paid great attention to Taylor."

The intimacy between Taylor and Johnson continued, without interruption, until the latter was removed by death ; on the 13th of December, 1784. Dr. Taylor undertook the mournful task of reading the burial service over the remains of his lamented friend.*

---

*On his departure from Ashbourn, Boswell remarks, " I took my post-chaise from the Green Man, a very good inn, at Ashbourn, the mistress of which, a mighty civil gentlewoman, curtseying very low, presented me with an engraving of the sign of her house ; to which she had subjoined, in her own handwriting, an address, in such singular simplicity of style, that I have preserved it pasted upon one of the boards of my original journal at this time, and shall here insert it for the amusement of my readers :—

"' M. KILLINGLEY'S *duty waits upon Mr. Boswell ; is exceedingly obliged to him for this favour ; whenever he comes this way, hopes for a continuance of the same. Would Mr. Boswell name the house to his extensive acquaintance, it would be a singular favour conferr'd on one who has it not in her power to make any other return but her most grateful thanks, and sincerest prayers for his happiness in time and a blessed eternity.*

"' *Tuesday morn.*' "

Dr. Taylor was remarkable for having the finest breed of milch cows in Derbyshire, or perhaps in England. Boswell remarks, that he and Dr. Johnson rode out to survey their host's farm, and were shown one cow which he had sold for 120 guineas, and another for which he had been offered 130 guineas. Dr. Taylor died in April, 1788. The house in which he resided is situated in Church-street, directly opposite the Grammar School : it is shewn in the view of the *West Entrance into Ashbourn.* A fine portrait of Dr. Johnson, by Sir Joshua Reynolds, is still to be seen there.

CHAPTER IV.

Memoir of Mr. Richard Cadman Etches.—His Mercantile Speculations.—His exertions for the Release of 12,000 British Prisoners.—Capture of his Vessels by the Spaniards, in Nootka Sound, and threatened rupture with Spain, in consequence.—His Release of Sir Sidney Smith, when a Prisoner in the Temple.—His Services to the British Government.

One of the most pleasing provinces of the historian is to discover neglected merit, and to bring before the public, extraordinary actions and eminent services, which, having been neglected by the governments or individuals for whose benefit they were performed, have remained unknown, except to a few private persons. Ashbourn has been the birth-place of a family, one of whom, even in the stirring times of the first French revolution, distinguished himself above others, by the most persevering activity to serve his country, and by a daring, disinterested, and happily successful effort to rescue from prison in a hostile land, one of the most celebrated of our naval commanders. The person referred to, was Mr. Richard Cadman Etches, son of Mr. William Etches, formerly a wine-merchant, in the Market-Place, Ashbourn, and whose family have resided in the town for several generations. He left Ashbourn whilst a youth, and entered a large mercantile firm in London. In process of time he became himself the head of an extensive wine establishment, was a large and spirited ship-owner, and for thirty-six years remained a livery-man of the cor-

poration of London.   He was the first merchant who perceived the commercial advantages that were to be derived
from the discoveries made by Captain Cook, and his immediate successors and coadjutors, in the South Seas. Captain
Cook had received from the barbarous natives of those
regions, with whom he had established a species of barter,
some valuable specimens of furs, for European commodities of a far inferior nature.   The hope of procuring a considerable quantity of these rare and costly skins, for the
sale of which a very advantageous market presented itself
at Canton, in China, was the principal inducement to Mr.
Etches to fit out an extensive expedition.   Animated by
such views, and having received the most affirmative marks
of the protection of government, previous to departure,
Mr. Etches caused to be fitted out from London, five ships,
in 1785, and the two succeeding years.   Four of these vessels, after doubling Cape Horn, arrived safely on the north-
west coast of America.   The sanguine expectations that
had been entertained of effecting a lucrative exchange of
commodities with the natives, were fully and speedily realised.   Cargoes of the finest furs were procured, and sold to
the Chinese, even under great commercial discouragements,
and pecuniary impositions, at so high a price, as amply to
reimburse and enrich the adventurers.   Other attempts of a
similar nature were made from Bengal; and two vessels were
successively dispatched from the Ganges to the same coast,.
in 1786.   A factory was established at Nootka Sound, and
possession of it was solemnly taken in the name of the
sovereign and crown of England.   Amicable treaties were
concluded with the chiefs of the neighbouring districts, and
a tract of land was purchased from one of them, on which the
new proprietors proceeded to form a settlement, and to construct storehouses.   Every thing bore the appearance of a
rising colony, and each year opened new sources of commerce and advantage.

Spain, however, claimed an exclusive right to the whole
of this part of the continent of America, and an admiral of

that nation, M. Martinez, stated that he had the king of Spain's authority to seize all vessels that should be found trading on the coast. He seized some of the English vessels, and in other ways interfered with the success of the adventurers. This act of aggression nearly led to a rupture between this country and Spain. In defence of the commercial interests of the country, the British government acted promptly and decidedly. Within one week after full intelligence of the transaction had been received, a positive demand of satisfaction aud restitution was sent to Madrid, and the most active warlike preparations were made. At the expense of three millions sterling, a formidable armament was fitted out. The nation awaited, in painful anxiety, the result of the pending negociation; deprecating the dreadful alternative of appealing to the sword for the vindication of their rights, yet confident of the justice and ultimate success of their cause, when the agreeable intelligence arrived, that an amicable convention had been agreed upon between his Britannic Majesty and the King of Spain. The plenipotentiary, by whom, on the part of Great Britain, this important treaty was conducted and ratified, was Alleyne Fitzherbert, Esq. (now Lord St. Helens.)

Mr. Etches, finding his views and speculations with respect to the fur-trade with China obstructed, immediately turned his attention to continental matters, both commercial and political. Having been made a citizen of Denmark, at Copenhagen, in 1789, he was enabled, as a Danish subject, to visit France frequently during the first great revolution, and he became personally acquainted with the different ministers of Paris, their secretaries, &c., from whom he ascertained, that far more might be effected with the French government by private, rather than by public negociation. He soon perceived that one of the gigantic projects of France was, to separate the British wholly from commercial intercourse with the continent; and this was the reason that the French Government resisted, with so much pertinacity, every proposition, whether by exchange or otherwise, for the release of our merchant-seamen taken by them in the commencement of the war.   Our Government felt their release to be a great national object, and Sir Frederick Morton Eden received the fullest powers to treat with the French government on the subject. Though a man of ability, he failed in his mission, and no representation he had made, no language he had held, made any impression on the rulers of France. Mr. Etches, through the medium of his friend Mr. Nepean, made a proposal to Lord Spencer, to the following effect: that he (Mr. Etches) was willing to repair to Paris, at his own expense, to see what he could do towards the release of the 12,000 prisoners. His proposal was approved of, and in the summer of 1795 he went to Paris, and had influence enough to procure a decree of the Convention, for an exchange of prisoners, without any interference on the part of the respective governments. Before he quitted France, he had the satisfaction of seeing upwards of 12,000 British prisoners restored to their country, at an expense not exceeding six hundred pounds. Mr. Etches was severely wounded whilst a spectator of the dreadful carnage that took place in the streets of Paris, when Buonaparte, under the order of the Directory, cannonaded the sections, who were marching on the Convention.

Mr. Etches, never losing sight of commercial objects, shortly afterwards visited Holland. The Dutch, he well knew, could only be swerved from British interests by force. Those of commerce, he considered, to be useful or profitable ought to be mutual, otherwise they could not be lasting, and Mr. Etches was determined to ascertain by the means of personal observation, the true state of public feeling in Holland with respect to this country. Whilst he was thus engaged, he acquired a knowledge of the most important military facts.

Residing as a merchant in Holland, he ascertained that all the small craft throughout the United Provinces had been put in requisition for transporting a large French army commanded by General Bournonville, which was to be disembarked on the coasts of Essex and Suffolk, with the avowed intention of surprising and destroying the British capital. The defenceless state of the coasts of those counties was well known to France. Possessed of this most important information, Mr. Etches determined upon visiting all the ports, and surveying the inland waters of Holland, in order to ascertain a list of the vessels put in requisition, their tonnage, and every preparation that was making for the intended expedition. Having done so, he embarked in a fishing-boat for England, and submitted to the English government an ample detail of the means by which, judging from accurate local knowledge, he conceived the expedition might be frustrated. The lords of the Admiralty adopted, forthwith, his ideas; and an armament, commanded by Sir Richard Bickerton, as chief naval, and by Colonel Doyle, as chief military officer, was fitted out, and immediately sailed for the Texel, with a view to attack and bring out the fleet. Mr. Etches embarked as a volunteer on board the *Ramilies*, and it was in a great measure through his instructions, that the French project of invasion fell to the ground.

In the following December, Mr. Etches again went to Paris, and from thence communicated to his government at home the real object of the immense naval and military preparations that were taking place in France, and which had been so long and so profoundly kept a secret. Our East India possessions, according to French calculation, were most vulnerable by attacking them through Egypt. The English government, however, received subsequent information, which it considered to be better founded than than that of Mr. Etches; but the landing of Buonaparte and his army some months afterwards, in Aboukir Bay, his movements from thence to Alexandria and Damietta, his ascending the Nile to Cairo, his intention of proceeding to the cities of Ginnah and Corsire on the Red Sea, convinced the British ministers of the accuracy of Mr. Etches' details. The practicability of transporting an army from the coasts of the Red Sea to India may be doubted, but Mr. Etches

was an eye-witness that many large prize-ships in the ports
of France were transferred to Americans, who were appointed to the command of them.   These ships were man-
ned with Americans and with British prisoners, the latter
being furnished with certificates to prove them native
Americans, and they were dispatched, under American
colours, to sail round the Cape of Good Hope. They were
to rendezvous at the French islands, in the oriental ocean,
to await there the arrival of the French army, and to proceed up the Red Sea to the port of Corsire, and to transport
it to the coast of Malabar.   In consequence of the failure
of the French expedition in Egypt, the further employment
of this fleet was rendered unnecessary.

It will be recollected, that in the year 1797, two distinguished British officers, Sir Sidney Smith and Captain
Wright, were prisoners in the Temple, at Paris. Every
effort had been made by the Transport Board at home to
effect their release, but in vain, and the project of obtaining
it by negociation was entirely abandoned. Mr. Etches
resolved, if possible, to liberate them.   He learned at Rotterdam, from an American, whose brother was confined in
the Temple, the circumstances of Sir Sidney Smith's deten-
tion. He immediately repaired to Paris, and under guise
of being a friend to the American prisoner, he obtained
frequent access to the Temple.   In that portion of the
gardens of the Temple allotted to English prisoners, he
repeatedly saw Sir Sidney, but dared not, for fear of discovery, openly accost him.   At length, by means of a note
inclosed within an orange, which he conveyed to Sir Sidney,
he informed that officer who he was, acquainted him with
his designs, and begged to be told how they could be most
surely carried into effect. Sir Sidney communicated to him
in reply, that the wife of the *concierge*, or gaoler, must be
bribed. Mr. Etches undertook to do so, and gained the
woman over to his views, by means of a splendid silver
coffee-service. She so far prevailed on her husband, that
Sir Sidney Smith, Captain Wright, and the French colonel

Philippeaux, also a prisoner, were allowed, though always accompanied by the gaoler, to visit nightly the different theatres of Paris. At those places of public resort, Mr. Etches frequently met them, and concerted with them measures for their ultimate escape. Through the instrumentality of a lady, he obtained a counterfeit order for their release; the order was intended for the release of others, but the minister, in the hurry of signing it, took no notice of the names of the prisoners that were inserted in it. There was therefore little difficulty in getting them out of the Temple, but the great point was, to procure them disguises, and get them clear of the capital and its police. Mr. Etches hired a mob, to assemble round the carriage that was to await at the gate of the Temple; to convey the prisoners away. As soon as they were in the carriage, and it began to move, a female, who was in the secret, threw herself before the horses, and by her loud cries, intimated that she had received a serious injury. The mob surrounded her, the attention of all who were near the prison was immediately directed to the supposed sufferer, and in the confusion, Sir Sidney Smith, Captain Wright, and Colonel Philippeaux quitted the carriage, and escaped to an appointed rendezvous in Paris. They then obtained the necessary disguises, and Mr. Etches, who had preceded them to London, having made every necessary preparation for their flight through France, and for their embarkation at Calais, they left the French Capital, adopted the plan and route he had traced out for them, and safely arrived in England. The Directory having learned that Mr. Etches was the immediate instrument of their release, his return after that time to Paris, became impossible, as he was condemned, in his absence, to be shot. The following is an extract of a letter written in the decline of life, by Mr. Etches, and referring more minutely to the circumstances of the above-mentioned memorable escape:

"At the time Sir Sidney Smith and Captain Wright were prisoners in Paris, in the Temple, I was at Rotterdam.

Being present at a public dinner with a party of Americans, one of whom had a brother imprisoned in the Temple, I heard him say that Sir Sidney's usual money-allowance was stopped, whereby he and Captain Wright, and several other prisoners, who were intimate with him, were very much inconvenienced. I immediately determined, on hearing this information, to go to Paris, for the purpose of serving Sir Sidney. On my arrival, I obtained an order for fifty louis on Messrs. Herries & Co. and conveyed it to him, with a note, enclosed in an orange. I resolved to ascertain whether I could promote Sir Sidney's release by means of bribery, and finding it certain that I could, I hastened to London, to communicate with Lord Spencer, and the other Lords of the Admiralty. They highly approved of my proposed attempt, but as every endeavour and application hitherto made had failed, they doubted the practicability of my efforts. I was confident, however, that money, properly made use of in Paris, would effect almost any undertaking. I returned, therefore, to Paris, and soon got access to the Temple and the prisoners. I so managed, that Sir Sidney and Captain Wright were enabled to come out of the Temple at night, accompanied, however, by the *concierge*. Aided by the advice of Colonel Philippeaux, we had several private interviews, at which the practicability of my plans was clearly ascertained, and Sir Sidney delivered me a letter for Lord Spencer. I again returned to London, in full confidence that the necessary funds would be advanced to me, on account of the very flattering manner in which my project had been received at the Admiralty. It appeared that it was to the Transport Board that any application for an advance of money for such a project as that of mine ought to be made. I made the necessary application to that Board, but it was refused, on the ground that every feasible effort had already been made unsuccessfully. I was, notwithstanding, assured by Mr. Nepean, that if I could myself raise the funds, and bring about the release of Sir Sidney, whatever amount of

money I should spend in the undertaking, would be repaid
to me by Lord Spencer. I once more returned to Paris, and
succeeded in all my arrangements. I confidentially engaged
Mr. Keith, cashier of the banking-house of Messrs. Herries
and Co., and I introduced him to Sir Sidney at one of our
nightly meetings at the theatre; and he was of the greatest
service in the proper management of the funds. This gentleman afterwards accompanied Sir Sidney in the *Tigre*.
Just as every thing was ready, a lady in the secret, wife of
one of the French government secretaries, informed me that
I had been denounced, for having held certain communi-
cations with Sir Sidney, and that I must leave Paris next
day. On the following morning, I set off without a single
article of luggage, arrived safely at Calais, and instantly
embarked for my own country. Whilst off the pier, two
French couriers arrived from Paris with orders to arrest
me, which assuredly would have been effected, by recalling
the vessel in which I was, had not, fortunately, a British
cruiser been between us and the pier. Had I been taken,
my destination was certain,—I should have been shot,
without judge or jury. On my arrival in London, I communicated my arrangements [for the prisoners' release] to
Mr. Nepean; and on the Saturday following, I received a
letter, in cipher, from my friend Keith, which had been
transmitted open in the dispatches of the French Minister
of Marine, to Mr. Otto, Commissioner for French prisoners
in London. Mr. Otto kindly affixed his official seal to it,
and sent it me by a confidential servant. I took it to the
Admiralty, where it was considered as a document that
referred to provisions, (for the names of different sorts of
meat were used to designate the fugitives. I deciphered
it, and confidently pronounced that Sir Sidney would arrive
within twenty-four hours. He did arrive, and dined the
following day at Wimbledon. I ascertained on the evening
of that day, at Camelford House, that he would sleep at
the Prince of Wales's Hotel, Conduit-Street. On Monday
morning I called at the Hotel. The instant Sir Sidney saw

7

me, he took me in his arms, and carrying me from one
extremity of the coffee-room to the other, he placed me
on a table, and embracing me affectionately, exclaimed
several times, in the presence of many gentlemen that were
in the room, ' *Here is my Deliverer!*'

In 1797, Mr. Etches again proved how anxious and disinterested he was in his efforts to serve his country.   In
that year, he repaired to Holland, and having ascertained
the force, military and naval, in that country, and having
obtained, from official sources, manuscript charts of the
Zuyder Zee, and of the inland waters, together with plans
and drawings of the fortifications, the number and force
of the shipping, &c. belonging to the States of Holland,
he embarked for England with this body of most important information.   On his arrival in London, he submitted to the Lords of the Admiralty, a plan, not only for
an attack upon the Texel, but also a plan for conducting a
naval force, to be accompanied by troops, throughout the
inland waters, from the Texel to the Western Scheldt.
This plan had the merit of perfect originality, as the question of the practicability of successfully attacking Amsterdam from the Texel had never been previously agitated,
save to be decidedly negatived.   But Mr. Etches was no
visionary schemer ; he never recommended a plan unless
he was thoroughly satisfied of its practical working, and on
this occasion he had ascertained the depth of the different
waters, the rocks, bridges, and shoals, from the entrance of
the Texel to Flushing ; and every other point that would be
essential to the success of such an expedition.   It is necessary to remark, that at this time Amsterdam had adopted
no means of defence.

The plan was accepted by the Admiralty; and it was
immediately resolved, that an expedition, under the command of Admiral Mitchell and General Abercrombie should
forthwith sail.   Mr. Etches accompanied the force, as a
volunteer ; and when at sea, on board the *Isis,* he had the
high satisfaction to find that the Admiral and General had

his identical plans, charts, and drawings on board, for their guidance on the expedition. When off the Dutch coast, the only doubt the Admiral had, was whether they could obtain pilots acquainted with the Texel passages; upon which Mr. Etches assured him, that as soon as the sand-hills of the Helder Peninsula were carried, Texel pilots could be procured, who would carry the fleets safely in. Mr. Etches, in company with the General, was present at the attack on these sand-hills, all of which were carried.— The next morning, he went with Admiral Mitchell into the Texel, and had the gratification of witnessing *the complete capture of Admiral Storey's fleet, and of every ship of war specified in his own list.* Their number amounted to forty-four. Mr. Etches likewise volunteered his services in the ensuing campaign; he was present in every engagement, and in one of them he received a severe wound. After the retreat from Alkmaar, and before the General re-embarked at the Texel, he sent for Mr. Etches, and asked him if he had preserved his " red book." This book was a diary of the information he communicated to the Admiral and General, and also contained the observations he (Mr.E.) had made during the expedition. He informed the General that he had preserved the book in question, upon which the General said that he should give him a letter to Lord Spencer, stating the importance of his services. The Admiral, who put the same question to him, also gave him a similar letter to Lord Spencer. On Mr. Etches' arrival in London, he presented the letters to Mr. Nepean, and informed him that he still preserved the book containing the remarks he had made on the expedition. Mr. Etches was then told that it was the order of his Majesty's minister that he should retire into the country, and write his own opinions respecting all the operations of the expedition. He was also told not to conceal his sentiments as to the conduct of any one engaged in the expedition, that he need not fear the displeasure of any one connected with it, as his observations were intended for the inspection of the highest

authority in the empire. Mr. Etches obeyed the command,
and wrote a narrative of the expedition, extending to 70
pages, not a syllable of which has ever publicly transpired.

It was in consequence of Mr. Etches's suggestions that
so many successful attacks were made upon the Dutch
shipping within the Vlie, and also within the inlands north
of the Texel. The taking possession of Heligoland, which,
from his local knowledge, Mr. Etches represented to be a
Gibraltar in miniature, also entirely originated with him.
The commercial importance of this island throughout our
long struggle is well known.

On the fitting out of the expedition which had for its
object the attack on the Danish fleet in Copenhagen-roads,
Mr. Etches transmitted to the British Admirals, (Nelson
and Parker) some valuable information relative to the state
of the fortifications, and the naval preparations of the Danes.

In the year 1804, a project was submitted to the British
government, for ruining the navigation of the harbour of
Boulogne, and for dispersing the immense flotilla which
Buonaparte had there assembled, for the invasion of Great
Britain. Mr. Etches was requested by the Secretary of
State, to give his opinion of the project. From his knowledge of the flotilla, the harbour, the currents, and set of
the tides, he felt bound to state, that if such a plan were
adopted, the vessels by which it must be carried into execution would be removed during the ebb of a single tide. He
stated further, that if it were the intention of the government to make an attempt of the kind, he would, if desired,
submit a project of his own; and he was immediately
requested to do so. His proposal was, to equip three large
vessels, of small draught of water, and to erect on them a
solid body of masonry, united with cement, and so clamped
with iron plates, screws, collars, &c. as to withstand the ebb
of many tides: they were to be rigged as fire-ships, with a
heavy tonnage of floating fire-works on board of each. The
plan was highly approved by his Majesty's ministers, and
in the presence of several of them, Mr. Etches was asked,

'if it were adopted, whether he would superintend its execution?' He answered, that 'he had never submitted a project, which he had not volunteered his services to carry into effect.' He was then ordered to attend on the following morning, and to furnish an estimate of the probable expense of the undertaking. He did so, and such was the confidence which the ministers reposed in his ability and integrity, that to enable him to commence operations, the sum of £10,000 was placed to his credit, at the banking-house of Messrs. Hammersleys & Co. on that very day.— The project, however, was eventually given up by the government, although there was little reason to doubt but that it would have been successfully executed. It was admitted that Mr. Etches had done his duty, and he was completely exonerated from all responsibility in the affair.

From the foregoing narrative it will be seen that no inconsiderable share of the success which attended the British arms in their defence of the great commercial interests of the country, and in the efforts directed against the common enemy at this eventful period, is to be attributed to the ability, the zeal, the local and general knowledge, the intrepidity and integrity, of Mr. RICHARD CADMAN ETCHES. It has seldom fallen to the lot of a biographer to record a series of services of more real importance than those which have now, for the first time, been detailed; there is every reason to believe that had Mr. Etches chosen to adopt the military profession, (for which, it is abundantly clear, his genius was well adapted,) that his name would long since have been recorded in the fairest page of his country's annals. The compilers of this work feel gratified that they are now enabled in some measure to do justice to his memory.

Mr. Etches died in London, in the year 1817—18.

At the termination of the Peace of Amiens, in 1803, the French troops then in possession of St. Domingo, were compelled, through the general rising of the black population on the' one hand, and the blockade of the ports by a British naval force on the other, to evacuate and abandon that island. The French General Rochambau concluded a treaty of capitulation with the British commodore, by which it was agreed that the French officers and troops, amounting to about 8,000, should be sent to Jamaica as prisoners of war, and their wounded to, France and America. About 5,000 of these prisoners were dispatched to England; and the General himself, with 300 of his officers, resided, for several years, on parole, at Ashbourn.

CHAPTER V.

The town of Ashbourn is situated in a deep, rich well-wooded valley, in the southern and most fertile division of the county of Derby; 139 miles north north-west of London, and on the great road from that city to Manchester. Approaching Ashbourn from Derby, the traveller passes through a pleasant, undulating country, whose general aspect, however, presents no very remarkable features. When he arrives within a mile of the town, he perceives a striking change in the character of the landscape. In the back-ground are visible, in bold relief, the abrupt hills of Dovedale, forming the first portions of the mountainous ridge which extends northward, through the Peak; while immediately beneath lies the town, well sheltered from the boisterous winds, by the hills which appear to overhang and embosom it. The view from the descent has often been characterised as extremely picturesque, and it is to this point that allusion is made in the well-known and often-quoted motto prefixed by Sir Walter Scott to the first chapter of his 'Heart of Mid-Lothian.'

> "So, down thy hill, romantic Ashbourn, glides
> The Derby dilly, carrying six insides."*

The Schoo, or Henmore, a small tributary stream of the

---

*See *View of Ashbourn, from the Derby Road.*

river Dove, flows through the valley, dividing the town
into two parts;* that portion situated to the south of this
brook, is denominated Compton, anciently *Campdene*.†

Ashbourn has usually been ranked immediately after the
two corporate towns of the county, but anciently, it was
equal in point of importance to either of those places. As
early as the 13th century the town contained 1,000 inhabitants of the age of sixteen years and upwards; and if to this
be added the number of children under that age, it will
appear, on the most moderate computation, that the population at that time exceeded 2,000. This is a fact worthy
of particular notice, since it is found that in the reign of
Edward III., at least one hundred years later, the entire
population of the kingdom did not exceed 2,500,000. In
the year 1377, Richard II. caused a capitation-tax to be
levied on all persons above the age of fourteen years, beg-
gars only excepted. From the record which has been
preserved of the number of contributors to this tax, it is
inferred that the population of the metropolis did not then
exceed 35,000; and many ancient towns, were at that time
but little, if at all, in advance of Ashbourn. Among them
may be mentioned, Winchester, Worcester, Nottingham,
Ipswich, Exeter, Northampton, Hull, Carlisle, Newark,
Lichfield, and Derby, none of which places had more than
2,500 inhabitants, and several of them not exceeding 1,000.
Ashbourn, like many other inland towns in the centre of
agricultural districts, has not shared to any great extent in
the increase of population which has since taken place.

*In its ordinary course this is an insignificant rivulet, but after heavy rains in
the uplands it becomes a furious torrent, completely flooding the lower parts of
the town, and occasioning the inhabitants much loss and inconvenience.

†Thomas Bedford, a non-juring divine, the learned editor of 'Simon Dunel-
mensis, and author of the 'Historical Catechism,' resided in Compton: he died
there in 1773, and was buried in Ashbourn church.

In 1782, died Francis Millward, of Compton, aged 108. He served under
William III. in the Irish wars, and afterwards with the Duke of Marlborough
and Prince Eugene.

The following table exhibits the state of the population of the parish of Ashbourn, in the years 1801, 1811, 1821, and 1831, with the acreage of each township and hamlet, and the estimated annual value of the real property as assessed in April, 1815:*

PARISH OF ASHBOURN.	Population.				Acres.	Rental.
	1801	1811	1821	1831		£.
Ashbourn township	2006	2112	2188	2246	55	4988
Clifton and Compton township....	627	663	768	839	1002	2932
Hulland chapelry and township ..	146	214	221	234	909	1796
Newton Grange liberty..........	9	15	38	41	737	1410
Offcote and Underwood liberty....	220	257	341	328	1809	5821
Sturston hamlet	360	387	561	578	925	2779
Yeldersley and Painter's-Lane....	187	210	202	226	1456	2085
Broadlow Ash					405	—
	3555	3858	4319	4492	7298	21811

The chief support of the town is derived from its well-reputed markets and fairs, which afford a ready disposal for the agricultural produce of the neighbourhood.‡ The land for many miles round Ashbourn is principally occupied by dairy farmers, and a large quantity of cheese is made in the district. This article is of first-rate quality, and obtains high prices in the London and other markets. The market is held on Saturday, and is mentioned as existing in the year 1296, but as the charter has not been discovered, the exact date of its establishment is not known. The fairs were well attended in the reign of Edward I.,† at which time there were two, each held for three days, at the Festivals of St. Oswald and St. John the Baptist. The

---

*The Township of Ashbourn is situated chiefly in the Hundred of Wirksworth. The east or Sturston side of Compton-street and Spital Hill, is in the Hundred of Appletree; and the west, or Clifton side forms part of the Hundred of Morleston and Litchurch. The Town of Ashbourn (including Compton) contained at the last census 502 houses.

On the passing of the Reform Act in 1832, Ashbourn was appointed a polling-place for the election of Members of Parliament for the Southern Division of the County.

†The Burgesses of Derby then complained that "the bailiff of Thomas Touchet distrained upon those who traded to the fair of Esseburne."

8

charter of King Charles I. enumerates five fairs, but several others have since been established.*

Sir William Boothby, as lord of the manor, receives a toll upon all cattle and goods offered for sale in the markets and chartered fairs. He holds a court-leet annually, at which the constables and other town-officers are appointed.

The vicinity of the town to Dovedale, and the scenery of the Peak, occasions an influx of travellers during the summer months, and few places can boast of better inns for their accommodation. Many genteel families reside in the town and neighbourhood, and there are several highly-respectable and well-conducted schools.

The air of the town, and particularly of the surrounding hills, is very salubrious, and the water pure and wholesome.

The very ancient game of foot-ball still continues to be played in Ashbourn, on Shrove Tuesday and Ash Wednesday. "The mode of playing this game in Ashbourn and Derby," says Glover† "differs very much from the usual practice. The players are young men, from the age of eighteen to thirty and upwards, married as well as single, and many veterans who retain a relish for the sport are occasionally seen in the very heat of the conflict. The game commences in the market-place, where the partisans of each parish are assembled, and, about noon a large ball is tossed

---

*The Fairs are supplied with horses, horned cattle and sheep, and are attended by dealers from all parts of the kingdom. They are held on the 1st Tuesday in January, 13th of February, April 3d, last Thursday in April, May 21st, (a great pleasure-fair,) July 5th, August 16th, October 20th, November 29th. The February fair begins (with the sale of horses,) two days before the date; that in October three days before. The fairs of April and May are in great repute for the sale of milch cows; those in August and November, for fat cattle. The Cheese Fairs are held on the 2nd Tuesday in March and the 3d Tuesday in September; the day preceding each is a fair for horned cattle, sheep, horses, &c. The statutes (and fair) are held on the 15th of December, and the annual *wakes* commences on the First Sunday after August 16th.

No manufactures exist to any extent in the town; but at Hanging Bridge, Mayfield, and Wood Eaves, in the immediate vicinity, there are Cotton Factories, which employ a number of hands.

†History and Gazetteer of the County of Derby, vol. 1. p. 310.

Published by Dawson & Hobson, Ashbourn.

ASHBOURN HALL,

The Seat of Sir William Boothby Bart.

up in the midst of them. This is seized upon by some of the strongest and most active men of each party. The rest of the players immediately close in upon them, and a solid mass is formed. It then becomes the object of each party to impel the course of the crowd towards their particular goal. The struggle to obtain the ball, which is carried in the arms of those who have possessed themselves of it, is then violent, and the motion of this human tide heaving to and fro, without the least regard to consequences is tremendous. Broken shins, broken heads, torn coats, and lost hats, are among the minor accidents of this fearful contest, and it frequently happens that persons fall in consequence of the intensity of the pressure, fainting and bleeding beneath the feet of the surrounding mob. But it would be difficult to give an adequate idea of this ruthless sport: a Frenchman passing through Derby remarked, that if Englishmen called this playing, it would be impossible to say what they would call fighting. Still the crowd is encouraged by respectable persons attached to each party, and who take a surprising interest in the result of the day's sport. The shops are closed, and the town presents the aspect of a place suddenly taken by storm." The game is supposed to have been played in Derby at a very early period. It was general in England in the reign of Henry II., but its introduction into Ashbourn is of more recent date.

ASHBOURN HALL, the seat of Sir William Boothby, Bart. is situated at the eastern extremity of the town, on a gentle declivity, overlooking the park and gardens, which are laid out with so much taste, as amply to compensate for the absence of more picturesque scenery. The house is of modern erection, and although not possessed of any external architectural decorations, its interior is elegant and commodious. It contains some good pictures, among which is that most extraordinary production of Fuseli's, *The Nightmare;* and the allegorical painting by the same artist, in memory of the daughter of Sir Brooke Boothby.

This picture is well described in one of Sir Brooke
Boothby's sonnets:—

" My Fuseli ! before thy ken of thought,
Imagination's world expanded lies ;
And to ideal shapes, in orient dies,
To give a breathing form thy art has taught.
    Witness yon bright illusion though hast wrought
With pictured bliss to cheat these weary eyes,
And raise my drooping spirit to the skies,
On fancy's wing to scenes celestial brought.
    'Tis immortality that sounds the call !
Lo, the mild angel to receive her bends !
    From the dark disk of this terraqueous ball,
In spotless shade to her own heaven ascends,
The towering day-star, smiling points the way
To glorious regions bright with cloudless ray !

ASHBOURN CHURCH.—At the remote period of the Norman Conquest Ashbourn possessed 'a priest and a church.'
The present edifice, which is supposed to have been erected
on the site of the ancient one, was probably completed
in the early part of the thirteenth century.   This supposition is founded on a Latin inscription engraved on a brass
plate, discovered on repairing the church some years ago.
The following is a translation:—"In the year from the
incarnation of our Lord, 1241, on the eighth of the kalends
of May, this church was dedicated and this altar consecrated, in honour of St. Oswald, king and martyr, by the
venerable father, Hugh de Patishul, lord Bishop of Coventry."*   The building, at its original foundation, was purely
gothic, and its chief parts present now specimens of the
Early English style of architecture, but they are very much
interspersed with various alterations, additions, and insertions, of later styles.   It is built in the form of a cross, with

*"*Anno ab incarnatione Dno MCCXlj viii. die Maij dedicata est hœc eccia et hocal-
tare consecratum in honore sci Oswaldi regis et martiris, a venerabili patre Dno Hugo-
ni de Patishull Coventrensi Episcopo." In the Harleian manuscript No 1486, folio
49, 6, is a copy of this inscription (differing in a few letters only) which is then
said to be written in an old Saxon character, in brass, in Mr. Cokaine's house
at Ashbourn.   This brass was probably fixed up in the church at the time the
ancient hall was taken down.—Glover.

Drawn & Printed by Rayner Derby.

ASHBOURN CHURCH
FROM THE SOUTH.

Published by Dawson & Hobson, Ashbourn

a square tower in the centre, the battlements of which have trefoil openings. The whole is surmounted by a lofty octagonal spire, extremely light, and of beautiful proportions, enriched with crockets at the angles, and pierced by twenty Decorated windows. The chancel has lancet-shaped windows north and south, also two in the Decorated style, and a fine Perpendicular one of seven lights fills the east end. The ancient acutely-pointed roof, the altitude of which may be seen from the weather-moulding, has given place to a flat one. The nave is in the transition style between the Early Pointed and the Decorated; its piers and arches, and those of the transepts are remarkably fine; several of the windows are modern insertions. The North transept has two large Decorated windows; the south transept another, and adjoining it is one in the Perpendicular style. The windows exhibit numerous shields of arms in stained glass, of the Ferrers, the Cokaynes, the Boothbys, and other eminent families. In the south wall of the chancel are three stone stalls, and nearly opposite, within the north wall, is a large canopied arch resembling that of a tomb. This was the *holy sepulchre*, where at Easter certain rites commemorative of the resurrection were anciently performed with great solemnity. The font dates with the earliest part of the fabric. The tower contains a peal of eight fine-toned bells; and there is a powerful organ.

A thorough renovation of the interior is now (1839) taking place, under the able superintendence of L. N. Cottingham, Esq. The whole of the unsightly and ill-arranged pews and galleries are removed, the mutilated windows and pillars, with their elaborate ornaments, restored, and the fabric re-pewed in oak. Under the new arrangement a gallery is proposed to be carried round the nave, and the organ placed in the south transept. The partition which completely cuts off the nave from the chancel (the earliest and best-preserved portion of the edifice,) is to be removed and the whole thrown open, thus presenting an uninterrupted view from east to west of 179 feet in extent. Due effect will then be given to the massive proportions of the edifice, and when completed, Ashbourn Church will doubtless rank among the finest existing specimens (for a parish-church) of that beautiful style of architecture, the Early English. At the same time, the inconveniences resulting from the peculiarities of its structure are so far obviated, that the amount of accommodation will be increased by several hundred sittings, a great proportion of which will be free. The funds for effecting these improvements are raised by voluntary contribution.*

MONUMENTS.—A portion of the north transept is screened off, and forms the cemetery of the later lords of the manor. Within it are several monuments to members of the Cokayne and Boothby families, some of which merit accurate descriptions. One of the most curious of these monuments is affixed to the wall, or within a window-place, near the northern corner of the transept. It represents, in an arched niche, a knight and lady in antique costume, kneeling opposite to each other, and with clasped hands in the attitude of prayer, offering up their devotions over what appears to be a miniature altar-piece. On a tablet in front is inscribed,

" *Hic jacent sepulta corpora Thomæ Cokaini Militis et Dom Dorothæa uxoris ejus. Christi mors nobis vita.*"

On a lower compartment are ten little figures, in bas relief, rudely sculptured, representing the ten children of the knight and lady, three sons and seven daughters, kneeling opposite to each other. The following is the inscription:

" *Nomina liberorum Thomæ Cokaini Mil et Dom Dorothæa uxoris ejus, Franciscus, Thomas, Edward, Florentia, Dorothæa, Ha. Johannes, Johanna, Jane, Maud.*"

Beneath this monument, to the right as the spectator examines it, is a large embattled altar-tomb, profusely decorated on its sides with quartrefoils and shields of arms.

---

*During the alterations the remains of a stone coffin, and several large stone slabs, bearing on the surface the cross and other sculptured devices, have been discovered. Also, on the walls, traces of several inscriptions, chiefly passages of Scripture, in large old English characters. The porch on the south side of the nave (shown in the plate) is taken down, the inner doorway removed, and a window inserted uniform with those on each side.

On the upper surface of this altar-tomb lie, with their feet
towards the wall, two large and rude effigies, in alabaster;
the one to the right is meant to represent an armed knight
in plate armour, with pointed helmet, and having a richly-
mounted short sword by his side. His arms, three cocks,
are carved upon his breast, the figure of an animal, appar-
,ently of a small lion supports his feet, and the pillow upon
which his head rests is supported by angels. On the left
side of this figure is represented another, that of an old man
in a close cap, with a short beard, dressed in a tunic, with
a robe enveloping his left shoulder and side. A purse and
dagger are suspended from his girdle, and his feet rest on a
dog *couchant*. It is evident that these figures are meant for
the representatives of some of the earlier members of the
Cokayne family, and it is probable that the figure of the
armed knight is that of John Cokayne, who was for a time
knight of the shire, and whó died in 1375.

On the left side of the former, is another altar-tomb, also
of alabaster, with full-length effigies of a knight of the
Cokayne family and of his lady. These figures are sculptured more elaborately and less rudely than the former.
Each side of the tomb is richly decorated with gothic carving and tracery, and with figures of angels, bearing before
them shields of arms. The knight is habited in plate armour, with a collar round his neck. The head of this
figure is supported by a large close helmet, surmounted by
the family crest (a cock's head) and lamberquin. The
costume of the lady consists of a close gown and mantle,
and a curious reticulated head-dress. These figures are
supposed to represent Sir John Cokayne, (who was slain at
the battle of Shrewsbury) and his lady. The following
inscription is said to have been engraved on this tomb, but
no traces of it are now discernible:—

" *Tumuli alabastrini Johannis Cokain primo capitalis Baronis de Scaccario, deinde
unius Justiciarum de Communi Banco sub rege Henrico IV. accurata effigies.*"

In the corner of the transept, adjoining the monument
last described, is a large and elevated altar-tomb; on its

upper surface are carved lines representing two whole-
length figures, with the following quaint inscription, in old
English characters:—

> " Here lyeth Sir Thomas Cockaine,
> Made knight at Turney and Turwyne :
> Who builded here fayre houses twayne,
> With many profettes that remayne :
> And three fayre parks impaled he,
> For his successors here to be :
> And did his house and name restore,
> Which others had decay'd before .
> And was a knight so worshipfull,
> So vertuous, wyse and pitifull,
> His dedes deserve that his good name
> Lyve here in everlasting fame.
>
> Who had issue III. sonnes and III. daughters."

Next to this tomb, nearer the door of the transept, is
another, apparently of greater antiquity than any hitherto
described. Its upper surface is inlaid with brass, on which
are traced several curious and intricate designs. This tomb
has suffered much from the hand of time; and it is impossible from the few remaining letters of the inscription,
accurately to discover to whom the frail tenement belonged.
The sides exhibit many traces of ancient carving, in a state
of rapid decay, together with the figures of eight angels,
holding shields of arms.

The most deservedly-celebrated monument in the church
is that executed by the sculptor T. Banks, R.A. in memory
of the only daughter of Sir Brooke Boothby. This exquisite piece of sculpture does the highest credit to the acknowledged abilities of the artist. In consequence of a
wooden covering, kept constantly locked, the monument is
in the freshest state of preservation. It represents a child
of delicate and amiable features, who has long suffered from
slow and incurable disease, lightly but rather restlessly
reclining on her right side. The position of the meek and
lovely sufferer shows that she has but just assumed it in
order to seek temporary relief from pain, or from the

Published by Dawson & Hobson, Ashbourn.

ASHBOURN CHURCH
VIEW OF CHANCEL.

weariness that a protracted horizontal position, even on the softest materials, eventually causes. The little patient is extended in the posture just described, on a marble mattress and pillow, to which the hand of the sculptor has communicated the apparent texture of the softest down. The expression of the countenance is slightly indicative of pain, felt even in the intervals of slumber, and the little hands lifted towards that countenance, plainly show that the slumberer has so placed them in order that they and the arms may in some measure be a support to the body, and relieve it from the aching tenderness caused by long contact with the couch on which it rests. Around the head is bound in loose folds a handkerchief, which allows the artist greater scope to exhibit the child's features. The body-costume of the lamented child is a low-fronted robe, with short sleeves, and confined—but perhaps rather too tightly for an invalid—around the waist, by a broad riband, most gracefully sculptured. The whole of the drapery is executed in the most finished style, and the ease and softness of the folds are an admirable proof of the delicate chiselling of the artist. He has also shown his natural and pure taste in the manner in which he has placed the beautiful naked feet. The entire position of the figure is faultless, and it represents, with refined fidelity to nature, the female infant form patiently and slowly perishing beneath the steady, undermining progress of irresistible decay. He who has in a mixed agony of hope and despair, long watched over an infant withering beneath the blight of disease, will feel grateful to the sculptor who had the talent to execute, and to the parent who had the affection to erect a monument which faithfully places before his view the representation of sufferings which time allows him to remember and to contemplate with melancholy satisfaction.

On the oblong-square pedestal and slab that support the monument are four inscriptions, in English, Latin, French, and Italian.

1. *Left hand on the slab.*—" I was not in safety, neither had I rest, and the trouble came."

Beneath on the pedestal.—" To Penelope, only child of Sir Brooke Boothby and Dame Susannah Boothby, born April 11th, 1785: died March 13th, 1791. She was in form and intellect most exquisite. The unfortunate parents ventured their all on this frail bark, and the wreck was total."

II. *Latin side, at her head on the slab.*—" Omnia tecum una perierunt gaudia nostra."*

Beneath on the Pedestal.—" Tu vero felix et beàta Penelope mea, Quæ tot tantisque miseriis una morte perfuncta es."†

III. *French side, end of the slab.*—" Beaute, c'est donc ici ton dernier azyle."‡

Beneath on the pedestal.—" Son cercueil, ne la contient pas toute entiere; Il attend le reste de sa proie: Il ne l'attendra pas longtemps."§

IV. *Italian side.*—" Lei che'l ciel ne mostra terra n'asconde."

" Le crespe chiome d'or puro, lucente,
E'l lampeggiar dell Angelico riso,
Che solean far in terra un Paradiso,
Poca polvere son che nulla sente."‖

This monument probably suggested to Sir F. Chantrey the execution of that master-piece of art, the group of the two children, which is now the grace and ornament of Lichfield Cathedral, and the boast of modern sculpture.‡‡ It appears that it was at an inn, in Ashbourn, after a visit to Miss Boothby's monument, that Sir Francis designed that justly-celebrated group.

There are several other monuments to different members of the Boothby family; two of them have remarkably pleasing inscriptions, which are said to have been written by Miss Seward and Sir Brooke Boothby:

All our joys are perished with thee alone.

†*But thou art happy and blessed, my dear Penelope, who, by one touch of Death hast escaped so many and so great miseries.*

‡*Beauty, this then is thy last asylum!*

§*Her tomb does not yet contain all; it waits for the rest of its prey:—it will not wait long.*

‖*Those that descend into the grave are not concealed from Heaven. Thy curling locks of pure shining gold, the lightning of thy angelic smile, which used to make a Paradise on earth are now become only a little senseless dust.*

‡‡*Rhodes's Derbyshire Tourists' Guide.*

A monument of alabaster.—" Sacred to the memory of Sir Brooke Boothby, Bart. and Dame Phœbe his wife, daughter and heir of William Hollins, Esq. of Moseley in the county of Stafford. He was born November 2nd, 1710, and died April 9th, 1789. She was born October 4th, 1716, and died May 5th, 1788. They were married in 1742, and left issue two sons and one daughter, Brooke, born June 3d, 1744; William, born May 4th, 1746; Maria Elizabeth, born February 16th, 1758.

> Here blameless pair, with mild affections blest,
> Beloved, respected, much lamented, rest:
> Life's sheltered vale secure in peace ye trod,
> Your practice virtue, your reliance God.
> Long days, long love, indulgent heaven bestow'd,
> And sweet content to gild your calm abode :
> Friends who through life their faith unalter'd kept;
> Children who loved, who honoured, and who wept;
> Heroes and kings, life's little pageant o'er
> Might wish their trophied marbles told no more"

A monument.—" Sacred to the memory of Hill Boothby, only daughter of Brooke Boothby and Elizabeth Fitzherbert, his wife; born October 27th, 1708; died January 16th, 1756.

> Could beauty, learning, talents, virtue, save
> From the dark confines of th' insatiate grave;
> This frail memorial had not asked a tear,
> O'er Hill's cold ashes, sadly mouldering here :
> Friendship's chaste frame her ardent bosom fired,
> And bright religion all her soul inspired :
> Her soul too heavenly for a house of clay.
> Soon wore its earth-built mansion to decay.
> In the last struggles of departing breath,
> She saw her Saviour gild the bed of death;
> Heard his mild accents tuned to peace and love,
> Breathe a blest welcome to the realms above;
> To those bright regions, that celestial shore,
> Where friends, long lost, shall meet to part no more.
> " Blest Lord, I come," my hopes have not been vain :
> Upon her lifeless cheek, extatic smiles remain."

In the south transept, is an old altar-tomb, without effigy or date, probably belonging to some member of the Bradburne family.

To the right is another fine altar-tomb, in excellent preservation, with whole-length effigies in alabaster, of Sir Humphrey Bradburne, knight, of Lea, near Bradburne, and Dame Elizabeth his wife, daughter of Sir William Turvill, of Newhall, Warwickshire, knight. Obiit 1581.

Adjoining this tomb is another, of greater antiquity, and much dilapidated. On the wall immediately above it, is a tablet inscribed to a member of the Bradburne family.

In the chancel is a white marble cenotaphic monument, with an inscription

"In memory of Lieut. Colonel Philip Bainbrigge, fourth son of the late Thomas Bainbrigge, Esq. of Woodseats, Staffordshire. He commanded the 20th regiment of foot at the battle of Egmont-op-Zee, on the 6th of October, 1799, which terminated the expedition to Holland, where he was killed, in the 44th year of his age, leaving a widow and eight children to mourn their irreparable loss. His body was buried by his brother soldiers, in the church-yard near the field of battle."

The church contains many other monuments; but those which have now been described are the most remarkable.

In the reign of Richard II. a chantry was founded at the altar of St. Mary, in Ashbourn church, and endowed by Henry de Kniveton, rector of Norbury. Another chantry, in honour of St. Oswald, was founded in or about the year 1483, by John Bradburne and Anne his wife.

These chantries were private religious foundations, established for the purpose of keeping up a perpetual succession of prayers for the prosperity of some particular family while living, and the repose of the souls of those members of it who were deceased, but especially of the founder and other persons specifically named by him in the instrument of foundation. "Chantries were usually founded in churches already existing; sometimes the churches of the monasteries, sometimes the great cathedral or conventual churches, but very frequently the parish church, whether in a town or in a rural district. All that was wanted was an altar with a little area before it, and a few appendages; and places were easily found even in churches of small dimensions in which such an altar could be raised without interfering inconveniently with the more public and general purposes for which the churches were erected. An attentive observation of the fabric of the parish-churches of England will often detect where these chantries have been, in some small remains of the altar, which was removed at the Reformation, but more frequently in one of those ornamented niches, called piscinas, which were always placed in proximity with the altars. Sometimes there are remains of painted glass which it is easy to see has once been the ornament of one of these private foundations, and more frequently one of those arched recesses in the wall, which are called Founders' Tombs, and which in many instances no doubt were actually the tombs of persons to whose memory chantries had been instituted. In churches which consisted only of a nave and chancel with side aisles, the eastern extremities of the north and south aisles were often seized upon for the purpose of these foundations. [It is very probable that the chantry founded by the Bradburne family, in Ashbourn church, was situated in this position in the south transept.] In the larger churches, having the platform resembling the cross on which the Saviour suffered, the transverse beams were generally devoted to the purpose of these private foundations. It was by no means unusual to have four, five, or six different chantries in a common parish-church; while in the great cathedral churches, such as old St. Paul's, in London, the Minster at York, and other ecclesiastical edifices of that class, there were at the time of the Reformation thirty, forty, or fifty such foundations. When the fabric of a church afforded of itself no more space for the introduction of chantries, it was usual for the founders to attach little chapels to the edifice. It is these chantry chapels, the use and occasion of which are now so generally forgotten, which cause so much of the irregularity of design which is apparent in the parish-churches of England. Erected also as they generally were, in the style of architecture which prevailed at the time, and not in accommodation to the style in which the original fabric was built, they are a principal cause of that want of congruity which is perceived in the architecture of different parts of the parish-churches. When chapels were erected for the special purpose of the chantries, they were usually also the places of interment of the founder and his family, whence we sometimes find such chapels belonging, even to this day, to particular families, and adorned with monuments of many generations."*

These extracts are valuable, as they serve in some degree to point out the causes which have led to the mixture of styles in the architecture of Ashbourn Church.

The rectory of Ashbourn, together with the chapels, lands, tithes, and other appendages, were granted by William Rufus to the church of St. Mary, at Lincoln, and to the bishop of that see and his successors; but by some arrangement at a later period, it was attached to the Deanery of that see, and it is now leased out by the Dean. The present lay impropriator is George Henry Errington, Esq. and the annual amount of tithes from the whole parish exceeds £2,000.

The vicarage has been augmented by a parliamentary grant of £600, and its present value is about £100 per annum. The rectory of Mappleton is annexed to the vicarage, and the Rev. Samuel Shipley has been for many years the incumbent.

There is an afternoon-lectureship attached to the church; the present lecturer is the Rev. Evan Thomas.

An evening service takes place in the chancel, which is fitted up for public worship. The duty is performed gratuitously by the vicar.

Near Ashbourn Hall, there formerly stood a chapel dedicated to St. Mary. Its remains were taken down some years ago, previously to which time it had been used as a malt-house. Sir John Cokayne, by will dated in the 13th year of the reign of Henry IV. charged his manor of Budsley Endsor, in Warwickshire, "to find as many priests singing to the world's end for his soul, his wife's, his children's, and all his ancestors' souls, as the rent thereof would maintain, viz. in St. Mary's chapel, Polesworth, five pounds to one priest; in St. Mary's chapel, near Ashbourn, seven

---

*Cyclopædia of the Society for the Diffusion of Useful Knowledge.

marks to another priest, and the remnant to be spent in waxen vigils and alms deeds on the eve and day of his obit." Sir Thomas Cokayne, (the warrior before-mentioned) " by his testament, bearing date April 8th, in the 28th year of Henry VIII. bequeathed his body to sepulture in our lady's Quire at Ashbourn, (where his ancestors lie interred) before the image of St. Modwin."

The NATIONAL AND SUNDAY SCHOOL, is a substantial edifice of stone, situated on an eminence north of the church. The expenses of its erection were defrayed chiefly by the proceeds of a bequest to the Church Sunday School, from a Miss Taylor, formerly a resident in Ashbourn. This bequest was augmented by the contributions of the inhabitants, and by a grant from the National Society. The operations of the school are conducted on the Society's plan. The Sunday School is under the direction of members of the Established Church. The building was opened in 1823.

COUNTESS OF HUNTINGDON'S CHAPEL.—At the southeast end of the town, on the Derby road, is a neat and substantially-erected chapel belonging to the Countess of Huntingdon's Connexion. This chapel and the six almshouses adjoining were erected and endowed in the year 1800, by Mr. John Cooper, a native of Ashbourn. In early life, Mr. Cooper followed the laborious occupation of brickmaking, but becoming disgusted with the employment, he removed to London, and by frugality and persevering industry, acquired a considerable property.

The Chapel is well attended, and contains accommodation for about five hundred worshippers. It is also provided with an organ. The Rev. Alexander Start is the present minister.

WESLEYAN METHODIST CHAPEL.—In 1822, a commodious chapel was erected by the Wesleyan Methodists. 1 is a neat brick building, situated in Compton, and contains six hundred sittings. This chapel was built by voluntary contribution, and its ministers are supported in a similar manner.

In connexion with both these chapels are Sunday Schools, conducted gratuitously, on a similar plan to that belonging to the Establishment.

The Presbyterians formerly possessed a place of worship in Compton. The building is now converted into dwelling-houses.

In 1826 a chapel was erected for the use of a congregation of General Baptists, but it has for some time been closed.

Drawn on Stone by S. Rayner.

ASHBOURN

W. ENTRANCE, SHEWING THE GRAMMAR SCHOOL.

Published by Dawson & Hobson Ashbourn.

CHAPTER VI.

The Free Grammar School—Its Foundation and Endowments.—Almshouses, and other Charitable Institutions.—Miscellaneous Notices connected with the Town of Ashbourn.

Near the church stands the FREE GRAMMAR SCHOOL, a fair specimen of the less-ornamented structures of the Elizabethan age, and a noble evidence of the philanthropy and munificence of the former inhabitants of Ashbourn. The School was founded in the reign of Queen Elizabeth, under letters patent, dated the 15th of July, 1585. The recital of the charter states that Sir Thomas Cokaine, of Ashborne, knt., William Bradborne, of the Lee, Thomas Carter, of the Middle Temple,* Thomas Hurt, and William Jackson, of Ashborne, and other persons inhabiting the same town, purposed to found and establish there a free grammar school, for 'the better information, instruction, and education of the youth of the country near that place.' Her Majesty, on the petition of the said Thomas

---

*By a passage from the ancient topographer Stow, it would appear that the founders of the School were chiefly citizens of London:—

" Divers well-disposed citizens of London, desirous (as yet) not to be named being born in or near to Ashburne, in the Peake, in the county of Derby, combining their loving benevolence together, have builded there a faire schoolhouse, with convenient lodgings for a master, and liberal maintenance allowed thereto."—*Stow's Survey of London and Westminster.*

10

Carter, desiring to promote the said purpose, granted and
ordained that there should be a free grammar school in
Ashbourn, for the education and instruction of boys and
youths in grammar and other good learning, to continue
for ever, which should be called *The Free Grammar School
of Elizabeth Queen of England.* Her Majesty also granted
that there should be three discreet, good and honest men,
to be called Governors of the possessions, revenues, and
goods of such school; and twelve discreet, good and
honest men, to be called Assistants to the said Governors,
Her Majesty also ordained that Thomas Cokaine, son of
the said Sir Thomas Cokaine, John Alsop, of Alsop-in-the-
Dale,* and Robert Hurt, vicar of Ashbourn, should be the
first Governors; and that Robert Whithall, Thomas Alsop,
Roger Hurt, and nine others, parishioners of Ashbourn,
should be the first Assistants.† That the said Governors
and Assistants should be a body corporate, and when by
death or removal a vacancy should occur among the Governors or their successors, it should be filled up from the
Assistants; and that vacancies among the latter body
should be supplied from 'the more discreet and fit men inhabiting the parish of Ashborne.' Her Majesty granted
that the said Governors and Assistants should have a
common seal, and that they and their successors should
have the power of making statutes for the management and
direction of the school. Her Majesty also granted to the
said Sir Thomas Cokaine, knight, William Bradborne,
Thomas Carter, Thomas Hurt, and William Jackson, and
the survivors and survivor of them, and after their death to

---

*Until the last few years Alsop-in-the-Dale formed part of the parish of
Ashbourn.

†The present Governors are Mr. Christopher Harland, Mr. Robert Docksey
Goodwin, Sir William Boothby, Bart.; and Assistants, Mr. Thomas Wise, Mr.
Samuel Dawson, Mr. John Whitham, Mr. Robert James Hartshorn, Mr. John
Nicholson, Mr. Rupert Toogood, Mr. William Tyson, Mr. John Dawson, Mr.
Septimus Bradley, Mr. Peter Bainbrigge Le Hunt, Mr. John Harry Buxton,
and Captain Thomas Archer; Treasurer, Mr. Philip Dawson.

THE SEAL

Of the Governors and Assistants of the Ashbourn Free Grammar School.

the said Governors and Assistants and their successors, or the greater part of them, with the advice and consent of the heirs-male of the before-mentioned persons, power and authority to appoint a master and under-master of the school, so often as those offices should become vacant; and in case the said founders, and after their deaths the Governors and Assistants, should not, within thirty days after such vacancy, appoint other fit and learned persons to perform such offices, then the Bishop of Lichfield and Coventry for the time being should have the power of appointment. It was also ordained that every master and under-master so appointed, should hold and enjoy the said School, and should remain and be without any other presentation or investiture to be thereupon made, for the term of his life, according to the ordinances and statutes of the school; that every master, under-master, governor, and assistant should be removable, and might from time to time be removed, according to the said ordinances and statutes; and that the school should be donative and collative, and not by any means presentative.

The first statutes for the government of the School appear to have been made in the year 1796, in consequence of certain abuses having crept into its management. A letter previously addressed to the Bishop of the Diocese, by the Governors and Assistants, requesting his advice and assistance, states that the head-master had at that time only one free-scholar, and had had only two or three for many years past; and that the under-master taught a private school in his own house, and neglected the few free-scholars. These statutes were revised and amended in the year 1836.

The school is open, under certain restrictions, to the boys of the town and neighbourhood; and admission is obtained by a certificate from one of the Governors or Assistants. The scholars are to be instructed gratuitously in the Greek and Latin classics, ancient and modern history, geography, English grammar and composition, the mathematics, and the principles of the Christian religion;

reference being duly had to the age, ability, and acquirements of each boy. For writing and arithmetic, the under-master receives a stated sum quarterly from each scholar.

The Masters are allowed to take as many boarders as their houses will properly accommodate; subject to the visitation and control of the Governors and Assistants.

The facilities which this school has afforded for the acquirement of a sound classical education,—facilities perhaps equal to those of any similar establishment,—have obtained for it some reputation amongst the gentry of Derbyshire and the adjacent counties. The edifice having recently undergone considerable improvements, its means of accommodation for boarders are thereby increased; while at the same time the views and intentions of its founders with respect to gratuitous instruction are more effectually carried out.

The Rev. George Edward Gepp, M.A. was appointed head-master in 1837, and the Rev Thomas Gibbs, second-master in 1818.

The whole annual revenue of the school amounts to £255 0s. 4d.; of which sum, (after deductions for the repairs of the building, and other expenses,) two-thirds are paid to the head-master, and the remaining third to the under-master. Each master has besides a good house and garden.

The Charity Commissioners' Report contains a lengthened account—extending to nearly forty folio pages,—of the donations and bequests which have at different periods been made for the support of the Free Grammar School, and the other charitable foundations belonging to the town. That account is too diffuse for general readers, and a careful abridgment of it, with such corrections and additions as the lapse of time and other circumstances have rendered necessary, will probably best serve the purposes of those to whom it is of more immediate interest.

CHARITIES.

FREE GRAMMAR SCHOOL.—*Thomas Hurt* gave the land (three roods) on which the School is erected.

Sir Thomas Cockayne, Knt. by deed, on the 21st September, 1585, granted to the Governors and Assistants of the School, a yearly rent-charge of £4 out of all his estate in Ashbourn. This payment has long since ceased, and it is supposed that Sir Thomas Cockayne substituted four tenements in the Middle Cale for the rent-charge. The property now produces the yearly sum of £15 9s.

Thomas Carter, by deed, 13th September, 1586, granted a rent-charge of 40s. for the support of the School and the Master and Under-master thereof, out of his premises in Ashbourn. The sum of £1 12s. is now paid by the owner of the premises in the Market-place late the property of Mr. William Sutton; 8s. having been deducted from the original sum for land-tax.

Philip Okeover, by deed, 15th September, 1586, granted a rent-charge of 20s. annually out of his lands in Mappleton, for the support of the school and the Master and Under-master thereof. This sum is now paid out of the same lands.

Gilbert, Earl of Shrewsbury, Robert Booth, and Thomas Cooke, by deed, granted a rent-charge of £5 per annum for the use of the school, out of an estate at Glossop. It is paid by the Duke of Norfolk, the present owner of the estate.

Humphrey Street gave at different times, in or about the year 1608, as much as £100 to the school.

Sir Anthony Ashley, and *Mrs. Storer*, in the year 1608, each granted a yearly rent-charge of 20s. out of property in London, for the use of the school; both these payments have long ceased, and are now lost.

Roger Owfield, by will, dated 28th January, 1610, gave £70 to be laid out in land for the benefit of the school.

Johane Denton (wife of Richard Denton) by deed, 10th June, 1619, granted, for various charitable purposes, a rent-charge of £5 annually, out of lands in Sturston, Compton, and Fenton, of which the annual sum of 10s. was to be paid to the Governors and Assistants, for the use of the school.

Edward Shawe and *Johane Denton*, on the 1st of March, 1625, granted, for charitable purposes, a rent-charge of £5 annually out of lands in Bradley, Sturston, Compton, and Fenton, of which the annual sum of 10s. was to be paid to the Governors and Assistants, for the use of the school. This payment is now made by Mr. Robert James Hartshorn, the owner of two fields in Compton.

Paul Taylor, by will, dated 24th December, 1640, gave several sums amounting to £27, to be applied to various purposes connected with the School. He also gave twenty nobles towards making a loft in the church for scholars and others to sit in. Also three nobles and twelve crowns to buy fifteen handsome walking staves, for the Governors and Assistants ' to put them in mind of his desire and a conscionable performance of all things belonging to them in their places.'

George Taylor, by will, dated 2nd May, 1668, gave out of his land in the Long-Doles, £1 per annum for the increase of the school-master's salary. The present tenant of the field pays £5 annually as rent for one-half of the land (about two acres) which is applied as directed by the will. The rent of the remaining part is applied to another purpose. [See a subsequent page.]

Christopher Pegg, by will, dated 12th June, 1669, directed certain premises in Ashover and Wingerworth, to be conveyed to the trustees of the school for augmenting the revenue of the head-master, usher, and under-master. In 1777, these lands were exchanged (by virtue of an Act of Parliament passed for that purpose in 1772,) for an estate in the parish of Brailsford, containing A.157 0R. 19P. now in possession of Hamlet Yates, and producing the yearly rent of £197. Two-fifths of this rent are paid to the school account; the remainder is otherwise applied. [See page 81.]

John Hanson, by will, dated 13th January, 1678, gave to the Corporation of the school, a yearly rent-charge of £6 13s. 4d. out of his tithes of lead-ore arising out of the parishes of Bakewell, Tideswell, and Hope, for increasing the head-master's salary. This payment is now made by the Duke of Devonshire, the owner of the tithes.

Elizabeth Buxton, by will, dated 11th July, 1730, gave 10s. yearly to purchase Bibles for the free-scholars.

The Estate belonging to the school, situated at Shirebrook, was purchased by the trustees on the 8th of January, 1613, for the sum of £180, subject, however, to an annuity of £5 payable thereout. This annuity was afterwards purchased by the trustees, for £95. The estate comprises a farm-house, outbuildings, and 103 acres of land, and is now held on lease by William Bowmar, at the yearly rent of £141.

OWFIELD'S ALMSHOUSES.—*Roger Owfield,* by will, dated 28th January, 1630, gave £100 to erect an Almshouse for poor inhabitants of Ashbourn, but that sum not being sufficient, the buildings were completed by his widow, Thomasin Owfield, at her own expense.

Thomasin Owfield, by deed, 28th January, 1630, made over the sum of £100 to the Governors and Assistants of the School, to be placed out at interest for raising £8 per annum, to pay the eight poor alms-people £1 each.

Samuel Owfield, (son of Roger and Thomasin Owfield,) by deed, 2nd November, 1640, granted to the trustees of the School, the eight newly-erected alms-houses, in trust, to maintain the same for eight poor people of the town of Ashbourn.

Paul Taylor, by will, dated 24th December, 1640, gave £12 10s. that the interest thereof, if it would make so much) should be paid by 2s. 6d. each to the poor almspeople every Good Friday: but as it was not sufficient for that purpose, it was made up by Robert Webster, as will be seen subsequently.

John Owfield and *William Owfield,* on the 1st of June, 1652, granted to the Governors and Assistants of the School, in trust for the benefit of the inhabitants of these almshouses, two pieces of land, situated in Mappleton, containing about seven acres. This land is supposed to have been substituted for the £100 given by Thomasin Owfield, as before mentioned. It is now occupied by William Chawner, and the rent is applied as above directed.

Part of the ground belonging to these almshouses is let as a garden to

William Webster, Esq, at the annual rent of £4, which is equally divided among the alms-people of this charity.

Robert Webster, by deed, 28th March, 1659, granted a rent charge of £1 yearly out of a field in Offcote, to the Governors and Assistants of the School, to enable them to pay £1 yearly to the eight alms-people as directed by Paul Taylor's will. This rent-charge is now paid by Sir William Boothby, Bart. the owner of the field.

George Taylor, by will, dated 2nd March, 1668, gave to the Governors and Assistants of the School £100 to be lent out at interest, and to pay thereout 1s. annually to each of the alms-people. It is not known how this £100 was disposed of, but Mr. William Etches pays £5 yearly as a charge for interest out of a field of his in Offcote.

Jane James, by will, dated 13th July, 1669, gave a rent-charge of £2 yearly out of two fields in Roston, for the benefit of these alms-people. The rent-charge is duly paid by the tenant of the land, and is applied as directed in the will.

Richard Peters, by will, dated 18th of May, 1708, gave out of his lands in the parish of Uttoxeter, the yearly sum of £4, to be distributed to the eight inhabitants of these almshouses, every Midsummer-day. This sum is paid by John Harrison, Esq. of Snelston, the owner of the property at Uttoxeter, and it is applied as directed in the will.

Nicholas Spalden, by will, dated 16th April, 1710, gave to the Governors and Assistants his lands in Parwich, in trust, for the benefit of the inmates of these almshouses. The lands contain A.13 0R. 34P. and are held by William Ellis, at the rent of £39 per annum.

The whole rents allow the weekly sum of 2s. 6d. each to the eight alms-people, and the overplus of £5 is applied for repairs of the houses, &c.

These almshouses are situated on the south side of Church-street, and are inhabited by eight poor persons, widows or widowers, of the township of Ashbourn. When vacancies occur either in these or the other almshouses under the management of the Governors and Assistants, they are filled up at a meeting holden after notice given, at which the candidates attend, and the election is decided by a majority of the Governors and Assistants present. The persons thus chosen are such as are not in the receipt of parochial relief.

PEGG'S ALMSHOUSES.—*Christopher Pegg,* by will, dated 12th June, 1669, directed six almshouses to be erected on property of his in Ashbourn, for six poor persons inhabiting the town, to be chosen by the Governors and Assistants of the School, with the consent of his trustees. And for their maintenance he gave his farm, &c. at Ashover and Wingerworth, occupied by Matthew Briddon, in trust, that the Governors and Assistants should pay the rents thereof by even portions to the six alms-people. He also gave another farm in Ashover and Wingerworth, in possession of William Needham, in trust, that half the rent thereof should be paid in even portions to the said alms-people.

These farms were in 1777 exchanged, (as before stated) for lands in Brailsford. Three-fifths of the rent is applied towards the support of the alms-people, and the remainder is paid to the school account.

11

German Pole, by will, dated 6th October, 1682, gave to the Governors and Assistants several pieces of land lying near Mercaston Mill, in trust, to apply the rents towards the maintenance of these six almspeople. This property contains A.29 OR. 30P. and is occupied by George Mounteney, and the rent is applied as above directed.

Part of the ground belonging the almshouses is let as a garden to Edward Walker, Esq. for two guineas a year, which sum is equally divided among the six almspeople, and is in addition to seven shillings per week which they each receive from the rents of the Brailsford and Mercaston estates. Twenty shillings' worth of clothing is also given to each poor person every two years out of the surplus.

These almshouses are also situated in Church-street, contiguous to the last-mentioned. They are occupied by six poor widows or widowers of the township of Ashbourn. The mode of choosing the almspeople in this and the other foundations has been already described; but as those in Pegg's almshouses enjoy greater advantages than those in Owfield's, it is the practice, on the occurrence of a vacancy in the former, to fill it up with the person who has been the longest time in the latter.

SPALDEN'S ALMSHOUSES.—*Nicholas Spalden*, by will, dated 16th April, 1710, gave to the Governors and Assistants of the school, all his messuages, lands, &c. in Dublin or elsewhere in Ireland, in trust, to purchase land, in Ashbourn, and build thereon ten almshouses, to keep the same in repair, and pay each of the almspeople a weekly sum of 2s. 6d. and give them each yearly, clothing of the value of £1.

Thomas Chatterton, by will, dated 20th February, 1811, gave money in the funds to the Governors and Assistants, for increasing the allowance of the poor persons in Spalden's almshouses. The only money, however, derived from this bequest was £80; but through the gift of Mr. Chatterton's next of kin, and a public subscription in the town of Ashbourn, a sufficient sum was raised to purchase £500 stock in the then four per cents, now new three and half. The dividends thereof, amounting to £17 10s. are paid in weekly sums of 8d. each to the ten alms-people; the balance is equally divided among them.

These almshouses adjoin the churchyard. The persons appointed to them are married men belonging to the town of Ashbourn; but when an alms-man dies, his widow is usually permitted to remain in the house in which her husband resided, and to receive the benefit of the charity.

CLERGYMEN'S WIDOWS' ALMSHOUSES.—*Nicholas Spalden*, by will, dated 16th April, 1710, directed the Governors and Assistants, in case there should be any surplus arising out of certain property mentioned in his will, to purchase land, and build thereon 'four neat and pretty houses for entertaining the widows of four clergymen of the Church of England', and to pay £10 yearly to each of such widows so long as each woman should continue a widow.

The surplus was sufficient for this purpose, and the four houses were erected on the south side of Church-street. They are occupied as directed by the will, and the £10 paid annually to each of the widows.

Isaac Hawkins, by will, gave a sum of money to trustees, to be laid out in charitable uses as they should think proper, and part thereof was in 1804, laid out in the purchase of £400 stock in the four per cents, (now reduced to three and half) in the names of three of the Governors and Assistants; the dividends, being £14, a year, are duly paid to the widows, in equal shares, as directed by the will.

The clergymen's widows are appointed to these almshouses, by the Governors and Assistants, as vacancies occur, without any restriction, or reference to the place of residence of their deceased husbands; notices of such vacancies are given by public advertisement.

SPALDEN'S SCHOOLS.—*Nicholas Spalden,* by his will, directed the Governors and Assistants of the Free Grammar School, out of any residue arising from his will, to purchase land, and build thereon a school-house for the instruction of thirty poor boys, children of the inhabitants of the town of Ashbourn, until they should be fit to go to the Free School of Ashbourn; and to pay the School-master £10 yearly. Also to purchase land and build thereon another school-house for the instruction of thirty poor girls, children of the inhabitants of Ashbourn, until they should be twelve years old; and to pay the school-mistress £10 yearly.—There was sufficient to establish these schools, and they are carried on as directed by the will. The master and mistress have each an allowance of 30s. a year out of the overplus, for coals.

FIELD-RENTS.—In the year 1625, some disputes arose in consequence of certain persons having claimed a right to enclose some open lands, near Ashbourn-Green, to which lands the inhabitants of Ashbourn alleged they had a right of common. In order to settle these disputes it was decreed by the Duchy Court of Lancaster, on 10th February, 1625, that it should be lawful for all owners of lands within [or adjoining] the said open fields, to inclose the same, on paying yearly for the benefit of the town of Ashbourn, to the Governors and Assistants of the Free Grammar School there, the sum of 1s. 6d. per acre for every acre of the said fields so inclosed within twenty years past.— By another decree of the same Court, on the 8th May, 1630, it was ordered that a further sum of sixpence per acre should be paid in addition to the before-mentioned 1s. 6d.

The quantity of land liable to this charge is A.146 2R. 20P., and the annual sum received is £14 8s. 8d., which is usually applied (together with the surplus of Spalden's charity) in purchasing coals to be distributed to the poor inhabitants of the town of Ashbourn, in the winter season, as ordered by the vestry-meeting on Easter Tuesday.

BREAD CHARITY.—*Nicholas Hurt,* by deed, in 1637, gave a yearly rent-charge of £5 out of his estate at Castern, in Staffordshire, to the Governors and Assistants, to be laid out in bread, to be distributed weekly to twelve poor persons of Ashbourn and Compton. The rent-charge is applied as directed.

Paul Taylor, by will, dated 24th December, 1640, gave to the Governors and Assistants £50 to be laid out in land, the yearly rent thereof to be given weekly in bread to six of the poorest people of the town of Ashbourn, which poor people are to enjoy the same during their lives.—The proceeds of this bequest, amounting to £4 16s annually, are paid out of Little Field Close, now the property of Sir William Boothby, Bart.

Edward Pegge, by will, dated 31st March, 1666, gave £5 4s. annually out of his lands in Sturston, one half to be given weekly, in bread, to six poor inhabitants of Ashbourn; the other half to be given in like manner to the poor of Osmaston, near Ashbourn. The sum of £2 12s. is paid out of the Gravel Pits Farm, in Sturston, the property of Miss Bradley, and is expended as directed in the will.

George Taylor, by will, dated 2nd March, 1668, gave to the Governors and Assistants, and inhabitants of Ashbourn £100 to be placed out at interest, and from the profit thereof he gave £2 12s. yearly, to be dealt every Sunday in bread, to twelve poor inhabitants of the town.

LECTURESHIP.—About the year 1630, Robert Bateman, Esq. and 'divers other charitable persons inhabiting within the city of London, and counties of Derby and Stafford,' raised the sum of £400 by voluntary contributions, towards purchasing an annuity for the maintenance of an able, pious, and orthodox preacher, who should weekly preach two Sermons or Divinity Lectures in Ashbourn : but if anything should happen that the said pious work should be hindered, then the said Lectures should be preached at some other convenient town in Derbyshire, not above five miles from Ashbourn; and in case of disturbance at Ashbourn, or in any other place as aforesaid, then the said annuity to go towards the relief and maintenance of the poor of the town of Ashbourn. The money was about the year 1651 increased by other contributions, and laid out in the purchase of an annuity of £40 per annum, out of property at Walton, near Chesterfield, to be applied to the maintenance of a preacher, to be appointed by certain trustees or their successors. The rent-charge is paid by Sir Henry Hunloke, the owner of the property at Walton.

Paul Taylor, by will, dated 24th December, 1640, gave £10 towards the maintenance of Thursday Lecture, but if the lecture did not continue, the sum was to go towards the maintenance of the lecturer for the time being. He also gave the sum of £20 towards the maintenance of the lecturer to preach a sermon on Good Friday, for ever.

Nicholas Spalden, by his will, gave £340 to trustees to place out at interest, and to pay thereout the yearly sum of £8 to the lecturer for reading divine service every day in the week next preceding the first Sunday in every month, and preaching a Sermon in the parish church on the last Friday in every month. [In case these directions should not be complied with, see further instructions on a subsequent page.]

MISCELLANEOUS CHARITIES.—*Johane Denton*, (wife of Richard Denton,) by deed, 10th June, 1619, granted a rent-charge of £5 annually out of lands in Sturston, Fenton, and Compton, of which £3 was to be distributed (with the advice of the minister for the time being) amongst the poor widows and fatherless children inhabiting Ashbourn and Compton.

Also to pay a preacher at Ashbourn 10s. yearly.

To the Governors and Assistants, for the instruction .of poor children 10s. yearly.

To the Churchwardens, for repairing the church, 10s. yearly.

To the Constables, for the repairs of the three Bridges, the Market-Cross, the Common Well, and the Highways of Ashbourn, 10s. yearly.

Edward Shaw and Johane Denton, out of the rent-charge before-mentioned ordered the yearly sum of £2 10s. to be distributed, with the advice of the Governors and Assistants and the Minister, amongst the poor widows and fatherless children of Ashbourn and Compton; and after the decease of two persons mentioned in the deed, the further sum of 10s. yearly, to be distributed in like manner.

Also to the Preacher at Ashbourn, 30s. yearly for ever.

To the Governors and Assistants, for teaching poor children, 10s. yearly.

Paul Taylor, by his will, gave the Governors and Assistants £20 towards the maintenance of the Lecturer.

Also £15, the profit thereof to be distributed among the poorest widows, widowers, and impotent people of Ashbourn, on Good Friday for ever.

Also 20 marks towards raising a stock to set poor people on work.

Also five marks to buy Books of Acts and Monuments, to be laid safe in some convenient place in the church.

Robert Webster, by deed, 28th March, 1659, in consideration of a sum of money paid to him by Paul Taylor's widow, granted a rent-charge out of his land, 52s. of which was for bread for six poor people weekly; 24s. for poor widows, widowers, and impotent people, of Ashbourn, on Good Friday; and 20s. for the poor of Owfield's Almshouses. The consideration given to Robert Webster for this rent-charge, was the £12 10s. given by Paul Taylor, for the use of the poor in Owfield's almshouses; the £50 for bread; and the £15 for the poor widows, &c.

The money is now paid by Sir William Boothby, Bart., the owner of the land charged with the same.

George Taylor, by his will before-mentioned, gave to the Governors and Assistants, and inhabitants of Ashbourn, £100 to be lent on good security to ten young tradesmen, at five per cent, out of which interest 52s. was to be paid weekly in bread, to twelve poor inhabitants of the town; 8s. to the poor in Owfield's almshouses; 20s. to be given by the overseers to forty poor housekeepers, yearly every Christmas; and 20s. yearly to the Vicar or Minister to preach a sermon annually, in which the legacies given by himself and his brother Paul Taylor, should be mentioned, to stir up the charity of others. And in case good security could not be given for the money, then he empowered his executors to buy so much land as would pay £5 annually till his heir came of age, and then settle the said annual rent out of his own lands for ever, he receiving the £100.

It is not known how this £100 was disposed of, but a yearly sum of £5 is paid by Mr. Etches, out of Sole Meadow, which formerly belonged to the Taylors.

He also gave out of his Long.doles land, 20s. yearly for the repairs of the church and steeple; and 20s. yearly out of the same land for the increase of the Schoolmasters' salary, provided that the said land should never be inclosed, and the poor barred of the right of putting in their cattle. Sampson Gather holds the land, and pays £5 as rent for two acres, (one-half the field) which is applied to the Schoolmasters; the rent of the remaining half of the field, is received by the Churchwardens for the repairs of the church, as directed by the will.

Christopher Pegge, by will, gave to the Governors and Assistants, certain lands in Ashover and Wingerworth, (subsequently exchanged for land in Brailsford,) of which half the profits were to be distributed yearly to the most indigent people of Ashbourn. The sum of £18 18s 2d. (the proportion) is paid in small sums to the poor of the town on St. Thomas's Day.

John Hanson, by will, dated 13th January, 1610, charged his lands in Ashbourn with the payment of £5 annually to the Churchwardens, to be by them distributed at Easter and Michaelmas, to such poor of the town as they should think in most need.

Nicholas Spalden, by will, gave £340 to Trustees to be placed out at interest, to pay £8 yearly to the Vicar of Ashbourn, for reading divine service morning and evening, every Wednesday and Friday throughout the year.

Also to pay £8 yearly to the Lecturer.

Also to pay 20s. yearly to the person appointed to ring the bell on those occasions.

If the above directions should not be complied with, then he gave 40s. a year to the poor of Snelston, 20s. to the poor of Clifton, 40s. to the poor of Mayfield, 20s. to the poor of Mappleton, and the remaining £11 to be laid out in coal for the poor of Ashbourn in the winter season.

If there should be any surplus after all his legacies and bequests were performed, he gave the same to the Governors and Assistants, to be disposed of by them, for the public benefit of the Town of Ashbourn, and they to give an account in writing, of their management and transactions, every year on Easter Tuesday, at a public meeting of the parish, in the church, to be read and perused by the inhabitants of Ashbourn.

Catharine Port, by a codicil to her will, 9th February, 1724, confirmed all the charities given by her father, John Port, Esq., one of which was £5, to be given in wool, or money, to the poor of Ashbourn, annually.

This payment is now made by Jesse Watts Russell, Esq.

Elizabeth Buxton, by will, dated the 11th July, 1730, gave to the Vicar of Ashbourn, 10s. yearly, to preach a sermon; also 5s. yearly to the Ringers, to ring a solemn peal; and 20s. yearly for forty poor housekeepers of the Township of Ashbourn, to be distributed by the Overseers by 6d. each.

Mr. Ralph Toplis of Winster, (the owner of the property in Ashbourn charged with these payments) pays these sums for the sermon, &c., on St. Swithin's day.

GISBORNE'S CHARITY.—This Charity was founded by the Rev. Francis Gisborne, by deed, dated 1817, and was afterwards augmented by will, dated 1818. It consists of a large sum of money in the funds; the dividends of which are divided in equal portions, among one hundred rectories, vicarages, and curacies, in the county of Derby, to be applied by each Rector, &c., in the purchase of flannel and woollen cloth, to be distributed among the poor of each parish every Christmas. Among the places mentioned in the Schedule is Ashbourn, the vicar of which receives the sum of £5 10s. annually, which he distributes as above directed.

Dame Susannah Boothby, by will, dated 30th April, 1817, gave the remainder of her money in the Stocks, after payment of her debts, to be equally divided between four different Parishes there named, one of which is Ashbourn. Nothing has yet been received from this source.

COOPER'S CHARITY.—John Cooper, of Clerkenwell, London, by deed, dated Jan. 5, 1801, gave £3,500 in the three per cents, stock, and a further sum of £1000, to be invested therein; to the trustees of Lady Huntingdon's College, Cheshunt, Herts, in trust, for the maintenance, of six poor persons inhabiting the six alms-houses, which he had previously erected; and for the support of the Minister and the maintenance of divine worship, in the Zion Chapel, adjoining.

Out of the dividends, the almspeople receive each ten guineas yearly; the remainder is applied for the support of the minister, the maintenance of divine worship and to defray other necessary expenses.

The minister of the chapel and the alms-people are appointed by the trustees of Cheeshunt College. The committee for the management of the chapel have usually the nomination of the person who succeeds to an alms-house, on the occurrence of a vacancy.

In addition to the Charities already mentioned, there is a well-regulated Dispensary for the poor of the town and neighbourhood. The number of patients on the books in the year 1837, exceeded one hundred.

The Bible and Missionary Societies, and other religious Institutions (connected both with the established Church and with congregations of Dissenters,) have each their several branches in the town, and large sums are annually contributed to their support.

There are in the town a flourishing Savings' Bank, and several Benefit Societies. Also two News Rooms, a Moral and Religious Permanent Library, two Book Societies, and several Circulating Libraries.

The Banking House of Messrs. Arkwright and Co., and the Commercial Bank of England have branches in the town.

CHAPTER VII.

Ancient Families.—Particulars of the Mining Inquisitions held in the Town.—
Conference for the suppression of " Tutbury Bull-Running"—Description of
the Sport.—Bull-baiting.

Among the first families besides those of the lords of
the manor already mentioned, that seem to have acquired possessions or to have held estates in Ashbourn,
is that which derives its name from the place; but the
times in which its first members lived being so remote,
but few particulars can be discovered relative to their
history. On the granting of a charter to the town of
Uttoxeter, in the 36th year of the reign of Henry III., by
William de Ferrers, Earl of Derby, a Robert de Esseburne
is one of the principal witnesses. In the fourth year of
Edward I. this Robert de Esseburne or his immediate
descendant was possessed of *Campdene Street*, [Compton]
which was then a country village,* and had most likely
been granted to him or his ancestor by one of the lords of
Tutbury. A Robert de Essebourn represented the county
in three several parliaments of Edward I. In the succeeding reign flourished Thomas Ashburne, a celebrated divine.
"He was born" says Dr. Fuller, "at that well-known
market-town in the county of Derby, and not in Staffordshire, as others have mistaken. He became an Augustinian, went to Oxford and took his degree of D.D. He

*See page 11.

was a great opponent of Wickliffe, and in the synod where-in his doctrines were condemned for heresie, by ten bishops, twenty lawyers, and forty-four divines, he was one of the latter number. Yet once he did some good, or rather diverted much evil. It happened that one Peter Patishull, an Augustinian, preaching in London, had some passages in favour of Wickliffe, which so displeased those of his own order, that they plucked him out of the pulpit, dragged him into the convent of Augustines, (near Broad-Street,) intending more violence to his person. This allarumed the Londoners, (amongst whom a considerable party of Wick-liffites) to rescue poor Patishull; In their rage they would have burnt the convent about the friars' ears, had not our Ashburne, with his tears and intreaties seasonably inter-ceded."*

One of the numerous branches of the family of *Beresford* has long been settled in Ashbourn. The name of this ancient family first appears in the train of William the Conqueror; and a John de Beresford was lord of Beresford, in the county of Stafford, in the reign of William Rufus. The illustrious Beresfords of Ireland are descended from Humphrey, the seventh son of Thomas Beresford, a warrior, who resided at Fenny Bentley in the time of Henry VI. Other branches also resided at Broadlow Ash and Newton Grange: the latter estate was sold by Richard, the uncle of the late John Beresford, Esq. of Ashbourn.†

The elder branch of the opulent family of *Hurt*, of Alderwasley and Wirksworth, (whose name is found in the foregoing list of benefactors,) flourished in Ashbourn for four generations previously to the visitation ordered by the Heralds' Office, in the reign of Elizabeth, A.D. 1569. The pedigree of the family was then entered by Thomas Hurt, gent. of Ashbourn. This branch terminated about the close of the seventeenth century, by the marriage of the

---

*Fuller's Worthies. †For a more particular account of the different branches of the family, see "Fenny Bentley" and "Broadlow Ash."

12

heiress with a Byrom. The younger branches of the family were seated at Kniveton, Casterne, and Alderwasley. The latter estate has been in their possession for above one hundred and eighty years, and is now the property of Francis Hurt, Esq. M.P.

Another ancient family long resident in Ashbourn, is that of *Dale,* formerly of Flagg, in Derbyshire. Robert Dale, Esq. of Ashbourn, served the office of High Sheriff for the county in 1786. He was also commandant of the late Ashbourn Troop of Volunteer Infantry.

Edward Manlove, Esq. Steward of the Barmote Court for the lead mines within the Wapentake of Wirksworth, in the seventeenth century, was a resident in Ashbourn. He published a curious work in verse, on the customs and rights of the miners of Derbyshire, compiled from the Exchequer Rolls, and from inquisitions taken in different reigns.

The lead-ore, which forms the chief natural product of Derbyshire, was a very important article of commerce under the government of the Romans. The fact is proved by the numerous pigs or blocks of lead, bearing Latin inscriptions, which have been discovered in the mining districts. " In Britain" says Pliny, "in the very upper crust of the ground, lead is dug up in such plenty, that a law was made on purpose to stint them to a set quantity"* The mines in the Peak and in the Wapentake of Wirksworth were regarded as the peculiar domain of the crown at a very early period, and as such they are mentioned in Domesday-Book.

The Kings of England were always jealous of their mineral rights, and several of them after the Conquest, would not suffer their mines to be wrought. In 1246, Henry III. executed a writ of enquiry as to his mineral possessions in Derbyshire; and the inquisition was held at Ashbourn. It was then given for the King, that the mines in the

---

*Gibson's Translation of Camden.

High Peak, in the county of Derby, and those in the forest
of Mendip, in the county of Somerset, were the prerogative
royal of the crown, and not the property of those who had
long worked them; but the King permitted the miners to
proceed till further order, on condition that they paid to
him every thirteenth dish of lead-ore. In the 16th year
of Edward I. another inquisition was held at Ashbourn,
when it was again proved that the right to the minerals
was vested in the crown. The following is a translated
copy of the writ of inquisition, from the Exchequer Rolls:

"DERBY.—*Edward*, by the grace of God, King of England, lord of Ireland,
and duke of Acquitain, to the sheriff of the county of Derby greeting: Know ye
that we have assigned our faithful and well-beloved *Reynold of the Ley* (Lea)
and *William of Memill* (Meynell) to inquire by the oaths of good and lawful
men, of your county, by the which the truth may be best known, of the liberty
which our miners do claim to have in those parts, and which they have hitherto been used to have, and by what means, and how, and from what time, and
by what warrant. And therefore we do command, that at a certain day and
place, which the said Reynold and William shall appoint thee, Thou shall
cause to come before them so many, and such good and lawful men of thy
bailiwick, by the which may there the best be known in the premises by the
inquiry, and that thou have there the writ. Witness our well-beloved cousin,
Edmund Earl of Cornwall, at Westminster, the 28th day of April, in the sixteenth year of our reign. By *William* of *Hambleton*, and at the instance of
Hugh of *Cressingham*, the day is appointed at ASHBOURN, upon Saturday next,
after the feast of the *Holy Trinity.*"

The rule established by Henry III. and confirmed by his
successor, was extended by other Kings till the time of
Philip and Mary. Queen Elizabeth, in the 16th year of
her reign, granted all her mineral possessions in this
county to a society or corporation. *

*The mineral laws and customs are very curious. They consist of a body of
regulations, framed upon ancient rights, customs, and immunities, applying
particularly to that portion of the county called "the King's Field," which comprises the hundreds of the High Peak and the Wapentake of Wirksworth, with
the exception of some few estates. These laws originally authorised any man
or set of men to enter at any time any part of the King's Field, to dig or search
for veins of lead-ore, without being accountable to the owner or occupier of the
soil for any damage which they did to the surface, or even to the growing crops.
At present, however, it is held, that unless a miner procures ore enough from

In the year 1778, a meeting or conference took place at
Ashbourn, attended by fifteen deputies from each of the
counties of Derby and Stafford, to concert measures for the
suppression of a barbarous custom long practised in the
town of Tutbury.   The custom alluded to, that called
"*bull-running*," is supposed to have been instituted by
John of Gaunt, in imitation of the bull-feasts of Spain, the
native country of his Queen, who for some time resided
at the Castle of Tutbury; and it appears originally to have
formed the concluding scene of a festival held in that town,
denominated "The Minstrels' Court."   Though the more
pleasing part of that festival has long ceased to exist, its
cruel and revolting features have survived till a comparatively recent date.   "As the minstrels' court fell into disuse,
a mixed multitude of the inhabitants of each county joined
in this dangerous amusement: all authority was set at

---

any search he may make after a vein to free the same, that is to pay the King
or his lessee a dish of ore, he is liable to the occupier for all damage he may
have done him.   In the King's Field are certain officers appointed, called bar-
masters, and mineral courts are held, at which a jury of twenty-four miners de-
cide all questions respecting the duties payable to the King or his lessee, and
to the working of the mines by those to whom the bar-master has given possession.   When a miner has found a new vein of ore, provided it be not in an
orchard, garden, high-road, or churchyard, he may obtain an exclusive title to
it, on application to the bar-master.   In general, a thirteenth part of the ore
is due to the King or his lessee, but the proportion taken is seldom more than a
twenty-fifth.   The brazen-dish by which the measures of the ore are regulated,
is deposited in the Moot Hall, at Wirksworth.   It bears the following inscription :—

"This Dishe was made the iiij day of October the iiij yere of the Reigne of
Kyng Henry the viii before George Erle of Shrowesbury Steward of the Kyng's
most Honourable household and also Steward of all the honour of Tutbery by
the assent and Consent as wele of all the Mynours as of all the Brenners within and Adioyning the lordshyp of Wyrksworth percell of the said honour. This
Dishe to Remayne In the Moote Hall at Wyrkswyrth hangyng by a cheyne So
as the Merchanntes or Mynours may have resorte to the same at all tymes to
make the trw mesure after the same."

The mineral duties of the King's Field are let on lease, the present farmer
of those in the High Peak, is the Duke of Devonshire; and of those in the Low
Peak, Richard Arkwright, Esq.—*Glover's History of Derbyshire.*—*Beauties of
England and Wales.*

defiance; this feast of harmony was disgraced by the discordant brawlings of drunken revellers; the peace of the place was perpetually broken; and every friend to humanity and good order anxiously desired the abolition of a custom equally productive of cruelty and outrage."* In 1778 the usual day of 'running the bull' happened on the Sunday, and although of course the ceremony was deferred until the morrow, the bull was paraded round the town, and the sacred day polluted by the drunkenness and quarrelling of the assembled crowds; during which one individual lost his life. This occurrence afforded a fit opportunity for attempting the suppression of the custom. A petition setting forth the evil effects resulting from it, was presented to the Duke of Devonshire,† who consulted the king on the subject; and at the recommendation of govern-

---

*Sir O. Mosley's History of Tutbury.

The custom of the bull-running was celebrated on the feast of the Assumption, in the following manner: " All the minstrels within the honor came early on that day to the house of the bailiff of the manor of Tutbury, and from thence to the parish church in procession; the king of the minstrels for the year past, walking between the steward and bailiff of the manor, attended by the four stewards of the king of the minstrels, each with a white wand in their hands, and the rest of the company following in ranks of two and two together, with the music playing before them. After service was ended, they proceeded in the same order from the church to the castle hall, where the said steward and bailiff took their seats, placing the king of the minstrels between them, whose duty it is to cause every minstrel dwelling within the honor who makes default, to be presented and amerced. The court of the minstrels is then opened in the usual way, and proclamation made, that every minstrel dwelling within the honor of Tutbury, in any of the counties of Stafford, Derby, Nottingham, Leicester, or Warwick, should draw near and give his attendance; and that if any man would be assigned of suit or plea, he should come in and be heard. Then all the musicians being called over by a court-roll, two juries are impanelled, one for Staffordshire, and one for the other counties, whose names being delivered in to the steward, and called over, and appearing to be full juries, the foreman of each is sworn, and then the rest of them in the manner usual in other courts. The steward then proceeds to charge them, first commending to their consideration the antiquity and excellency of all music, both on wind and stringed instruments; and the effect it has upon the passions, proving the same

†High Steward of the Honor.

ment, the meeting at Ashbourn was called, which led to its final abolition.

Another sport, that of *bull-baiting*, closely allied, in its character and effects, to that just mentioned, was for many years practised in Ashbourn. The period of its introduction is unknown, but there is strong reason to suppose, from the connexion anciently existing between the two

---

by various examples; how the use of it has always been allowed in praising and glorifying God; and skill in it esteemed so highly, that it has always been ranked amongst the liberal arts, and admired in all civilized states; exhorting them, upon this account, to be very careful to make choice of such men to be officers amongst them as fear God, are of good life and conversation, and have knowledge and skill in the practice of the art.   After the officers for the next year have been elected, the jurors depart out of the court, and the steward with his assistants, and the king of the minstrels, in the meantime partake of a banquet, during which the other musicians play upon their several instruments: but as soon as the jurors return, they present the new king whom they have chosen; upon which the old king, rising from his seat, delivers to him his wand of office, and then drinks a cup of wine to his health and prosperity; in like manner the old stewards salute the new, and resign their offices to their successors.   The court then rises, and all repair to another large room within the castle, where a plentiful dinner is provided for them; after which the minstrels went anciently to the priory gate, but after the dissolution, to a barn near the town, in expectation of the bull being turned loose for them.   This bull was formerly found by the prior of Tutbury, but afterwards by the Duke of Devonshire, who enjoyed the priory lands.   The animals horns were sawed off, his ears cropped, his tail cut off to the stump, all his body smeared over with soap, and his nostrils blown full of pounded pepper : whilst this inhuman preparation is in progress, the steward makes proclamation that all manner of persons should give way to the bull, no person coming nearer unto him than forty feet, except the minstrels; but that all should attend to their own safety, every one at his peril : thus enraged to the utmost, the poor animal is then turned out to be taken by the minstrels, and none else within the county of Stafford, between the time of his being turned out, and the setting of the sun on the same day. If the bull escapes, he remains the property of the person who gave him ; but if any of the minstrels can take and lay hold of him, so as to cut off a small portion of hair, and bring the same to the market-cross, in proof of their having taken him, the bull is then brought to the bailiff's house, where a collar and rope are fastened to him, by which he is brought to the bull-ring in the high street, and there baited with dogs; after which the minstrels had him for their own, and might sell, kill, and divide him amongst themselves, as they thought fit.—*Plott's Staffordshire.*

places, that it was established in imitation of the "bull-running" at Tutbury.* The annual *wake* was the season at which this disgraceful exhibition took place. The bull, provided expressly for the purpose, was tied or chained to a ring in the market-place, and in that situation was subjected to the repeated attacks of dogs of the most ferocious breed. The reader may be spared a recital of the cruelties inflicted on the unoffending animal, or of the sufferings of his canine assailants; it is sufficient to state that they were such as grievously outraged the feelings of every friend of the brute creation. The town was on these occasions the resort of the idle and the dissipated of the surrounding country, and the scene presented was in many respects analogous to that which has been described as having occurred at Tutbury.

On a calm review of the past, it will appear surprising to every unprejudiced mind, that a custom whose obvious tendency was to foster and encourage the worst passions of our nature, and whose practice was always productive of intemperance and disorder, should in later times have been supported or tolerated. Its existence for so long a period after it had been rendered penal by act of Parliament, shows in a remarkable manner how slowly and unwillingly obedience is rendered to enactments which, as in this case, are opposed to the mistaken prejudices of the people.

It is proper to remark, that the majority of the inhabitants of Ashbourn participated not in the brutal pastime, and that many strenuous though abortive efforts were made by them to wipe away this stain in the character of the town. More stringent legislative enactments have at length effected its suppression, and since the passing of Mr. Pease's act in 1835, the practice has been discontinued.

---

*Bull-baiting was prevalent in England as early the twelfth century. A still more cruel sport was then sometimes exhibited, in which a horse, haltered to a stake or tree, was baited by dogs.

It has been supposed by some that Ashbourn had anciently a mayor and corporation, and that evidence of their existence may be traced in the annual celebration of the *mayor's feast*, which formerly took place in the town. This custom, however, it is well known, prevails in many small towns and villages, which could never have been incorporated. It was observed at Ashbourn in the year 1741, as appears from the following note of invitation, addressed "To John Borrows, Esq. at Derby" :—

" Sir Nathaniel Curzon (present Mayor of Ashbourne) intends to have the annual ffeast for the Corporation at the Black's Head, on Thousday, the 15th Day of September, when and where he desires your company to dine with him and assist in choosing his successor. Sir, your humble servant,

" 9th September, 1741."   "Jo : ALLSOP, Recorder."

CHAPTER VIII.

Notices of Offcote and Underwood, Clifton, Edlaston, Yeaveley, Hungry Bentley, Alkmanton, Longford, Brailsford, Shirley, Osmaston, Bradley, Hulland, Atlow, Kniveton, Hognaston, Bradbourn, Tissington, Parwich, Fenny Bentley, Thorpe, and Broadlow Ash.

OFFCOTE* and UNDERWOOD, a liberty belonging to and adjoining Ashbourn, contains about 328 inhabitants, who are chiefly engaged in agricultural pursuits. The manorial rights of the liberty are vested in the daughter and heiress of the late John Hayne, Esq. of Ashbourn-Green Hall.

One mile north of Ashbourn, on the Buxton-road, (in the same liberty,) is Sandy-brook Hall, an elegant modern erection, the seat of Sir Matthew Blakiston, Bart.†

CLIFTON, with the west side of Compton, form a township and constabulary in the parish of Ashbourn, in a detached part of the hundred of Morleston and Litchurch. The village of Clifton is situated about a mile and-a-half south-west of Ashbourn. At the time of the Domesday survey it was found that " *In Cliptune Leuric and Levenot had three carucates of land to be taxed, land to three*

Ophidicotès, (Offcote,) a berwick of Ashbourn, was in possession of the King at the Norman survey.

†Sir Matthew Blakiston, Bart. is descended from Matthew Blakiston, Esq., an eminent merchant of London, who was elected an alderman of that city in 1750, sheriff in 1753, and lord mayor in 1760. In 1759 he was knighted, and was afterwards created a baronet.—*Debrett's Baronetage.*

ploughs, eight villanes and five bordars have now there four ploughs and four acres of meadow.   Value in King Edward's time 40s. now 10s., and then belonged to Ralph Fitz Hubert."

The manors of Great and Little Clifton belonged to the Cokaynes,* of Ashbourn, in the reigns of Henry VII., Henry VIII., and Queen Elizabeth; they are said to have held them under the Fitzherberts, of Norbury.   The manors afterwards came to the family of Hayne, and Miss Hayne is the present proprietor.

The ancient chapel at Clifton was taken down about the year 1750, and part of the materials were used to repair the chancel of Ashbourn church.

EDLASTON, in Domesday-Book written *Edolveston*, a village, township, and parish in the hundred of Appletree, is about three miles south of Ashbourn.   The manor was given by one of the Ferrers family to the Priory of Tutbury. Henry VIII. granted it to William, Lord Paget, who sold it soon afterwards to Sir Edward Aston, knight.   It then came to the Eyres, of Hassop, who sold it to Mr. Daniel Morley, of Ashbourn, and from his devisee in trust it was bought by the ancestor of the Rev. Thomas Gisborne.   The

---

*What is now termed " Ashbourn Lodge Farm," in the parish of Clifton, was probably one of the " three fayre parks," impaled by Sir Thomas Cokayne, in the time of Henry VIII.   See ante p. 64.

Ashbourn and Clifton were in 1645 visited by that fearful malady the Plague.   In the accounts of the churchwardens and constables of Uttoxeter, the following items occur:—

" 1645.   August 26th: Paid to Ashburn by the Churchwardens of Uttoxeter when the town was infested with the Plague, £3."

" Paid to the inhabitants of Clifton, when the Plague was there, £5."

A monumental inscription in Chesterfield Church, to the memory of Paul Webster, a native of Ashbourn, states that ' his removals from Ashbourn were occasioned by the plague and civil wars.' [The ancient registers, and other public documents of the parish of Ashbourn, which it is reasonable to suppose would contain some information relative to these events, have most unaccountably disappeared.]

CHARITIES.—The sum of 13s. 4d. is paid annually by the lady of the manor to the overseers of Clifton, who distribute it in bread to the poor of the township.

present lord of the manor is John Harrison, Esq., of Snelston Hall. The church is an ancient structure, dedicated to St. James. The parish, including the hamlet of Wyaston, contains about 225 inhabitants; and the annual value of the property is assessed at £1,784.

YEAVELEY, anciently *Gheveli*, is a chapelry and township in the parish of Shirley, (hundred of Appletree.) Here there was formerly a Hermitage,* which with the lands and appurtenances, were given in the reign of Richard II. to the Knights Hospitallers, whereupon it became a preceptory to that order.† It was dedicated to St. Mary and St. John the Baptist. Sir William Meynell,

---

*Tradition states that this Hermitage stood by the road-side in the village; and a dwelling-house, evidently built on the foundation of an ancient building, is still shewn as its site.

"Solitude was an essential characteristic of hermitages, and they were particularly seated in the forests. The hermitage of Warkworth was one of the sweetest retirements in the known world, being a most elegant cavern hewn out of a rock; but that at Tottenham was, I believe, a house with apartments, unless these were modern. The hermitage of S. Briavel was a chantry of two monks; and had demesne lands, on which corn was grown. Gardens were appendages to them, and it seems hermits were in the habit of labouring in agriculture. (Fiacre, the eminent hermit, thought it necessary " to make a grete gardin, where he sholde have alle manere of herbs good for to make potage with for to fede the poure." Wulfa, a Dane, near his hermitage cultivated gardens. Another made a turning bridge over a ditch. Sometimes they had allowances from the crown. Some were placed in churches to look after them; Godric, of Finchall, maintained himself by a small field, which he dug himself and gave away as much besides as he could: they are also coupled with laymen in respect to living by different trades and manual labour. Alms-boxes were annexed to them. They were the great *emporia* of the village news : and were to be near towns or abbies, where they could meet with sustenance. But sometimes they were neither the solitary nor comfortable habitations which might from the preceding description, be supposed."—*Fosbrooke's British Monachism.*

†Hospitals were originally designed for relief and entertainment of travellers upon the road, and particularly of pilgrims : and therefore were generally built upon the road's side. In later time they have always been founded for fixed inhabitants.—*Dugdale's Monasticon Anglicanum.* [The Hospital of Yeavely or Stydd, appears to have been of the latter description. Its revenues were partly derived from property in Ashbourn. See ante p. 11. The steep ascent to the south of the town on the road to the Hospital, is termed in ancient deeds, ' *The 'Spital Hill.*']

lord of the town, was in 1268, a great benefactor to this hospital. At the dissolution of the monasteries in the reign of Henry VIII. it was granted, together with the preceptory of Barrow, in Cheshire, to Charles, Lord Mount-joy. Some remains of a chapel which is supposed to have belonged to the Hospital, are still existing near Stydd Hall. They consist of part of the south wall, having seve-ral pointed windows in the style of the thirteenth century, with the pillars clustered, and their capitals beautifully foliated; the whole being in fine preservation. Near these ruins, and corresponding in date, is a remarkably curious font.

Stydd Hall, once a substantial edifice, has been suf-fered to fall into decay, and is at present tenanted as a farm-house.

HUNGRY BENTLEY, so called to distinguish it from Fenny Bentley, is a small village, township, and constabulary in the parish of Longford, four miles south-west of Ashbourn. The manor, at the Domesday Survey was part of the immense possessions of Henry de Ferrers. It afterwards descended to the Blount family, and from them to the Brownes, who had here 'an old house and a large park.' The representative of the family now resides at Chester-field. Sir Robert Wilmot, Bart. is the present lord of the manor.

ALKMANTON, is a village, township, and constabulary also in the parish of Longford. This lordship was part of the lands of Henry de Ferrers. In 25 Edward I. Ralf de Bakepuize and his descendant Galfred de Bakepuize held it. After which it came to the family of Blount, and continued in it till it came either by marriage or purchase to William Barnsley, Esq., of Alkmanton. The estate afterwards came in succession to the Brownes, Earl Ches-terfield, and Earl Stanhope; by the latter it was sold to the late Thomas Evans, Esq. of Derby, and it is now the property of his grandson, William Evans, Esq. of Allestree,*

---

*See Glover's Derbyshire, Vol. i. p. 15, 16.

Between the villages of Bentley and Alkmanton there stood another religious house,—the Hospital of St. Leonard. Walter Blount, (Lord Mountjoy,) in 1474, bequeathed £10 per annum to the Hospital, for the maintenance of seven poor men, not under 55 years of age; (old servants of the lord of the manor of Barton, or other lordships belonging to the patron of the college to be preferred.) These pensioners were to have pasture for seven cows in Barton Park, fuel from Lord Mountjoy's manors, and every third year a gown and hood of white or russet cloth, alternately marked with a cross of red. They were to pray for the souls of Lord Mountjoy, his family and ancestors; the Duke of Buckingham, Earl Rivers, Sir John Woodville, and the ancient lords of the hospital, and to repeat the psalter of the Virgin Mary twice every day in the chapel of the Hospital. Lord Mountjoy directed also that a chapel dedicated to Saint Nicholas, should be built at Alkmanton, and that the master of the Hospital should say mass in it yearly, on the festival of St. Nicholas. Dugdale states that there are now no remains of the Hospital or of the chapel of St. Nicholas.* At Bentley, however, some vestiges of a church are to be seen.

LONGFORD, anciently, *Laganford,* a village, township, and parish in the hundred of Appletree, was formerly the seat of a family who seem to have derived their name from the place. Nicholas de Langeford represented the county in the seventeenth parliament of Edward II.; Nicholas de Longford in the 5th of Henry IV. and Sir Ralph Longford was sheriff for Derbyshire in the year 1501.† Some time after the death of the last of the Longfords (in the early part of the seventeenth century,) the seat came into the possession of a descendant of Sir Edward Coke, Lord

---

*Monasticon Anglicanum.

†Longford, of Longford. Fourteen generations of this family are described in the visitation of 1569. *Magna Britannia, Derb.*

Chief Justice of England in the time of James I. Edward
Coke, Esq. of Longford, was created a baronet in 1641,
and he served the office of Sheriff for the county in 1646.
He married Catharine, the grand-daughter of the Lord
Chief Justice Dyer; and was succeeded in his title and
estates by Sir Edward his fourth son, who died without
issue. Longford then became the property of Edward the
second son of Edward Coke, Esq. of Holkham, a lineal
descendant of the Chief Justice Coke. Dying unmarried in
1733, he left the estate to his younger brother, Robert
Coke, Esq. who was vice-chamberlain to Queen Caroline.
He married lady Jane, eldest sister and co-heiress of
Philip, Duke of Wharton. On the death of the last-
mentioned possessor, the estate descended to his nephew,
Wenman Roberts, Esq., who took the name and arms
of Coke, and in 1772, was chosen one of the representatives in Parliament, for the Borough of Derby.*—
Thomas William, his eldest son, not only succeeded his
father in the possession of his estates in the counties of
Derby and Lancaster, but afterwards became heir to the
vast property of Viscount Coke, Earl of Leicester. The
estate and manor of Longford, were however, enjoyed by
Edward Coke, Esq., the second son, who for many years
represented the borough of Derby in Parliament, and who
was nominated High Sheriff of the county in 1819. On
his death the estate and manor again reverted to Thomas
William Coke, Esq. of Holkham, created, 21st July, 1837,
Earl of Leicester and Viscount Coke.

Longford Hall, the family seat, is a spacious fabric
with wings, and seems to have been erected at two different
periods. It is now undergoing great improvements. The
Park and grounds, pleasantly situated in an agreeable
country, are laid out with considerable taste.

The church, an ancient structure, exhibiting marks of
several distinct styles, consists of a chancel, nave, and side

*Pilkington's view of the present state of Derbyshire, 1803.   vol. 2.

aisles, surmounted by a massive square tower. The arches of the north aisle are semi-circular, supported by heavy cylindrical piers, and apparently of early Norman construction: those of the south aisle, are pointed, in the style immediately succeeding. In the south wall of the chancel, are three stone *sedilia*, or stalls; anciently appropriated in Catholic worship, to the use of the officiating priest or his attendant ministers, the deacon and sub-deacon, who retired thither during the chanting of some parts of the service. In a small niche adjoining, is the *piscina*, a hollow and perforated basin of stone, into which the priest emptied the water after washing his hands, which he was accustomed to do during the ceremony. The holy water which by any means had become defiled, was also dismissed through the same channel. In the north wall of the chancel, within a gothic arched canopy of stone, is a whole length effigy in alabaster, in a recumbent position, greatly mutilated, and without date or inscription. In the wall of the south aisle, is another gothic stone canopy, of larger dimensions, and more richly and elaborately ornamented, and within it a figure in alabaster, repesenting a knight of the fourteenth century, in chain armour, his head resting on a helmet, and his feet supported by a dog. Near this is an elevated altar-tomb, of very early date, with another effigy of a knight in armour, and a dog *couchant* at his feet. Part of the north aisle has been partitioned off, and is now used as the vestry-room. It contains several monuments, and on the wall is a mural tablet with this inscription :—

" Edwardo Coke Arm: de Longford Edwardi ex Agro Norfolciensi Filio natu Secundo Qui Obiit XII. Auguste Æt: XXXII. A. D. MDCCXXXIII. Robertus Regina Carolinae Vice Camerarius Fratrii Meritissimo hoc Monumentum libens lubensq posuit."

On a stone slab in the floor is an inscription, partly defaced, marking the burial place of Sir Edward Coke, who died in 1669. Over another marble tablet is the following:

"Here lyes the body of Sir Edward Coke, late of this place, Bart. who died the 20th September, 1727, aged 79, and by his will directed this monument to be erected, in memory of Sir Edward Coke, Bart., his father, and of Dame Catherine his mother, who was grand-daughter to the Lord Chief Justice Dyer; and of their children, whose names were Edward, Catharine, Robert, Richard, Anne, the last Sir Edward, Clement, and Theophila, who all died without issue."

In recesses in the west wall are three whole-length figures, in alabaster, removed from their original recumbent position, and standing upright. One represents a knight, in armour, in good preservation; another an old man, with a beard, and the third a female. To none of these effigies nor to those before described, can the slightest traces of any date or inscription be discovered: and consequently it is impossible to state with certainty to whom they belonged. There can however be little doubt but that they represent some of the Longford family before-mentioned.

The living is a rectory, and the church is dedicated to St. Chad. It is said to have been given by Nicholas de Griesly, alias de Longford, and Margaret his wife, to the monastery of Kenilworth, in Warwickshire.

BRAILSFORD, a considerable village, in the hundred of Appletree, is situated nearly mid-way between Ashbourn and Derby. "*In Brailesford*" (at the Doomsday survey,) "*Earl Wallef had two carucates of land to be taxed. Land to two ploughs. There are now in the demesne two ploughs, and twenty-four villanes, and three bordars have five ploughs. There is a priest and half a church, and one mill of 10s. 8d., and eleven acres of meadow. Wood pasture one mile long and one mile broad. Value in King Edward's time 60s. now 40s. Elfin holds it.*" The manor was given to Henry de Ferrers, under whom Elfin, ancestor of the ancient family of *Brailsford* held it. In 25 Edward I. Ralph de Bakepuize had this and other estates belonging to the Ferrers family, under some agreement, to cover them after Earl Robert's attainder, which lands were held by Henry de Brailsford, who was fined in the reign of Edward I. for refusing to be made a knight. About the year 1380, Sir John Bassett, of Cheadle, married the heiress of Sir Henry de Brailesford, and became possessed of the estate. Sir Ralph Shirley, by his marriage with the heiress of Bassett, of Cheadle and Brailsford, obtained the manor: he died about 1443, and left it his son, Sir Ralph, who died in 1469, and is said to have been buried at Brailsford. The manor remained in possession of the noble family of Shirley, until within the last fifty or sixty years. Earl Ferrers sold the manor and several farms to Mr. John Webster, a banker of Derby. The estate then came into the hands of William Drury Lowe, Esq., of Locko; and it has since passed by purchase to William Evans, Esq. of Allestree, the present proprietor.

The parish, including the villages of Burroughs,* Culland,† and Ednaston,‡ contained in 1831, about 780 inhabitants; and the estimated annual value of the buildings and land is £6,912.

The church is a Norman structure, with an embattled tower, around the string courses of which are some rudely sculptured heads. Between the nave and chancel is a round pillar, of very ancient date, behind which there appears to have been a passage to a confessionary. In a wall of the chancel are three stone *sedilia*. On the floor are several alabaster slabs; two of them have effigies, in scroll lines, of knights in armour; and on a third is the representation of a priest in his vestments. The inscriptions are nearly effaced, and but a few words of each can now be decyphered. At the foot of one, " *Rauf*

---

*OVER BURROUGHS HALL and estate formerly belonged to the Bradburnes. Early in the seventeenth century they were sold to the Ferrers family, who appear not to have held them long, for the family of the present possessor, William Osborne, gent. have been proprietors for about two centuries.

†CULLAND, in 1498, belonged to the family of Shaw, and afterwards to the Drapers. It is now the property of Edward Soresby Cox, Esq.

‡The manor of Ednaston which had been given to the priory of Tutbury, by Robert Earl Ferrers the elder, was granted in 1540, to Sir John Gifford, who conveyed it to Francis Shirley, Esq. ancestor of the present noble proprietor, Earl Ferrers.—*Glover.*

14

*Shirley, esquire, and Dame Alice, his third wife, on whose
sowles God have mercy.*" The church is dedicated to All
Saints. The living is a rectory, and the Right Hon. Earl
Ferrers is the patron.

SHIRLEY.—The village of *Shirley,* (derived from the
Saxon,signi fying " a clear place or pasture,") four miles
south-east of Ashbourn, is memorable for giving name to
a family who for ages have been considered one of the most
honourable among the most ancient houses of the county
of Derby. This place however, is not the original seat
of the *Shirleys;* even before the conquest, as we learn from
Domesday-Book, they were seated at Eatington, in Warwickshire; and it is remarkable that both these places
still remain the inheritance of their first recorded lords;
the manor of Shirley being (anno 1838) the property of
the Right Hon. Washington Shirley, Earl Ferrers, who
represents the elder line; and Eatington, the seat of
Evelyn John Shirley, Esq., one of the Knights of the
shire for the county of Warwick, chief of the younger
branch of the family.

The first establishment of the *Shirleys* in the village
from whence they afterwards assumed their name, seems
to have been in the reign of Henry I. when the Prior
and Convent of Tutbury granted to Fulcher, son of
Sewallis, with the consent of Robert Earl Ferrers, (his
lord) four ox-gangs of land in " Sirlei" (Shirley) and a
mill at Derby, at an annual rent of 10s. 8d. to be paid
on St. John Baptist's Day. Shirley did not however
become the principal seat of this family until the reign of
Henry III., nor does it appear to have long remained so,
for few houses obtained larger possessions by marriage
with heiresses than the ancient lords of Shirley; and
among other manors about the middle of the fifteenth
century, by the marriage of Ralph, son and heir of Sir
Ralph Shirley, with Margaret, sister and sole heir of
Thomas Staunton, they became possessed of the manor of

Staunton Harold, in the county of Leicester, which has ever since continued the chief seat of the *Shirleys*.

Sir Hugh Shirley, of Shirley, fought under Henry IV. at the battle of Shrewsbury, (anno 1403;) and Sir Ralph Shirley, of Shirley, accompanied the succeeding monarch (Henry V.) to France, in 1415, and greatly distinguished himself at the Battle of Agincourt. Of the Ferrers family, so far as they were connected with the town of Ashbourn, some interesting particulars are recorded in the first chapter of this work.

A moat, now partly filled up, surrounding a farm-house which bears but few traces of antiquity, marks the site of the ancient manor-house of Shirley: it lies in a hollow, mid-way between the parsonage-house built by the present Rev. W. A. Shirley, vicar of Shirley, and the village-church which crowns the opposite hill.

The church, consisting of two aisles and a chancel, contains but little to interest the antiquary, and the sepulchural remains at present existing here are few. In the chancel, on an alabaster slab, the figure of an ecclesiastic can be traced, with the remains of an inscription in black letter. In the principal or north aisle is a large alabaster slab, whereon the word " *quidem*" can now alone be made out: this is probably sufficient to identify it with the tomb of William Pope and Agnes his wife, who died about the year 1508, and were buried in this church.* The font is octagonal, of the date of the fourteenth century. The tower formerly of wood, was rebuilt in 1832. In the churchyard, near the south porch, stands a remarkably fine yew tree,—dating perhaps with the Conquest.

The family estates at Shirley, which formerly comprehended the whole parish, were much diminished by Washington, fifth Earl Ferrers, who sold considerable property here about fifty or sixty years ago; and what is particularly to be lamented, he alienated (to use the quaint

*Dodsworth's MSS. vol. 82, p. 55, B.

description of Sir Thomas Shirley, in the reign of Charles
I.,) "the two antient stately parks, of a large extension,
and most pleasant to behold, which for the large compass
of ground, and great plenty of high stately oaks in them,
may be more aptly termed a Forest."*

The parish of *Shirley*, including the townships of
Yeavely and Stydd, contained in 1831, 602 inhabitants:
and the estimated annual rental is £4,223.

OSMASTON, *(Osmundestune)* a village, township and
parish in the hundred of Appletree, contains about 289
inhabitants. At the Conquest it was in the same hands
as Brailsford; and it has usually been considered as forming part of that parish, though not included therein in the
last population returns. Osmaston was long the chief
residence of the *Pegges*, branches of whose family also
resided in Shirley, Yeldersley,† and Ashbourn. Dr.
Samuel Pegge, the well-known antiquary, was of Osmaston, where his ancestors had resided in lineal succession
for four generations. He died possessed of the patrimo-
nial estate there. Christopher Pegg, a considerable
benefactor to the poor of Ashbourn, was an eminent
attorney in that town.

The church, dedicated to St. Martin, is ancient, having
a square Norman tower.

The annual value of the property in the parish is assessed
at £1,752.

YELDERSLEY, a hamlet in the parish of Ashbourn, contains about 226 inhabitants, and the estimated annual rental is £2,085.

---

*Edward Soresby Cox, Esq. and Francis Wright, Esq. have considerable
estates in Shirley Park.

†Thomas Pegge, Esq., of Yeldersley, near Ashbourn, married a daughter of
Sir Gilbert Kniveton. Their daughter (Katharine) went abroad, and while
there became the mistress of Prince Charles, afterwards King Charles II.
She bore the prince two children: a son, named Charles Fitz Charles, created
in 1675, Earl of Plymouth, who died at the siege of Tangier; and a daughter
who died in her infancy.

STURSTON, a hamlet in the parish of Ashbourn, belonged at the Domesday survey to Henry de Ferrers, under whom it was held by one *Roger*. Two parts of the tithe of this demesne were granted to the priory of Tutbury, and the grant was confirmed and renewed by Robert de Ferrers, the second Earl of that name.* The Cokaynes had lands here in the time of Henry VII. The estates afterwards passed to the Meynells, of Bradley, and the manorial rights of both Sturston and Yeldersley are still vested in that family. The entire hamlet (including part of Compton,) contains about 578 inhabitants, and the annual rental is estimated at £2,779.

In this hamlet, one mile and a half north-east of Ashbourn, is *The Grove*, formerly a seat of the Meynells, and now the residence of John Silvester, Esq.

BRADLEY, a village, township and parish in the hundred of Appletree, is seated in a valley three miles east of Ashbourn. The manor belonged to the Ferrers from the time of the Doomsday survey till the fall of that great family, when it became part of the possessions of the Duke of Lancaster, under whom it was held by Ralph de Shirley, in 21st Edward I. In the fourth year of the same reign Ralph de Okeover held lands here. At a very early period Bradley became the property of the ancient family of *Kniveton*. After the elder branch of the Bradley Knivetons had become extinct, the manor passed to Sir Gilbert Kiveton, bart. of Mercaston, whose ancestors had been there settled for several generations. His son and successor, Sir Andrew, (governor of the castle of Tutbury in the time of Charles I.) suffered much in his fortunes through his devotion to the royal cause. He sold Bradley in 1655, to Francis Meynell, Esq. Alderman, citizen, and goldsmith, of the city of London, and in his family it has ever since continued. The first mention of the name occurs in the " Roll of Battle Abbeie ;" and it is certain that a family

---

*Sir O. Mosley's History of Tutbury, p. 248.

of the Meynells were seated in Derbyshire as early as the reign of Edward I., for the name of Giles de Meynell is found among the very first recorded members of parliament for the county. The Meynells of Bradley however, are said to be descended from a very ancient family of the same name seated at North Kilvington, in the county of York.

Glover gives the following pedigree of the family from the time they became possessed of the Bradley estates :—

Francis Meynell, esq. sheriff and alderman of London, who purchased this estate, had three sons, Godfrey, Francis, and Richard, the two latter died without issue. The eldest son, Godfrey Meynell, of Bradley, esq. married twice: first, Margaret, daughter of George Vernon, esq. by whom he had no issue; secondly, Elizabeth, daughter and heiress of Edward Littleton, esq. by whom he had issue one son and one daughter: he was sheriff in 1681, and died in 1708. Littleton Poyntz Meynell, esq. the only son, married Judith, the daughter of —— Alleyne, of Barbadoes, esq. by whom he had three sons and two daughters. To his eldest son, Godfrey, he left an annuity of £100, but better provision was afterwards made for him by act of parliament, he married and left three daughters; the eldest daughter was wife of E. M. Mundy, of Shipley, esq.; the second daughter, Harriet, wife of Sir John Caldwell, of Castle Caldwell, bart.; and the third daughter, ——, wife of —— Bland, of Kippax, esq. To Hugo Meynell, esq. his second son, he devised all his estates. This gentleman was Member of Parliament for Lichfield, and high sheriff for the co. of Stafford in 1758: he married twice; first, Ann, the daughter of John Gell, of Hopton, esq. by whom he had one son, Godfrey; secondly, Ann, the daughter of Thomas Boothby Scrimpshire, of Tooly Park, Leicestershire, esq. by whom he had two sons, Hugo, and Charles. Godfrey Meynell, esq. the late lord of the manors of Bradley, Yeldersley, &c. married Susanna, the widow of —— Estridge, esq. by whom he had no issue. Hugo Meynell, of Hoare Cross, esq. the second son, and half brother to the said Godfrey, married the Honourable Elizabeth Ingram, daughter and co-heiress of Lord Viscount Irwin, and had issue Hugo Charles Meynell, now of Hoare Cross, esq., Elizabeth, and other children, and died in 1801. Charles Meynell, esq. the third son lived at the Grove near Ashbourn; he married Elizabeth, daughter of —— ——, and left issue. Hugo Charles Meynell, esq. married Georgiana, daughter of F. Pigou, of Hill-Street, Berkley Square, esq. and has issue several children. This gentlemen was high sheriff for the county of Stafford in 1826.

The old hall at Bradley, the seat of the family, was taken down many years ago, and stables and offices were built for an intended new mansion, which however was not completed.

The church, (dedicated to All Saints,) is a plain building
of early date. In the chancel are the arms of the Meynells,
and several monumental tablets to different members of the
family. There is also a fine circular gothic font. The
Dean of Lincoln is patron of the living, and the Rev.
William Skinner is the rector.

In the early part of the 17th century resided at Bradley
Thomas Bancroft, a poet and writer of epigrams. Sir
Aston Cokayne, of Ashbourn, with whom he was on terms
of great intimacy, makes frequent allusion to him in his
writings. He (Sir Aston) remarks that Bancroft " was
surnamed *the small poet*, by way of ironie, but worthy to
be ranked among the best classicks." Many of his
epigrams have considerable point, and the poetry, though
tinctured with the alloy of the times, is far from being
destitute of merit.

In 1762, Dr. Kennedy, rector of Bradley, published an
elaborate and important work on the chronology of the
Scriptures.* It contains a long series of connected calculations, in which is attempted to be fixed the precise date
of the creation, and of some of the principal events
recorded in the sacred writings. Dr. Kennedy thus ex-
plains the leading proposition on which his reasoning is
founded :—

---

*" A complete system of Astronomical Chronology unfolding the Scriptures; in
which the Chronology of the Masoretic Hebrew Text is proved, by astronomical arguments, to be genuine and authentic, without error, and without cor-
ruption; The date of the Creation is fixed; The year, month, day of the
month, and day of the week, in which the Israelites went out of Egypt are
ascertained; It is clearly proved, that at the going out of Egypt the original
Sabbath was changed by Divine Legislative authority: It is proved that our
Saviour rose from the dead on the seventh day of the week, in the uninterrupted
Series of Weeks from the creation, and that the original Seventh Day or
Patriarchal Sabbath, revived with him; It is proved that our Saviour gave up
the Ghost upon the cross, on the very month, day, hour and minute, on which
the Paschal Lamb was ordered, by the law, to be slain; The Chronology of
the five books of Moses is completed in all its particulars; The astronomical
Epocha of the Gospel, and the year, month, and day of Christ's death are
determined."

" I .have employed many pages, and made a great variety of calculations
to prove the fundamental proposition of this scheme, which is, that Moses has
recorded in his Pentateuch, *the position of the sun and moon to each other* at
the creation, and in the first year after the flood, or in the beginning of the old
world and the new.   This *revealed position* of the sun and moon at the creation,
I call the *scriptural astronomical era.*   By the assistance of this era, together with
some other principles to be mentioned in another place, I find myself able to
keep even pace with the course of the two great luminaries, from the first
year of the world to that which is current.   Nor will it be thought presump
tion to take it for granted that no intelligent person will be inclined to call in
question the truth of these conclusions, which are confirmed by the joint
attestations of the sun and moon, *the two faithful witnesses in the heavens.*"

According to Boswell, the learned author received some
assistance from the powerful pen of Dr. Johnson: " In
1762" (says Boswell) " he wrote, for the Rev. Dr. Kennedy, rector of Bradley, in Derbyshire, in a strain of
very courtly elegance, a dedication to the King, of that
gentleman's work, entitled, ' A Complete System of
Astronomical Chronology, unfolding the Scriptures.' He
had certainly looked at this work before it was printed;
for the concluding paragraph is undoubtedly of his composition, of which let my readers judge:"

" ' Thus have I endeavoured to free religion and history from the darkness
and difficulties of a disputed and uncertain chronology; from difficulties which
have appeared insuperable, and darkness which no luminary of learning has
hitherto been able to dissipate.   I have established the truth of the Mosaical
account, by evidence which no transcription can corrupt, no negligence can
lose, and no interest can pervert.   I have shewn that the universe bears
witness to the inspiration of its historian, by the revolutions of its orbs and
the succession of its seasons : *that the stars in their courses fight against* incre-
dulity, that the works of GOD give hourly confirmation to the *law,* the
prophets, and the *gospel,* of which *one day telleth another, and one night certifieth
another ;* and that the validity of the sacred writings never can be denied, while
the moon shall increase and wane, and the sun shall know his going down.' "

This extraordinary work on its first appearance was the
occasion of much controversy.   If it be true that the
author's conclusions have never yet been satisfactorily
refuted, they are worthy of some attention in the present
day, when the assertions of certain geologists in reference
to the age of the earth, would seem directly to impugn
the accuracy of the scriptural account of the creation.

HULLAND, or HOLLAND, anciently *Hoilant,* a chapelry and township in the parish of Ashbourn, was in the possession of Geoffry Alselin at the Domesday survey. In the seventeenth century a branch of the ancient family of *Borough* or *Borrow,* originally *De Burgh,* settled here, and became the owners of Hough Park, a manor lying within Hulland. John Borrow, Esq. of Hulland, was High Sheriff for the county of Derby in 1688. The present proprietor of the estate is John Charles Burton Borough, Esq. of Chetwynd Park, Salop.

Hulland had formerly a chapel of ease; it was standing and was used for divine worship in the year 1712.

The new district-church erected in 1837, is a stone structure, in the plain gothic style, having a tower at the west end. It is dedicated to Christ, and was consecrated on the 29th of August, 1838. The interior contains about 300 sittings, of which 138 are free. The funds for its erection and endowment (amounting to upwards of £2,300,) have been raised by the voluntary contributions of a few private individuals, aided by a grant of £245 from the Diocesan Church Building Society. This church was built for the accommodation of the inhabitants of Hulland, Hulland Ward, Ward-Gate, Biggin, and some detached parts of Turnditch. The patronage is in the alternate gift of J. C. B. Borough, Esq. and the representative of the late John Blackwall, Esq. of Blackwall. The Rev. Charles Evans is the minister.

Richard Paul Joddrell, Esq. is lord of the manor of Hulland and Hulland Ward.

ATLOW, a village, township and constabulary in the parish of Bradbourn, lies about three miles east of Ashbourn. The manor was held under Henry de Ferrers or his immediate heirs, by the ancestor of the very ancient family of *Okeover,* and it has ever since continued to form part of the possessions of that family.* The chapel is a

---

*See under the head " Okeover."

plain building, presenting little that is worthy of notice.
The living is a vicarage, in the gift of the Okeover family,
who have considerably augmented its revenues. The Rev.
R. E. Aitkens is the present incumbent.

The number of inhabitants is about 157, and the annual
rental is estimated at £1,603.

KNIVETON, a village, township and parish in the hundred of Wirksworth, is three miles north-east of Ashbourn. Its name at the time of the Domesday survey, was
written *Cheniueton*, and it was then in the hands of Hugh,
Earl of Chester. "Kniveton" says the learned antiquary
Camden, "hath given both name and seat to the famous
family of *Kniveton*, from whence the *Knivetons* of Mercaston and Bradley, of whom is St. Loe Kniveton, [also an
antiquary] to whose study and diligence I am so much
indebted." The first recorded parliamentary representative for the county of Derby was Henry de Kniveton, who
served that office in the 23rd parliament of Edward I.

The parish contains about 342 inhabitants, and the
estimated annual rental is £3,275.

The church is a plain building, and the living is a perpetual curacy.

At Mudge Meadow, a short distance to the south of
Kniveton, is a sulphureous spring.

HOGNASTON, at the time of the Norman Conquest was a
berwick of Ashbourn, and as such was held by the King.
The church is ancient, but has nothing remarkable. The
living is a rectory, in the gift of the Crown. The number
of inhabitants is 271, and the annual value of the property
in the parish is assessed at £2,181. Philip Gell, Esq. of
Hopton, is lord of the manor.

BRADBOURN, a village, township and parish in the hundred of Wirksworth, is six miles north-east of Ashbourn.
This manor belonged to the Earls Ferrers, and was held
under them at an early period by the family of *Caus* or *De
Cauceis*. After the fall of the Ferrers family, it was held by
the Bakepuizes. In the reign of King John the manor was

conveyed to Godard de Bradburne, and it continued in that
family until the reign of Edward VI. In 1207, Roger de
Bradburne held lands in Hough and Offdecote (Offcote)
and the manor of Bradburne. Henry de Bradburne, eldest
son of Roger, was executed at Pomfret, in 1322, for his
adherence to Thomas, Earl of Lancaster; upon which the
manor passed to his younger brother, John, and his
descendants. The last male-heir of the family (Sir Humphrey) lies buried in Ashbourn church. His co-heir, Jane,
marrying Sir Humphrey Ferrers, of Tamworth, was mother
of Sir John Ferrers, who died in 1633. From him the
estate descended to the Baroness de Ferrers, who married
George, Marquis of Townshend. In 1809, the manor was
sold by the latter family to Philip Gell, Esq. of Hopton,
for the sum of £85,000. It has since been re-sold, and is
now in the hands of several proprietors.

The church is ancient, having an embattled Norman
tower. In one of the chancel windows are the arms of
Ferrers. There are several monumental inscriptions to
members of the ancient family of *Buckston*, originally of
Buxton,* who settled here about two centuries ago. The
Rev. German Buckston, the representative of the family, is
the vicar. In the year 1205, the church was given to the
Priory of Dunstable, by Sir Geoffery de Cauceis, whose
gift was confirmed by William de Ferrers, Earl of Derby,
as chief lord of the fee.†

---

*The first of this family on record is Henry de Bawkestone, mentioned in a
deed of the year 1256; and one Thomas Buxton was high sheriff for Derbyshire
in 1415—Henry Buxton, Esq. of Bradborne, born in 1670, espoused Dorothy
sister of the Right Honourable Sir Richard Levinge, knt. and bart., lord chief
justice of the court of Common Pleas in Ireland, and daughter of Richard
Levinge, Esq. of Parwich, by Anne, his wife, daughter of George Parker, Esq.
of Park Hall, in Staffordshire. The Rev. George Buckston, M. A. Rector of
Shirland and Vicar of Bradbourn (who died in 1826) married Frances, daughter
of Moreton Walhouse, Esq. of Hatherton, in Staffordshire, by Frances, his
wife, daughter of Sir Edward Littleton, bart of Pillaton.—*Burke's Commoners.*

†The Chronicle of the priory of Dunstable states, that "When the church
was given to the priory, it had a rector and two vicars. In 1214 the prior had
a suit in the court at Rome, with the rector and vicars, with a view, it is

The township of Bradbourn contains about 195 inhabitants, and the annual rental is estimated at £3,624.

The parish includes the chapelry of Atlow, the townships of Aldwark, Ballidon,* and Brassington, and the hamlet of Lea Hall.

TISSINGTON, a village, township and parish in the hundred of Wirksworth, is situated about four miles north-east of Ashbourn. At the conquest, *Tizinctun* belonged to Henry de Ferrers ; and the Herthulls and Meynells afterwards held estates here. The manor of Tissington then

---

supposed of displacing them. It was alleged, that Robert, the rector, was son of Godfrey, a former rector; that Henry, one of the vicars, was son of John, his predecessor, in one mediety of the vicarage; and that William, the other vicar, kept a concubine publicly, and went a hunting, forsaking his tonsure and clerical duties. When the church became vacant, the convent sent one of their canons who resided at Bradbourn, under the name of a *custos* or warden, accounted with the Priory for the profits, and provided for the church and its chapels many years before the rectory was actually appropriated to the Priory." The prior kept a great flock of sheep in this parish, and in the Annals before referred to it is stated that 800 died in the year 1243.—*Magna Britannia, Derb.*

*Ballidon, a township in the parish of Bradbourn, six miles north-east of Ashbourn, came into the possession of the Cokaines of Ashbourn early in the fifteenth century, by the marriage of Elizabeth, heiress of Sir Giles Herthull, to Edmund Cokayne of Ashbourn; a branch of whose family was settled at Ballidon for several generations. The estates passed by sale into other hands, and a large portion is now the property of William Webster, Esq. of Ashbourn, to whom it was bequeathed by Dr. John Taylor. *See Glover's Derb.* vol. 2. p. 76.

Near the road leading from Brassington to Pike-hall is an ancient *barrow* called Mininglow. Mr. Pilkington, who in 1788, described it, states " that the higher part of the mount seems to have been removed, several of the vaults being fully exposed to sight. The diameter is about forty yards, and the vaults appear to be carried round the whole circumference. The stones of which they are formed are very large. One of the. vaults which I measured is between six and seven feet long, three wide, and six deep. It consists of only five stones; one on each side and end, and the other for a corner. Some of them are a foot, and others half a yard thick. What number of vaults there are, I am not able to ascertain; but I imagine, if they are continued throughout the whole circumference, they must amount to forty. If these vaults were receptacles for the dead, it is evident from their size that many must have been buried here. But I cannot positively affirm that they were used for this purpose, having never heard that bones have been found in them." *Pilkington's Derbyshire,* vol. 2. p. 294—5.

TISSINGTON HALL.

The Seat of Sir Henry Fitzherbert Bart.

Printed by T.W. & C.Fairland, London.

Published by Dawson & Hobson, Ashbourn.

came into the possession of a descendant of the ancient and
honourable family of *Fitzherbert,* through his marriage
with the daughter and coheir of Robert Frauncis, Esq. of
Foremark. From this marriage Sir Henry Fitzherbert,
Bart. the present lord of the manor, is lineally descended.*
John, a younger son of Sir Nicholas Fitzherbert, of Tissington, was High Sheriff of Derbyshire in 1602; his son,
Sir John, served the same office in 1624; William Fitzherbert, Esq. of Tissington, was member of Parliament for
the borough of Derby in 1762, and in 1768 Recorder for
the same place, and a lord of Trade and Plantations. He
was on terms of intimacy with Johnson, Burke, Garrick,
and many of the most eminent *literati* of the last age. His
only surviving son is the Right Honourable Alleyne Fitzherbert, Lord St. Helens. William, his eldest son was
Recorder of Derby, and in 1783 was created a baronet; he
was succeeded by Sir Anthony Perrin Fitzherbert, who
died in 1799. The title and estates then devolved upon his
brother, the present baronet.

The entrance-gate to the ancient family mansion opens
to a very fine avenue, more than half a mile in length.
The house is of stone, and was most probably erected in the
latter end of the reign of Elizabeth; a few alterations in
the windows are observable, but otherwise its original character is preserved. The carriage-front (towards the village)
has before it a court, enclosed by a wall, and a curious
gateway, coeval with the house, consisting of an arch surmounted by a bold cornice, almost concealed by the wood-
bine which has entwined the fret-work of the parapet.
Over the entrance-porch on this side the mansion, is a
square compartment, sculptured with the family arms;
within the porch are several pieces of old armour, and the
heraldic bearing again, blazoned in proper colours. The
porch opens to a very handsome dining-room, panelled with
oak, but coloured white. The chimney-piece, (of Hopton-

---

*Burke's Baronetage.

stone, reaches to the ceiling, and is very much admired, both for its elegance of design, and for the beauty of its workmanship. The western drawing-room is of modern construction, and is furnished in very good taste. Among the pictures are—A very good copy of *Raphael's* Holy Family—A portrait, by *Hudson*, of Mrs. Fitzherbert, wife of William Fitzherbert, Esq. M. P., and daughter of Littleton Meynell, Esq. of Bradley Hall; [this is the lady of whose understanding and talents Dr. Johnson speaks in such high terms]—A portrait of the late Sir William Fitzherbert, painted at Rome by *Battoni*—A portrait of Sir William's sister, Selina, wife of the late Henry Gally Knight, Esq.; and another of Lord St. Helens; both by *Angelica Kauffman*—Two full-length portraits of George III. and his consort, by *Romney*—A portrait of the present Lady Fitzherbert, by *Sir William Beechey.*—There is also an excellent bust of Lord St. Helens, by *Nollekens*, one of the latest works of that eminent sculptor.—The grounds in the vicinity of the Hall are well-wooded, and on the garden front is a fine open view of the country towards Ashbourn.

Tissington church is most picturesquely seated, on the brow of a gentle eminence, nearly opposite the mansion. It bears evidence of having been originally constructed in the early Norman style, though in the repairs and renovations of its interior almost every trace of antiquity has been swept away. Like many other village churches of small dimensions, it consists of a nave and small chancel, without supporting pillars or side-aisles, and having a square tower at the west end. The south doorway (within the porch, which is of modern date) is clearly Norman, having underneath the semi-circular arch some grotesque heads and figures, exhibiting the elaborate workmanship of that age, in tolerable preservation. This church is the burying-place of the Fitzherberts, and there are several highly-wrought monuments to different members of the family. The one that attracts most attention is extremely lofty, reaching to the roof of the building. It is divided into two compartments, in the lower of which are three figures, habited in dark costume, and kneeling, in the attitude of prayer, over a tablet, bearing the following curious inscription:—

" Francis Fitzherbert, Esq. departed this life the 4th of January, Ætatis Suae 80, Anno Domini 1619.

" Love, justice honoure here
All at once in one appeare
Let the reader silent be
And do homage on his knee:
To this Reverend Esqvire
Yt hath now his full desire:
Of that peace he ever loved
In his life and death approved:
Layd here with his two loyal friends,
Most renowned in their ends."

In the upper compartment are two figures, kneeling over a similar tablet, inscribed to Sir John Fitzherbert, Bart. who died on the 2nd of August, 1642, aged 43.   This monument has some very curious decorations, and the whole is surmounted by the family arms, carefully blazoned.

The church is dedicated to St. Mary; and Sir Henry Fitzherbert, Bart. is the patron.

Tissington was the scene of a severe and decisive contest between the royalists and parliamentarians, during the civil wars in the reign of Charles I., in which the former were completely defeated, with considerable loss.*

This retired village is perhaps best known as the seat of a very pleasing rural custom,—a relic of the olden time— (said once to have extensively prevailed in this country,) called *well-flowering* or *well-dressing*.   Holy Thursday is the day chosen for the festivities.   The wells or springs, (five in number) that supply the villagers with water, are tastefully decorated with the flowers of the season, disposed in elegant and fanciful devices.   The figure intended to be represented, (often that of an architectural pediment) is first cut out in wood, the outer surface of which is then covered

*See page, 19, 20.

with moist clay; into this the stems of the flowers are closely inserted, and a brilliant *mosaic* is thus prepared, forming, as it were, a ground work for various ornamental designs, as of crowns and stars, and appropriate mottoes, chiefly from scripture, which are most ingeniously introduced. The devices when prepared, are so placed in the spring that the water appears to issue from beds of flowers. There is a service at the church, from whence the inhabitants go in procession, preceded by a band of music, to the different wells, where the collects for the day are read in succession, and psalms and hymns are sung. The villagers entertain their friends on the occasion; and the festival is numerously attended by the gay and the fair of the surrounding country; the green is covered with booths, and the whole scene is one of extraordinary enjoyment.

The custom of *well-flowering* is undoubtedly of the highest antiquity. It was common among the Greeks and Romans. The latter had their *Fontanalia*, in honour of the nymphs of their wells and fountains: and " in Catholic times" remarks a topographer of the last century,* "great respect was paid to such wells as bore a reputation for curing distempers upon the saint's day whose name the well bore, the people diverting themselves with cakes and ale, music and dancing."

The practice of *well-dressing* has some affinity to that of sprinkling rivers with flowers, so beautifully alluded to by the poet Milton :—

> " The shepherds at their festivals
> Carol her good deeds loud in rustic lays,
> And throw sweet garland wreaths into her stream,
> Of pansies, pinks and gaudy daffodils." *Comus.*

The decorating of wells and fountains has lately been revived or introduced at Bradley, Wirksworth, Belper, and Youlgreave, in this county.

---

*Rev. Stebbing Shaw, in Gentleman's Mag.

The Rev. Richard Graves, a writer of some talent, well known in the literary world as an associate of the poet Shenstone, resided for several years in the family of Mr. Fitzherbert, of Tissington. He is the author of a humorous burlesque, published in 1773, under the title of "The Spiritual Quixote," several of the scenes in which are laid in Ashbourn and Tissington. The work is based on that of the renowned Cervantes, and its chief aim is to satirize and expose the followers of Wesley and Whitfield, some of whom at that time carried their enthusiasm on religious subjects to a most extraordinary height. In the author's 'apology' prefixed to the work, its object is thus explained:

"The following narrative was intended to expose a species of folly which has frequently disturbed the tranquillity of this nation. The author, indeed, by no means considers ridicule as a proper test of religious opinions. But they are the practices, rather than the principles, of the people in question, which he thinks exceptionable. And the following work is so far from ridiculing religion, (as perhaps may be objected,) that he flatters himself it has a direct tendency to prevent religion becoming ridiculous by the absurd conduct of such irregular teachers of it. And he does not see how the honour of God is any more concerned in an attempt to expose the ill-judged zeal of a frantic enthusiast, than the authority of the king would be in our laughing at the absurdities of some pragmatical country justice or petty constable."*

---

*Whatever might be the author's intention, and however plausible his reasoning, his warmest admirers must admit, that in ridiculing the practice of these 'irregular teachers,' he has done much to bring religion itself into contempt. He trifles systematically with all that is sacred, and his profane irony is displayed by an indiscriminate travesty of the language of inspiration, as well as of those peculiarities of expression, the use of which, in the opinion of the admirable essayist, *Foster*, is to be considered as one of the causes why persons of taste have occasionally shown so lamentable an indifference to evangelical religion.

A late writer remarks, that "it is to be feared he (the author) descended into the grave without leaving behind him a single expression of regret for having polluted the clerical name with a performance which directly attacked christianity, under the shadow of a pretence, merely to display the human weaknesses of such persons as Whitfield, Wesley," &c.†

The talent for description, and the keen sense of the humorous evinced throughout the work, will remind the reader of some of Goldsmith's happiest efforts, and will cause him to regret that its tendency is of so reprehensible a character. That portion of the work which appears to have been written during the author's residence at Tissington, is for the most part a record

†Signature "J. L." in *Christian Observer*, Jan. 1831.

16

of actual occurrences, and the characters who took part in them are represented under feigned names. The hero of the tale, (*Wildgoose*) in the course of his pilgrimage arrives at 'Ashburne in the Peak,' attended by his trusty *squire*, *Tugwell*. Here he has some curious adventures, and *Tugwell* is taken into cus-tody ; " for being in his political principles rather attached to the Stuart family, and the town of Ashburne, since the late march of the rebels through that place, being divided into two parties (who persecuted each other with great vio-lence), *Tugwell*, it seems had somewhat imprudently taken the part of an honest barber, who, as he was drinking his morning cup [at the inn] had fallen into a dispute about the rebellion, with a dissenting baker, that was very zea-lous for the government, and upon Tugwell's interfering had charged the con-stable with him as a disaffected subject." Wildgoose is also charged with being a jesuit in disguise, and both are carried before the magistrate, (Mr. Boothby,) who, being a sensible man, and endeavouring as much as possible to preserve peace among his neighbours, dismissed the case. ' The Jacobite barber, whose cause *Tugwell* had espoused, as soon as his worship was out of sight, clapped *Jerry* (Tugwell) on the shoulder by way of triumph, and said as he himself was acquainted with the butler, and *Tugwell* he found was a curious man, he would shew him a curiosity. The barber then got his friend the butler to take him up the back stairs into a long gallery, which led to the principal bed-chamber, on the doors of which had been written by the quarter-master in chalk, (and after-wards traced over with white lead by way of curiosity) the names of the Prince, Lord Ogilvy, Pitsligo, and other rebel chiefs, who in their way to Derby, having halted one night in Ashbourn, had been quartered in this gen-tleman's house.' [This is strictly true : on the departure of the chiefs from Ashbourn Hall, their names were found so written on the doors.]

The reverend author thus portrays the character of his host, Mr. Fitzherbert : " *Sir William Forester* was a gentleman of fine sense; and (what is not always a consequence) of fine taste, not only in the polite arts, music, painting, architecture, and the like, but in life and manners. He had the art of making every company happy; and the greater art of making himself happy in every company. Some of his wise neighbours indeed were a little scandalized at his admitting people of inferior rank so frequently to his table; but *Sir William*, like Swift's virtuoso, who could extract sunbeams from cucumbers, had the skill of extracting entertainment from the most insipid companions; of discovering humour in the most phlegmatic divine, or solid sense in (the most trifling of all characters,) a country dancing-master." [Dr. Johnson has characterized his friend in terms of similar import :—" There was" said he, " no sparkle, no bril-liancy in Fitzherbert, but I never knew a man who was so generally accepta-ble. He made every body quite easy, overpowered nobody by the superiority of his talents, made no man think worse of himself by being his rival, seemed always to listen, did not oblige you to hear much from him, and did not oppose what you said. Every body liked him. He was an instance of the truth of the observation, that a man will please more upon the whole by negative qualities than by positive, by never offending than by giving a great deal of delight."]

The number of inhabitants in the parish of Tissington, is about 459, and the estimated annual rental is £5,450.

PARWICH, a village, township and parish in the hundred of Wirksworth, seven miles north of Ashbourn, was a royal demesne at the time of the Norman survey. In this manor was included a subordinate yet more valuable one, which belonged to the Fitzherberts, of Norbury, and afterwards to the Cokaynes, of Ashbourn, who sold it in the time of James I., in whose reign it was purchased by Thomas Levinge, a descendant of a Norfolk family. In the year 1814, Sir Richard Levinge sold the manor, after it had long ceased to be the seat of the family. The present proprietor is William Evans, Esq. of Allestree.

At a place called Lombard's Green, about half a mile north of Parwich, are some vestiges of what is said to have been a Roman encampment.* The supposed camp or station is of an oblong form, covering a level piece of ground near the summit of a very high eminence. It occupies a space of nearly half an acre, and consists of several divisions made by walls, the foundations of which have been dug up. About sixty or seventy years ago, a labourer who was searching the ground for lead-ore, found, at the depth of two feet and a half, a military weapon, a considerable number of coins, and an urn of great thickness, in which they had most probably been deposited. These coins, principally consisting of Roman

---

*A writer in the *Archæologia* has thrown some doubt on the supposition. "It must be owned," he says, "that the names ' Lombard's-Green,' and ' Parwich,' (*Parvus Vicus*) might warrant the conjecture: and the distance, which is about half-way from Buxton to Little Chester, [Roman Stations] would suit well for an intermediate station. But with all these advantages, the distance of two miles and a half from the Roman road, and an apparent want of connexion with it, is an objection not to be got over. If, indeed, a way from Buxton to Rocester should be found in the direction of the present Ashbourn turnpike-road, Parwich, being then in the space between two Roman roads, might have some right to be considered as a station to accommodate both; but until such a discovery is made, an antiquary of any experience must be inclined to suspend his opinion."

denarii, were in good preservation, and seventy-four of them were formerly in the possession of Mr. Rawlins, of Ashbourn. They were stamped in the upper empire; and are some of them as high as the triumvirate of Octavius, Lepidus, and Mark Antony; and others as low as the Emperor Aurelian. Near the encampment, at the summit of the hill, is a bank, about two feet high, running two miles to the west into the Ashbourn-road, and half a mile eastwards to a mere of water.*

Parwich was formerly a chapelry in the parish of Ashbourn. The church, a plain building, of very early date, is dedicated to St. Peter.

The parish contains about 544 inhabitants; and the estimated annual value of the property is £5,080.

FENNY BENTLEY, a village, township and parish in the hundred of Wirksworth, is situated two miles north of Ashbourn, in a valley watered by a small brook to which it gives name. The manor of Bentley was part of the crown lands at the time of the Domesday Survey; and in the 25th year of Edward I. Edmund, Earl of Lancaster, held it.— In the reign of Henry VI. a younger branch of the ancient family of *Beresford,* of Beresford, in the county of Stafford, settled here, and their descendants for many generations held the manor. Thomas Beresford, of Bentley, served under Henry VI. in his wars in France, and he is reported to have raised a troop of horse, consisting of his sons and his own and their retainers, for the service of that unfortunate monarch. He is also said to have been present at the battle of Agincourt, in the preceding reign. The elder branch of the Beresfords soon became extinct in the male line; the heiress married Edmund Beresford, Esq. of Beresford; whose daughter and heiress married Sir John Stanhope, of Elvaston; and the heiress of Sir John Stanhope married the celebrated Charles Cotton, at whose death the manor again came into the hands of the Beresford family. In the 13th of Henry VII. William Basset, Esq. of Meynell

---

*Pilkington's Survey of Derbyshire.

Langley, died possessed of lands here, which he had held under the Honor of Tutbury. In the time of Henry VIII. two families of Beresfords owned estates in the parish; and the Bradburnes had also property here. The manor passed away from the Beresford family, and is now in various hands.* Sir Henry Fitzherbert, Bart. owns an estate formerly belonging to the Beresfords; and John Goodwin Johnson, Esq. has considerable landed property in the neighbourhood.

In Bentley Church there are several monuments to members of the Beresford family. On the north side of the chancel is a large altar-tomb, belonging to Thomas Beresford, Esq. (the warrior before mentioned) and Agnes his wife. On the upper surface are extended two alabaster effigies, completely enveloped in shrouds; at the sides are twenty one smaller figures, habited in a similar manner, representing their children. The inscriptions are in English and Latin :

" Thomas Beresford, Esq. the sonne of John Beresford, late lord of Beresford, in the county of Stafford, esq. and Agnes, his wife, the daughter and heir of Robert Hassel, in the county of Chester, esq. who had issue sixteen sons and five daughters. Thomas died 20th March, 1473; and Agnes, 16th March, 1467. Also Heughe, third sonne of the said Thomas and Agnes.

As you now are, soe once were wee,
And as wee are, soe shall you bee.

Quem tegat hoc marmor si forte requiris,
Amice, nobili Beresford tu tibi nomen
Habes, luce patrum clarus proprio sed
Lumine major, de gemino merito nomine luce capit Largus militis.

Doctus, amans, alvit, coluit recreavit musas : ius vinctos sumptibus, arte domo excellens, strenuus dux, fortis et audax, Francice testatur, curia testis Agen."

The church is dedicated to St. Mary Magdalen. The living is a rectory in the gift of the Dean of Lincoln, and the Rev. Jervase Brown is the rector.

In 1831 the parish contained 308 inhabitants; and the estimated annual rental is £2,000.

Fenny Bentley is a place of great antiquity. Degge, the antiquary, who resided here, supposed that the Roman

*History and Gazetteer of the County of Derby, vol. II.

Road passed through the village, for he had an urn, some coins, and other remains, which had been found in the neighbourhood.

Part of the old manor-house, anciently the residence of the Beresfords, is still standing, and is converted into a farm-house. It appears to have been a castellated building, and some traces of a moat are discernible.

At the hamlet of Woodeaves, a short distance north-east of Fenny Bentley, is a cotton factory, in which a number of hands are employed.

BROADLOW-ASH, an estate and manor three miles north of Ashbourn, is situated partly in the parish of Ashbourn, and partly in that of Thorpe. This manor was a royal demesne at the Domesday survey. It was afterwards held by the Cokayne family, and in the 37th Henry VIII. George Beresford held it. In 1608 it was granted, with other estates, to Robert Cecil, Earl of Salisbury, in exchange for lands in Hertfordshire. In 1613, the Earl sold the manor to Dame Judith Corbet, widow of William Boothby, citizen of London, by whose bequest it passed to her grandson Sir William, who was created a baronet, in 1660. The Boothbys had here a fine park, and a good mansion, which was for several generations the chief residence of the family—In 1754 they sold the estate to Mr. Nicholas Twigge, and two other persons. Mr. Twigge afterwards became sole proprietor, and from him it descended to his grandson, the Rev. Thomas Francis Twigge, late of Derby, who devised it F. T. Foljambe, Esq. and the Spend-lane estate to William Bourne, Esq. of Hull.—The ancient mansion was taken down in 1795.*

---

*History and Gazetteer of the County of Derby, vol. II.

Robert Millward, a celebrated warrior, was born at Broadlow-Ash. He served in Spain, and is said to have engaged in single combat with a Spaniard. ' They first fought with quarter-staves and then betook themselves to sword and dagger. The Spaniard soon afterwards lost the use of his left arm, and then his life.' Robert was eldest son of John Millward, Esq. who died in 1632, and lies buried in Thorpe Church. Colonel John Millward, of Snitterton, Derbyshire, who served with the Royalists in the time of Charles I, was youngest brother of the warrior.

THORPE, in Domesday Book called *Torp*, a village, township and parish in the hundred of Wirksworth, lies about four miles north-west of Ashbourn. At the Norman survey it was a royal possession, and it appears afterwards to have belonged to the Ferrers family, for they granted five parts of the tithe to the priory of Tutbury. Francis Cokayne, of Ashbourn, who died in 1538, was possessed of this manor. The present proprietor is Ralph Adderley, Esq.

The ancient church, being situated on the brow of a hill, and surrounded with trees, is a very pleasing object. The living is a rectory, and the patronage is in the hands of the Dean of Lincoln. The church is dedicated to St Leonard.

The tourist, approaching Thorpe from the south, will mark an extraordinary and almost instantaneous change in the aspect of the country. Leaving behind him the 'brown heath and the richly-cultivated meadow,' he enters upon new and very different scenes. From the rising grounds which have grown, as it were, insensibly beneath him, starts in bold abruptness, *Thorpe Cloud*, a detached, cone-shaped hill, of steep ascent, and of considerable elevation. At its base, winds the most frequented road to that secluded and wildly-beautiful glen, DOVEDALE.

CHAPTER IX.

THE river DOVE, " one of the most beautiful streams that
ever gave charm to a landscape," takes its rise between
what are termed ' the Great and Middle Axe-Edge hills,'
about four miles south-west of Buxton, near the point where
meet the three shires of Chester, Derby, and Stafford,
and it forms in its course one of the natural boundaries
between the two latter counties.   There are, perhaps, few
districts in England, of a similar extent, that exhibit scenery
of a more diversified character, than the valley through
which flows this romantic and far-famed river.   At the
sterile region of its source, the tourist may contrast the barren elevations of the Peak, with the widely-extended, fertile, and thickly-peopled plain, denominated, not inaptly,
"The Vale Royal of England." For several miles the Dove

---

*The Great Axe-Edge, is the highest point of a line of lofty hills, extending
across the boundaries of the county into Staffordshire. *Farey* estimates its
height at 1875 feet above the level of the sea. *Whitehurst* states that it has an
altitude of 2,100 feet above the town of Derby.

is a small but rapid streamlet, and in its progress so far, over a wild, uninteresting country, it bears a strong resemblance to most other rivers that have a mountainous origin. Acquiring strength and vigour from its numerous auxiliary springs, it then courses through rock-girt dells and deep ravines, displaying combinations of scenery,—of wood, water, and rock,—singularly wild, fantastic, and picturesque. Escaping from its rocky confines, the Dove expands, and after enlivening and beautifying one of the most fertile and luxuriant vales of which this country can boast, pours its waters into another and a larger stream.* But the Valley of the Dove has attractions apart from its inherent natural beauties. The more southern portion of this district, owing to its extreme fertility, and consequent fitness for the abodes of men, would be peopled at a very early era;† and accordingly its antiquities, and the historical incidents connected with them, are of an interesting character, involving, as they do, much that is curious and valuable in reference to the manners and customs, the religion and condition of its inhabitants in past

---

* " The Dove," says Cotton in ' The Complete Angler,' " is so called from the swiftness of its current, and that swiftness occasioned by the declivity of its course, and by being so strained in that course betwixt the rocks, by which, (and those very high ones) it is for four or five miles confined into a very narrow stream; a river, that from a contemptible fountain which I can cover with my hat, by the confluence of other rivers, rivulets, brooks, and rills, is swelled before its fall into the Trent, a little below Eggington, where it loses the name, to such a breadth and depth as to be in most places navigable, were not the passage frequently interrupted with fords and weirs; and has as fertile banks as any river in England, none excepted. And this river from its head for a mile or two, is a black water, as all the rest of the Derbyshire rivers of note originally are, for they all spring from the mosses; but it is in a few miles' travel so clarified by the addition of several clear and very great springs, bigger than itself, which gush out of the limestone rocks, that before it comes to my house [Beresford Hall] which is now but six or seven miles from its source, you will find it one of the purest crystalline streams you have seen."

† " The fertile vallies of the Dove and Trent were the favourite resorts of the Mercian Kings."—*History of Tutbury.*—The small market-town of Repton, near the junction of the two rivers, was the metropolis of the kingdom of Mercia, and several of the kings were buried in the abbey there.

17

ages. Some of the erections of modern date in its immediate vicinity, and the objects of art contained within them, displaying the opulence or taste of their respective proprietors, are also of a highly attractive order.

It is these peculiar features that have obtained for the Valley of the Dove such a wide-spread celebrity. The painter, by the productions of his pencil, the poet,* through the efforts of his muse, and the topographer, by his graphic descriptions, have each and all contributed to disseminate a knowledge of its beauties. But the sketches of most previous writers have been in great part confined (perhaps of necessity,) to that, the most picturesque division of this valley, to which the name of DOVEDALE has been applied; while the scenery above and below that limited portion has been overlooked, neglected, or at best but partially described. In the present work it is the writer's intention to describe the objects of attraction, natural and artificial, in the Valley of the Dove, as nearly as possible in the order they would present themselves to one who had resolved to explore the stream downwards, from its source to its fall.†

*" The Tour of the Dove," a poem by Edwards, has passages evincing great descriptive power, and the versification is smooth and harmonious: take for example, his stanza on reaching the source of the stream :—

" At length 'tis gain'd, the heathy cloud-capt mountain !
Not at the hamlet of Dove-head I rest,
But higher up, beside a bubbling fountain,
That makes within a little well its nest.
Here springs the Dove ! and with a grateful zest,
I drink its waters that first serve the poor.
O, when shall they repose on ocean's breast?
How long must their rough pilgrimage endure ?
They ask not, but commence their wild romantic tour."

†This, though the obvious and natural route, can only be pursued by a pedestrian. It is here followed for the convenience of description.

Those who explore *Dovedale* only, commonly proceed through the pleasant village of Mappleton, by Thorpe to Ilam, where an excellent Inn, (*The Izaak Walton*) has been erected specially for their accommodation; or, they follow the Buxton-road, and turning to the left at Sandy Brook, go through Spend-lane, where there is another well-known inn, *The Dog and Partridge.*

Taking the Buxton road from Ashbourn, through Fenny
Bentley, leaving Tissington (one of the most pleasing rural
seclusions in Derbyshire,) half a mile to the right hand, we
enter upon a bleak, monotonous country, intersected by
stone walls. At no very distant period this was a wild open
waste, and even now, though the hand of improvement has
been exerted, its aspect is cheerless and cold. Near the fifth
mile-stone, the scene changes, a deep narrow dell, in a
high state of cultivation, opening to the east.   At one
end of this dell, almost shut out from the traveller's
view, is a little village, consisting of a few farm-houses,
the church, and the remains of the ancient manor-house, to
which has been given the appropriate name, of *Alsop-in-the
Dale.** In this neighbourhood it was that THOMAS BECON,
one of the most laborious and useful preachers and writers
among the British Reformers, took refuge from the furious
persecution of his enemies during the reign of Henry VIII.
He was a disciple of Latimer, and was apprehended by
Bonner in 1544, when he was compelled to make a public
recantation at Paul's Cross, and to burn his little treatises,
which had then begun to attract some notice. Finding
there was no safety for him in London, Becon travelled into
Derbyshire and Staffordshire, where he remained in seclusion till the accession of Edward VI.   During this interval
"he educated children in good literature, and instilled into

---

*In 1086, Alsop and Eaton were berewicks to the manor of Parwich. Alsop
which had been parcel of the ancient demesnes of the crown, was granted to
William de Ferrers, Earl of Derby, who, in the reign of King John, granted
Alsop to Gweno, son of Gamel de Alsop, to hold by homage and service of 10s.
per annum, and suit to the wapentake of Wirksworth. His descendants enjoyed
the manor for seventeen generations, until the close of the seventeenth century,
when Anthony Alsop, Esq. sold estates here to John Borrow, Esq. of Derby,
and Sir Philip Gell, Bart. The Beresfords and Milwards afterwards held it,
and having since passed by sale through various hands, it is now the property of
Walter Evans, Esq. Cold Eaton is said to have belonged to the Vernons, of
Haddon, and a fourth part was many years in the Boothby family. The
church at Alsop has some remains of Norman architecture. The living is a
perpetual curacy, in the gift of the freeholders.—*Hist. & Gaz of Derbyshire.*

their minds the principles of Christian doctrine." " When neither by speaking nor writing," he remarks, " I could do good, I thought it best not rashly to throw myself into the ravening paws of those greedy wolves, but for a certain space to absent myself from their tyranny. Leaving mine own native country, I travelled into such strange places as were unknown to me and I to them.* I found the people of very good wits and apt understandings. In a little village called Alsop-in-the-Dale, I chanced upon a certain gentleman called Alsop, lord of that village, a man not only ancient in years, but also ripe in the knowledge of Christ's doctrine. When we had saluted each other, and I had taken a sufficient repast, he shewed me certain books, which he called his jewels and principal treasures. To repeat them all by name I am not able, but of this I am sure, that there was the New Testament after the translation of that godly learned man, Miles Coverdale,† which seemed to be as well worn by the diligent reading thereof, as ever was any mass-book among the papists. In these godly books, this ancient gentleman, among the mountains and rocks, occupied himself both diligently and virtuously. But all the religion of the people consisted in hearing matins and masses, in superstitious worshipping òf saints, in hiring souls' carriers to sing trentals,‡ in pattering upon beads, and such other Popish pedlary. Yet the people where I have travelled for the most part are reasonable and quiet enough, yea, and very conformable to God's truth. If any be stubbornly obstinate, it is for want of knowledge, and because they have been seduced by blind guides."§

---

*At this period many of the inland secluded districts were scarcely accessible to travellers, and far less known to the inhabitants of the southern counties than some parts of the continent.

†His was the first Testament in English, printed about twenty years before.

‡Roman Catholic priests who repeated masses for thirty days to deliver souls from purgatory.

§Becon's Jewel of Joy. Lives of British Reformers.

We now pursue our route, hitherto an almost continuous ascent, to Newhaven, where we meet with a spacious inn, erected by the late Duke of Devonshire, for the reception of travellers to and from Buxton.* A turn to the left leads to the village of Biggin, whence we suddenly descend into a deep glen, on the one hand rising a lofty verdant range of hills, at intervals beautifully covered with wood, and on the other grey and naked rocks, piled one above another, having a dismal air of blank and lonely desolation. Down this glen we wind for nearly three miles, its aspect becoming continually more impressive; the hills lifting their heads to a greater elevation, and their decorations of wood and verdant declivities growing more animatedly beautiful. At length we reach the Dove,† and now a scene breaks upon us, which, under the influence of a poetic imagination, has been termed 'grand and bewildering.' Towers, and spires, and rugged domes, crowned with pinnacles, are some of the forms to which the rocks and precipices may here be likened: showing in many points, a striking resemblance to the more imposing scenery lower down the dale.

At HARTINGTON,‡ a considerable village, a little to the north-east of Biggin, there is said to have been in former times a castle, and some remains of ancient works have

---

*Newhaven is well known for its fairs, two of which are held annually, and notwithstanding the wildness of the country, they are attended by an immense concourse of people. 'The ground where the booths and tents are pitched is so broken and diversified, as to resemble the site of an ancient encampment.

†Higher than Hartington there is but little to interest the tourist: from this point then we descend with the stream.

The reader will observe that the form of expression is occasionally changed.

‡HARTINGTON, in Domesday-Book called *Hortedun*, is a very large parish, extending nearly twelve miles along the western boundary of Derbyshire. The manor belonged to the Ferrers family, and was afterwards annexed to the Duchy of Lancaster. In the reign of Charles I. Villiers, Duke of Buckingham, held it, but in the following reign it passed to the Cavendish family, and the Duke of Devonshire (who also derives his second title from the village,) is now the chief proprietor. The living is a vicarage, and the church is dedicated to St. Giles. In 1831, the number of inhabitants in the entire parish was 2,103.

been discovered. Several traditions of battles having been fought here are current among the inhabitants. On Hartington common the Britons are reported to have had a sharp conflict with the Roman general, Agricola, but the tale is uncorroborated by any historical evidence.* It is however certain that a skirmish took place here in the time of Charles I.† Many musket-balls, washed from the hills by heavy rains, have been found at different periods.

In the vicinity of Hartington there are several of those primitive sepulchral monuments, which in the northern districts are termed *cairns*, but in Derbyshire, *barrows*, or more commonly, *lows*. The most remarkable of these, situated on a hill, south-east of the village, is exactly circular, and rises about three feet above the surface of the ground. It is formed by stones of various sizes, the smallest being the most outward. Its circumference, measured at the base, is nearly seventy yards; and its diameter at the top is about ten yards; in the centre there is a cavity one yard deep, and three yards wide.

This and most other *lows* found in Derbyshire are supposed to have been constructed by the ancient Britons, perhaps even before the Roman invasion. Being among the only remaining works of the aborigines of this country, they possess a high degree of interest to the historian and the antiquary. A short summary of the chief peculiarities in the structure and uses of these and similar remains may not be unacceptable to the reader:—

"Those affections that have cherished a friend or relative when living, are generally expressed for his lifeless remains in a great variety of forms; and as love and friendship are most intense among the uncivilized, the rudest tribes are found to present the most striking indications of these passions, in their funeral ceremonies and modes of burial. The intensity of their feelings on such

---

*Beauties of England and Wales. Pilkington's Survey of Derbyshire.

†See page 19.

occasions, the ancient Britons have sufficiently announced
to posterity, in the numerous barrows and cairns that exist
in the island. What particular ceremonies they used in
the interment of their dead we know not; but from the
contents of the graves, we find that, like other rude nations,
they buried with the body whatever they accounted most
valuable. Weapons of war and of the chace, ornaments of
every kind, and even articles of jewellery were thus deposited; and frequently also the relics of dogs and deer, are
found mixed with human bones. All this had, doubtless,
a prospective view to the existence of the departed individual in a future state; he was thus not only arrayed for
that other scene in a manner befitting his rank and former
estimation, but furnished with the means of defence subsistence, and amusement. The prodigious labour with which
the old British barrows were evidently constructed, by soil
in many cases brought from a great distance, and the care
and ingenuity displayed in their forms, excite the wonder
of modern ages. These strange sepulchres exhibit great
variety both in size and shape, and by this, in some cases,
we can conjecture not only the period of their construction,
but also the condition of those whom they were designed
to commemorate. Thus the immense mounds of earth of
an oblong form and rude construction, some of which are
about 400 feet in length, but containing few bones and
fewer valuable relics, were probably the earliest graves of
the island, and designed for chieftains, who could more
easily obtain the labour of a thousand vassals, than the
possession of a single trinket. Next to these may perhaps
be classed the bowl-shaped barrows, as they are called,
which are plain hemispheric mounds of earth. The bell-
shaped barrow is evidently of still later date, being an
improvement upon the former, having its sides gracefully
curved inward, immediately above the surface, and exhibiting greater skill and labour in their construction. To these
may be added what have been improperly termed the
Druid-barrows; these are the most elegant of the whole

series of graves, and appear to have been in general occupied by females, from containing trinkets of a finer and
more feminine character, and bones of a smaller size than
those of the others.   It is conjectured also that these vast
piles were reserved only for chiefs and personages of elevated rank; while the common people, as in other coun-
tries, were buried in those more humble receptacles whose
traces are soon erased.

"The bodies of the dead were placed in the tombs in a
variety of positions.   It appears also that the practice of
consuming them by fire, sometimes prevailed, for in many
of the barrows, the half-burnt bones have been discovered.
A still more classical mode of burial was frequently followed among the Britons.   When the body had been
consumed on the pile, the ashes were carefully collected,
inclosed in a linen sheet, which was secured by a brass
pin, and deposited in an urn.   Some of the barrows, on
being opened, are found to contain these urns, which are
placed, in most instances, with the bottom uppermost."*

To the south of Hartington, on an eminence in the
midst of meadows, two or three hundred yards from the
Dove, stands BERESFORD HALL,† once the residence of the
well-known Charles Cotton.   The hall is a stone building
of very plain exterior, apparently erected about two centuries ago, and it has for many years past been occupied
as a farm-house.   Some of the offices have fallen into ruins,
but the front is still kept in tolerable order.   The ancient
furniture has disappeared, and the wainscotting, ceiling,

---

*Pictorial History of England, vol. i. p. 130, 131.

†The shortest and most convenient route for the visitor to Beresford Hall, is
(on quitting Ashbourn) to follow the Buxton-road as before directed, but turn
ing to the left near the fifth mile-stone, for the village of Alstonfield, instead
of proceeding onward to Newhaven.   The approach to Alstonfield is a steep
and narrow defile, skirted by rugged rocks, and from it we catch a pleasing view
of the church on the opposite hill.   Beresford Hall is about a mile and a half
distant, and the foot-path which leads to it, through several pasture-fields, rich
in so wild a situation, winds round the base of a hill, from which on the left
is seen a large circular valley, bounded by the lofty moorland elevations.

and interior decorations, have suffered from the mouldering hand of time. The "hall," now used as the
house-place, is of large dimensions, and on the ancient
carved-wood chimney-piece appears the cypher of Cotton.
The chief object of curiosity, especially to anglers, is
Cotton's fishing-house, a small building, situated on an
angle of the Dove. On the key-stone of the arch over the
door-way, the original cypher, C.W.C. (the initials of
Walton and Cotton) still remains undefaced; but the inscription above that, "*sacrum piscatoribus*" (sacred to fishermen,) has been lately renovated. Some idea of the
original state of the fishing-house may be formed from the
following description of it, written for Sir John Hawkins.
"It is of stone, and the room inside a cube of about fifteen
feet; it is also paved with black and white marble. In
the middle is a square black marble table, supported by
two stone feet. The room is wainscotted with curious
mouldings that divide the panels up to the ceiling; in the
larger panels are represented in painting, some of the most
pleasant of the adjacent scenes, with persons fishing; and
in the smaller, the various sorts of tackle and implements
used in angling. In the further corner on the left is a fire-
place, with a chimney; and on the right a large beaufet
with folding doors, whereon are the portraits of Mr. Cotton,
his boy-servant, and Walton, in the dress of the times.
Underneath is a cupboard, on the door of which are the
figures of a trout, and also of a grayling, well portrayed."
All these decorations have disappeared, and nothing remains of the furniture of the room but the marble table and
a few chairs. The site of this building is very happily
chosen, and the portion of the river that flows beneath it
has all the appearance of a good fishing-stream. In one of
the rocks that overhang the river, is a small cavern, of difficult approach, in which it is said Mr. Cotton used to
secrete himself when pursued at the suit of his creditors, by
the unrelenting perseverance of bailiffs. A faithful female
dependant, it is related, brought him his food while he was

18

in this place of concealment. The depth of the cave is about fifteen yards, but even in this small space there are several intricate windings, which being difficult to explore, make it well adapted for Cotton's supposed purposes of concealment.

Some years since Beresford Hall was purchased by Lord Beresford, the general who distinguished himself in the Peninsular war. By his orders some repairs and alterations have taken place in the building, and several planta-ations have been laid out around it.

The manor of Beresford, (anciently *Berreford or Bar-riesford*,) was for several centuries the inheritance of the family of Beresford, who first appear in the train of William the Conqueror; and a John de Beresford held the manor as early as the year 1087. The illustrious Beres-fords of Ireland are descended from this family.

In the reign of Edward IV. the manor was granted, in trust, to John, Lord Audley, but was afterwards released, and in course of time came into the possession of the Cotton family.

Charles Cotton the elder, who married the daughter of Sir John Stanhope, of Elvaston, (ancestor of the present Earl Chesterfield,) was a person of great talents and varied accomplishments. He was on terms of friendship with the celebrated Lord Clarendon, whose character of him is thus elegantly expressed:—"Charles Cotton was a gentleman born to a competent fortune; and so qualified in his person and education, that for many years he continued the great-est ornament of the town, in the esteem of those who had been best bred. His natural parts were very great, his wit flowing, in all the parts of conversation; the superstructure of learning not raised to a considerable height; but having passed some years in Cambridge, and then in France, and conversing always with learned men, his expressions were ever proper and significant, and gave great lustre to his discourse on any argument, so that he was thought by those who were not intimate with him, to have been much better acquainted with books than he was. He had all those qualities which in youth raise men to the reputation of being fine gentlemen; such a pleasantness and gaiety of humour, such a sweetness and gentleness of nature, and such a civility and delightfulness in conversation, that no man in the court or out of it appeared a more accomplished person: all these extraordinary qualifications being supported by as extraordinary a clearness of courage and fearlessness of spirit, of which he gave too often manifestation. Some unhappy suits in law, and waste of his fortune in those suits, made some impression on his mind: which being improved by domestic afflictions, and those indulgences to himself which naturally attend those afflictions, rendered his age less reverenced than his youth had been, and gave his best friends cause to wish he had not lived so long."

The younger Mr. Cotton was born at Beresford Hall, on the 28th of April, 1630. He received his education at Cambridge, and was esteemed one of the brightest ornaments of that seat of learning. In 1656, before any patrimony had descended to him, he married a distant relation, Isabella, daughter of Sir Thomas Hutchinson, knight, of Owthorp, Notts. The distress in which this step might have involved him, was in some measure averted by the death of his father, in 1658, which gave him possession of the family estates; but from the character of his father as given by Lord Clarendon, it may well be supposed they were encumbered with mortgages. In the year 1670 having been honoured with a commission in the army, he visited Ireland, which event he has recorded in some lines entitled "*A Voyage to Ireland*,"* carelessly written, but abounding

---

*In this poem, he relates with singular pleasantry, that at Chester, coming out of church, he was noticed by the mayor of that city, for his rich garb, and particularly for a gold belt that he then wore; and by him invited home and very hospitably entertained.

in humorous description.   Tempted by the vicinity of his
residence to one of the finest trout streams in the kingdom,
Mr. Cotton chose angling for his chief recreation, and looking upon it to be what Walton terms it, " an art," he applied himself to the improvement of that branch of it, fishing with an artificial fly. To this end he made himself
acquainted with the nature of aquatic insects, with the
forms and colours of the flies that are found on or near
rivers, the times of their appearance and departure, and
the methods of imitating them with furs, silks, feathers,
and other materials : in all which researches he exercised
much patience, industry, and ingenuity.   The publication
of Izaak Walton's " *Complete Angler*," probably excited
in him a desire to become acquainted with the author, for
in the year 1676, they were united by the closest ties of
friendship.   These were no doubt the inducements that
led Cotton to write the second part of the *Complete Angler*,
and therein more fully to explain the art of fly-fishing.
The book, as the author assures us, was written in the
short space of ten days ; and first came abroad, with the
fifth edition of the first part, in 1676, and ever since the
two parts have been considered as one book.   The second
part of the *Complete Angler* is apparently an imitation of
the first ; and besides the instruction there given, and the
beautiful scenery of a wild and romantic country therein
displayed, the urbanity, courtesy, and hospitality, of a well-
bred country gentlemen, are represented to great advantage.
This book might be thought to contain a delineation of the
author's character; and dispose the reader to think that he
was delighted with his situation, content with his fortunes,
and in short one of the happiest of men ; but his next publication speaks a very different language ; for living in a
country that abounds, above all others in this kingdom, in
rocks, caverns, and subterraneous passages (objects that to
some minds, afford more delight than stately woods and
fertile plains, rich enclosures, and other the milder beauties
of nature,) he seems to have been prompted by no other

than a sullen curiosity to explore the secrets of that nether
world : and surveying it rather with wonder than philo-
sophical delight, to have given way to his disgust, in a
description of the dreary and terrific scenes around and beneath him, in a poem, called "*The Wonders of the Peak*,"
which he published in 1681. This has been with perfect
justice described as a mean, splenetic composition. During
the whole of his life Mr. Cotton was involved in difficulties,* arising chiefly from the debts that incumbered
his paternal estate, and a certain easiness of disposition,
which laid him open to the arts of designing men. It is
said, that his pecuniary embarrassments drew upon him the
misfortune of personal restraint; and that, during his confinement in one of the city prisons, he inscribed on the
wall of his apartment therein the following lines :—

> " A prison is a place of care,
> Wherein no man can thrive,
> A touch-stone sure to try a friend,
> A grave for man alive."†

It might be supposed that Cotton's second marriage, with
the Countess Dowager of Ardglass, who possessed a join-
ture of fifteen hundred a-year, would have extricated him
from his difficulties; but the supposition seems to be con-
tradicted by a fact which the administration of his effects
on his decease discloses, namely, that his estate was granted

---

*In his epistle to Sir Clifford Clifton, speaking of himself, are the following
lines :—

> " He always wants money which makes him want ease;
> And he's always besieged, tho' himself of the peace,
> By an army of duns, who batter with scandals,
> And are foemen more fierce than the Goths or the Vandals."

†In the notes to Cotton's Life in The Complete Angler, it is doubted whether
he really did write these lines : they are said to have been found inscribed in
the Old Tolbooth, Edinburgh, with the following additional stanza :—

> " Sometimes a place of right,
> Sometimes a place of wrong,
> Sometimes a place of jades and thieves,
> And honest men among."

to his principal creditor, his widow and children first renouncing. He died in the year 1687, in the parish of St. James's, Westminster.

Mr. Cotton's moral character is to be collected, and does indeed naturally arise, from the sentiments contained in his writings, and more especially from his poems, which comprehend odes and epistles to his friends, translations from several French writers, and some burlesque verses. Many of these are inexcusably licentious, and will induce a suspicion that the author was but too well practised in the vices of the town. On the other hand, there are, in his "*Poems on several Occasions*," verses, to ladies in particular, of so courtly and elegant a turn, that allowing for their incorrectness, they might vie with the productions of Waller and Cowley. Others there are that bespeak him to have had a just sense of honour, loyalty, and moral rectitude. One of our most distinguished living poets has adduced several passages of his "*Ode upon Winter*," for a general illustration of the characteristics of fancy. " The middle part of this ode contains a most lively description of the entrance of Winter, with his retinue, as a 'palsied king,' and yet a military monarch, advancing for conquest with his army, the several bodies of which and their arms and equipment, are described with a rapidity of detail, and a profusion of fanciful comparisons, which indicate, on the part of the poet, extreme activity of intellect, and a correspondent hurry of delightful feeling." This recommendation from the hand of Wordsworth, will make the reader anxious to become acquainted with a volume which, " though stained with some peculiarities of the age in which the author lived," ought yet to form a part of all future collections of English poetry.*

The following verses, written at Beresford Hall, in one of his happiest moods, will give some idea of his habits and acquirements.

---

*Life of Cotton, prefixed to Sir John Hawkins's edition of Walton and Cotton's Angler. Professor Rennie's Notes.

THE RETIREMENT.
STANZES IRREGULIERS, TO MR. IZAAK WALTON.

Farewell, thou busy world, and may
    We never meet again;
Here I can eat, and sleep, and pray,
And do more good in one short day
Than he who his whole age out-wears
Upon the most conspicuous theatres,
Where nought but vanity and vice appears.

    Good God! how sweet are all things here!
    How beautiful the fields appear!
      How cleanly do we feed and lie!
    Lord what good hours do we keep!
    How quietly we sleep!
      What peace, what unanimity!
    How innocent from the lewd fashion,
Is all our business, all our recreation!

    Oh, how happy here's our leisure!
    Oh, how innocent our pleasure!
    O ye valleys! O ye mountains!
    O ye groves, and crystal fountains!
    How I love, at liberty,
    By turns to come and visit ye!

    Dear Solitude, the soul's best friend,
That man acquainted with himself dost make,
    And all his Maker's wonders to intend,
    With thee I here converse at will,
    And would be glad to do so still,
For it is thou alone that keep'st the soul awake.

    How calm and quiet a delight
      Is it, alone,
    To read and meditate and write,
      By none offended, and offending none!
    To walk, ride, sit, or sleep at one's own ease,
And, pleasing a man's self, none other to displease.

    O my beloved nymph, fair Dove,
    Princess of rivers, how I love
      Upon thy flowery banks to lie,
    And view thy silver stream,
    When gilded by a summer's beam;
      And in it all thy wanton fry,
      Playing at liberty,
    And with my angle, upon them
      The all of treachery
    I ever learn'd industriously to try!

Such streams Rome's yellow Tiber cannot show,
The Iberian Tagus, or Ligurian Po,
The Maese, the Danube, and the Rhine
Are puddle water all compared with thine;
And Loire's pure streams yet too polluted are
With thine, much purer, to compare;
The rapid Garonne and the winding Seine
   Are both too mean,
    Beloved Dove, with thee
    To vie priority;
Nay, Tame and Isis, when conjoined submit,
And lay their trophies at thy silver feet.
O my beloved rocks, that rise
To awe the earth and brave the skies,
From some aspiring mountain's crown,
   How dearly do I love,
Giddy with pleasure, to look down;
And from the vales, to view the noble heights above!

O my beloved caves! from dog-star's heat,
And all anxieties, my safe retreat;
What safety, privacy, what true delight,
   In the artificial night
    Your gloomy entrails make,
    Have I taken, do I take!
How oft, when grief has made me fly,
To hide me from society,
E'en of my dearest friends, have I
   In your recesses' friendly shade,
   All my sorrows open laid,
And my most secret woes intrusted to your privacy!

Lord! would men let me alone,
What an over-happy one
   Should I think myself to be;
Might I in this desert place,
(Which most men in discourse disgrace,)
   Live but undisturbed and free!
Here, in this despised recess,
   Would I, maugre winter's cold,
And the summer's worst excess,
Try to live out to sixty full years old;
  And, all the while,
   Without an envious eye
  On any thriving under fortune's smile,
Contented live, and then contented die.

           C. C.

It is sufficiently evident that the great defect in Cotton's character was inconsistency. At one time he is devoted to the innocent pleasures of retirement; at another, emulous of distinction as a ribald and profane writer in the most immoral period of our literary history.*

Of the future fortunes of his descendants little is known, save that to his son, Beresford Cotton, was given a company in a regiment of foot raised by the Earl of Derby for the service of King William; and that one of his daughters became the wife of that eminent divine, Dr. George Stanhope, Dean of Canterbury.

---

*The tone of pleasantry pervading the following passages from " The Complete Angler," in which Cotton figures as *Piscator*, is strangely at variance with the exhibition of spleen in his " Wonders of the Peak :"

" *Piscator.* You are happily overtaken, sir : may a man be so bold as to inquire how far you travel this way ?

Viator. Yes, sure, sir very freely; though it be a question I cannot very well resolve you, as not knowing myself how far it is to Ashborn, where I intend to night to take up my inn.

Piscator. Why then, sir, seeing I perceive you to be a stranger in these parts, I shall take upon me to inform you, that from the town you last came through, called Brailsford, it is five miles; and you are not above half a mile on this side.

Viator. So much! I was told it was but ten miles from Derby, and methinks I have rode almost so far already.

Piscator. Oh, sir, find no fault with large measure of good land, which Derbyshire abounds in, as much as most counties of England.

Viator It may be so; and good land, I confess, affords a pleasant prospect: but, by your good leave, sir, large measure of foul way is not altogether so acceptable.

Piscator. True, sir; but the foul way serves to justify the fertility of the soil, according to the proverb, " There is good land where there is foul way : " and is of good use to inform you of the riches of the country you are come into, and of its continual travel and traffic to the county town you came from; which is also very observable by the foulness of its road, and the loaden horses you meet every where upon the way.   *   *

But we have already talked away two miles of your journey; for, from the brook before us, that runs at the foot of this sandy hill, you have but three miles to Ashborn.

Viator. I meet every where in this country, with these little brooks; and they look as if they were full of fish: have they not Trouts in them ?

19

Piscator. That is a question which is to be excused in a stranger, as you are : otherwise, give me leave to tell you, it would seem a kind of affront to our country, to make a doubt of what we pretend to be famous for, next, if not before, our malt, wool, lead, and coal; for you are to understand, that we think we have as many fine rivers, rivulets, and brooks, as any country whatever; and they are all full of Trouts, and some of them the best (it is said) by many degrees, in England.

Viator. I was first, sir, in love with you; and now shall be so enamoured of your country, by this account you give me of it, as to wish myself a Derbyshire man, or, at least, that I might live in it: for you must know I am a pretender to the angle, and, doubtless, a Trout affords the most pleasure to the angler, of any sort of fish whatever; and the best Trouts must needs make the best sport; but this brook, and some others I have met with upon this way, are too full of wood for that recreation.

Piscator. This, sir! why this, and several others like it, which you have passed, and some that you are like to pass, have scarce any name amongst us; but we can shew you as fine rivers, and as clear from wood, or any other encumbrance, to hinder an angler, as any you ever saw; and for clear beautiful streams, Hantshire itself, by Mr. Izaak Walton's good leave, can shew none such, nor, I think, any country in Europe.

Piscator. Sir I think myself happy in your acquaintance; and, before we part, shall entreat leave to embrace you. You have said enough to recommend you to my best opinion; for my father Walton will be seen twice in no man's company he does not like, and likes none but such as he believes to be very honest men, which is one of the best arguments, or at least of the best testimonies I have, that I either am, or that he thinks me one of those, seeing I have not yet found him weary of me.

Viator. You speak like a true friend, and, in doing so, render yourself worthy of his friendship. May I be so bold as to ask your name?

Piscator. Yes, surely, sir; and, if you please, a much nicer question : my name is ———, and I intend to stay long enough in your company, if I find you do not dislike mine, to ask yours too. In the meantime, (because we are now almost at Ashbourn,) I shall freely and bluntly tell you, that I am a brother of the angle too, and, peradventure, can give you some instructions how to angle for a Trout in a clear river, that my father Walton himself will not disapprove, though he did either purposely omit, or did not remember them, when you and he sat discoursing under the sycamore tree. And, being you have already told me whither your journey is intended, and that I am better acquainted with the country than you are, I will heartily and earnestly entreat you will not think of staying at this town, but go on with me six miles farther to my house, where you shall be extremely welcome; it is directly in your way; we have day enough to perform our journey, and, as you like your entertainment, you may there repose yourself a day or two, or as many more as your occasions will permit, to recompense the trouble of so much a longer journey.

*   *   *

I will tell you, that my house stands upon the margin of one of the finest rivers for trout and grayling in England—that I have lately built a little fishing house upon it dedicated to anglers, over the door of which you will see the two first letters of my father Walton's name and mine, twisted in cypher—that you shall lie in the same bed he has sometimes been contented with, and have such country entertainment as my friends sometimes accept, and be as welcome too, as the best friend of them all.

    *   *   But sir, we are now going down the Spittle hill into the town; and therefore let me intreat you suddenly to resolve, and most earnestly not to deny me.

Viator. In truth, sir I am so overcome by your bounty, that I find I cannot, but must render myself wholly to be disposed of by you.

Piscator. Why that's heartily and kindly spoken, and I as heartily thank you. And being you have abandoned yourself to my conduct, we will only call and drink a glass on horseback, at the Talbot, and away. * * What will you drink, sir,—ale or wine?

Viator. Nay, I am for the country liquor, Derbyshire ale, if you please; for a man should not, methinks, come from London to drink wine in the Peak.

Piscator. You are in the right: and yet, let me tell you, you may drink worse French wine in many taverns in London, than they have sometimes at this house. What! ho! bring us a flagon of your best ale.—And now, sir, my service to you: a good health to the honest gentleman you know of, and you are welcome to the Peak."

The course of the Dove in the vicinity of Beresford is marked by scenery of a prettily romantic character,—a kind of miniature representation of a part of Dovedale. 'Pike-Pool,' ' Beresford's enchanting glen,' and the objects adjacent, Mr. Edwards has thus described:

" But who can paint the beauties of Pike pool?
Thy Duddon, Wordsworth, in its splendid route
Has nought so soft and green, so shadowy cool.
'Tis haunted by the grayling and the trout;
And from the sleeping water rising out—
Fairer than workmanship of elfin hands—
Appears an obelisk, a rocky sprout;
Like those of coral seen on Indian strands;
Or shapely pine that sole in some deep valley stands.

" Shrubs and steep crags a crescent skreen have drawn,
That on its southern side the river bounds;
The fellow bank is a smooth slip of lawn,
Skirted abrupt by bold romantic mounds,
With foliage hanging as from garden grounds:
These lead the eye to open fields of grass
But loveliest is that pool the glen surrounds.
High above all rears a stupendous mass,—
A rock-built range of towers that frown upon the Pass.

"Enough, methinks, is told of Nature's grace,
Poured freely on this stream, to anglers dear.
Diviner worth has sanctified the place.
That Fishing House amid those firs which rear
Their tops above it, leads me to revere
The seal of Friendship warm as filial love.
Twined in one cypher, on the front appear
Walton and Cotton's names; there fixed to prove
A record of affection near their favorite Dove.

          "Cheerful, sage, and mild,
Walton's discourse was like the honey balm
Distilled by flowers. Along these waters wild,
Smit with the love of angling, he beguiled,
With his adopted son, the hours away :
While Cotton owned the fondness of a child
For him, in whose glad company to stay,
Had made the whole year pass like one sweet month of May."

Leaving Beresford, and pursuing our tour in a south-
westerly direction, we enter a wild confined glen, called
Narrow-dale, so very narrow, Dr. Plot, the historian of
Staffordshire affirms, 'that the inhabitants there, for that
quarter of the year when the sun is nearest the tropic of
Capricorn, never see its face at all; and that at length,
when it does begin to appear, they never see it till about
one o'clock, which they call the "Narrow-dale noon,"
using it proverbially, when they would express a thing
done late at noon.'

          "Valley of Shadow ! thee the evening moon
          Hath never visited : the vernal sun
          Arrives too late to mark the hour of noon
          In thy deep solitude."   *Edwards.*

A portion of one of the elevated limestone ridges south-
west of Beresford, is termed 'Ecton Hill.' At the base of
this hill, on that side of it skirted by the Manifold, a river
having many characteristics in common with her sister-
stream, the Dove, is the entrance to *the deepest mine in
Great Britain.* That part of the hill in which the mine is
situated is of a conical form; its perpendicular height is
estimated at seven hundred feet, and the diameter at its
base, from the Manifold westward, is about half a mile.
The mine was doubtless wrought at a very remote period;

tradition states, as early as the Conquest. Dr. Plot, in the History of Staffordshire, published in 1686, informs us that it was wrought by the Earl of Devonshire, in the early part of the seventeenth century; and afterwards by Sir Richard Fleetwood and some Dutch miners, but they had all given it up as unproductive. After their efforts had ceased, it would appear from the accounts of a later topographer,* that all traces of the mine were lost.† He says that in the following century it was again *discovered* by a Cornish miner, who, passing over the hill, found a piece of copper-ore, annexed to some fine spar, to which that metal usually adheres. On examining the hill he concluded that it might contain vast quantities of copper-ore, and that no place could be more convenient for working it. He therefore communicated his discovery and his sentiments to some adventurers at Ashbourn, who approved of the project, and applied to the Duke of Devonshire for a lease to search for copper in the hill. The required permission was granted; upwards of £13,000 were expended before any profit was realized, and several of the adventurers, despairing of success, sold their shares at a heavy loss. The remaining shareholders persevered in their researches, and were more fortunate: for after sinking a shaft of about two hundred yards deep, and driving in a level, they found copper-ore in rich abundance, the quantity increasing, the lower they descended. They thus acquired considerable fortunes. At the termination of the lease, the mine reverted to the Duke of Devonshire, and for many years it produced him from £8,000 to £10,000 per annum.‡ A tourist who visited and explored the Ecton mine, about fifty or sixty years ago, (the period of its highest prosperity,) has furnished a description of the interior, as it then

---

*Beauties of England and Wales—Staffordshire.

†The accuracy of this statement may with good reason be doubted.

‡Popular report says much more: it is affirmed and believed by some, that the cost of erecting the range of buildings called the Crescent, at Buxton, was defrayed out of one year's proceeds! It is almost needless to observe that this is an exaggeration.

appeared, together with some information on the manner of working the mine :*—

"In descending to view this extensive mine, we enter [as before remarked] at the base of the hill by the river, and proceed almost four hundred yards in a direct line. About sixty yards from the entrance, the level is nearly five feet high, walled on each side with masonry. Beyond this point its height varies, and in some places rises to six feet. At the centre there is a spacious timber lodgment for landing and receiving the ore from below. After being drawn up to this lodgment, it is conveyed through the level on four-wheel carriages, each carriage containing about a ton and a half. These vehicles, which have brass wheels, run along the passage in grooves, being drawn by boys. Thus far it is easy to pass, with the assistance of lights; but below there is such a horrid gloom, rattling of carriages, noise of workmen boring the rocks and blasting the more obdurate and impenetrable strata, under the very feet of the beholder; while from this apparently frightful gulph resounds the distant and hollow voices and murmurings of labourers, that if Milton had wished for a place from which to have drawn his picture of Pandemonium, he could not better have described it, than by a representation of this stupendous mine. From the platform the descent is nearly two hundred yards, through different lodgments, by ladders, steps, and cross-pieces of timber, let into the rock. In passing down, the constant blasting of the rocks, making a noise much louder than the loudest thunder, seems to agitate the whole mountain. When at the bottom, strangers take shelter in a niche, as the miners generally give a salute of half a dozen blasts in quick succession, by way of welcome to these horrid mansions. The monstrous cavern above, the glimmering light of candles, and the suffocating smell of sulphur, all conspire to increase the stranger's surprise, and to heighten his apprehensions.

* Gentleman's Magazine, vol. xxxix.

" There is something in the position, situation, and inclination, of this mine different, it is said, from any yet discovered in the known world : for the amazing mass of copper ore with which this hill abounds, does not run in regular veins, courses, or strata, but sinks perpendicularly down, widening, and swelling out at the bottom, in the shape of a bell. Let the reader suppose himself nearly three hundred fathoms deep, in the bowels of a mountain, in a great hollow, of immense diameter; then let him suppose an impenetrable wall of limestone rock, interspersed with small veins of copper ore, yellow, black, and brown, intermixed with spar, marcasite, mundic, and other sulphureous compositions, of all colours; and at the same time figure to himself the dark complexions of the miners, their labour, and miserable way of living in those subterraneous regions, and he will then be apt to fancy himself in another world. Yet these inhabitants being trained up in darkness, labour and confinement, are not perhaps less happy or less contented, than those who possess the more flattering enjoyments of light and liberty."

The writer states, that though the works were then two hundred yards below the bed of the river, the quantity of water was inconsiderable, and that four horses, working six hours each at a common engine, were sufficient to keep the mine clear. The number of men then employed was about three hundred, who wrought night and day, in parties of seventy men each, relieving each other every six hours. Besides these, many women and boys were occupied in carrying, sorting, or washing the ore.

" When the ore is emptied from the carriages before mentioned, it is broken into small pieces by large hammers, and is then conveyed in hand-barrows, to a shed, where it is sorted into three different qualities. Being then beaten to a fine sand, the ore is removed to the buddles for washing, and is afterwards exposed for sale in the open air, in heaps, ticketted according to the quality. It is sold to the proprietors of the smelting-houses often in a manner resembling a public auction."

Since the mine has ceased to yield that enormous amount of mineral riches for which in past days it was so famous, public curiosity has died away, and of late years but little has been made known, respecting it. The scene described by the writer just quoted cannot now be witnessed, the operations of the few remaining adventurers being conducted on a limited scale; to the lover of enterprise, however, a visit to the mine in its present state will be amply gratifying, though the descent is a task of difficulty, not unattended with danger.

In the autumn of the present year (1838) we (the writer and a friend) determined upon exploring it. On reaching the entrance we prepared for the adventure by enveloping ourselves in coarse miners' frocks; thus equipped, and being furnished with lights, we entered the horizontal shaft, or level, accompanied by two or three of the most experienced miners. The passage for some distance is floored with boards, placed across sleepers, beneath which flows a current of water, a few inches deep. Proceeding along this level for about three hundred yards, we arrived at the point of descent, which is accomplished by the ladders before mentioned. Their sides are formed of wood, and the staves chiefly of iron, some of which are loose, and others so worn away by the repeated treading of the miners, as to convey a fearful sense of insecurity to those who were unaccustomed daily to make trial of their strength. We now found out the utility of the miners' substitute for a candlestick, (a lump of moist adhesive clay into which the candle is thrust;) this we could place securely against the side of the shaft, while the hand that held it was at liberty firmly to grasp the iron hooks and stays, which in the most hazardous situations have been driven into the rocks to assist descent. After descending what appeared to us an almost interminable number of ladders, and after groping our way through several cavernous passages, hewn out of the solid rock, and scarcely high enough in some places, to admit of our standing erect, we landed, within forty yards of the bottom of the mine, in a gloomy excavation of great extent, and very considerable height. In the dense and overwhelming obscurity which reigned around us, scarcely broken by the feeble glimmer of our lights, we were unable to form any probable estimate of its proportions; if we state its altitude to be in some parts not less than fifty or sixty feet, it is certainly not overrated. We were now buried, as it were, in the very bowels of a mountain, at the depth of at least fifteen hundred feet beneath its summit. The situation itself is one of appalling loneliness, and even in the company of the miners, who, from the force of habit, beheld the scene with careless indifference, it is hardly possible to shake off the apprehensions which it is so well calculated to inspire. But these imaginary dangers vanished before a real one. Just before our arrival the miners had effected a blast, the shock of which had loosened some pieces of rock, suspended, and almost detached from the roof. Some of these now fell within a few feet of the spot in which we were resting, causing us, it is needless to say, to make a hasty and precipitate retreat. The reverberation through the cavern occasioned by these falling fragments of rock, was loud and startling, what it would be in the case of an explosion, we had not then an opportunity of discovering. The rich bed of ore, in excavating which this vast chasm has been formed, is now exhausted; and thin leafy veins are all that remain for the miners to work upon; as one of them remarked to us, (rather expressively) "the trunk and the branches were exhausted,—they were then at work on the twigs." The air of the mine is close, but to those who are accustomed to it, not inconveniently so. We were informed that the workmen are subject to no more disease, and perhaps even less, than those who are exposed to every change of temperature in the open air. That this was the fact, their muscular frames and healthy appearance clearly indicated. One of our guides however stated, that in the course of forty years' experience as a miner, he had seen

20

many of his fellow-workmen drawn up to the entrance in a mangled and often lifeless state, arising from falls, or from injuries received in the dangerous process of blasting. Our guides next led us through a narrow passage on one side the cavern, to the mouth of a shaft leading to the bottom of the mine; but being told that the passage was insecure, we did not risk a further descent. Proceeding a short distance, we arrived at the great perpendicular shaft; on looking upwards the sky at the summit of the mountain was distinctly visible. Having gratified our curiosity to its full extent, we prepared to retrace our steps. The miners, in number perhaps a dozen, now left their labour, and each with his feeble light, defiled up the ladders before us. The effect produced by the motion of their dark forms, brought into strong relief amid the thick gloom in which all beside was enshrouded, was striking,—almost unearthly, and we lingered some moments to observe it. On reaching the upper level, we heard the sound of running water, and turning off to one side were suddenly conducted to an immense water-wheel, of extraordinary power; its diameter being thirty-two feet, and its width across the staves about six. By a singular exercise of ingenuity, this wheel is put into motion by the water collected in the upper parts of the mine, while its power is employed in drawing off that which would otherwise accumulate in the lower. Nothing we had hitherto beheld surpassed, for startling effect, the scene now before us. The revolution of this enormous wheel, and the action of its appendant machinery over a dark and apparently unfathomable abyss, added to the deafening roar of waters, increased in a ten-fold degree by the echo of the cavern, might serve for the reality of some one of those scenes deemed to exist only in the imagination of the poet. It must be witnessed to be appreciated,—to describe or to paint it is almost impossible. Near the wheel there is a capstan, with a rope equal in strength to a ship's cable, used for raising heavy weights. To preserve the rope from the effects of damp, fires are sometimes kept burning,

often for months together. Passing along the level by
which we entered, we emerged into the light of day, after an
absence of about an hour and a half.

The actual depth of Ecton mine is stated to be 1,650 feet.
In the year 1835 an assertion, perhaps never yet contra-
dicted, was put forth in a newspaper, and from it copied
into other publications, that a shaft at Monkwearmouth
colliery in Sunderland was the deepest in the kingdom,
being then extended to 1,600 feet below the surface of
the ground.* This statement must have been made in ignorance of the Ecton shaft, which then exceeded it by fifty
feet, and has now it is believed, for aught that yet appears,
a perpendicular depth surpassing that of any mine in Great
Britain.

The supposition, founded on the existence of volcanic
fires and hot water springs, that the internal heat of the
globe becomes more intense, in proportion to the depth
we penetrate from its surface, has in Ecton as well as other
mines, received strengthening testimony. Under the direction of Mr. Hopkins, the able geologist, who has bestowed
so much labour in surveying the strata of Derbyshire and
the adjoining counties, some experiments by means of
thermometers, are now being conducted in different parts of
the mine. The results already ascertained are decidedly
favourable to the truth of the supposition. These results
may be regarded as more conclusive than those obtained
from the like observations in coal-mines, in which other
causes have been assigned for an increase of temperature,
independently of the presumed subterranean heat.

The miners now engaged here have a lease from the
Duke of Devonshire, by which they are empowered to work
the mine for their own benefit, on paying to him a tribute
amounting to one-tenth of the ore procured.

The elevated ridges contiguous to Ecton are conceived
with strong probability, to be rich in mineral treasures

*Durham Advertiser.

Two companies, ("The Burgoyne" and "The North Staffordshire,") are now prosecuting operations vigorously.

The geologist is here presented with a wide and interesting field of observation and discovery. The strata, when bared to view, are often found to lie in the utmost confusion, exhibiting traces of some remote yet mighty convulsion of nature. The course of the Dove passes thrice over what geologists have termed 'the great limestone-fault,' consequently intersecting rocks of the earliest formation. Through Beresford-dale its course is upon the fourth limestone; but in the valley particularly denominated Dovedale it rushes amid precipitous rocks, and opens to the inquisitive eye of the scientific student more of the general series of strata than is any where else to be contemplated in the same limited extent throughout England.* To the miner, and to those engaged in mining pursuits, a knowledge of the facts revealed to us by geological investigation is of the highest importance, when it is considered how materially it will aid their researches, and what a vast amount of labour and capital it may hereafter save them. In the notes of a very recent survey of this district, we are presented with some details in reference to its aspect and formation, which may interest the general reader:—†

"If we draw a line from Ashbourn to Derby, and continue it thence to Nottingham, we shall have marked out a very important and striking natural division of the district. Any one who has passed through the country and crossed this line, even on the top of a stage coach, must have been struck with the difference that exists in the aspect and character of the country to the north of it and to the south. South of that line, the country is a complete plain—fertile and beau-

* History and Gazetteer of Derbyshire, vol i. p. 36.
† "A Popular Sketch of the Geology of Derbyshire," by J. B. Jukes, B.A. F.G.S. From Nos. 24 and 25 of "The Analyst" a valuable literary and scientific journal. Our brief extracts from Mr. Jukes's survey are somewhat out of order, inasmuch as they trench upon ground we have already described; but for this little apology is requisite when the interest of the subject is duly estimated.

tiful indeed, and frequently varied with gentle undula-
tions—but, upon the whole, a broad level space, stretching
east and west between the hills of Leicestershire on the one
hand, and those of the north of Derbyshire on the other.
In a level and cultivated tract, like this, where every bank
is clothed with grass, and nothing deeper than a gravel-pit
is anywhere visible, a man may pass his life without a
thought of what lies beneath the soil he tills. If, however,
we cross the line before mentioned, towards the north, the
scene is quickly changed: the country becomes gradually
bolder in its features, till we find ourselves at length winding among the deep and lovely valleys of the Peak, environed on every side by lofty hills. Here every one becomes
a practical geologist, so far as the composition of the different rocks and their range at the surface goes; and no
one, however unacquainted with the science he may be,
can traverse the country without having the subject forced
upon his mind. He will sometimes cross the high bleak
moors of gritstone, dark with the foliage of the fern and the
heather, or covered with long plantations of fir trees, where
dreariness itself has something of grandeur from its very
extent. From these he will look, on the one hand, over
the coal district, composed for the most part of longitudinal
ridges, furrowed by transverse valleys, frequently well wooded, and, where not actually deformed by smoky chimneys
and heaps of cinders and rubbish, containing many lovely
spots. Turning his back upon the coal-field, and proceeding towards the limestone district, he will generally find
the gritstone terminate in an abrupt descent, with a line of
rough beetling crags overlooking a narrow fertile valley.
On the opposite side of this valley, the hills rise with a
smooth but sometimes steep ascent, to a height equal or superior to that on which he stands. This valley is composed
of shale, and has most commonly a brook winding among
a strip of lovely meadows, and the hills opposite are limestone, and on them is no heather, no fern, and but few trees;
but they are clothed with a short light-green turf, and their

outlines, though not peaked ; are yet lighter and more de-
licately traced than the heavy lumpish forms of the gritstone.
But the chief beauties of the limestone district are its dales.
The brooks and rivers run in narrow winding valleys, with
precipitous walls of white limestone hung with the richest
festoons of creepers, and from every ledge juts a dark yew,
or a bending ash, with thick woods of other trees on the
green slope at the foot of the cliffs.   The flashing waters of
the brook as it foams over the ledges of rock that cross its
path below, and the hoar cliffs that rear their heads into
the sky above, form scenes to enchant the eye of the painter
or the poet, as well as to delight and instruct the mind of
the geologist."

After sketching each of the geological formations of the
district, the writer proceeds to show the situations they
respectively occupy, starting on a position which he appears
to have successfully established, that there is a sub-stratum
of mountain-limestone existing over the whole of Derbyshire and the adjoining counties to the east, west, and
north, for an indefinite and unknown extent, sometimes
forming the surface of the country, at others buried to a
great depth under other materials.   In examining the coal
measures, he expresses his positive conviction, "that in all
the country bounded by lines drawn through Wirksworth,
Ashbourn and Derby, there is not the most remote probability of coal being got.   Some persons, (he adds) deceived by
the resemblance of the limestone shale to coal measures,
and by the occurrence of nodules of coal in a diluvial clay
near Biggin, have been induced to sink and bore for coal
between Ashbourn and Turnditch—an absurdity, from the
expense and disappointment attendant on which the slightest knowledge of the structure of the district would have
saved them, and which sufficiently shows the want of a
greater spread of correct geological knowledge."*   In

---

*A similar attempt with the like results, was made a few years ago, between
Ashbourn and Fenny Bentley.

concluding his survey of the formation and position of the different strata, he remarks, " if we look from effects to their cause, and let the facts we have examined briefly speak for themselves, they tell us that over all this district which is now the county of Derby (and did we extend our examination we should be obliged to extend our expression to nearly the whole of England), at the remotest period to which we can trace its history, there existed a deep sea. In this sea abundance of animals lived and moved and had their being, peopling its tranquil depths with the happiness of existence, the old gradually dying, the young coming into life,—life frequently cut short by accident or violence, everything in short proceeding as we know the business of existence now to proceed in similar situations.   How long this state of things existed we know not, but sufficiently long for beds of limestone many hundred feet in thickness to be deposited, and for generation after generation of these creatures to be born, to live their appointed time, and perish one after the other, each race leaving its relics entombed in the successive beds of rock that gradually accumulated at the bottom of the sea."

Resuming our tour, we will leave the ' silver Dove' for a space, and follow the course of the Manifold.   This river, a little below Ecton, flows with glassy smoothness beneath a perpendicular range of rocks, clothed with many-hued foliage, forming a picture that strongly reminds us of Matlock.   Ascending the hill leading from the small vil- lage of Wetton to Alstonfield, we enter upon a scene that for bold and picturesque wildness may be fairly compared with any in Dovedale—we had almost said, in Matlock. High up in the face of an immense cliff, forming one of the boundaries of a deep and richly-wooded, but wide and bold-featured dell, opens a stupendous natural cavern, having a lofty vaulted entrance. Crossing the once deserted channel of the Manifold, whose sides exhibit several ver- dant spots, of extreme fertility, we scale the precipice,—a task more fatiguing than difficult—to explore the cavern.

Its height, at the entrance, and for a little way inwards, is probably between thirty and forty feet. The interior has several divisions, and to the right, there opens a remarkable fissure in the rock, of great height, but only wide enough to admit of a passage, and to catch a glimpse through it of the vale below. Further inwards, on an elevated portion of the floor, is a detached mass of rock, bearing some resemblance to an altar. The whole interior has been likened, with more of fancy than reality, to a gothic church. Tradition, with her often faithless tongue, says that the cave was the resort of the ancient Druids. The name given to it by the inhabitants of the district, (namely "Thur's-house") has been interpreted to mean the 'house of the god Thor,' and it is said that human victims were here sacrificed to that idol.* No one, after inspecting the place, will feel disposed to question the fitness of so wild a situation for the performance of these sanguinary barbarities, but in the absence of confirmatory evidence, the truth of the story has been doubted. That the ancient Britons inhabited the district, is proved by the discovery of their burial-places before mentioned, and from the fact that with-

---

*" These works of darkness Christianity extirpated; yet has the place recently become associated in the minds of the vulgar with new terrors, by occasion of a fatal catastrophe which happened here about February, 1825. Tissington Mycock, a man of some notoriety as a coal-carrier, having neglected his charge to indulge in liquor at the public alehouse, lost his asses. When the fit of inebriation was over he went the next day in search of the strayed animals; but instead of finding them, he became himself bewildered in the snow which then covered the ground; and wandering to the verge of the precipice above the cavern, fell from its tremendous height. He was dashed upon one of the rocky spines that branch out on the left side of the steep, and was thence hurled into the recess of the aperture already described, where, after a lapse of four days his mangled lifeless body was discovered. Since then, a report has prevailed amongst the peasantry of the neighbourhood, that the place is haunted by his ghost; strange noises, it is rumoured, have been heard issuing from the dark cavities that extend within to unexplored heights and depths; and the farmer's boy when at the hour of night-fall he collects the straggled herd, avoids with superstitious dread the gloomy mouth and frowning precincts of this mountain cavern."—Notes to " Edwards's Tour of the Dove."

in a few miles' distance there exists a Druidical circle.* We learn too, from the testimony of the early Roman writers, that caves, woods, and the depths of forests, were the chosen resorts of the British priesthood, and that a stream of water was always essential to the performance of their superstitious rites. With this strong collateral evidence in support of the tradition, the charge of credulity brought against Dr. Darwin, for having in the following lines assumed its truth, cannot well be sustained:

> " Where Hamps and Manifold, their cliffs among,
> Each in his flinty channel winds along;
> With lucid lines the dusky moor divides,
> Hurrying to intermix their sister tides.
> Where still their silver-bosomed Nymphs abhor,
> The blood-smeared mansion of gigantic Thor,—
> —Erst, fires volcanic in the marble womb
> Of cloud wrapped Wetton raised the massy dome;
> Rocks reared on rocks in huge disjointed piles
> From the tall turrets, and the lengthened aisles;
> Broad ponderous piers sustain the roof, and wide
> Branch the vast rainbow ribs from side to side.
> While from above descends in milky streams
> One scanty pencil of illusive beams,

---

*The *Arbor-Lows*, near Middleton, between two and three miles north east of Newhaven. This interesting remain consists of an area, encompassed by a broad ditch, which is bounded by a high mound or bank: its form is that of an ellipsis, or imperfect circle, measuring forty-six yards from east to west, and fifty-two from north to south. The width of the ditch which surrounds the area on which the stones are placed, is six yards; the height of the bank or vallum, on the inside, is from six to eight yards; but it varies throughout the whole circumference. The bank seems to have been formed from the earth thrown up from the ditch; which is not carried entirely round the area: but both at the northern and southern extremities they terminate, and allow a level passage or entrance of about fourteen yards wide. On the east side of the northern entrance, is a barrow standing in the same line of circumference, but entirely detached from it. This barrow was opened some years ago, and in it were found a stag's horns. The stones which compose the circle within the area are rough and unhewn masses of limestone, about thirty in number. Most of them are about five feet long, three broad, and one thick; these however are variable and their respective shapes are different. They all lie on the ground and generally in an oblique position. In the middle of the area are three large stones, which it is probable composed originally but one, the *Maen Gorsedd*, (Stone of Assembly.—*Davies, Pilkington, Beaut. of England and Wales.*

21

Suspended crags and gaping gulphs illumes,
And gilds the horrors of the deepened glooms.
—Here oft the Naiads, as they chanced to play
Near the dread Fane on Thor's returning day,
Saw from red altars streams of guiltless blood
Stain their green reed-beds, and pollute their flood;
Heard dying babes in wicker prisons wail,
And shrieks of matrons thrill the affrighted gale;
While from dark caves infernal Echoes mock,
And Fiends triumphant shout from every rock!
—So still the Nymphs emerging lift in air
Their snow-white shoulders and their azure hair;
Sail with sweet grace the dimpling streams along,
Listening the Shepherd's or the Miner's song;
But, when afar they view the giant-cave,
On timorous fins they circle on the wave,
With streaming eyes and throbbing hearts recoil,
Plunge their fair forms, and dive beneath the soil.—
Closed round their heads reluctant eddies sink,
And wider rings successive dash the brink.—
Three thousand steps in sparry clefts they stray,
Or seek through sullen mines their gloomy way;
On beds of lava sleep in coral cells,
Or sigh o'er jasper fish, and agate shells.
Till, where famed Ilam leads his boiling floods
Through flowery meadows and impending woods,
Pleased with light spring they leave the dreary night,
And mid circumfluent surges rise to light;
Shake their bright locks, the widening vale pursue,
Their sea-green mantles fringed with pearly dew;
In playful groups by towering Thorp they move,
Bound o'er the foaming wears, and rush into the Dove.

—Botanic Garden.

A little below, and almost within sight of " Thor's Cave,"
the Manifold, after a serpentine course of several miles,
forsaking the channel through which it has for ages flowed,
suddenly disappears beneath the cavernous fissures in the
limestone, and pursuing a subterranean route for about
four miles, emerges in the grounds at Ilam. "The junction of the wet and dry channels of the river," says Mr.
Edwards, in the notes to his ' Tour,' " affords a most interesting point of view. Below, is the empty water-course,
strewed with pebbles of every size, and fragments of rock,
worn with the attrition of the billows, and mellowed with

all the hues of vegetation, impressing the mind even in
their repose and silence with thoughts of agitation and tumult: above is the refreshing gleam and the soft murmur
of the cool pellucid stream, flowing amid green meadows,
embayed with cliffs and copses, and backed by the lofty
grey hills in the distance." Since this was written, some
attempts have been made, with partial success, to force the
river into its ancient course, by closing the fissures of the
rock through which it escapes.

For the distance of about two miles below Beresford, the
Dove is a succession of clear and rapid streams, forming
the chief charm in the somewhat dull scenery of this portion
of the valley. On the west, or Staffordshire side, stands
Alstonfield, a considerable village, containing some substantial farm-houses, and one or two respectable inns.
"Alstonfield" writes the old topographer, Erdeswick, "is
a great large seignorie, hath many hamlets; hath also of
old time been forest-lands, and hath many privileges belonging unto it." No man affecting to seat himself in that
wild country,* Alstonfield was divided into many parts.
For though in 9 Ed. II. Hugo le De Spencer and Nichol
Audley are only said to be lords thereof, yet were there
divers other lords which, their purparty being but small, were
omitted to be spoken of in the record. The most whereof

*" The admiration of picturesque scenery which characterizes the present age,
and the English nation in particular, has not at all times been displayed, as
may be evidently shewn from the topographical writings which antiquarians
have left us. If the splendid reign of Edward III. has, in the choice of situation for the numerous abbeys that were then founded, supplied sufficient
demonstration of fine taste and fondness for romantic seclusion; yet a strange
reverse of feeling must have been in operation, during what has been called the
golden age of our Elizabeth. The following extract from the " Survey of Staffordshire, containing the antiquities of the County," by Sampson Erdeswick,
Esq. (who died in 1603) will show that this most beautiful dale of the Peak was
at that time held in no estimation."

" Dove having past by the side of Alstonfield, for three or four miles, *without
any matter worth the noting*, at last receiveth on the west side, a pretty brook, for
its many turnings (by reason of the mountains, and the unevenness of the ground)
called Manifold, which taketh its beginning within a mile of the head of Dove,
and, fellow-like, keepeth its course with it, not being above two miles from it
until they meet."—*Notes to " Edwards's Tour of the Dove."*

are now come by purchase to Harper of Swareston, in Derbyshire." The church is a gothic structure, with a square tower, a nave, chancel, and side-aisles. The roof is supported by large pointed arches; and there is a fine east window, richly ornamented. Alstonfield parish extends to the length of fifteen miles, and has a population of nearly 5,000 inhabitants.

The landscape improves as (following the stream) we approach Mill-Dale, a little hamlet, curiously situated on the margin of the river, at the base of the hills that bound it on the Staffordshire side.

> " In this romantic region wandering on,
> (Where every living cry can stir the mind,)
> Recurs the bold rock-scenery : anon,
> A rustic bridge appears, and lodged behind,
> A group of cottages, with mill to grind
> Their slender harvest. Gladly did I hail
> The sight, in this lone place, of human kind :"*
>
> —*Edwards.*

From Mill-Dale, for the distance of rather more than a mile, the sides of the valley exhibit occasionally round tower-like rocks, with verdant slopes between them, otherwise preserving their wild yet monotonous aspect. The vale contracting, the river takes an abrupt turn ; and now 'a change comes over the scene,'—we enter at once a glen of surpassing beauty, furnishing an endless variety of ever-changing ever-varying views.

The first remarkable object that presents itself is a tall rocky precipice, on the left or Derbyshire side, perforated at its base by two caverns, of inconsiderable depth. The largest has a span of between fifty and sixty, and a perpendicular height of about thirty feet. These caverns have obtained the local appellation of "the Dove-Holes."† Seated on the turfy declivity that gently slopes to the margin of the river, we see on its banks directly opposite, several large masses of isolated rock, which seem to have

---

*Mr. Edwards, it must be observed, traces the stream upwards to its source.

†Beyond this point, travellers who *ascend* the stream rarely proceed.

A ravine on the left immediately above " Dove-Holes" leads into the Buxton road, by the farm of Hanson-Grange.

DOVE DALE
N. Entrance

Drawn on Stone by S. Rayner.

Published by Dawson & Hobson, Ashbourne

been hurled thither by some effort of nature; downwards, to the south-west, the eye wanders over a lengthened and winding range of mountains, profusely and thickly covered from their summit to their base, with various plants, shrubs, and trees, of mountain growth. The vale now enlarges, the river assumes a wider and deeper aspect, and the footpath winds through a rich and verdant plot of ground, skirted on the left by a grove of hazles. Lower down, on the right side, is another curious detached rock, rising to a considerable height from the very edge of the river, so closely, that at a distance one would imagine it stood in the middle of the stream. This cliff forms a kind of portal, which is considered as a distinct entrance into another division of the dale. In consequence of its projection, the stream is much contracted, and appears to force its way onwards with difficulty. On the opposite side there is a cluster of several remarkable rocks, one of which bears the appearance of a lofty cone, having a small cavernous aperture at its base. On a slope near the summit of one of the largest and most elevated of these, is a large detached piece of stone, of oblong-square form, apparently suspended by so frail a thread that a blast of wind might precipitate it into the bed of the river, or over the head of the spectator below. This rock has been frequently described and painted, and its parasite portion has received the fanciful designation of " the watch-box." From the middle of this ravine, which is in itself one of the most beautiful spots in the vale, we obtain views on all sides uniting nearly every object that can compose perfect landscape scenery. Entering now a thickly-wooded glen, we perceive the hills on the right to rear their heads to a greater elevation, and to be more plentifully clothed with trees, than those on the opposite side, still preserving that sylvan character which has hitherto distinguished them. A little further down we arrive at two stupendous cliffs, that rise abruptly on each side the river. The chasm here is so very narrow, that when by heavy rains the stream is swollen, the passage through it becomes almost impracticable. This defile is appropriately styled "Dovedale-Straits." Advancing a few paces, we see the naked cliffs on the left, bearing a singular resemblance to portions of ruined towers, take an expansive sweep round the mountain to the verge of the river, forming a wide natural amphitheatre. The Dove here loses her general character of a swift-running stream, flowing smoothly and placidly for several hundred yards. Just beyond this amphitheatre of cliffs, and as it were in the base of one of its wings, rises a vast and finely formed natural arch, pierced through the solid rock. We pass through this arch by a very steep ascent over loose sand and shale, to "Reynard's Hall," a large cavern, about thirty feet in height and fifteen in breadth. For the space of about forty feet this cave may be explored, but beyond it contracts to a narrow opening, supposed by some persons to communicate with other caverns, and to terminate near Parwich, between two and three miles distant. To the left, a little above, is another cavern, of smaller dimensions, called "Reynard's Kitchen." Descending to the arch, and looking through it we have views of the wildest and most splendidly-picturesque description. Retracing with the eye, as far as practicable, those divisions of the dale already passed, they form a deep winding ravine, in which the circular hill of the back ground—its outlines being softened by the distance—contrasts strongly with the rugged crested cliffs beneath and around. Far below is the Dove, running placidly along through the 'woody wilderness,' and sending aloft on the ' wings of the wind' her chastened murmurings. A little verdant island divides the stream, and beyond on the opposite hills, rises a lofty pile of rocks, with tall towering spires and pointed arches,—a group which has been likened to ' a magnificent abbey in a beautiful wood.'

> "Thou venerable Fane! thy walls were reared,
> Thy ivied arches springing roofed the void,
> Thy fretted spires above the trees appeared,
> Ere Science one fair Order had employed,
> One metal, gold or silver unalloyed,

To shape and ornament her piles with grace.
And yet the high emotions here enjoyed,
The humbling thoughts that human pride abase,
Might well befit the service of a holier place.

" I glance around the dale from right to left;—
It seems as Paradise were passing by,
And I beheld it from this secret cleft.
Flowers yield their fragrance; trees, luxuriant, high,
Climb the rude rocks; and in the orient sky
O'er yonder peak the sun reveals his fires.
The sparkling stream of Dove has caught his eye;
His glory lightens all the cliffs and spires;—
I see, I feel, my spirit glows with rapt desires."

—*Edwards.*

It is supposed that it was in attempting to scale an
acclivity near "Reynard's Hall," that Dean Langton met
with the accident that occasioned his end. The circumstances of the fearful catastrophe, as detailed in the jour-
nals of the time, are briefly these :—In July, 1761, Mr.
Langton, (then Dean of Clogher) being on a visit at Longford Hall, the seat of Wenman Coke, Esq., formed one
of a party to visit Dovedale. After viewing the scenery,
and partaking of refreshment in a spot near "Reynard's
Cave," they prepared to return, by way of Tissington, it is
supposed, for the Dean proposed to ascend on horseback a
steep hill over which a path led to that village; and Miss
La Roche a young lady of the party, agreed to accompany
him on the same horse. Mistaking the road, the Dean unfortunately followed a sheep-track on the right of the eminence, which he found too steep to ascend. In attempting to
turn about, the horse, overpowered by the burden imposed
upon him, fell backward down the hill. The Dean being
precipitated to the bottom, was taken up so dreadfully
bruised that he died within a few days, and was buried in
Ashbourn Church. Miss La Roche, whose fall was broken
by her hair becoming entangled in a thorn bush, escaped
with some severe contusions, though for two days she continued insensible. The horse, more fortunate than his
riders, was but slightly injured.—Dean Langton was of an

ancient family in Lincolnshire. He was chaplain to the
third Duke of Devonshire, when that nobleman was Lord-
Lieutenant of Ireland, and by him was presented with the
Deanery of Clogher.*

The Dove is now for some distance a varied succession
of almost still waters, rapid streams, and small cascades;
occasionally intersected with little islands, and studded
with fragments of limestone-rock, torn apparently from the
cliffs above. Further onwards, we pass, (on the Derbyshire
side) a hill almost separated from the mountain-range, the
sides of which are surrounded by several divisions of rock,
curiously rising one above another, obtaining from their
form and locality, the appellation of "Tissington Spires."
The Staffordshire side the dale continues to preserve its
distinctive sylvan character; its acclivities being shaded
with the rich foliage of the mountain-ash, the hazle and
the hawthorn; its rugged cliffs clothed with lichens, the
creeping ivy, and an innumerable variety of odoriferous
flowering shrubs. To the botanist the whole valley teems
with attractions, and he may here enrich his collections
by specimens of many rare and indigenous plants and
flowers with which it abounds. The fickle and whimsical
Rousseau, who resided for a time at Wootton Hall, in his
occasional rambles visited Dovedale, and is said to have
sown the seeds of some curious foreign flowers in the
neighbourhood. Whether any of these are yet in existence
is a matter of uncertainty.

The path now winds upwards through a thick grove of
trees, by the ruins of a hovel, which with the exception
of a fishing-house on the other side the river, are the only
traces of the innovating hand of man to be met with in the

---

*The Dean preached at All Saints Church, Derby, on the Sunday before his
death. ' His discourse' says a chronicler, 'was pathetic and much approved by
his hearers. The text was, "It is appointed unto all men once to die"—an
awful theme, prophetic of his end.'

He died on the 28th, July, 1761. An inscription on a flag in the south transept of Ashbourn Church, marks the place of his interment.

dale. All else is nature, wild and unbroken—and long may it so continue!* The path just mentioned leads to a round elevation, covered with smooth and flowery turf, and which overhangs, at an immense height, the river. Here, again, is a spot that is often chosen as the rendezvous and resting-place of visiters, and many a merry rural repast has been enjoyed beneath the shade of the clumps of trees by which the hill is crowned. The view from this point is perhaps the most extensive and imposing in the dale, possessing it, has been said, some of the bold and peculiar features characteristic of continental scenery. As the southern entrance of the glen is approached, the precipices which form its boundaries are perceived to lose their luxuriant aspect; they are no longer covered with trees, and but scantily clothed with verdure. The Dove, however, widens in her course, and taking a sudden turn to the right, at the base of Thorpe-Cloud, escapes from her confinement. Traversing several fertile meadows, she then forms a junction with the Manifold.

Romantic beauty amidst unbroken wildness, is the great charm of this far-famed dale. Its prominent and most striking features,—its rocks and precipices,—are bold, in some degree approaching in magnitude to the vast; but at the same time the general effect of the whole cannot with propriety be termed " awful," "sublime," or " transcendently grand," —epithets which some writers have injudiciously and indiscriminately lavished upon it. By the dim moonlight, indeed, when all is hushed save the never-ceasing murmur of the waters, when the lengthened shadow of some tall precipice casts a gloom,—a palpable obscurity, on the dell below,—it may then impress the mind with awe by its solitude; it then possesses sublimity from its very indistinctness; and when occasionally 'the queen of night' throws off her mantle of dark black clouds, and illumines for a moment with a flood of pale and silvery light the scene around, the effect of the magical transition is indisputably grand. At such a time, and under such aspects, the scenery of

22

Dovedale scarcely can be over-drawn. But Dovedale has *beauty* at all times and in all seasons: at the still and solemn hour of midnight, and in the broad and sunny glare of open day; at the dawn of the year and at its close; in the full bloom and luxuriance of summer, when vegetation exhibits a thousand varied hues, and amid the naked wildness and hoar frosts that march in the train of stern and dreary winter. Whatever then is thus really and truly beautiful, needs not the adventitious aid of highly-wrought and over-strained description to bring into notice. We have preferred therefore, to place the scene as it exists before the reader, leaving him, (if he have a heart and an eye to appreciate the picturesque) to form his own estimate of it, rather than to heighten his expectations by indulging at every stride in high-flown raptures, which to the sober imagination are but so many foolish fantasies.

Of all those who, in describing this delightful scenery, have evinced the possession of a high poetical temperament, no one appears to us to have painted its beauties in more warm yet generally faithful colouring than the gifted and imaginative William Howitt.* A native of and long resident in the vicinity of the wild scenery of the Peak, he has proved in his own inimitably graphic and pleasing manner, that to the 'warm heart and the vivid imagination' the contemplation of what is beautiful in nature never satiates nor cloys:

"Dovedale (he says) is undoubtedly one of the finest parts of the Peak. Its rocks do not, perhaps, equal in altitude and individual magnitude some of those at Matlock, but the scenes of Matlock wear a monotony, or at least a strong resemblance to each other, which soon deprives them of much of their effect, by familiarizing the eye, after seeing a part, to the character of the whole. But here besides the singular character of the scenery, its novelty is perpetuated to the very last. You are at once transported into

* Author of "Rural Life in England," 2 vols. 12mo. London: 1838.

a land of enchantment. Every object that surrounds you,
though you have but just left the other most striking parts
of the Peak, is strange and wild, and wondrously unlike all
other features of creation. The river, about every quarter
of a mile, takes a sudden turn round the feet of the mountains, and throws open before you as you follow it, another
scene different from the last, so that your mind is continually exerted by fresh emotions of astonishment and delight,
—which can only be felt in silence, and that make us
sensible how poor, how feeble is all human language.
Upon the whole Dovedale is a place so full of romantic
beauty, that happy should I be to see the spot that
surpasses it. If the man who enters it possesses the
least latent admiration of nature; if he have a soul capable of being moved in any degree by an assemblage of the
most wild, awful,* and sublime images, he will not see it

---

*Rather overdone—at least in our estimation. Professor Rennie, verging to
the opposite extreme, says that " it is utterly ridiculous to talk of the *grandeur*
of Dovedale. My impression (he continues) on visiting it in 1817 was, that
it was prettily romantic—on so small a scale that it might almost be artificially
imitated." Truly the Professor has a gigantic soul! As a set off to his flippant
remark, we adduce the opinion of *Byron*, than whom, all must admit, few men
were more capable of appreciating natural scenery. Writing to Moore, who
was then rusticating at Mayfield, the poet says, with an obvious reference
to Dovedale, " There are things in Derbyshire as noble as in Greece or Swit-
zerland."—*Sir Richard Phillips* calls Dovedale " one of the natural wonders of
the nation; nothing (he adds) can be conceived more picturesque, astonishing,
and even sublime : and a visit will repay every traveller and lover of nature in
its rude and grand features.—" It is, perhaps, (observes *Mr. Gilpin*, in his ' Northern Tour,') one of the most pleasing pieces of scenery of the kind we any
where meet with. It has something peculiarly characteristic. Its detached
perpendicular rocks stamp it with an image entirely its own, and for that reason it affords the greater pleasure. For it is in scenery as in life: we are most
struck with the peculiarity of an original character, provided there is nothing
offensive in it."—*Mr. Edward Dayes*, recapitulating the merits of Dovedale,
says that " it possesses an union of grandeur and beauty, not to be equalled by
anything I ever beheld. It is of that high cast of character which Pallas holds
among the females in poetry. Borrowdale in Cumberland, is sublime from its
magnitude; yet being destitute of wood, it wants the power to please : all there
is barren and desolate : but here beauty reigns triumphant. Happy is the man
who, divested of care, finds himself enabled to retire to such scenes as these,
and who at the same time possesses sensibility to enjoy their excellence."

without emotion. But to the warm heart and the vivid imagination it is a world in itself. In this lonely and astonishing seclusion, you cannot divest yourself of the impression
that it is all a dream, or a creation of magic: and the
awakened fancy speedily peoples it with a swarm of ideal
beings. I could almost fancy, as I reclined on a rock, and
looked down into the vale, that I saw ages pass before me,
with all their change of character. Do you not see here
the ancient Briton seeking an asylum from the Roman—
the Saxon from the Dane? Do you not see the knight and
the peasant of feudal times pass wandering through its
then savage obscurity?—the anchorite in his wretched
weeds, erecting his hut in its gloomy glens, or tenanting
its caves?—   *   *   *   or in
later and more lucid years, honest Izaak Walton and his
friend Cotton throwing into many a clear deep, some cunning bait for their favourite trout, as they sauntered down
by the Dove banks from Beresford Hall? Or the proud
and melancholy Rousseau, from his retreat at Wootton,
botanizing among its cliffs, and indulging delectable
remembrances of his native mountains.   *   *   *
There is nothing here to undeceive the sophisms of the
fancy; there are no traces of art to check its excursions, all
is wildness, loneliness, and peace, except when some brilliant party breaks in upon your musing; for such parties
the justly-increasing celebrity of the place brings every day
in summer." In illustration of the last remark the tourist
adds "We were sauntering along, imagining ourselves the
only human beings in this sequestered place, except an old
woman or two from Mill-Dale gathering sticks, when suddenly we saw scarfs, parasols, and feathers, glancing among
the rocks, and a troop of ladies climbing aloft over the
cliffs. In one place in the valley was a gay party, which
Horace and Burns would have liked to join, seated on the
turf, with music and the bottle, in all that merriment and
good humour which such scenes and times inspire: in
another, agile young lasses in white, sylyh-like, running

along by the river, with their bonnets in their hands, and
glowing with exercise; in another, portly dames, of a more
advanced age, walking sedately along the smooth path at
the bottom, wondering at the frolics of the young folks; in
another genteel youths handing girls up the stony heights
to the caves,—their companions at a distance calling to
them to take care ;—and laughter, and shrieks of moment-
ary terror, and silver voices heard from different rocks, that
at once converted this lately silent glen into a happy valley
of some brighter world."*

On the attractions of the Dove to the angler, and of its
celebrity as a fishing stream, it is not our province to dilate.
Not being an adept in the craft, we are unable to say
from experience wherein those attractions consist.   If an
opinion may be formed from the reports of others, who are
well qualified to judge, it would be that there is scarcely
a river in the kingdom that surpasses it.   From the time
of Cotton (and for aught we know long before) the Dove has
been the chosen resort of fishermen :

> "Of all fair *Thetis* daughters none so bright,
> So pleasant none to taste, none to the sight,
> None yields the gentle angler such delight."
> —*Wonders of the Peak.*

In later days, Sir Humphrey Davy, when visiting at Ilam,
pursued his favourite recreation on the clear pools and lim-
pid rills in the vicinity.—The number of anglers who resort
hither during the season testifies that the reputation of the
stream is yet spreading far and wide.

We now (on leaving Dovedale) traverse a foot-path at
the base of Thorpe-Cloud, still keeping the left bank of the
river. Crossing the stream by a rustic bridge some distance
lower down, we soon reach a level road.   An entrance-
gate to the right leads to that excellent hostelry erected by
the affluent proprietor of Ilam, and felicitously named after
'the prince and father of anglers.' From the carriage-drive,

---

*From " A Pedestrian Pilgrimage of Five Days through some of the most
Romantic Parts of Derbyshire, by Wilfred Wender" (William Howitt.) North
Staffordshire Mercury, August, 1824.

over the side of an elevation termed 'Bunster-Hill,' the
traveller is presented with a commanding view of the splendid and imposing exterior of ILAM HALL.

The site of this building is most happily chosen. Its
'towers, turrets, and embattled parapets' rise proudly out
of an angular valley, bounded and inclosed on all sides save
the front by hills of a nearly mountainous height and appearance, darkened and shaded by the sombre yet luxuriant
foliage of a thick overhanging wood. Partial glimpses of
the Manifold, sometimes a rapid brilliant stream, having
its banks skirted with ash and alder trees, complete the
harmonious whole of this delightful picture.* " The principal part of the building, with its large bay windows, octagonal projections, and richly-ornamented parapets, is in

---

*Mr. Rhodes, who visited Ilam in 1820, (before the present mansion was
erected,) thus describes it :—" The hills about Ilam have a magnificent character; they are thrown together in irregular forms, and with one exception only
in connected masses. Some of their mighty steeps are covered with noble wood,
others with a smooth glossy verdure, and in the space between them lies the
sweet vale of Ilam. A village of a few houses only, scattered amongst trees,—
a country church, with a tower nearly covered with ivy—verdant meadows,
watered by a busy stream, everywhere sparkling with light—and on a gentle
eminence, a venerable mansion rising out of, and backed by luxuriant foliage,
are the principal features of this lovely spot, which is one of the most romantic
little vales that nature ever formed. No glen in the Alps was ever more beautiful, more picturesque, or more retired. As I approached Ilam, and contemplated the landscape around me, I felt as if I had been treading on fairy
ground. The parts were so beautiful, and so exquisitely combined, and the
whole so rare and unexpected, that it seemed more like a scene of enchantment
that might soon pass away, than anything real and permanent. When this
train of feeling had a little subsided, I entered the house, which I found a
good commodious ' building made with hands,' and the residence of the elegan-
cies as well as the comforts of life. The principal entrance, agreeably to the
fashion that once generally prevailed, was a square hall, in the centre of the
building, which communicated with the adjoining apartments : a massy, old-
fashioned fire-place, admirably adapted for winter, with a huge, unlighted log
of wood, and some faggots of wood in the grate, occupied nearly one side of
the room; in a niche opposite hung a Chinese gong, whose loud and sonorous
sound summoned the company at Ilam to dinner : bows, arrows, and targets,
a fine old organ, and some antique chairs, completed the remaining part of the
furniture of this apartment.—*Peak Scenery.*

Drawn & Printed by Rayner, Derby.

Published by Dawson & Hobson, Ashbourn.

ILAM HALL

The Seat of Jesse Watts Russell, Esq.

that peculiar style of architecture, which was fashionable
in the reign of Elizabeth; but there are portions of this
structure that nearly assimilate with the gothic, both in
character and ornament, and these are decidedly the finest
and most imposing parts. The whole appears to be admirably contrived both for picturesque effect and convenience;
but the most beautiful feature in this noble mansion is the
circular gothic lantern by which it is surmounted. It is
not a paltry thing, made merely for the purpose of admitting light; its dimensions are ample, and perfectly in proportion with the capacious base whereon it rests. The
circle of which it is composed presents to the eye a series of
pointed arches, resting on appropriate shafts: these, in
connexion with each other, describe a magnificent circle,
and constitute the frame-work of the lantern. Where light
is wanted in the central part of a building, the dome is
sometimes so constructed as to be -a noble ornament; but
the lantern at Ilam is a more novel contrivance, and is one
of the most tasteful and elegant architectural ornaments
that ever adorned a building."*

The chief entrance to the mansion is not, as is usual,
constructed in its front, but rather on one side its principal
wing. A portal of gothic shape and fine proportions, surmounted by the family arms in relief, leads the visitor immediately to the *hall*. On each side the steps ascending
to it is a figure of natural size, in complete armour; one
wielding a formidable lance, and the other resting on a long
two-handed sword. The *hall* contains a curious and valuable collection of ancient arms and armour—firelocks, swords,
dirks, lances, scymitars, cuirasses, helmets, shields, and all
the trappings and instruments pertaining to the profession
of the warrior. These are not a meagre or scanty collection,
but include specimens of various dates and nations. This
apartment is also enriched by some fine pieces of ancient

---

*Rhodes's Peak Scenery, Part iv. p. 93.

carved furniture,—a set of massive, old, and elaborately-ornamented oak chairs, are particularly deserving of notice. To complete the scene, there stand on either hand of the door-way at the further end, two other figures, armed *cap-a-pie*, one hoisting the union-jack, and the other a large yellow flag.

On quitting the *hall*, the *vestibule* is entered. It is of square form, and the pavement is of tesselated marble. A large window, of coloured glass, on the right side, throws a peculiarly soft and mellow light over the apartment.

The *dining-room*, though not of very large dimensions, is tastefully furnished. The objects that first strike the eye are a magnificent Chinese screen, and a large dining table of the finest grained oak, of divers natural colours, curiously figured and inlaid. In this room is preserved the massive silver candelabrum, presented to Mr. Watts Russell, by the Conservatives of North Staffordshire, on the 29th of August, 1834. From a tri-lateral pedestal, around the extreme base of which sweeps a bold and richly-worked scroll, rises the stem or shaft, terminated at the summit by a foliage of Acanthus leaves, out of which spring eighteen branches, richly wrought with intertwining tendrils and foliage, and each supporting a light. Around the base of this stem is a classical group, executed in full relief, representing the arming of Achilles for battle. The hero is in a sitting posture, in the act of drawing the sword conferred by his goddess-mother, who stands at his side. The car and horses from which she has descended complete the group. The latter are studies from the Elgin marbles; and in composition and execution, the whole group may be termed a *chef-dœuvre* of art. On one side of the pedestal is a masterly *basso relievo*, exhibiting the combat of Hector and Achilles; another shews the armorial bearings of Mr. Russell; and on a third is engraved the following inscription:—

" A tribute of respect and gratitude to Jesse Watts Russell, Esq. of Ilam
Hall, from a numerous body of friends and supporters in the contested election for North Staffordshire, A. D. 1832, to perpetuate in his family their
sense of the public spirit which prompted him to undertake that contest, the
steady perseverance and strict honour with which he conducted it to its close,
and the opportunity he thus afforded to 3,387 electors to record by their votes
(of which 2,400 were undivided) their conservative principles, and their determination to maintain the ancient institutions of the British monarchy in
church and state."

The value of this splendid testimonial is estimated at £1,200.

The next apartment on the right, formerly the *billiard-
room*, is now appropriated as a *study*, and leads to the
library. The books include a choice selection of ancient
and modern literature. Among the many costly and elegant
works of art, is a fine bust in Chantrey's best style, of the
late Mr. Watts; and another, by the same talented sculptor, of the late Marquis of Londonderry. From the middle
window of this delightful apartment, the spectator commands a view, extensive, varied, and beautiful, bounded
on the left by Thorpe-Cloud, and the wild scenery that
fronts the southern entrance into Dovedale; while before
and around him lies a living landscape of hills, woods, and
verdant lawns.

The *music-room* is tastefully and elegantly furnished,
and contains, besides other instruments, an organ, of considerable size, and of fine tone.

Connected with these apartments is the *gallery*. There
is scarcely a picture among the many costly ones in the
collection that is not a good one, and that does not merit a
special description; our notices will however be confined
to a few of the principal ones.

A fine portrait of Mrs. Watts Russell, by *Phillips*, is
clearly and beautifully coloured, and has the reputation of
being an excellent likeness.

Over the door is a painting by *Romney*, from the collection of the late Lord de Tabley, representing a scene
from Shakspeare's "Midsummer Night's Dream,"—Tita-
nia, Puck, and the Changeling:

23

Puck: "——She, as her attendant hath
A lovely boy, stol'n from an Indian king;
She never had so sweet a changeling :
And jealous Oberon would have the child
Knight of his train, to trace the forests wild ;
But she, perforce, witholds the lov'd boy,
Crowns him with flowers, and makes him all her joy."

The celebrated Lady Hamilton, painted so often by Romney, was the model for the representation of the fairy queen.

On the right and left of the chimney-piece are two of *Howard's* finest productions. One of them is a representation of the solar system, from Milton :

"Hither as to their fountain, other stars
Repairing, in their golden urns draw light,
   *   *   *   *
  *   *   * that move
In mystic dance, not without song resound
His praise, who out of darkness call'd up light."

The other picture, " The Pleiades disappearing," is especially worthy of the reputation of the artist. He has vividly embodied the conception of our great poet :—

" First in his east the glorious lamp was seen,
Regent of day, and all th' horizon round
Invested with bright rays jocund to run
His longitude through heav'ns high road : the gray
Dawn, and the Pleiades before him danc'd,
Shedding sweet influence."
                     —Paradise Lost.

Near the last-mentioned picture hangs a large one by *E. Landseer,*—" Alpine mastiffs reanimating a distressed traveller." One of these mastiffs is said to be a portrait of that famous one which received and had hung round his neck, several medals, as a testimony of the number of persons he had rescued from perishing, when exposed to sudden Alpine snow storms. It is still to be seen stuffed in the convent of the charitable monks of Mount St. Bernard. This dog is painted, the size of life, in the fore-ground of the picture. A traveller, all but lifeless, lies nearly overwhelmed in the snow. The dog, with a little keg of brandy attached to his decorated collar, is licking the hands of the dying traveller, and eagerly endeavouring, by all the means in his power, to restore him to animation. Another mastiff, of the same noble breed, is painted a little behind, seemingly in the act of barking with all his might, and appears to have aroused the attention of the monks, one of whom is visible distant in the back-ground, hastening to the rescue. The landscape is a dreary one, befitting such a scene, and it serves to heighten our admiration of the group in their disinterested devotion to a high and generous purpose —the preservation of human life. The graphic pencil of *Landseer*, though it has since painted many more generally popular subjects, has never undertaken a more noble one than this.

The well-known description in Spenser's 'Faerie Queen;' of "Una among the satyrs," is well embodied in a large picture by *Hilton*, and it is said to be one of the most successful efforts of that clever historical painter :

> " So from the ground she fearlesse doth arise
> And walketh forth without suspect of harm.
> They, all as glad as birds of joyous pryme,
> Thence lead her forth, about her dauncing round
> Shouting and singing all a shepheard's ryme ;
> And with green braunches strewing all the ground,
> Do worship her as queene ;
> And all the way their merry pipes they sound,
> That all the woods with double echo ring ;
> And with their horned feet do weare the ground,
> Leaping like wanton kids in pleasant spring."

A well-executed and very interesting piece, called "The Fortune-Teller," by *Owen*, hangs near the picture last described. The all-believing simplicity of the cottage-girl, who no doubt expects to become the wife of her young squire, is plainly delineated in the countenance of the beautiful village victim. The assumed simple seriousness of the gipsy woman, betrayed by the insuppressible cunning of the eye, shews her to be a wolf well disguised in sheep's clothing; and the artist has given a signal proof of his skill, in softening down, as it were for the purpose of more easy deception, the generally sly expression of her features into that of matronly interest and affection.* This is unquestionably one of the best pictures in the gallery.

There are two small landscapes by *Salvator Rosa*, but by far the best and most valuable painting of this wonderful man,—this great painter, poet, player, musician, conspirator, (his admirers would say patriot) is his own portrait, painted by himself. The countenance is remarkably noble, of a sombre and rather severe cast; yet those who look into it will see that it is one of those that at fitting times could relax into buoyant hilarity. To surpass the beauty of drawing and colouring evinced in this admirable picture is, we think, scarcely possible.

There is a very beautiful marine painting,—" Dutch Fishing-boats running foul,"—and any comment on the excellency of its execution will be unnecessary when it is stated that *Calcott* is the painter.

A small picture by *Fuseli*, conveys a correct notion of the wild and daring yet not very pleasing style of that eminent painter. The incident which forms the subject is selected from Milton, but the ideal being is better known under the name of 'Robin Goodfellow,' in the " Midsum-

---

*" Whilst black-eyed Susan ply'd her murmuring task,
   A rural prophetess by chance pass'd by.
  Now, now's my time!—my future fate I'll ask :
   Be seated, Dame, and tell my fortune try :
  Her wheel within thy brain she twirls—that's known ;
  Then with an idle elbow stopp'd her own ;
  Her fingers, too full willingly resign,
   Their open palm perused in every line.
  We say no more, but if her ear's deceived,
  Observe her eyes; the flattering tale's believ'd :
  For though she tells of gibbets to the rabble rout
  Of noisy laughing rogues who dare to doubt,
   'Mongst anxious girls for ever in employ,
' She tells a sweeter tale, and all their dreams are dreams of future joy."

mer Night's Dream," and the artist appears in his delineation more to have followed the dramatic poet:

> " *Fairy.* Either I mistake your shape and making quite,
> Or else you are that shrewd and knavish sprite,
> Call'd Robin Goodfellow. Are you not he
> That fright the maidens of the villag'ry,
> Skim milk, and sometimes labour in the quern ;
> And bootless make the breathless huswife churn;
> And sometimes make the drink to bear no barm,
> Mislead night wanderers, laughing at their harm."

The following, among others, are of various degrees of
excellence:

Christ the Good Shepherd—*J. Northcote, R.A.*

View of the Castle of Dordrecht, with the river and
shipping—*Vander Capella.*

School-Mistress—*J. Opie, R.A.*

Portrait of Charles the First's Jeweller—*Vandyke.*

The Fisherman's Return ; A morning scene—*Collins, R.A.*

View on the Arno—*R. Wilson.*

The Cottage-Girl—*Opie.*

Portrait of two of Mr. Watts Russell's Children, and a
Favourite Pony—*T. Phillips, R.A.*

Cottage Girl—*M.A. Shee, R.A.*

Wood Scene; the church and village of Cornard, near
Sudbury, Suffolk, in the distance—*T. Gainsborough, R.A.*

View of a Scene in Norway—*Ruysdael.*

Two Landscapes—*Salvator Rosa.*

Two Landscapes with Figures—*Murillo.* The only
pictures of the kind by the master.

Portrait of Mr. Watts Russell—*J. Jackson, R.A.*

A View of Oxford, from the Abingdon-road—*Turner, R.A.*

Our Saviour and St. Peter—*Sebastian Ricci.*

Four Pictures—subject, the History of Tobit—*Stothard.*

Portrait of the late David Pike Watts, Esq.—*Sir W.
Beechey, R.A.*

A View of the High-street, Oxford—*Turner, R.A.*

The Last Supper—*Sebastian Ricci.*

Sketch from the Ballad of Chevy Chase—*E. Bird, R.A.*

A Landscape—*Claude Lorraine.*

Portrait of the late Lord Radstock—*J. Northcote, R.A.*

A Girl crossing the Brook—*H. Thompson, R.A.*

Copy from Vandyke—*Old Stone.*

A Baccante; figures engaged in sacrifice occupy the distance—*Benjamin West.*

The Fall of Phaeton—*J. Ward, R.A.*

Portrait of Lucius Francois, Painter—*Vandyke.*

A Cattle Piece—*Van Stry.*

A marble bust of George the Fourth, by *Chantrey.*

A bust of a Greek Girl, by *Gibson.*

An Ebony Cabinet (from the Fonthill collection,) the folding-doors representing two well-known Roman historical subjects.

The gallery contains several fine models of ruins, chiefly of structures famed iu classic story. Among them are—Remains of the Sepulchre of Scipio Africanus; Ruins of part of the ancient walls of Rome; Temple of Minerva Medica; Temple of Peace; The Sepulchre of Cæcilia Metella in the Court of the Farnese Palace at Rome; The Temple of Vesta at Tivoli; The Sepulchre of the Horatii and Curiatii, at Albana; The Temple of Janus, &c.

One of the chief curiosities in the gallery is the Font of Raphael, originally in the Florence Gallery. The following detailed description was written by the late Noel Jennings, Esq.: "The magnificent laver of an oval form, with a recurved edge and pointed bottom, which as well as the raised zone on the belt encircles the middle of the outside, is wrought in fluted or gadrooned work. Each side is ornamented with a laughing cornuted satyr's head; two grotesque sphinx-like figures, half satyr, and half dragon, with each a double tail, serve as supporters: their arms are extended to the edge, and their hind parts with wings expanded underneath resting on an oval base which has a hollow gadrooned edge. The whole is painted in the most lively colours, and glazed. On the inside, within a gro-

tesque border, is represented a Roman naval engagement.
The boarding of two ships by a number of soldiers in boats,
sword and shield in hand; sailors fixing their grappling
hooks, to facilitate the entrance of the assailants, who are
opposed by soldiers on board the ships, armed in like
manner. The exterior is enriched with grotesque figures,
supporting festoons of flowers, interspersed among which
are birds, military achievements, foliage, &c. &c."

The other apartments in this mansion of almost baronial
splendour, it is impossible, within our limits, properly to
describe. We must content ourselves with saying that
they form parts of a well-defined, comprehensive, and
magnificent plan, creditable alike to the genius of the
master-mind that designed it, and to the good taste of him
who had the perseverance to carry it into effect.*

From the terrace in front of the hall, the verdant lawn
slopes gracefully down to the river and the village church,
by which a path leads into the gardens and pleasure-ground.
Ascending several winding flights of rustic stone steps,
hewn out in the side of a mass of disjointed rocks, we
reach a splendid conservatory, well stocked with choice
exotic plants and flowers. In a calm sequestered recess in
the rocks below, is the grotto, with roughly-formed stone
seats, and table of the same obdurate material, in which
it is said, that Congreve, when a youth at the age of nine-
teen, wrote his celebrated comedy of the "Old Bachelor,"
and a part of the "Mourning Bride."† Near this spot,
bubbles upwards from its dark fathomless channel, the long
hidden Manifold; and about twenty paces further on,
within a kind of cave at the foot of the rock, rises the
Hamps. The latter stream forsakes its natural course, and
disappears underground, in a way precisely similar to the
Manifold, at the Waterhouses, a village several miles distant, about mid-way between Ashbourn and Leek. The

---

*Ilam Hall was built from designs by J. Shaw, Esq.
†Congreve was of a Staffordshire family. Beaut. of England & Wales.

waters of both rivers now unite with that division of the
Manifold which has retained or been forced to retain its
ancient channel, round the amphitheatre of rock and wood
in front. The re-appearanee of these two subterranean
streams in this surprising manner, within a few yards of
each other, constitutes a phenomenon that will by many
be deemed too marvellous to be real. The identity of the
two streams in their secret course, is said however to have
been correctly determined by experiment,—casting in corks
and other light floating bodies at the chasms where the
respective streams disappear, and which are stated to have
been found at the points where they emerge.*

"The united rivers (observes Mr. Rhodes) become a powerful stream, that within a few yards of the place where
they first appear, is precipitated over an artificial barrier,
where it forms a cascade of considerable extent and great
beauty. This river is one of the beauties and one of the
blemishes of Ilam. From the cascade in the garden, to its
junction with the Dove it is all play and sparkle ; above it
is an inactive pool, unless occasionally in winter, when it
is inundated with heavy rains, or the breaking up of a
snow-storm : then its subterranean passage, not being of
sufficient capacity to admit so large a body of water, it flows
into its former channel, and becomes an impetuous and
ample stream. It is then in harmony with the scenery of
Ilam, and the noble woods that decorate its banks; but
during three-fourths of the year it is far from being an object of beauty. Everything about it, with the exception
of water only, has the appearance and character of a
river. To behold this element still and lifeless, amongst
lofty and precipitous hills, with which the mind naturally
associates impetuous streams and foaming cataraets, seems
something like an anomaly in nature, and we are always
dissatisfied at her deviation from her accustomed habits."†

*"That they do not intermingle is evident from the difference in their tem-
perature, which on trial with the thermometer in October, 1802, I found to be
two degrees."—*Brayley's Notes to Dayes' Picturesque Tour.*   †Peak Scenery.

Mr. Rhodes then asks 'whether the river where it first commences its subterraneous career cannot be divided, and a part of it made to flow continually along its obvious channel?'* To this, Mr. Edwards remarks, 'it may be replied, that probably it is the case with the Manifold as with the Hamps, that there is a number of fissures occurring in the course of its passage, which would render the proposed attempt abortive. Neither, (he adds) in my humble opinion, is such a change desirable. The *whole* of the stream would afford but a scanty pittance for the supply of the channel here, which the volume of its occasional floods has rendered both ample and deep. The floods sometimes happen very suddenly : in the midst of summer when the bed of the stream is dry, a heavy thunder-storm on the hills above will bring down in the space of ten or fifteen minutes a tide of water several feet in depth, impetuously rolling its billows beneath the amphitheatre of woods that incloses the upper part of the vale. But this noisy spectacle disturbs the harmony of the secluded pastoral nook, and serves to weaken the impression of its own romantic charms. The sandy stony track of the empty channel is prevented by the bushes and trees growing along its banks from being an obtrusive object; and a casual glimpse of this phenomenon in British scenery, strikingly accords with the strangeness and novelty here displayed.'†

From the level plot of open verdant meadow, forming the left bank of the river, the eye takes in a picture of mingled wildness, beauty, and repose. Mr. Rhodes, whose description of Ilam scenery is at once accurate and poetical, portrays it with his accustomed force and feeling: "It was morning; the sun shone brightly in the heavens, and the rain which had fallen in copious showers the preceding day, had given a delightful freshness to the verdure of the fields, and a livelier tone of colouring to every object around me. My right, looking towards Thorpe, was a

*As we have stated, the attempt has since been made.
† Notes to " The Tour of the Dove."

24

steep and lofty hill, covered with wood, and involved in
shadow; another wood, still more beautiful, that glowed
with the bright effulgence of the newly-risen sun, lay on
my left: in distance, rising behind a mass of trees, Thorpe
Cloud reared his magnificent head; a beautiful light rested
on the side of this lofty eminence, and some thin white
clouds played about its summit. The cattle that were
grazing near—the freshness of the herbage on which they
fed—the smoke rising slowly from a cottage chimney at the
extremity of the wood on my right—were all pleasing incidents in the delightful morning picture that was here
presented. Delight was not the only emotion with which I
gazed upon this tranquil scene. I heard around me accents
of joy and sounds of pleasure only. Every object that had
life seemed to be freely and fully partaking of the benefi-
cent gifts of heaven, and for a while I forgot the works, the
employments, and the cares of man, in the contemplation
of that Being who has made so fair a world, and filled it
with happiness; who reared the mightiest barriers of rock
and hill with a word—adorned the vales with verdure—
clothed the woods with beauty, and led the streams through
pleasant pastures."*

In the churchyard, which is separated from the grounds
by an ornamental border of flowering plants, there is a
stone pillar, of great antiquity, bearing traces of some
rudely-sculptured decorations. This monument is supposed
by some to be of Danish, and by others of Saxon construction.† The church, originally a structure of early date, consisting of a tower, nave and chancel, is an extremely picturesque object. A thick mantling of ivy almost obscures the
stone-work of the tower, and the dial of the clock is nearly
buried in foliage. The interior contains some remains of

---

*Peak Scenery, Part iv. p. 91.

†Alfred the Great, who divided England into counties, hundreds, and
tythings, erected a number of crosses or landmarks, which no man was permitted to remove, and, to give them a sacred character, they were sculptured
with religious allusions, and the symbols of his faith."—*Ibid.*

high antiquity. A capacious and curiously-figured gothic
font will immediately attract the visitor's notice. Near it
is a large altar-tomb, without effigy, date or inscription,
which popular tradition affirms is the tomb of St. Bertram,
who is said to have led an eremitical life in this village.*

On a very curious altar-tomb there are two full-length
figures in alabaster, and on a tablet beneath is inscribed:

"Here lyeth the bodies of Robert Meverell, Esq. and Elisabeth his wife,
daughter of Sir Thomas Fleming, knt. and lord Cheife Justice of the King's
Bench, by who he had issue only one daughter, who married Thomas, Lord
Cromwell, Visconte Lecaile, which Robert died the 5th of February, an. 1626,
and Elisabeth departed the 5th of August, 1628."

Above this monument, attached to the wall, is a kind of
marble canopy, beneath which kneels an effigy, habited in
crimson, with a dark flowing head-dress; on a pedestal are
four smaller figures, representing children, with clasped
hands.

On a tablet affixed to the wall in the chancel, is an in-
scription (almost illegible) to Mary, wife of a member of the
Port family, of Ilam, and "daughter of William Fitzher-
bert, Esq. of Tissington, and his vertuous lady, Lady Mary
Cromwell, of the familie of Throwley." She died the 23d
May, 1685.

Among other monuments of the Port family is one "To
the memory of Lieutenant George Rowe Port,† of the Royal
Navy, and of Lieutenant Beville Port,‡ of the 19th Light
Dragoons, who were snatched away in the morning of life,
in the service of their country."

---

*" Ilam parish is also noted for the tomb, well, and ash of St. Bertram, who
is said to have confirmed the truth of his religious faith by many stupendous
miracles in this county. The sacred ash was formerly much venerated, and
taken great care of by the common people, who had a notion that it was highly
dangerous to break a bough of it. Little, however is now thought of either the
saint, or his tomb and well.'—*Beaut. of Eng. & Wales, Staff.*

† Died at Antigua, June, 1794. ‡ Died at Bangalore, June, 1801.

The ancient and loyal family of *Port* have been seated at Ilam for several
generations. Rowe Port, Esq. served the office of High Sheriff for the county
of Derby, in the reign of George II. (anno 1730.)

On a tablet to the memory of Robert Port, Esq. is inscribed a copy of verses from the pen of Charles Cotton:

> " Virtue, in those good times that bred good men,
> No testimony craved of tongue or pen;
> No marble columns nor engraven brass,
> To tell the world that such a person was;
> For then each pious act, to fair descent,
> Stood for the worthy owner's monument:
> But in this change of manners and of states,
> Good names, though writ in marble, have their fates;
> Such is the barbarous and irreverent rage
> That arms the rabble of this impious age.
>
>   Yet may this happy stone, that bears a name
> Such as no bold survivor dares to claim,
> To ages yet unborn, unblemish'd stand,
> Safe from the stroke of an inhuman hand.
> Here, reader! here a poet's sad relics lie,
> To teach the careless world mortality;
> Who while he mortal was, unrivall'd stood,
> The crown and glory of his ancient blood;
> Fit for his prince's and his country's trust;
> Pious to God, and to his neighbour just;
> A loyal husband to his latest end,
> A gracious father and a faithful friend:
> Beloved he lived, and died o'ercharged with years,
> Fuller of honour than of silver hairs.
> And, to sum up his virtues, this was he
> Who was what all we should, but cannot be."

To the northern part of the chancel a small gothic
chapel has been added, destined to be the burying-place of
the family of Russell. This chapel is the receptacle of one
of the most successful efforts of modern monumental
sculpture,—a group in white marble, by Sir Francis Chantrey, to the memory of the late David Pike Watts, Esq.
The principal figure (representing Mr. Watts) rests in a
half-risen, half-reclined posture on his couch of sickness.
He holds a Bible open in one hand, and is in the act of
giving his final blessing to his daughter (the present Mrs.
Watts Russell,) who is kneeling by the couch. By her side
stand three little children, the two eldest of whom and the
lady have their countenances turned towards their sire, in
the attitude and with the expression of breathless attention.

The youngest clings to his mother's knees, and affected
with sorrow or affright at the melancholy scene, hides his
little face in her dress. The whole group represents most
naturally one of the most touching earthly circumstances,
—the departure of the revered and venerable head of a
family from his intensely-afflicted descendants. The first
criticism that a stranger might make would perhaps be,
that the dying figure, is not sufficiently emaciated for one
who is about to breathe his last. Such a judgment, which
in cases of death from the ravages of slow and lingering
disease would be correct, must be altered, when it is
known that Mr. Watts' sufferings were not of a protracted
or emaciating nature. This apparent defect is therefore a
real beauty. An exception might also be taken against
the attitude of the two elder children, who have their backs
turned towards the spectator. A moment's reflection will
convince any one that this too is a proof of the artist's consummate skill, and profound knowledge of nature. Called at
an age when the faculties are just budding into existence,
to take their final leave of a fondly-attached and indulgent
grandsire, the children cannot repress, even in the intensity of their grief, that curious, inquiring disposition
which nature has implanted in all. Lost to every other
object, they stand with their faces turned *full* upon the
dying figure. as if in the midst of sorrow they would
know something of that mysterious visitant death, whose
coming, they have been taught, is approaching, but of
whose nature they are yet ignorant, and whose terrors the
innocence of childhood has not yet learned to comprehend
or to dread.

James Montgomery, in one of his eloquent lectures,*
asserting the pre-eminence of poetry among the fine arts,
asks his audience " whether, among a hundred of the monuments in our cathedrals, and the statues in our public
places, they ever met with more than one or two that laid

---

* " Lectures on Poetry and General Literature."

hold of their imagination, so as to haunt it both in retirement and in society,—or most unexpectedly to

> flash upon that inward eye,
> Which is the bliss of solitude."   —*Wordsworth.*

The poet instances, as one of these rare productions, 'the
simple memorial of the two children in Lichfield Cathedral.'
If his remark be true of that celebrated monument, it is
emphatically so of the one we have been attempting to
describe. The same master-hand is present, working as by
a mystic spell, the same effects on our feelings, sympathies,
and affections, hurrying us from the examination of a
perishable evanescent work of art, to the contemplation of
the awful reality—the suffering, the tears, the solemnity of
the chamber of death; and leaving us not here, the sculptor
conducts us in imagination to that ' undiscovered clime,'
that

> " brighter world on high,
> Where hearts that here at parting sigh,
> May meet to part no more !"   —*Barton.*

It is perhaps necessary, and may not be altogether uninteresting, in illustration of the memorials of the dead
contained in our churches, briefly to trace the progress of
monumental sculpture from its first rude and simple efforts,
to the age that has produced those splendid compositions
of which the nation (and the county of Derby in particular*) has so just a reason to be proud. Monumental
remains, as specimens of art, are to the antiquary the con-
necting links between past ages and the present, and they
are further important from the information they furnish
relative to the costume and decorations of the times in
which they were executed.

Stone coffins are probably the earliest sculptured tombs
with which we are acquainted. They were sunk into the
ground, no lower than their depth, and the covering-stone,
of an angular shape, standing above the pavement, they
thus served for a memorial as well as receptacle of the dead.

---

*Sir Francis Chantrey, it will be remembered, is a native of Norton, a little
village of Derbyshire, bordering closely upon the county of York.

The sign of the cross, and other religious emblems, were their first ornaments. These stone coffins were in general use among the higher classes in the eighth, ninth, and tenth centuries. They were often placed entirely above ground, in which case the sides were sometimes sculptured. This may be considered as the earliest form of the altar-tomb.* Monumental effigies were at first sculptured on the covering slab in low relief, the ground being sunk into the stone; but a bolder style was soon adopted, and the effigies of the twelfth century are mostly in half relief. On the introduction of the Early English style of architecture, the arched stone canopy was introduced. This being united with the altar-tomb, which had now become general, and in which the body was deposited above ground, the mode of sepulture became a perpetual lying in state. The sides of these tombs are panelled, and filled up with shields of arms. Niches, containing effigies of the family of the deceased, were added before the end of the thirteenth century. The effigies of this and the following century are numerous and interesting. The sculptor Flaxman remarked of some of them, that though ill-drawn and deficient in principle, yet in parts there is a beautiful simplicity, and sometimes a grace excelling more modern productions.† Very little opportunity was given to the artist to expand and improve his ideas, as a slavish custom prevailed of placing all the figures in a posture of all others the most rigid and ungraceful, which was on their backs: under this obvious disadvantage our ancient sculptors executed many very excellent and interesting figures in beautiful transparent alabaster, although nearly all the males are represented in armour. As the effigies of distinguished persons are frequently accompanied by those of their consorts, more scope for genius and variety prevailed in the latter, and consequently we find females in the habits of the times, and represented in the rich ornaments of the sex; and making

---

*Stone coffins have been discovered at Alstonfield and at Hungry Bentley.
†Pictorial Hist. of England.

due allowance for the stiffness of their cumbent position,
the drapery is frequently placed in true and well-conceived
folds. The bas-reliefs on the sides of these tombs, representing the deceased person's children, bearing shields of
arms, or monks and nuns telling their beads, are frequently
well executed, and so far as to make us wish the artist had
been indulged to the full extent of his abilities.*

The engraved and inlaid monumental brasses which
abound in our churches, came into use about the year 1380.
The designs and embellishments of many of these memorials are extremely elegant.†

During the fifteenth and sixteenth centuries the recumbent effigy was varied by the introduction of the kneeling
attitude, and, exhibiting less taste and skill in execution
than those of the preceding era, the monuments of this
class were often disfigured by painting and gilding the
drapery. This mode of decoration was carried to the height
of excess.‡

In the indiscriminate destruction of church ornaments
at the Reformation, the memorials of the dead did not entirely escape; and there are few monuments of a date
prior to that event that do not bear marks of violence.
Sculpture, like her sister arts, had now lost between the
fury of persecution and the excitement of a great and triumphant *mouvement*, the ascendancy she had so slowly
acquired. The highest and noblest department of the art,
—that of preserving and perpetuating the memory of the
mighty, illustrious or benevolent,—had well nigh sunk
into oblivion.

At the Restoration, the practice of the art revived, but
in monumental effigies the taste had grievously degenerated.

---

*Introd. to Gould's Dictionary of Painters, Sculptors, &c. See the churches
of Ashbourn Longford, Norbury, &c.

†Some fine remains and specimens will be found in Blore, Okeover, and
Ashbourn churches.

‡See Ashbourn, Tissington, Blore, &c.

They are mostly clad in Roman armour, their heads and shoulders sustaining enormous wigs! From this date the fondness for large tombs with elaborate and fanciful decorations sensibly declines. Symptoms of an improved feeling now become apparent, though the eye is yet offended by exhibitions deficient in point of taste, as they are miserable in execution. The altar-tomb was nearly laid aside, and mural tablets, of every conceivable form, were substituted; some of which, and a few of the larger memorials in our cathedrals, are elegant in design, and rich in embellishment. But as yet monumental sculpture did not rise above mediocrity; and it was not till Bacon, Flaxman, Nollekens, Westmacott, Banks, and Chantrey had arisen, that the noblest branch of the art came to be understood or to be appreciated. It was reserved for these gifted names, and especially for the last mentioned, to show that a successful appeal to our sympathies is produced, not by gorgeously-wrought allegorical combinations, but by representations of nature, simple, free, and unadorned.

The hamlet of THROWLEY, a short distance west of Ilam, was the seat of the *Meverells*, "a very antient house of gentlemen, and of goodly living, equalling the best sort of gentlemen in the shire."* This family is of high antiquity, and appears to have been seated at Throwley for several generations. Arthur Meverell, of Throwley, was Prior of Tutbury, at the dissolution of the monasteries in the reign of Henry VIII. In the seventeenth century Wingfield, Lord Cromwell, Earl of Ardglass in Ireland, became possessed of the manor of Throwley, by inheritance from his mother Elizabeth, daughter and sole heiress of Robert Meverell, Esq.†

BLORE, a village on the brow of the hill south-west of Ilam, is chiefly remarkable as being the site of the ancient baronial mansion of the illustrious family of *Bassett*. In the

---

*Erdeswick.   †Beaut. England and Wales, Staff.

reign of William the Conqueror Edricus held it of Robert
de Stafford, and in 33d Henry III. William de Blore was
lord of the manor. The founder of the family of Bassett,
into whose possession it afterwards came, was Thurstan a
Norman baron. His son, Ralph Bassett, of Colston and
Drayton, was Lord Chief Justice under Henry I.

The following is an extract from the pedigree of that
branch of this illustrious family that was seated at Blore :

" Rafe Bassett of *New Place*, (and Blore) and after of Cheadle, 9 Henry IV.
who married Maud, daughter and heir of Thomas Beke, and Alice his first
wife who died 9 Henry V. and had issue, Ralph Bassett of Cheadle, and Blore
and Grendon, who married Margaret, daughter and sole heir of Sir Reginald
Dethick, Knt. (son of William, Treasurer of England) by Thomasine his wife,
daughter and coheir of Sir Hugh Meynil, Knt. (who was seised of the manors
of Langley, Kingley, Newhall, Hartishorne, and Staunton.) She afterwards
remarried Nicolas Montgomery son of Sir Nicolas Montgomery, knt. and died
1466. By her first husband she had issue Ciceley, wife of Hugh Erdeswicke,
(son of Henry) and William Bassett of Chedle, Blore, and Grendon, and of
Langley, Co. Derb. 34 Henry VI. who was father of William Bassett, sheriff of
Co. Stafford. 6 Edward IV. who died Nov. 12, 1498. He married Joan daughter
and coheir of Richard Byron, son of Sir John, and had issue by her John Bassett
eldest son, who married Elinor, daughter and heir of Sir John Aston, S. P.
Ralph third son who married Elenor, daughter of Hugh Egerton, of Wrine-hill,
and had Margaret his daughter and heir, wife of Sir Ralph Egerton of Ridley
(grandfather of lord Chancellor Egerton.) Nicolas Bassett, fourth son who married Elinor daughter of Sir Nicolas Montgomery, S. P. 1492. And William
Bassett of Langley and Blore, (second but eldest surviving son,) who in 21 Henry
VII. gave lands to Rocester Abbey, for the souls of William his father and Joan
his mother. He married Elizabeth daughter of Thomas Meverell, the younger
of Throwley (remarried to Henry Coleyne) by whom he had Thomas, father of
Thomas Bassett of Hintes in Staffordshire, (who married the daughter of
Chetwynd, 1583,) and Sir William Bassett, of Blore, Grendon, and Langley
(his son and heir) who married 1. Anne, daughter of Thomas Cockayne of
Ashbourn, Co. Derby, Knt. and 2. Isabel daughter and heir of Sir Richard
Cotton, by his third wife Helen, daughter of Thomas Littleton, by whom was
Maud wife of Ralph Oakover, of Oakover; but by his first he had Margaret,
wife of Richard Copwood of Tokeridge. Thomas Bassett (who married Helen,
daughter of Cotes of Wodcote, Salop, and was father of Thomas Bassett of Fald
Co. Staff. living in 1583) and William Bassett of Blore, Grendon, and Langley,
(his son and heir,) who married Elizabeth daughter of Sir Anthony Fitzherbert
of Norbury, knt. and had issue.

" William Bassett of Blore and Langley, living 1588, who married Judith,
daughter of Thomas Osten of Oxley in Staffordshire, Esq. (widow of William

Boothby, ancestor of the Boothbys, of Broadlow Ash, &c. baronets; and after her second husband's death, remarried to Sir Richard Corbett,) by whom he had issue—Elizabeth his sole daughter and heir, first married to Hon. Henry Howard, a younger son of the earl of Suffolk; and 2ndly to Sir William Cavendish, K. B. afterward duke of Newcastle, to whom she carried this estate, and of whose children she was mother. The Duke's 2nd wife, who wrote his life, says " that when he was 22 years old, his mother was desirous that he should marry, in obedience to whose commands he chose, both to his own liking and his mother's approving, the daughter and heir to William Bassett of Blore, Esq. a very honourable and ancient family in Staffordshire, by whom was added a great part of his estate." *

The ancient mansion was standing in the year 1662, but its site is now occupied by a modern farm-house.

The church, a gothic structure, with a square tower, nave, and small chancel, contains considerable remains of former embellishments. On the right side of the south door-way are the fragments of the *stoup*, or receptacle for holy water, into which each Catholic dipped his finger and crossed himself, when entering the sacred edifice. The roof is supported by pointed arches, and the chancel is separated from the nave by some fine carved oak screen-work. Of the richly-painted glass that once adorned the windows, only a few portions remain. In one of the south windows, was (in 1662) the effigy of William Bassett, in his surcoat of arms, with the arms of Cokayne quartered with Hèrthull, kneeling before a crucifix, and beneath an inscription in old English characters:—

" Orate Pro Bono Statu Willielmi Bassett armigeri et Anne uxoris ejus qui istam fenestram fieri fecerunt, et istam Cancellariam Reedificaverunt Anno Domini MDXIX.".

The same inscription, under a different coat of arms, was placed at the bottom of the east window; and at the bottom of the east window of the north aisle were the effigies of William Bassett, Esq. and Joan his wife; he in his surcoat of arms, and she with the arms of Biron on her mantle, both kneeling before Sir William, with this scroll on their lips:—

" O Sancte Willielme, Ora pro me."

*Beaut. England and Wales, Staff.

On a marble slab in the north aisle, are the remains of an
inlaid brass monument, with the effigies of a male and
female, and around the edges are some portions of the following inscription:—

"Orate Pro Animabus Willielmi Bassett Armigeri, Domini de Blore et
Langley et Joanne uxoris ejus unius filiarum et heredum Ricardi Buryn armiger
filii et heredis Johannis Buryn militis.   Qui quidem Willielmus obiit xii die
Mensis Nov. Anno Dni Millimo Dlxxxviii, et eadem Joanna Obiit Die Mensis
** Anno Dni *** Quorum Animabus Propitietur Deus.   Amen."*

At the upper end of the north aisle, within a kind of
chantry-chapel, is a noble altar-tomb of statuary marble.
Extended on a mattress, beneath a large square canopy,
are two effigies, one representing a gentleman in complete
armour, another, by his side, a lady in the costume of the
times; and a third figure of an old man in armour, is elevated on a slab about a foot higher than these.   At the
heads of the two lower figures, are two females, in a kneeling attitude, both habited in beautiful flowing costume,
with girdles, pointed handkerchiefs, and easy veils over
their faces. One of these ladies appears to be in the bloom
of youth and beauty, but the other is considerably older.
There is a chastened freedom of execution in these figures
by no means usual in the age of Elizabeth, when we may
presume the monument was executed.   On the pillars and
sides of the canopy are disposed numerous shields of arms,
and heraldic devices, fully blazoned.   Many of these ornaments have been sadly mutilated, and their gilding is tar-
nished or effaced through continued exposure to the action
of damp.   On a tablet at the back of the tomb is the
epitaph—

"Here lyes a courtier, souldier, handsome, good,
Witty, wise, valiant, and of pure blood
From William's conquest, and his potent sword
In the same lyne many a noble Lord,
That time hath lost in paying thus Death's debt,
In this unparallell'd William Bassett,
But thy high virtues with thy antient name
Shall ever swell the cheeks of glorious fame."

The monument is without date, but there is every reason to believe that it was erected in memory of William the last male heir of the Bassett family, who was living in 1588.

"Dove beginning at Blore to enlarge his banks, passeth on to OKEOVER, where is another fair old house, and a goodly demeasne."* The estate and manor of Okeover have been in possession of the family bearing that name for more than seven hundred years. At the Conquest, Ormus, or Orme, was lord of *Acover* and Stretton. From him the manor of Okeover descended in a right line to Thomas de Okeover, who died in the reign of Henry VI. possessed also of lands in Mappleton and Atlow. Members of this family are found to have filled offices of honour and trust in the counties of Derby, Stafford, and Nottingham, from a very early period. Philip de Okeover represented the county of Derby, in the fifth and fifteenth parliaments of Richard II.; Thomas de Okeover, in the ninth parliament of Henry IV., and in the eighth and ninth of Henry V.; Sir Philip Okeover, knight, was high sheriff for the counties of Derby and Nottingham in 1465, and Philip Okeover, Esq. in 1474. Humphrey Okeover, Esq. was sheriff for the county of Derby in 1631;† and Haughton Farmer Okeover, Esq. for the county of Stafford, in 1800. Among the many ancient and honourable houses with which this family became allied, are those of Bassett, of Blore; Bradburne, Aston, of Tixall; Leech, of Chatsworth; Longford, Dunham, Cheney, Cokayne, Ashley, (ancestors of the Earls Shaftesbury;) Bagot, Shirley, Hurt, Walhouse, Littleton,

---

*Erdeswick's Staffordshire.

†Bancroft, "the small poet," addresses one of his epigrams to " Humphrey Okeover, Esq.:"—

"I sometimes heard a kind of prophisie,
That your name should in fair longevity
Equal the tree of Jove—which may it bide
Like royal cedar, (never putrified)
Nor otherwise impaired: so sound a fame
To you I wish, and your well-timbered name."

Adderley, Anson, and others.   The present heir to the
estates is Charles Haughton Okeover, Esq.*

The vale of Okeover, seen from the hills which environ it,
forms a landscape rich and luxuriant, and not the less
pleasing because it is thoroughly English in its character;
Overlooking a fertile undulating park, thickly wooded,
and well stocked with deer, stands the family mansion, a
goodly structure of the last century, and close by, the village church, with its perpetual covering of ivy; the dark
hills of Dovedale close in the back-ground,—beneath and
to the south, scattered over the wide domain, are groups of
cottages and detached homesteads; and the winding Dove,
losing none of her power to charm, wanders in soothing
majesty, o'er a lengthened vista of 'fertile vales and dewy
meads'—

> "The stately homes of England!
> How beautiful they stand;
> Amidst their tall ancestral trees,
> O'er all the pleasant land;
> The deer across their green sward bound,
> Through shade and sunny gleam;
> And swan glides past them with the sound
> Of some rejoicing stream."   —*Hemans.*

The chief attraction in the hall is the celebrated picture,
ascribed to *Raffaelle*—"The Holy Family." The group
consists of five figures: the infant Jesus on his mother's lap;
St. Ann standing near—her eyes intently fixed on the holy
child; St. John behind; and Joseph still further in the
back-ground. At the first glance this picture may not appear to possess that transcendent degree of excellence
with which a previously-excited imagination will have
invested it. This absence of dazzling effect has been
remarked of other productions of the gifted painter whose
name it bears, and is attributed by some to a want of

---

*Pedigree of the family, Hist. of Derbyshire, vol. ii. p. 63, 4, 5.

Okeover Hall is now (1839) the residence of Robert Plumer Ward, Esq. the
talented author of "Tremaine." He married the widow of the Rev. Charles
Gregory Okeover.

Published by Dawson & Hobson, Ashbourn

OKEOVER HALL.
STAFFORDSHIRE.

strength in his colouring, and by others, with more justice, to his extreme fidelity to nature. It has been well observed, that 'an uncommon expression, strong colouring, or odd and singular attitudes of an inferior painter strike us at first sight because we have not been accustomed to see them elsewhere.' But in "The Holy Family," all is ease, grace, and dignity, and the longer we examine it, so much the more do its merits become apparent.

The value of this gem of art has been variously estimated —at from 1,000 to 2,000 guineas. It is said to have been discovered in an old lumber-room, where it is conjectured to have been hidden during the civil wars.

The dining-room contains several other good pictures, among which are *Vandervelde's* well-known pieces, "The Calm" and "The Storm;" "St. Veronica with the sacred handkerchief," by *Titian ;* "Christ meeting the Women in the Garden," by *Rubens ;* and others of less note.

The church, a small building with a square tower, is in good repair, and is furnished with an excellent organ.* The sepulchral remains are few ; on an alabaster slab is inscribed—

"Hic jacet Joliana Port, uxor Johannis Port Armigeri, filia omfredi Okor Armigeri, quæ quidem Joliana obiit III. die Februarii, Anno Dni MDXXIIII. cujus animæ propitietur Deus. Amen."

---

*Rowland Okeover, Esq. by indenture bearing date October, 1727, granted £60 yearly out of the rents of certain property in Atlow and Mappleton, for the support of an organist for the parish-church of Okeover, and also of twelve fit boys or girls to be choristers. He further directed his trustees to erect and endow out of the residue of the rents and profits of the said property, a neat and convenient house, divided into three dwellings for three widows of clergymen of the Church of England. These dwellings are pleasantly situated at Mappleton; the inmate of each receives the annual sum of £30. The appointment is vested in the trustees, and is made without limitation as to the county or diocese in which the deceased clergymen may have resided. About the year 1736, some proceedings are reported to have taken place in the court of Chancery respecting this charity, when it was established, except as to the maintenance of boys and girls as choristers. Twelve boys and girls of different parishes are now clothed out of the funds of this charity.—*Charity Commissioners' Report, July,* 1827.

Near this slab is a very fine inlaid brass monument, in excellent preservation, though the inscription round the edge is partly effaced. From what remains may be deciphered—

" Here under thys stone lyeth........Oker Esqueyer sumtyme Lord of Oker & Isabell hys wyfe daughter of John Aston Esquyer and Dame Elsabeth, hys wyfe the whiche Humfr....decessyd the xxii. day of Aprell the yere of our Lord...............Amen."

In the centre of the slab are engraven the effigies of the deceased; the head of the male rests on the trunk of a prostrate oak tree, on his left is a coat of arms, inscribed "The Armys of Oker and Aston." Underneath are the effigies of his children, viz.: "Philyp, Rauf, John, Willm. Roger, Nicolas, Robt. Thoms. Jane, Elsabeth, Mrgre," and two others not legible.

There are, besides, several mural monuments to members of the Okeover family, and in the chancel window are some remains of painted glass.

On an eminence about a quarter of a mile south of the hall is a square intrenchment, called the Hallsteads. The trench or moat is crossed on the north side by a stone arch in good preservation. This is evidently the site of a fortified building,—probably a seat of the ancient lords of Okeover.

The parish of Okeover contains about sixty inhabitants, and the annual value of the property is estimated at £1,029.

It is stated by a writer in "The Beauties of England and Wales," and by other topographers, that at some place in the vicinity of Okeover was born John Dudley, Duke of Northumberland, the accomplished statesman who acted so remarkable a part in the transactions of the eventful times of Henry VIII. and Edward VI., and who, in the following reign, perished on the scaffold for his unconstitutional attempt to raise Lady Jane Grey to the throne. This powerful nobleman, it will be remembered, was the son of Edmund Dudley, who, as a lawyer and statesman, rose to eminence under Henry VII., and who was the chief instrument employed by that monarch in the arbitrary extortions practised in the latter part of his reign. The character of the elder Dudley, and of his associate Empson, with their modes of procedure, are thus described by Lord Bacon:— "As kings do more easily find instruments for their will and humour, than for their service and honour, he (Henry) had gotten for his purpose two instruments, Empson and Dudley, bold men, and careless of fame, and that took toll for their master's grist. Dudley was of a good family, eloquent, and one that could put hateful business into good language, but Empson, that was a son of a sieve-maker, triumphed always in the deed done, putting off all other respect whatever. These two persons being lawyers in science, and privy councillors in authority, turned law and justice into wormwood and rapine. For first their manner was to cause divers subjects to be indicted for sundry crimes, and so far forth to proceed in form of law, but when the bills were found then presently to commit them: and, nevertheless, not to produce them in any reasonable time to them; but to suffer them to languish long in prison, and by sundry artificial devices and terms to extort from them great fines and ransoms which they termed compositions and mitigations." Soon after the demise of Henry VII. the popular clamour against Dudley and his associate became so strong, that they were attainted of high treason, and being found guilty, were both beheaded.

Contiguous to Okeover, on the opposite or Derbyshire side the river, is the pleasant village of MAPPLETON. At the Domesday survey *Mapletun* was a berewick of Ashbourn, and as such belonged to the crown. The Cokaynes of Ashbourn, had a seat here, and Francis Cokayne died possessed of the manor in 1558. In 1641, William Cavendish, Earl and afterwards Duke of Newcastle, (who married the heiress of Bassett of Blore) possessed lands in Mappleton and Thorpe. The manorial rights are vested in the Okeover family.

26

Mappleton Church is a small oblong building, surmounted by a dome and lantern. In the floor of the aisle is an alabaster slab, having round the edges some traces of an inscription in old English characters, and one of the windows contains a curious design in painted glass.—The living is a rectory, annexed to the vicarage of Ashbourn.

The parish contains about 180 inhabitants, and the estimated annual value of the property is £2,000.

CHAPTER X.

The Banks of the Dove—Their Extraordinary Fertility—Extract from a Sermon in praise of Derbyshire—Mayfield—Stanton, the Birth-place of Archbishop Sheldon—Snelston—Snelston Hall—Memoir of Michael Thomas Sadler.

IT has been previously remarked, that the tract of country we have undertaken to describe, (the Valley of the Dove) in its general aspect is of a highly diversified character. Its climate, soil, and degree of fertility are not less varied and remarkable. The lofty elevations amid which the Dove and some of her tributary streams take their rise are bleak, cheerless, and barren in the extreme; but over the limestone-district of Derbyshire and Staffordshire, which these streams intersect, a pasturage is produced of excellent quality. On their junction in the vale of Ilam, the full tide of luxuriant fertility sets in, and DOVE BANKS, (which, setting aside the local limitation of the term, may be understood to comprehend the whole valley from Ilam downwards) are a succession of meadows and pastures, of unexampled richness and beauty. The soil is a deep mellow loam, the greater part strongly impregnated with a calcareous deposit from the overflowing of the river; the herbage is very fine, with scarcely any admixture of rushes or aquatic plants. A sudden rain, or the melting of snow on the Moorland or Peak hills, is sufficient to inundate large breadths of this valley, and the river, in the space of twelve hours, has swollen so rapidly, as to produce the most devastating effects, carrying off sheep, cattle, and produce, to the great loss of the inhabitants. The floods, however, owing to the declivity of the river's channel, speedily subside.

In the very midst of winter (writes Dr. Plot, in his Natural History of Staffordshire, anno 1680) the banks of the Dove are adorned with a pleasant verdure, "and when the river overflows them in the spring, it enriches them as the river Nile doth Egypt, and makes them so fruitful that the inhabitants thereabout usually chante this joyful ditte :

'In April Dove's flood, is worth a king's good.'

" From which limestone hills, and rich pastures and meadows, the great dairys are maintained in this part of Staffordshire that supply Uttoxeter mercat [market] with such vast quantities of good butter and cheese, that the cheesemongers of London have thought it worth while to set up a factorage here for these commodities, which are brought in in so great plenty, that the factors many mercat days (in the season) lay out no less than five hundred pounds a day in these commodities only."

To these remarks, which have reference chiefly to the Staffordshire side the Dove, we may append an eulogium of higher antiquity, on the county of Derby generally, part of which, at least, may apply with peculiar force to the vale we are describing. This quaint panegyric is an extract from a sermon said to have been preached in London, before a congregation of Derbyshire men, by Dr. Gardiner, rector of Eckington. It is a fair specimen of the strange digressions in which preachers of the day sometimes indulged :

" If you fall out amongst yourselves, you'll discredit the country that bred ye. For give me leave to tell you, there is hardly a county in England where faction and division lesse thrive than in Derbyshire. Nay, you will also disho-

nour this honourable city, as if this place and aire, (which
has great influence on men's bodyes and mindes, say physi-
cians) had much altered your naturall temper and disposition. It was the county of Derby (as I am credibly
informed) that first of all revived these love-feasts,* which
by reason of our late civill dissensions, were layd aside. By
this you may see the naturall genius and disposition of your
county, and may easily judge how like ye are still unto
yourselves.

"And now I have mentioned Derbyshire, it may possibly
be expected by some that I should make a long description
and commendation of it. But that is the business rather
of a topographer than of a preacher, of the mappe than of
the pulpit. And indeed, why should I goe about to describe or commend it unto you, who know it as well as, yea
better than myselfe. Yet if any one be desirous to have a
sight of Derbyshire, they may see it as in a landskip, described by Moses, Deut. viii. 7, 8, 9, whilst he is setting
forth the choicest excellencies of that country that God
chose out of all the world to enfeoffe his own beloved people in :

7. "'It's a good land, a land of brookes of water, of
fountains and depths, that spring out of the hills.

8, 9. "'A land of wheate and barley,........where ye may
eat bread without scarceness........it's a land whose stones
are iron. A land wherein thou shalt not lack anything."'

"What's this but a description as in a type of our own
county, Derbyshire? What pen could have drawn it forth
more graphically and exactly? *It's a good land,* not a
hungry soile, that eates up the inhabitants, but one that
feedes even where it's most barren, in the mountainous
Peake, thousands of sheepe, and imploys a far greater
number of men.

"It's a land there richest where it's poorest by its mines

---

* " The party seem to have dined together after a sermon. In one place he
mentions in the margin, ' as condescending to mix with the inferior sort,' H. L.
Mansfield, Sir S. Sleigh, Sir J. Curzon, Jer. Poole, Esq. and Alderman Ireton."

and grooves: where its surface promises least, it yields most, and what is wanting in nature, is supplied by miracles or wonders.

"It's a land also (like that which flowed with milke and honey) full of brookes of waters, of depths and fountaines, that springe out of the hills. It is not like the dry deserts of Arabia, or the barren sands of Lybia, but like the delicious plaines of Jordan. A land well watered even like Paradise, the garden of the Lord. *Quot tubera, tot ubera.* Every exuberant hill is as one of nature's springing duggs, always running to meete and refresh the thirsty traveller. In short *naturœ gaudentes opus,* a country wherein nature sports itself, leaping up and down, as it were, in the pleasant variety of hills and valleys, until being weary it recreate itselfe, at Chatsworth, Boulsover, or Hardicke.

"It's a land whose stones by indefatigable industry are turned into iron, and by labouring men, for their own work and sustenance, into bread. Out of whose hills more lead is digged in a yeare, than Canaan afforded brass in ten.

"What shall I say more! for time would fail me sooner than matter. A land of wheate and barley, oates, and pease, that affords seed to the sower, and bread to the eater, who takes paines to get a good stomacke.

"In a word, and what can be said more! Derbyshire is a county where there is a lacke of nothing, *sibi sufficit unus.* It's England's cornu-copiæ, having almost all necessaries within itselfe, and supplying with its abundance the wants of other places. It enjoys good aire, fertile ground, pleasant waters, fire and fuel of the best; neighbouring counties fetch her coals from farr, who being warmed by her fires, cannot but wish and call her blessed. Cattell, corne, sheepe, mill-stones, iron, lead of all sorts and colours, these are her native commodities, which enrich even the Indies, and visit the uttermost coastes of the earth.

"I might go on even to the tyring both of you and myself, yet after all I must still leave Derbyshire even as it is, most of her worth and riches hid under ground, in the place of silence. In truth it's almost a pity to breake up so rich a Haddon Field* of discourse, unless we had more time to worke it. I shall onely adde that Derbyshire is a county that lyes in all counties, yea, in all parts of Christendome, and beyond ; the sun's county, where it never setts, but upon which it shines perpetually. She parts with her entrayles, and without complaintes suffers her bowells to be continually torne out, to serve the necessities of all nations under heaven."

It is supposed that a collection was made at the feast for the benefit of the poor natives of the county resident in London, for after the last observation there follows, as very naturally to be expected, an inference or exhortation :—

"Let us be children resembling our deare mother. Let us draw forth our soule, [Isa. lviii. 10.] our bowels of mercies, our purses at least, to supply out of our sufficiency the necessitie of others : I shall not propose, much less prescribe, I would have it a free-will offering."†

From Okeover the Dove rolls on to MAYFIELD, (in Domesday Book written *Mavreveldt*, afterwards *Matherfield*, and *Mathfield*,) a considerable village chiefly occupying a rising ground on the Staffordshire side the river. There is reason to suppose that the Romans had a settlement here.‡ To some of the numerous *barrows* formerly existing in the vicinity, traces of which may yet be discovered, antiquaries have assigned a Roman origin; coins,

*Haddon Pastures are famed for their excellent herbage.
†Gentleman's Magazine, April, 1776.

‡‘ It may reasonably be concluded, from the Roman coins that have sometimes been found in *Dale close*, between *Oakover* and *Mayfield*, and a Roman urn dug, now about one hundred years ago, out of a bank in *Church Townfield* in *Upper Mayfield*, &c. that the barrows hereabouts may for the most part, be esteemed Roman. Particularly *Harlow Greave*, a little north-west of *Mayfield*, and that other in a field near the left hand the way as you pass between *Mayfield* and *Ellaston*, near *Colwich Common*, without name, and another larger over against it, at the other end of the common, which they call *Rowlow*, perhaps the sepulchre of some petty king, *Rowlow* importing as much as *Regale Sepulchrum.'—Plot's Staff.—Beaut. England & Wales, Staff.*

also, and other tokens of equal antiquity have been found
implying, at least, that the place was known to the
Romans, and that conflicts have occurred here between
the native Britons and their invaders. The reasons why
barrows and warlike instruments, certainly Roman, are
found so remote from the great military ways, may be
accounted for on the supposition that the natives drew their
assailants off, and skirmished with them as occasion presented.* At the Norman conquest Mayfield was a demesne
of the crown, but was granted to Henry de Ferrers, who,
about the year 1080, bestowed the church, tithe, and whatever belonged to them, on the Priory of Tutbury. In the
taxation of Pope Nicholas, taken in the year 1291, (temp.
Edward I.) that religious house was found to possess

	L.	S.	D.
" At Mayfield, one plough land of the annual value of	1	0	0
A mill there, worth by the year.........................	2	0	0
Pleas and perquisites there, producing yearly	0	4	0
The rent of assize there annually......................	2	0	0
Profitable stock there annually........................	2	0	0

One of the heirs of Henry de Ferrers made a further
grant to this Priory of the manor of Mayfield, and certain
privileges attached thereto, which in the 18th and 22nd of
Edward II. are thus stated:—

	L.	S.	D.
The manor of Matherfield	11	16	6
The clear annual value of the church there exclusive of £6 13s. 4d. received by the Canon of Lichfield from thence	2	0	0
The free-rent of Matherfield	6	7	8½
The rents of the naifes or natives there	9	0	0
The rents of the cottages there	1	10	8

At the dissolution of the Priory under Henry VIII., that
monarch granted its possessions at Mayfield, in exchange
for other lands, to Sir Edward Aston, knight, from whom
they passed into various hands.†

---

*Plot's Natural History of Staffordshire.
†History of the Town, Castle, and Priory of Tutbury.

Moore's Cottage, Mayfield.

The cottage in which Moore wrote his celebrated
"Lalla Rookh" is a small, plain-looking tenement, standing on an eminence, in Upper Mayfield. The poet appears
to have resided here at intervals between the years 1813—
1817.*

The traveller by the old mail-road between Manchester
and London, witnesses, on approaching Mayfield, one of
those agreeable and very striking changes of scenery peculiar to the district. From the town of Leek his route lies
over a wide expanse of inclosed moor-lands, dreary, cold,
scantily wooded, and as thinly inhabited, reaching almost
to the verge of the hills that bound the vale of Dove, into
which he passes by a rapid descent. From this declivity his
eye roams over a landscape that, for rural splendour, may
vie with the brightest and fairest spots even Dove's famed
banks present. Its constituent parts—the towering peaks
of Dovedale, the rich seclusions of Okeover and Mappleton, Ashbourn in the distance, the sparkling stream, the
busy village below, and the vale to the right stretching
into obscurity—already feebly painted, here unite in one
delightful picture, that claims and will receive the admiration of every sincere admirer of beautiful landscape scenery.

The river is crossed by a long stone bridge, of five arches,
from which we have (looking in the opposite direction) a
charming near view of part of the village,—in front some

---

*Lord Byron's letters to Moore during his residence here contain several
playful allusions to the country. One of these epistles concludes, "Ever, my
dear Moore, your'n (isn't that the Staffordshire termination?)" Another commences "When you next imitate the style of ' Tacitus,' pray add, ' de moribus
Germanorum;' this last [letter] was a piece of barbarous silence, and could
only be taken from the *Woods*, and, as such I attribute it entirely to your sylvan sequestration at Mayfield Cottage." In a third, (quoted before, p. 171)
dated "Venice, March 31st, 1817," he says, "I don't know whether to be glad
or sorry that you are leaving Mayfield. Had I ever been at Newstead during
your stay there (except during the winter of 1813—14, when the roads were
impracticable,) we should have been within hail, and I should like to have
made a giro of the Peak with you. I know that country well, having been all
over it when a boy."—*Moore's Life of Byron.*

beautiful overhanging nursery-grounds, on the right and left several neat cottage residences, and a row of picturesque tenements partly excavated out of a rock of red sand-stone that crowns the hill.

The current of the Dove is here available for manufacturing purposes, and is employed in two cotton spinning establishments, which afford occupation to a number of the inhabitants. J. D. Cooper, Esq. is the present proprietor of the Hanging Bridge factory, and J. Chambers, Esq. of the one at Mayfield, lower down the river.

Mayfield church is a neat structure, supported by semi-circular Norman arches. The tower, windows, and exterior walls are additions or alterations of later date. The living is a vicarage, in the gift of William Greaves, Esq. M.D. late of Mayfield Hall: the Rev. Court Granville is the present incumbent.

The parish, including Upper Mayfield, Middle Mayfield, and Church Mayfield; the townships of Butterton, Wood-houses, and part of Calton, contains 1,366 inhabitants, and the property therein is assessed at £7,151.

STANTON, a small village in the parish of Ellaston, two miles west of Mayfield, was the birth-place of *Gilbert Sheldon*, Archbishop of Canterbury. He was born on the 19th of July, 1598. His father was a menial servant to the Earl of Shrewsbury, who stood sponsor for him at his baptism, and gave him the name of Gilbert. Under the patronage of this nobleman, young Sheldon received a classical education, and took the degree of B.A. in Trinity College, Oxford, in the twentieth year of his age, and that of M.A. in 1620. He was elected Fellow of All Souls College, in the year 1622, entered into holy orders, and having attracted the notice of Lord Keeper Coventry, he was appointed domestic chaplain by that statesman, and in consequence of his abilities, employed in various affairs relating to both church and state. Lord Clarendon observes that Sheldon soon became distinguished for his

uncommon abilities and attainments, and was considered
by competent judges to be fully qualified to shine in any
ecclesiastical preferment. Lord Coventry recommended
Sheldon to Charles I. as a person versed in political as
well as theological knowledge. He was preferred to
several valuable livings, and in 1635, was appointed Chaplain in ordinary to the King, and afterwards Clerk of the
Closet. During the wars between the King and Parliament Sheldon adhered conscientiously to the cause of his
royal master, and in 1644, was deputed by his Majesty
to attend his commissioners at the treaty of Uxbridge, where
he argued earnestly and zealously in favour of the Church.

In April, 1646, he attended the King at Oxford, and
was witness to a vow made by his majesty, that if it should
please God to re-establish his throne, he would restore to
the church all lands or impropriations, which were taken
from any episcopal see, cathedral, &c.

In 1648, he was ejected from his wardenship of All
Souls College by the Parliamentary Visitors, and imprisoned by order of Parliament, with Dr. Hammond, at
Oxford. He was confined about six months, and then
liberated, on the hard conditions that he should not come
within five miles of Oxford, nor go to the King in the Isle
of Wight, and that he should appear before the Reforming
Committee at fourteen days' warning.

Dr. Sheldon now retired to the village of Snelston,
where he collected money by contributions from his
friends, for the use of the exiled King. Here he pursued his studies without interruption till the approach of
the Restoration. On the return of Charles II. Sheldon
met him at Canterbury, where he was most graciously
received by the sovereign whom he had so faithfully served.
Soon afterwards he was made Dean of the Royal Chapel,
and when Bishop Juxon was translated to the see of Canterbury, was elected Bishop of London, October 9, 1660.
He also held the Mastership of the Savoy, where the
famous Conference between the episcopal and presbyterian

clergy was held at his lodgings in 1661.   At this conference Dr. Sheldon exerted himself with his usual zeal and
ability in favour of the established church.   Upon the death
of Archbishop Juxon in 1663, he was elected to the see of
Canterbury; and thus, by a series of preferments most
honourably obtained, did the son of a lowly peasant
arrive at the very summit of episcopal power and authority.

In the year 1665, Archbishop Sheldon gave unequivocal
proofs of his magnanimity and charity by continuing at his
palace at Lambeth during the plague, and exerting himself
to the utmost of his power in aid of many afflicted and ne-
cessitous individuals.

On the 21st of December, 1667, the Archbishop was
elected Chancellor of the University of Oxford, which high
office he resigned in July, 1669.   After a long and active
life, the venerable prelate died at Lambeth, November 9th,
1677, in the eightieth year of his age.   His remains were
interred at Croydon Church, Surrey, where a monument
was erected to his memory, by his nephew and heir, Sir
Joseph Sheldon, the son of his elder brother, Ralph Sheldon, of Stanton.

From an impartial review of contemporary writers
respecting the public and private character of this eminent
man, it appears that he was more distinguished as a poli-
tician than as a divine.   His zeal for the church, made
him take a decided and severe part in the enactment of
penal laws against the non-conformists.

Parker says, "Archbishop Sheldon was a man of undoubted piety; but though he was very assiduous at
prayers, yet he did not set so great a value on them as
others did, nor regarded so much worship as the use of
worship, placing the chief point of religion in the practice
of a good life.   His advice to young noblemen and gentlemen, who by their parents' command resorted daily to him,
was always, "Let it be your principal care to be honest
men, and afterwards be as devout and religious as you will.
No piety will be of any advantage to yourselves or any

Drawn on Stone by S. Rayner.

Published by Jawson & Hobson, Ashbourn.

SNELSTON HALL.

The Seat of John Harrison Esq.

body else, unless you are honest and moral men." His worthy notions of religion meeting with an excellent temper in him, gave him that even tranquillity of mind by which he was still himself, and always the same, in adversity as well as in prosperity; and neither overrated nor despised life, nor feared nor wished for death, but lived agreeably to himself and others."

On the Restoration of Charles II. when the former members of the University of Oxford returned to their places and re-established the ancient institutions, Archbishop Sheldon liberally founded a theatre for the acts and exercises of the students, at a cost of £17,000. It appeared, by his private accounts, that in fourteen years he had bestowed £60,000 in public and private charities.

Dr. Plot says, that " going to visit the house of his nativity, in the very room where he was said to have drawn his first breath, he found the following iambics :

> " Sheldonus *illæ* præsulum *primus Pater,*
> Hos *inter ortus aspicit lucem* Lares,
> O *ter beatam* Stantonis *villæ casam !*
> *Cui canita possunt invidere Marmora.*"

These lines, it seems, were left there by the right Rev. father in God, Dr. John Hacket, lord bishop of Coventry and Lichfield, who, out of his extraordinary devotion to this great prelate, had purposely made a journey thither not many years before, to visit the place of his birth, "where, after he had given God thanks for the great blessings he had afforded the world in that place, he sate him down and wrote these verses."*

SNELSTON HALL, the seat of John Harrison, Esq., three miles south-west of Ashbourn, is an imposing modern structure, in the richly-ornamented gothic style. It was built from designs by L. N. Cottingham, Esq., and developes the talents of that architect, in the elaborate style which he has so successfully cultivated. The site of this mansion—in every way fitly chosen, and suffici-

---

*Biog. Brit. Beaut. England and Wales. Plot's Staffordshire.

ently retired to harmonise with the character of its architecture, was yet susceptible of improvements essential to
a well-ordered domain, the want of which the eye of taste
would not fail to discover. These improvements the
proprietor has effected, regardless of labour or expense,
and with a degree of success seldom equalled. Under his
judicious management the grounds have assumed a park-
like aspect, and the profusion of thriving timber by which
they are clothed, adds to the charms of the scenery, and as
it flourishes will complete the embellishment of this
representation of ancient splendour. The interior arrangements exhibit a corresponding degree of attention to
elegance and propriety. Some of the principal apartments are fitted up with ancient carved oak furniture, of
the most costly and curiously-wrought description. Nor
must we omit to notice the splendid stair-case—that noble
feature in the olden mansions of the great—it is an object
on which taste, skill, and elaborate workmanship have been
exerted, with a very pleasing effect. There is, too, a comprehensive unity of design pervading every part of this
seat, extending to the offices, lodges, and farm-buildings
erected on the estate, all of which are strictly in keeping
with the Hall.

A reference to our engraving of the mansion, will convey a better idea of its structure than pages of mere architectural description. Its bay windows, parapets, turrets,
and groups of picturesque chimneys, viewed from the south,
or from almost any other point, form a striking object in
the landscape.

The village church is a pleasing structure, clothed with
ivy. Within all is neatly arranged, but the antiquary will
find nothing of interest.

Snelston is a parochial chapelry in the parish of Norbury,
and county of Derby. John Harrison, Esq. is lord of the
manor. The number of inhabitants is about 484, and the
property is assessed at £2,969.*

*See Norbury.

In a plain farm-house, on Snelston Common, that amiable and accomplished senator, the late MICHAEL THOMAS SADLER, Esq., first drew breath. He was descended, on the side of his father, a respectable farmer, from the celebrated Sir Ralph Sadler,* one of Queen Elizabeth's ministers, and an important instrument in bringing about the Reformation. His mother's family were French refugees, at the revocation of the edict of Nantes.† The date of his birth is ascertained from the register of the parish, to be January 30th, 1780. He was educated principally at home, and exhibited extraordinary powers of mind in very early youth. His father intended him for one of the learned professions, but when about eighteen years of age, he was induced to join his brother in business at Leeds. The only memorial of his youthful days with which we are acquainted, is the following effusion, in which he gave vent to his overcharged feelings on leaving his native home. His affectionate parent to whom they refer, and to whom he was tenderly attached, died while he was very young:—

"ADIEU to the Banks of the Dove,
   My happiest moments are flown,
I must leave the retreats that I love
   For scenes far remote and unknown.

But wherever my lot may be cast,
   Whatever my fortune may prove,
I shall think of the days that are past;
   I shall sigh for the Banks of the Dove.

Ye friends of my earliest youth,
   From you how reluctant I part;
Your friendships were founded in truth,
   And shall ne'er be erased from my heart.

Companions, perhaps, I may find,
   But where shall I meet with such love,
With attachments so lasting and kind,
   As I leave on the Banks of the Dove?

---

*The family of Sadler, or Sadleir, is of considerable antiquity; they were seated at Standon, in the county of Hertford in the reign of Henry VIII.

†She was a daughter of the Rev. Michael Ferebee, rector of Rolleston, in the county of Stafford.

> Thou sweet little village, farewell!
>   Every object around thee is dear,
> Every woodland, and meadow, and dell,
>   Where I wander'd for many a year.
>
> Ye villas and cots so well known,
>   Will your inmates continue to love?
> Will ye think on a friend, when he's gone
>   Far away from the Banks of the Dove?
>
> But oft has the Dove's crystal wave,
>   Flow'd lately commixt with my tears,
> Since my mother was laid in her grave,
>   Where yon hallow'd turret appears.
>
> O Sexton, remember the spot,
>   And lay me beside her I love,
> Whenever this body is brought
>   To sleep on the Banks of the Dove.
>
> Till then, in the visions of night,
>   O may her loved spirit descend;
> And tell me, tho' hid from my sight,
>   She still is my guardian and friend.
>
> The thoughts of her presence shall keep
>   My footsteps, when tempted to rove;
> And sweeten my woes while I weep
>   For her, and the Banks of the Dove."

Mr. Sadler continued at Leeds, engaged in mercantile pursuits, but not to the exclusion of more congenial literary labours, till he was called into public life, by the ministerial proposition of the Catholic Relief Bill. He sat in two successive Parliaments for Newark-upon-Trent, and in a third, till the passing of the Reform Bill, for the ancient borough of Aldborough, in Yorkshire, and he afterwards contested the representation of Huddersfield and Leeds. In his public career, Mr. Sadler was generally associated with the old constitutional Tories, and with them he powerfully opposed the admission of the Roman Catholics to power, in one of the most eloquent and impressive speeches ever delivered within the walls of the British Parliament. By the confession of Lord Plunkett, an opponent in politics, yet a competent judge, Mr. Sadler was the most accomplished orator heard in the House of Commons, by the present generation. While, as a member of the legislature, he was the enemy of all those innovations, no matter how popular, which he regarded as dangerous to our institutions, he was the determined advocate of every measure which he believed would contribute to the happiness of the mass of the people, whose real interests he considered to be the main concern of every good government; and in and out of Parliament he ever spoke with indignation of those pretended patriots, who sought popularity by extending mere political privileges to the labouring classes, while they resisted every proposition for substantially bettering their condition. Under the influence of these feelings, he took very little share in any mere party measures, but was chiefly occupied in supporting whatever he thought would advance the happiness of the mass of society. The measures which he himself introduced into the legislature for this benevolent object were most comprehensive and important. He brought in a Bill to provide agricultural parishes with funds for allotting small portions of ground to their deserving poor, which, though it did not become a legislative enactment, was extensively circulated, and has been acted upon in several parishes with the happiest results.

For Ireland Mr. Sadler always expressed the deepest interest and sympathy. He twice introduced into Parliament the important measure of a Poor Law for that country, on the last occasion losing his proposition, against the overwhelming strength of the government, by a nominal majority only. Of this humane measure he was in public and private the powerful and unwearied advocate, and undismayed by the general opposition it provoked, he brought the cause of those who had none to plead for them again and again before the British public.

Mr. Sadler's propositions for the amelioration of Ireland, were given to the world in a deservedly popular work, entitled, "Ireland; its Evils, and their Remedies." This work was an introduction to a more voluminous one on

"The Law of Population," written principally with a view to controvert the theories of Malthus. "In his convincing refutation of the Malthusian system," writes one of his most enthusiastic friends, "he has overthrown a most elaborate series of dangerous arguments and insidious plausibilities, and in doing so, has justified the ways of God to man with an ability worthy of the cause he advocated. Yes, the system which represented the Creator of the universe as having constituted no other checks to the supposed superabundant population of his rational creatures, than vice and misery, famine, discord, and murder, is a libel on the power, the knowledge, and the beneficence of that Almighty Being, and therefore, the man who first dissipated the impious yet delusive reasonings of Malthus, merited the gratitude of the whole human race." The main dogma on which the Malthusian theory hinges,— that "there is a tendency in all animated life to increase beyond the nourishment prepared for it," Mr. Sadler conceived to be unscriptural in principle, and to disprove its truth he devoted the energies of his powerful mind. Without offering an opinion on the merits of a question which has been, on both sides, so warmly and so forcibly argued, it may be asserted, that "The Treatise on Population" is conceived and executed in a spirit of earnest, unfettered benevolence, before which the cold reasoning of his adversaries sinks repulsive into the shade.*

During the last session he sat in Parliament, Mr. Sadler was almost wholly occupied in prosecuting a Bill for the protection of children employed in our manufactories,— "The Ten-Hour Bill," as it was familiarly termed. This measure was referred to a select committee, of which Mr. Sadler was chosen chairman, and the toil and responsibility thus imposed upon him of collecting the vast mass of evidence contained in their report, probably laid the

---

*While health was continued to him, Mr. Sadler was diligently occupied in preparing materials for a third and concluding volume of this able treatise, which, however, he did not live to complete.

foundation of his long and fatal illness.   Neither did he succeed in passing this measure of mercy, although his opponents, in a subsequent session, brought one forward professedly similar.

Mr Sadler died (of disease of the heart, which he had for some time laboured under,) at his seat, New Lodge, near Belfast, July 29th, 1835, aged 55 years.

" Rich in science, replete with historic lore, Mr. Sadler's mind was a perfect treasury of sterling literature—a storehouse, as it were, of interesting facts, and such was the charm of his diction, such his pleasing facility of communicating knowledge, that it was impossible for any man of clear intellect to cultivate his society without deriving the most valuable information and the purest delight from his conversation.   Persuasion dwelt upon his tongue—truth, candour, philanthropy, virtue and religion, were the treasured inmates of his heart.   Mr. Sadler's virtues endeared him to a large and admiring circle of friends—he was affectionate, generous, affable, accessible, and an utter stranger to pride.   His appearance was remarkably that of a man of genius ; and there was an enthusiasm and an energy in his manner strikingly characteristic of an elevated and powerful mind.   It was said by Lord Bacon, at the close of life, " The poor have ever been precious in mine eyes," and no man could more fully adopt that sentiment than Mr. Sadler.   Public men have always been public property, but he ever felt himself emphatically the property of the poor, and his charity to them was unfailing, scarcely measured by his means, and he not merely gave the solicited alms, but made the sorrows and sufferings of the afflicted his own, and wept with those that wept—their wrongs, their sufferings, their privations, were his hourly conversation, and his days and his nights, and finally his life itself, were sacrificed to his intense and unwearied exertions to redress the grievances of unfriended poverty."

"Who" asks the editor of *The Standard*, in his obituary of Mr. Sadler, "does not forget his eloquence in the

memory of that enthusiastic benevolence perfectly without
example in the history of the world! As Burke said of
Howard, Mr. Sadler's philanthropy had as much of genius
as of virtue. It was a love of his fellow creatures on so
great a scale, that none but a great mind could have conceived it; and oh! how far was it from that benevolence
which is ever suspended in abstraction! It was our happiness and our greatest pride to enjoy his acquaintance,
and we can truly say, that whatever he sought for and
wished for on behalf of the whole human race, he no less
earnestly and vigilantly conferred by manners and conduct
upon all within his sphere. Without pretending to any
extraordinary sensibility, we declare it too painful to pursue
our recollection of the unrivalled charms of Mr. Sadler's
society. He has had his best earthly reward—he has died
" the death of the righteous," and almost without presump-
tion, we may anticipate that he has realised what a friend
predicted of him on that day when he was led into Manchester by 30,000 living and rejoicing infants,—" Sadler
will witness but one more such scene as this, and that will
be when he shall receive his reward in the resurrection of
the just." On this last point his friend, before quoted,
speaks decisively: "To all his estimable and endearing
qualities, Mr. Sadler added a far higher and more important distinction—he was a Christian, his mind was imbued with the deepest reverence for the will of God, and
his works abundantly testify that 'His word was his
meditation day and night;' and in his long and dreary
illness, when 'the days of darkness,' and they were many,
came upon him, his soul was sustained and comforted with
the hopes and promises of the Gospel, with the presence
and blessing of his God—and his end was peace."*

Mr. Sadler was elected a Fellow of the Royal Society on
June 7th, 1832. He married the daughter of the late

*The foregoing memorials of Mr. Sadler's life are derived chiefly from an
article in the *Belfast Guardian*, contributed by one who knew him well.

Samuel Fenton, Esq. of Leeds, who, and a family of seven children, survive him.

Mr. Sadler published a work under the title of "Jura Injuriæque Pauperum; or, a Defence of the Principles of the Poor-Laws of England; with Suggestions for their Essential Improvement."

Appended to his Treatise on Population is a Dissertation on "The Balance of Food and Numbers of Animated Nature,"—the substance of two lectures delivered before a literary society of which he was a member.—He is said also to have left behind him a number of manuscripts on various interesting subjects, some of which, it is hoped, may yet see the light.

20

CHAPTER XI.

THE Manor of NORBURY is situated within the parish of Norbury, which also comprises the parochial chapelry and manor of Snelston, the Hamlets of Darley-Moor, Roschintone, Rossington, or Roston, and Birchwood—in the Hundred of Appletree and Deanery of Ashbourn, from which town it is four miles distant.

In the reign of Edward the Confessor it belonged to the great Saxon thane Siward,* of which he was dispossessed by the Conqueror, who bestowed Norbury, together with 113 other manors in Derbyshire alone, upon Henry de Ferrers, and is thus described in Domesday Book :—

" *In Norbury and Rossington Siward has three carucates of land paying tax. The land contains three carucates. There are now two carucates in demesne, and seventeen villanes borderers having four carucates. There is a priest*

---

* " Siward being a potent Englishman, was kept prisoner with divers other persons of quality, till the end of the Conqueror's reign, who on his death-bed gave orders for their enlargement." *Roger Hoveden, Dugdale's Warwickshire.*

and a church, a mill* paying ten shillings, and twenty-four acres of meadow. A wood for pasture one mile in length and breadth.† In the time of King Edward, worth one hundred shillings, now sixty. Henry holds it.

" In Rossington one carucate paying tax. It belongs to Rocester. There are now two villanes."

Henry de Ferrers founded the monastery of Tutbury about the year 1080, but the first charter of foundation was not granted before the reign of William Rufus, (A.D. 1087—1100) by Robert, first Earl Ferrers. Among the numerous manors with which he endowed it, Norbury was included, but did not remain long in the possession of the Convent, for William the Prior of Tutbury by his charter, dated in the year 1125,‡ granted the manor of Norbury to William the son of Herbert,§ and to his heirs, to be holden in fee of the Priory of Tutbury, subject to the yearly fee-farm rent of one hundred shillings, and of five shillings annually in lieu of tithes for the lands in demesne and two bovates; subject also to the other feudal incidents of suit at the Prior's Court, and to contributing a proportionate aid towards the redemption of the body of the superior lord of Tutbury in the event of his captivity, towards the mar

*"No description of building is so frequently mentioned in Domesday-Book as water-mills. They were in every case the property of the lord of the manor, and his tenants were not permitted to grind at any other mill; a restriction which has not been abolished in some cases even at the present day." *Pictorial England.*

†The owners of woodland were accustomed to let at a fixed sum the right of turning in swine, which fed on the acorns and beech-mast; and the value of the wood was ascertained by the number of swine it would support.

‡" Anno ab incarnacione Dni milesimo centesimo vigesimo quto Willmo por Convent eccle sci mario Stotesbri dedit Willmo filio Herbti Norberiam in feodo et heredibus suis," &c.—*The Original Charter at Swynnerton.* [This deed is attested by Robert, the Bishop; Geoffrey, Abbot of Burton; Robert de Ferrers, Lord of Stotesbury (Tutbury) Hawise his wife, Robert his son, and William Piperell (Peveril?)

§It was a prevalent custom among the Normans to describe themselves as the son of some eminent ancestor, thus *Filius Herberti* (Latin) *Fils* (Norman) or *Fitz Herbert* became the patronymic of the family.

riage of his eldest daughter, and towards his "redeeming his honour," *(" Honorum suum re emerret.")* *

Sir William Fitzherbert, Knight, fifth lord of Norbury, by letters patent of 4th September, 1252, (36 Henry III.) obtained a grant of free warren in his manor of Norbury and Rossington.

Sir John Fitzherbert, Knight, seventh lord of Norbury, on a "*quo warranto*" tried at Derby in June, 1330, (4 Ed. III.) established his right to free warren in Norbury and Rossington, which had been granted to Sir William, his grandfather.

John Fitzherbert, thirteenth lord of Norbury, 16th July, 1493, (8 Henry VII.) procured letters patent exemplifying the record of pleadings on a "*quo warranto*" dated 1330, which was tried at Derby, when the verdict of the judge established the right of John Fitzherbert to free warren in Norbury and Rossington, which had been granted to his ancestor, before mentioned.

John Fitzherbert, lord of Norbury, obtained a license to inclose 300 acres of land in Norbury, Rossington, Snelston, and Cubley,† in the county of Derby, for a park and war-

---

*" In 26 Henry VI. Nicholas Fitzherbert and Ralph his son and heir apparent, gave to Thomas Gedney, the then Prior of the Monastery of the Blessed Virgin at Tutbury, all their lands, tenements, and rents in Osmaston, in the county of Derby, besides one messuage called the Hall Place, and 57 acres of land in Foston; one other messuage and twenty acres; one acre and two parts of an acre in Church Broughton, in the same county; in exchange for the reserved rent and other services which were due to the said Prior and Convent, out of the estates at Norbury."—*Register of Tutbury Priory. Sir O. Mosley's History of Tutbury.*

†Cubley, an agricultural village about seven miles south-west of Ashbourn, was anciently the seat of the family of *Montgomery.* William Montgomery, in 1251, obtained a grant of a market, which was held here on Mondays, together with a fair for three days at the festival of St. Andrew. The market has long been discontinued, but the semblance of a fair is still held on the 30th of November. John Montgomery, the last heir male, died in 1513, leaving three daughters, co-heirs, one of whom (Dorothy) brought Cubley and other estates to her husband, Sir Thomas Gifford, of Chillington, with whose heiress (Elizabeth) they passed to Sir John Port, of Etwall. Sir John Port had three daughters, co-heiresses, one of whom (Margaret) brought Cubley to Sir Thomas

ren, by letters of Privy Seal, dated 4th October, 1506, (22 Henry VII.) This was doubtless the origin of Birch-wood Park, the inclosure of which has long since been thrown down, and the land deparked, and cultivated as a farm.

There are, no doubt, numerous houses in England of equal antiquity to the knightly family of Fitzherbert, of Norbury. It is, however, to be apprehended that very few of them can establish, from authentic documents in their own possession, such irrefragable proofs of a lineal male descent from an ancestor living at the Con-quest. We have seen that William, the son of Herbert, had a grant of the manor of Norbury from the Prior of the Convent of Tutbury, in 1125, bestowed upon him, we cannot doubt, at the instance of his and their superior lord, Robert, Earl Ferrers—that identical valuable grant,* as well as the manor itself, are still, after a lapse of 714 years, fortunately in the possession of his *twenty-sixth lineal descendant*, the present Thomas Fitzherbert, Esq. of Swynnerton. During this long interval, they have invari-ably intermarried with families of their own knightly rank, without making a single derogatory misalliance.† They can boast of being able to make the proof, once so enviable

---

Stanhope, ancestor of the Earl of Chesterfield, the present lord of the manor and patron of the rectory.

The church, a gothic edifice, dedicated to St. Andrew, has a broad embattled tower, surmounted by pinnacles, and ornamented with thirteen shields of the armorial bearings of the Montgomery family and its alliances, and other sculp-tured devices. In the church were formerly some inscriptions to members of this family, and a rich altar tomb yet remains.

Michael Johnson, the father of Dr. Samuel Johnson, was a native of Cubley, where his family lived as day labourers.—*Glover's Derbyshire.*

*This precious document, and many other ancient deeds, together with the pedigree of the family, &c., have been admirably arranged in two M.S. volumes by Michael Jones, Esq. F.A.S.

†See Pedigree of the family, in " Burke's Commoners," furnished by Michael Jones, Esq. F.A.S.

and desirable in Germany, France, Italy, and other parts
of the Continent, of " sixteen quarters without a window."
They executed the honourable office of Sheriffs and Representatives in Parliament, and filled other stations of dignity
in their counties, till the laws of their country excluded
the professors of the Roman Catholic faith from all offices
of state.

On the 8th of May, 1818, an Act received the Royal
Assent for inclosing certain waste-lands in the manor of
Norbury, amounting to about 100 acres, in which it was
stated that Thomas Fitzherbert, Esq. was lord of the
manor; the Rev. Thomas Bingham, Clerk, was rector of
Norbury cum Snelston; and Mrs. Sneyd patron of the
living.*

Norbury Hall, the ancient mansion of the family, stands
upon a lofty cliff, which rises precipitously from the left
(Derbyshire) side of the river Dove, and was most probably
built by Sir Henry Fitzherbert, Knight, sixth lord of Norbury, about the period when in the 13th Edward I. he
obtained the King's license (the original at Swynnerton)
dated at Langley, 8th May, 1305, empowering him to obstruct and close a way through the court of Norbury from

---

* One fourteenth part of the waste was allotted to Mr. Fitzherbert as lord of
the manor, and the remainder was divided between the rector and other landed
proprietors of the parish. In consequence of this Act a map and survey were
completed in 1821, from which survey it appears that the manor contains
altogether 2298 acres, 1 rood, 28 perches ; of which 1011 acres, 1 rood, 6 perches
belonged to Mr. Fitzherbert. In the year 1824, March 31st, an Act received
the royal assent, for inclosing the waste lands in the manor of Snelston, (in
the parish of Norbury) containing about 160 acres. Sarah Ellen Evans and
Elizabeth Evans wife of John Harrison Esq. in her right, claimed to be lord
and lady of the manor, Mrs Sneyd claimed to be patron of the living of Norbury
cum Snelston; the Rev. Thomas Bingham rector. One-fourteenth of the waste
allotted to the lord of the manor.

The manor is bounded on the north and west by the river Dove, which
separates the counties of Derby and Stafford, by the manor of Snelston on the
neast, by the parish of Cubley on the south, by the parishes of Rocester, Marsto,
and Cubley, on the west.

Yeovely to Ethelaston, (Ellastone) to enable him to enlarge
" his said court, so that he made another road, through his
own lands, equally commodious for travellers."* The arch
and mullions of the upper windows in the wall facing the
west are of the form prevalent in the reign of Edward I.

There is an upper apartment which has, by constant tradition, borne the name of "Sir Anthony Fitzherbert's
study." On a great number of the panels are inscribed
sentences of scripture; on one of them is a death's head,
and "*memento mori.*"

An ancient barn still stands, probably built by Nicholas
Fitzherbert. The ends of the three principal beams are
ornamented with carved work, representing a quatrefoil,
a grotesque head, and an angel holding a blank shield, in
the style of the ceiling of the church.

In the year 1581, Laurence Bastock, a herald, or rather
perhaps a person in the employ of the College of Arms,
(for his name does not appear in Noble's History of the
College) in his progress from London into Cheshire, took
notes of the coats of arms then existing in the stained
windows in Norbury Hall. From their number, it is really
difficult to imagine where they were all placed.

The edifice has undergone much alteration, and is now
occupied as a farm-house. When in perfect repair, and in
the occupation of Sir Thomas Fitzherbert, in 1581, the
windows "so richly dight" must have presented a gorgeous
and beautiful display of heraldic devices.

Norbury Hall continued to be the residence of the Fitzherbert family until the death of Sir John Fitzherbert,
eighteenth lord of Norbury, which occurred at Lichfield,
January 13th, 1648. He died without issue, when Norbury
passed to William Fitzherbert, Esq., of Swynnerton, the
fourth in descent from William, a younger son of Sir
Anthony Fitzherbert, of Norbury, (the judge) who married
Elizabeth, youngest daughter and co-heir of Humphrey

---

*The original charter is preserved at Swynnerton. See also, " Rymer's
Federa," and " Abbreviatio Rotulorum Originalium."

Swynnerton, of Swynnerton, in the county of Stafford, and died 1578. The two estates have ever since the year 1649, been united, and Swynnerton Hall, the principal family residence.

The church of Norbury, from its situation, architecture, and beautiful stained glass, is one of the most remarkable in the county, and must be equally admired by the antiquary and the lover of the picturesque. From the various styles which it comprehends it has evidently been erected at different periods. The greater part, consisting of the nave, the walls, the windows of the chancel with curvilinear tracery, and the tower, are of the fourteenth century. The two chapels and entire roof, and the battlements of the south side of the chancel, which are differently formed from the usual battlements, thus are fashioned in the shape of the heraldic bearing of *Vaire*, evidently copied from the coat of arms of the Fitzherbert family,—"Argent a Bend Sable, over a Chief Vaire," and were added by Nicholas Fitzherbert, who died November 19th, 1473, on whose beautiful monument of alabaster, still in fine preservation, or perhaps on a white marble floor-stone, near to it, there existed the following epitaph, transcribed from "Le Neve's Monumental Inscriptions" :—

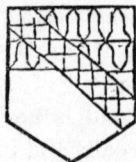

"An. CCCC. seventy and three
Years of our Lord passed in degree
The Body that bury'd is under this stone
Of Nichol Fitzherbert Lord and Patrone
Of Norbury with Alis the daughter of Henry Bothe
Eight sonnes and five daughters he had in sothe
Two sonnes and two daughters by Isabel his wife
So seventeen children he had in his lyfe
This Church he made at his own expense
In the joy of Heaven be his recompense
And in moone of November the nineteenth daye
He bequeathed his soule to everlasting joy."

Printed by T.W. & C. Fairland, London.   Published by Dawson & Hobson, Ashbourn.

NORBURY CHURCH, DERBYSHIRE.

The statement that "he made this church at his own expense," can only apply to his addition of the two chapels, and the roof, which is of the flat form prevalent in the fifteenth century, and was substituted for a previous roof of a much more acute pitch, which is manifest from the oak beams of the actual roof resting upon, and partly concealing the apex of the great east window, which point, no doubt, was many feet below the original high-pitched roof. The initials N. F., which appear on a great number of the lozenge panes of stained glass, clearly prove that the alterations and repairs of the church were made at the cost of Nicholas Fitzherbert.

The chancel extends 48 feet in length from the oak screen separating it from the nave, and 20 feet in width, and is lighted by eight large pointed windows, of three bays, with curvilinear tracery, four on each side, divided from each other by only the breadth of the buttresses which support the walls. The brilliant stained glass with which these windows are almost completely filled, is disposed in various beautiful devices, representing circles, frets, flowers, lozenges, and coats of arms of noble individuals, (among them the Fitzherberts) probably contributors to the erection of the church.* The great east window, occupying the whole width of the chancel, is divided by four mullions into five bays, the centre one wider than the others, and terminate in acute arches, without cusps. This window, no doubt, was originally filled with stained glass, like the eight lateral windows, but has unfortunately been destroyed, and the spaces are now filled up with plaster in a most unseemly manner. The clerestory windows abound with heraldic bearings and monumental portraits of the Fitzherbert family. In the window of the chapel at the southwest extremity of the nave, is a very curious representa-

---

*"The remains of painted glass in Norbury Church are in good taste, and evidently coeval with the building, which is of the style of the fourteenth century." See "Lysons' Magna Britannia," in which work appear some beautiful engraved specimens, selected from the different windows.

tion of the Trinity, in stained glass; and many of the lozenge panes contain the letters J. F., doubtless the initials of John Fitzherbert, whose monument is situated in the chantry chapel, which is supposed to have been built or founded by him. In the windows to the north of the west entrance, and in the four windows of the north aisle are represented the full-length figures of the twelve Apostles, and in scrolls above their heads, the Apostle's Creed, in Latin, written in old English characters, very perfect.

Among the armorial devices that appear in the windows, (besides the Fitzherberts') are those of Burgh, Earl of Ulster; Warren, Earl of Surrey; Plantaganet, Earl of Lancaster; the Constable of Chester; Kevelioc, Earl of Chester; Clare, Earl of Gloucester; Mandeville, Poynings, Acton, Audley, Bruce, St. Philibert, Heyforde, Chevent, Mowbray, Bassingbourn, Morville, Montgomery, Corbet, Somery, England, and others, unknown. In many of the windows the alternate lozenge pane of glass is ornamented with a golden star, *rose en soleil*, the cognizance of Ed. IV.

MONUMENTS.—On the north side of the chancel, near the east end, is a rudely-chiselled effigy of stone, the monument of Sir Henry Fitzherbert, sixth lord of Norbury. The figure, a recumbent one, is habited in chain mail, which envelopes nearly the whole body, and over it is thrown a surcoat; the right hand grasping a sword hilt, and the left bearing a shield. The head rests on a cushion, and the feet are supported by a lion.—Sir Henry Fitzherbert was Knight of the Shire of Derby in 1298 and 1307. The date of his death is not known.—On a stone five feet, in length, near this monument, appears a large cross.*

On a white marble floor-stone is engraved the figure of a lady, with a reticulated cap. Part of the inscription is legible :—" ....whos soule ....att off Henry Bothe Patrone of yis place........viii sones v daughters who had by

---

*Lysons in his " Magna Britannia," (Derbyshire) states that in the chancel of Norbury Church is the effigy of a crusader, in the act of drawing his sword. This is a mistake. Sir Henry Fitzherbert was not a crusader.

Printed by T.W.&C. Fairland London.

Published by Dawson & Hobson, Ashbourn.

CHANCEL OF NORBURY CHURCH,

Derbyshire.

bye........"—Most probably the monument of Alice Bothe, daughter of Henry Bothe, the first wife of Nicholas Fitzherbert.

Several other marble floor-stones in the chancel have their inscriptions defaced, except on one of them the words "sci mauri." Another bears the figure of a child, drawn in strong lines.

On the south side of the nave, beneath the eastern arch, is the fine altar-tomb of Nicholas Fitzherbert, who died in 1473. The effigy, a recumbent one, wears plate armour; the head rests on a helmet, and the vizor is punctured with round holes; lamberquin on a wreath; the crest, a clenched left hand within a gauntlet; chain gorget and reins; the belts ornamented with rosettes, from which are suspended the sword and dagger, both perfect. A chain of jewels, stars, and roses round the neck, to which is suspended the figure of a dog. The feet rest upon a lion. On one side of the tomb, beneath eight arched compartments, are the figures of eight monks in high relief, the first bearing on his dress several Maltese crosses. On the opposite side are similar small figures, the first representing a man in armour—an exact counterpart of the effigy on the upper surface of the tomb. The west end exhibits two figures of nuns, bearing blank shields.

On the northern side of the nave, opposite the last-mentioned tomb is the monument of Ralph Fitzherbert, son of Nicholas, and his lady. The cumbent male figure, exactly resembles that of Nicholas, excepting some difference in the chain armour about the neck; the crest also is a *right* hand, and he has no dagger. The right foot rests on the figure of a monk, seated on the back of a dog or lion. The chain round the neck is composed of roses and stars alternately, (the cognizance of Edward IV.) to which is suspended a figure resembling a boar. The lady wears a close bodice and gown, which have been painted green, and a robe painted red. Her cap is reticulated and gilt; the head-dress high and double-peaked. Encircling her neck is a chain, and jewel attached, representing the Virgin and Child. A row of beads is suspended from her girdle, and two little dogs at her feet bear her train in their mouths ; figures of angels support the cushion on which her head rests. Effigies of females and angels bearing shields, occupy the canopied sides of the tomb.

Both these altar-tombs are of alabaster, and exhibit traces of rich gilding and painting. They are in good preservation, but no arms nor inscriptions are now visible.* The following inscription, belonging to that last described, is preserved in Le Neve's Collection :—

> " The dart of death that no man may flee
> Nay the common Law of Mortalitie
> Hath demanded to be buried here
> The body of Rafe Fitzherbert Squiere
> Patrone of this Church and of this Towen Lord
> The whiche deceased yeares of our Lord
>   1483
> Of March the second day parted hee
> With him is laid upon this Sepulture
> Elsabeth his Wife begon in sure
> Daughter of John Marshall
> Esq. Lord of Upton and Sedsall
> 7 sonnes 8 daughters they had in fere
> In this lyfe together that whilst that they were
> Merciful Jesu that pitiest mankind
> In thy Blysse grant them a place to fynde
> Prestes ambobus Requiem Deus."

The name of Ralph Fitzherbert appears in the list of two Lords, nine Knights, fifty-eight Esquires, and twenty Gentlemen, who in the reign of Edward IV. 1474, entered into an indenture to aid and assist William, Lord Hastings, and his part to take against all persons, &c.*

*These monuments have, with the sanction of Mr. Fitzherbert, been lately removed by the present incumbent, the Rev. Clement F. Broughton, from the situations they are described as occupying, where they were unprotected, and consequently liable to injury. They have been cleaned and repaired, and are now placed at the eastern extremity of the chancel, along with other monuments. It is intended to portion off the space which they occupy, and to restore in a measure the appearance it exhibited when it formed a Lady Chapel. The altar is to be brought more forward into the chancel.

On a white marble floor-stone, covering the remains of Elizabeth Marshall,* only daughter and heiress of John Marshall, of Sibbesden, in the county of Leicester, is engraven an effigy enveloped in a winding sheet. At the four angles are shields of arms of the Fitzherberts and Marshalls.

In the south aisle, adjoining the chapel, is an altar-tomb of stone, on which is fixed a brass plate, inscribed

" Hic jacet corpus Johnis Fitzherbert, Armigeri quondam Deus huj. manneri q. obiit in Vigilia Sancti Jacobi Apostoli Ann. Dom. MCCCCC. tricesimo pmo. cuj. die. propiciet. De. Amen."

On a floor-stone in the north-east chapel, is inscribed

" Here lyeth the body of Ann Fitzherbert wife of William Fitzherbert Esq. & eldest daughter of Sir Basill Brook of Madely, in the county of Salop, she had seven sons and four daughters, and deceased the 9th of July, 1653."

At the east end of the nave is the monumental floor-stone of Sir Anthony Fitzherbert, Knight, the Judge, and of Matilda Cotton, his second wife. The inlaid brass figure of Sir Anthony has been removed; all but the head of his lady remains, whose tabard exhibits the armorial bearings of Fitzherbert, Cotton, Ridware, &c. The following inscription, some fragments of which now only remain, is found in Le Neve's Collection:—

" Of your charitie pray for the soule of Sir Anthony Fitzherbert knight one of the King's Justices of the common bench and sometyme lord and patrone of this towne and Dorithie his wife daughter of Sir Henry Willoughby knt. and dame Maude his last wife one of the daught. and heyr of Rychad Coton of Hamstall Rydware by which he had five sonnes and five daughters, which Sir Anthony deceased the XXVII of May, A. Dm. MCCCCCXXXVIII. and the said dame Maude."........

Sir Anthony Fitzherbert was born at Norbury in the year 1470. He was sent to pursue his studies at Oxford,

---

*Her will is dated October 20, 1494, in which she desires to be buried in the church of St. Barlok, in Norbury, near her husband Raufe Fitzherbert, or in the church of St. Sebastian near her father and mother, (probably in Sibbesden church.) She died in 1491. A figure of St. Barlok is represented in stained glass, in the window of the chapel on the south side or aisle. His name is not inserted in " Butler's Saint's Lives."

and from thence to one of the Inns of Court. By his great talents, judgment, and diligence, he rose rapidly in his profession. In 1511, he was called to the bar as a sergeant-at-law, and in 1516 received the honour of knighthood. He was afterwards made one of the Justices of the Common Pleas, in which honourable situation he spent the remainder of his life, discharging the duties of his office with such ability and integrity that he was universally respected as the oracle of the law. Two remarkable things are related of his conduct,—one, that he openly opposed Cardinal Wolsey in the height of his power, although chiefly on the score of alienating the church lands ; the other, that foreseeing on his death-bed, the changes that were likely to happen in church as well as state, he pressed his relations in very strong terms, to promise him solemnly neither to accept grants nor to make purchases of abbey lands. He died May 27th, 1538. Sir Anthony was author of the following works :—

·" Le Graunde Abridgment collecte par le Judge tres reverend Monsieur Anthony Fitzherbert." London : 20th Aug. 1577.

"L'Office & Auctorite des Justices de Peas." London, 1538 : 12mo. The first work on the subject ever printed.

" L'Office de Viconts, Bailiffes, Excheators, Constables, &c." London : 1538. 4to.

" Of the Diversity of Courts."

"Natura Brevium Novel." London : 1534. Afterwards translated into English, and often published, having been always in very high esteem.

" Of the Surveying of Lands." London : 1539, 8vo.

" The Book of Husbandry, very profitable and necessary for all Persons." 1534, 8vo.

The living of Norbury cum Snelston is a rectory, the annual value of which in the King's Books is estimated at £15 16s. 0½d., and yearly tenths £1 11s. 7½d. It is considered one of the most valuable in the neighbourhood, being endowed with the great and small tithes, and upwards of 100 acres of glebe-land. The Rev. Clement F. Broughton is the present incumbent, and also patron of the living; his family have possessed the advowson for a considerable time. The rectory-house stands near the church, and is a very good and commodious one, with extensive gardens and pleasure-grounds.* The situation is most beautiful, and for extent, richness, and variety of scenery, can be surpassed by few residences in the country. The lofty eminence on which it stands, looking down upon the Dove, is surrounded by a rich verdant lawn, sloping precipitously to the water's edge, delightfully broken by an abundance of remarkably fine timber-trees. The Valley of Dove at this point forms an angle, and the windows of the Parsonage command it in both directions. The tall spires of Ashbourn and Uttoxeter are seen at either extremity, and the towers of Rocester and Mayfield about midway in the valley; in front, Wever rears his lofty head, and forms a noble outline; Wootton Hall, and its romantic scenery lie on his sunny breast; while the picturesque village and church of Ellastone, and Calwich Abbey, with its lake and extensive ornamented grounds, are seen at his feet.

"The Vales of Wever," a descriptive poem, by John Gisborne, Esq., contains some very pleasing passages descriptive of the scenery in this neighbourhood, enlivened, too, by the introduction of such historical and antiquarian reminiscences as the locality affords. Of Norbury, Mr. Gisborne thus writes:—

"Sweet NORBURY, deck'd with rural smiles,
Gleams faintly through these silvan aisles;
'Mid Gothic grandeur soars serene†
O'er bold varieties of scene;
Sees Wever arch his giant crest,
And give the south his lawny breast;

---

*The parsonage was built by the late rector, Mr. Mills, whose happy taste in selecting the present situation cannot be disputed.—*Mr. Gisborne's Notes.*

†*'Mid Gothic grandeur.* The church at Norbury is a venerable pile of building, and from the banks of the Dove has a beautiful and highly picturesque effect.

Or when imperious winter scowls,
" And loud and long" the whirlwind howls,
With naked majesty control*
The frenzy of the northern pole;
Sees the connected vales unfold
Labour's rich realms of green and gold;
Sees at her feet the waters toil,
And drinks the thunder of Britannia's Nile."†

The following passage from a celebrated poet so nearly applies to the general
scenery about Norbury, that I cannot refrain from quoting it at length:

"———O ye dales
Of Tyne, and ye most ancient woodlands; where
Oft as the giant flood obliquely strides,
And his banks open and his lawns extend,
Stops short the pleased traveller, to view
Presiding o'er the scene some rustic tower
Founded by Norman or by Saxon hands."—*Akenside.*

With naked majesty. The summits of Wever occasionally assume a singular
and beautiful appearance during a violent snow-storm, when it happens that
the clouds are so directed by the currents of wind, that, while the vales are lost
amidst the driving vapour, these summits enjoy the full splendour of a meridian
sun:

†*And drinks the thunder of Britannia's Nile.* Dr. Plot and other writers have
given the Dove, in consequence of the great fertility of its waters, the appellation of the British Nile:

" Down yon mid vale the British Nile,
Fair Dove, comes winding many a mile."—*Mundy.*
—*Mr. Gisborne's Notes.*

NORBURY SCHOOL.—Thomas Williams, by his will bearing date Jan. 26th,
1687, devised to the Rev. Anthony Trollope, rector of Norbury, Godfrey Meynell
Esq., and Christopher Ley, gentleman, and their heirs, two closes called *Bill's
Neather Meadow and the Under Town Intack,* in trust, to dispose of the rents and
profits thereof for the maintenance of a school-master, to teach in the parish
church of Norbury all such children as should be born and resident in Norbury,
Roston and Snelston, to be disposed of amongst them at the discretion of the
Parson of Norbury for the time being, and he directed that in case the said
Godfrey Meynell and Christopher Ley should survive the said Anthony Trollope, that then they should convey the said two closes to the Parson of Norbury
for the time being in such a manner that he should be equally interested with
them or the survivor of them in disposing of the profits of the said closes upon
the trusts aforesaid, and the Parson of Norbury for the time being should be
always one of the said trustees, for disposing of the profits of the said closes.

Since the date of this will a house has been built for the school master, and
recently a school room for both boys and girls, erected with aid from the National
Society to which it was then united, and a mistress as well as master have since
been appointed. The annual rental of the closes named in the will is about £18.

The parochial chapelry of Snelston, (parish of Norbury) was held by Walter de Montgomery, under the Earl of Lancaster, in the reign of Edward I. It appears that Robert Docksey, Esq. was lord of the manor of Snelston in 1599. A good estate and mansion were purchased here in the year 1682, of the family of Bennet, by Ralph Docksey. About 1770—80 they passed to the daughter of Mr. William Bowyer, wife of the Rev. Thomas Langley, who describes himself as resident at Snelston, in 1799, in which year he published "A Serious Address to the Head and Heart of every Unbiassed Christian."*

---

* Pilkington's Derbyshire.

31

CHAPTER XII.

Calwich Abbey—Handel a Guest there—The Granville Family.—Ellastone.—
Wootton and the Vales of Wever—Wootton Hall, the retreat of Jean
Jacques Rousseau—Wootton Scenery—Wootton Lodge.

CALWICH ABBEY, the seat of Court Dewes Granville, Esq.
four miles west of Ashbourn, is the site of a Hermitage
which belonged to the Priory of Kenilworth. To that religious house it was given (says Tanner)* before the year
1148 by Nicholas de Gresley Fitz Nigell; and therein was
placed a small Convent of Black Canons (Carthusians.)†
The only names of Priors or Masters of this house which
have occurred are those of Hugh Bily, and Thomas de
Famcote, the latter of whom appears in the register of the
see of Canterbury about A. D. 1388. This house was
given, (27 Henry VIII.) to the monastery of Merton, Surrey,
in exchange for the manor of East Molsey, and as parcel of

---

*Notitia Monastica. Dugdale's Monasticon.

†The Carthusian monks were a branch of the Benedictines, whose rule,
with the addition of many austerities, they followed. Their discipline was the
most strict of any of the religious orders: never eating flesh, and being obliged
to fast on bread, water, and salt, one day in every week. None of the monks
were ever permitted to go out of the bounds of the monasteries, except the Priors
and Procurators, and they only upon the necessary affairs of their houses. Their
habit was all white, except the outward plaited cloak, which was black.—*Dugdale's
Monasticon Anglicanum.*

CALWICH ABBEY.

The Seat of Court. Dewes Granville Esq.

Printed by T.W. & C.Fairland, London.

Published by Dawson & Hobson, Ashbourn.

the same, was again granted (34 Henry VIII.) to John
Fleetwood, a member of the ancient Lancashire family of
that name, and in the possession of his descendants it continued for several generations.* The concise topographer, Erdeswick, writes (1660) " From Mayfield Dove
passeth to Calwich, whereof I can only make this report,
that being or belonging to a cell or house of religion, now
a Lancashire gentleman is owner thereof, who (as I have
heard) hath made a parlour of the chancel, a hall of the
church, and a kitchen of the steeple, which may be true,
for I have known a gentleman in Cheshire which hath done
the like."†

From the Fleetwoods Calwich passed to a branch of the
illustrious family of *Granville*, and afterwards to that of
Dewes, who have taken the name of Granville, and are
its present possessors.‡

The present mansion is of modern date, and is supposed
to occupy the site of the church that belonged to the Her-

---

*Harwood's Erdeswick's Staffordshire.

† A very curious letter, addressed to George Digby, Esq. of Sandon, entitled
" Observations upon the possessors of Monastery Lands in Staffordshire," by Sir
Simon Degge, (a zealous catholic) is appended to " Erdeswick's Staffordshire."
Sir Simon remarks—" 'Tis a wonder to see, that in sixty years (it being no
more since Mr. Erdeswick wrote this tract) one-half I believe of the Lands in
Staffordshire have changed their owners : not so much, as of old they were wont,
by marriage, as by purchase, and if it were not that I should tire out your patience, I could give you my conjecture of the reason : * * * The first reason I
conceive to be ; for that our ancient gentry were so guilty of Henry the Eighth's
sacrelegious robbing the church, that this mingled church lands with their
ancient inheritances, and 'tis no wonder to see the eagle's nest on fire that steals
flesh from the altar for her young ones."— Sir Simon then enumerates the misfortunes, real or supposed, which have befallen the possessors of Abbey-lands,
and among them the Fleetwoods of Calwich: " Calwich (he writes) is next in
order, bought by Sir Richard Fleetwood's grandfather, how unhappily it pros
pered with the grandson you have seen, and the children of that family have
been unfortunate."

‡ Mr. Dewes having married Miss Granville, who was mother to the last and
grandmother to the present possessor of the property, on which account they
took the name of Granville.

mitage, and which was converted by the Fleetwoods into a
family seat.   It stands at the base of a lengthened, woody
knoll, which, stretching east and west, forms the right
boundary of the vale of Dove.   The situation is rather
low, like that of monastic buildings in general, but
it is in no degree less beautiful on that account.   A rich
screen of fine forest trees shelters it on the north, and beneath is a fine verdant expanse of ornamental grounds, enlivened by a broad artificial sheet of water, fed from the
now ample current of the serpentine Dove.*

*Mr. Gisborne, in his "Vales of Wever" thus describes Calwich (1796):

"Come *Granville*, thou whose fostering hand
Guards the slow growths of Albion's land;
For thee, O friend, the placid spring
Wafts her pure balm on sweetest wing;
Thy lake's clear azure whispering curls
And Flora's tissued veil unfurls,
For thee the woodland kings display
The silvery gem, the golden spray,
Weave o'er thy banks a pensile wreath,
And cool thy twilight walks beneath.
Here amid black sequestered shades
That darkened once those sunny glades,
Frown'd a gray pile!†   The grass-grown walks
(Dire superstition's gloomy halls)
The roof, the towers, with ivy crown'd,
Damp horror spread his arms around.
Oft has this vale, when midnight drove
Her car in silence through the grove
Seen tremulous lights within the pile,
Pass and repass the cloister'd aisle;
Seen the funereal pall and bier,
Bedew'd with friendship's parting tear,
Seen the sad slowly moving bands
Pale tapers glimmering in their hands;
Heard the loud choir within the cave
Chant the sweet requiem o'er the grave."

†" There was formerly a large monastery at Calwich, and a part of the monk's
garden, and some of their fish-ponds are, I believe, still to be seen. During the
alterations in the grounds about Calwich in the late Mr. Granville's life, numbers of skulls and human-bones were frequently discovered; and large quantities
have lately been found by the work-people now employing at Calwich.—*Mr.
Gisborne's Notes.*

The ancient Hermitage has been converted into stables, but some portions of the original fabric yet remain. The north wall, with pointed gables, is nearly entire.

The interior of the mansion is commodiously arranged. From the windows of the front, (south-east) a fine prospect is obtained, taking in the vale, with the church, mansion and parsonage of Norbury, on the opposite heights.

The library comprehends an extensive selection of the best works in British, Continental, and classical literature. The possession of one memorial, which is here preserved, a prince might covet, namely—a large collection of the original manuscript music of Handel. The immortal harmonist was a frequent visitant at Calwich; and a fine-toned organ chosen by him, yet stands, surmounted by his bust, in the drawing-room of the mansion. On this instrument Handel was accustomed to perform; and there is perhaps nothing romantic in the assumption, that to his occasional residence in this calm seclusion, surrounded by the beauties of nature, and in the enjoyment of social intercourse with esteemed and admiring friends, we are indebted for some of those sublime compositions which are at once the delight and the admiration of all who have a soul to be moved by the 'concord of sweet sounds.'

The gallery and drawing-room—tastefully furnished apartments, contain a number of good pictures, and many excellent family portraits. A list of some of the most valuable we subjoin :—

A landscape by *Rembrandt*,—a lovely scene in some southern clime, is perhaps the gem of the collection. The colouring is warm, yet soft, and almost illusive in effect, perfectly characteristic of the style of the master.

Several smaller landscapes by *Ruysdael, Segers, Vandort, Poussin*, and *Wynants;* a " St. John in the Wilderness," by *Ludovico Carracci,* " A Sleeping Child," and " Boys with Fruit," from the pencil of *Murillo*, are of high degrees of excellence.

A fine portrait of Vice Chancellor Coke, by *Vandyck*, claims particular notice.   The countenance is a noble one, clear, thoughtful, and expressive, displaying that indescribable air of dignified ease, which the painter could so happily impart.

The Crucifixion—*Andrea Sacchi.*

The Holy Family—*Palma.*

Madonna and Child—*Howard: a copy from Caravaggio.*

Virgin at Prayer—*Velasquez.*

The Sacrifice of Iphigenia—*Santa Peranila.*

Two Monkeys—*Teniers.*

Man with a Flute—*Stone.*

Trumpeter—*Gerhard Douw.*

A Manege Horse—*Wouvermans.*

Narcissus—*Laurence de la Hire.*

Sir Richard Delabere presenting to the Black Prince the arms taken from the King of Bohemia, at the Battle of Cressy.

Portrait of *Michael Angelo*, in crayons, by his own hand.

Portrait of John Duke of Argylle.

A very fine miniature portrait of Shakspeare, in water colours, by *Ozias Humfrey*, miniature painter to the Duchess of Portland in 1775, copied from an undoubted original. This drawing was given by the Duchess of Portland to Mrs. Delany, known for her botanical drawings, and as having spent her last years with the Royal Family.

A " Holy Family," a " Madonna and Child," and a portrait of Charles I. after *Vandyke*, are from the pencil of Mrs. Delany, who appears to have been a lady of versatile talent.

A portrait of the late Rev. John Granville, and its companion, a portrait of Mrs. Granville, both by *Barber.*

Portrait of John Granville, Esq., their son—*Hoppner.*

Portrait of Colonel Granville, of Coulston, brother to Lord Lansdowne—*Wissing.*

Portrait of the Lady of Colonel Granville—*Soldi.*

Portrait of Mary, the wife of Dr. Delany, Dean of Down, and the daughter of Bernard Granville, Esq.

Portrait of George Granville, Baron Lansdowne, of Biddeford, in the county of Devon, one of the twelve peers created by Queen Anne, on the 2nd of January, 1711.

Portrait of Lady Stanley when a child, daughter of Bernard Granville, Esq., and niece to Sir Bevil.—*Houseman.* A finely-painted Cupid is introduced.

Portrait of Lady Joanna Thornhill—*Wright.*

Portrait of Vice Chancellor Coke's second lady—*Jervas.*

Portrait of Bernard, son of Bernard Granville, Esq. of Coulston, Wiltshire, and nephew to George, Lord Lansdowne.

Portrait of Sir Richard Greenville (or Granville) the intrepid seaman—*Cavaliero Moro.*

Portraits of Sir Bevil Granville, the warrior, and of his lady, Mary, the daughter of Sir George Smyth, Knight, of Exeter.

Portrait of Sir John Granville, created first Earl of Bath, in 1661.

Sir Richard Greenville, the friend and companion of Sir Walter Raleigh, was created Vice-Admiral, and entrusted with the command of two expeditions of discovery in America, in the last of which, during an engagement with the Spanish fleet, he lost his life. "This action of Sir Richard Greenville" says Hume, "is so singular as to merit a more particular relation. He was engaged alone with the whole Spanish fleet of fifty three sail, which had ten thousand men on board; and from the time the fight began, which was about three in the afternoon, to the break of day next morning, he repulsed the enemy fifteen times, though they continually shifted their vessels, and boarded with fresh men. In the beginning of the action he himself received a wound; but he continued doing his duty upon deck till eleven at night, when, receiving a fresh wound, he was carried down to be dressed. During this operation he received a shot in the head, and the surgeon was killed

by his side. The English began now to want powder; all
their small arms were broken or become useless; of their
number, which were but an hundred and three at first,
forty were killed, and almost all the rest wounded; their
masts were beat overboard, their tackle cut in pieces, and
nothing but a hulk left, unable to move one way or other.
In this situation Sir Richard proposed to the ship's company, to trust to the mercy of God, not to that of the
Spaniards, and to destroy the ship with themselves rather
than yield to the enemy. The master-gunner and many of
the seamen agreed to this desperate resolution, but others
opposed it, and obliged Greenville to surrender himself
prisoner. He died a few days after, and his last words
were: ' Here die I, Richard Greenville, with a joyful and
quiet mind: for that I have ended my life as a true
soldier ought to do, fighting for his country, queen, religion and honour. My soul willingly departing from this
body ; leaving behind the lasting fame of having behaved
as every valiant soldier is in his duty bound to do.' The
Spaniards lost in this sharp but unequal action, four ships,
and about a thousand men. And Greenville's vessel perished soon after, with two hundred Spaniards in her."

Sir Bevil Granville distinguished himself by his personal valour and activity in the service of Charles I., to
whose cause he was devotedly attached. Sir Bevil, with
other gentlemen of note and influence in the county of
Devon, had raised an army for the king, and after some
skirmishing, and a sharp engagement, in which the royalists had the advantage, the contending forces met on Lansdowne Heath, where they fought a pitched battle, with
great bloodshed, but no decisive result. In this conflict,
the gallant Sir Bevil was killed. His character is thus
described by Lord Clarendon: "He was indeed an excellent person, and his temper and affections so public that
no accident which happened could make any impression on
him, and his example kept others from taking anything
ill, or at least from seeming to do so. In a word, brighter

courage and a gentler disposition were never married together to make the most cheerful and innocent conversation."

The grandson of Sir Bevil, George Granville, Marquis
of Lansdowne, was a nobleman of high attainments, a fact
which his poetical works sufficiently attest.

Sir John Granville, also a firm adherent to the royal
cause, acted a conspicuous part in the negociations between
the last Parliament of the Commonwealth, and Charles II.,
which led finally to the Restoration. After the monarch
had been proclaimed, the Commons voted Sir John, who
was the bearer of His Majesty's most welcome proposals,
the sum of £500 to purchase a jewel.*

Calwich is a township in the extensive parish of ELLAS-
TONE, a village situated on the turnpike-road between Uttoxeter and Ashbourn, and distant about five miles from the
latter place.   In the 20th of William the Conqueror, the
manor of *Elacheston* was held by Woodman and Alfi,
under their superior lord, Robert de Stafford.   In the reign
of King John, William de Audley held of Robert de Stafford, *Athelarton*, with Blore, and Grendon.   In the time of
Henry III. Nigellus de Langford held it of the Baron of
Stafford; and in the 9th Edward II. Nicholas de Langford,
and Theobald de Verdon were lords of *Athelarton*.†   Henry
VIII. in the 34th year of his reign, granted to John Fleetwood, the rectory of Ellastone, and all lands and tithes belonging thereto.   That family eventually became possessed
of the entire parish, and they afterwards sold the manors of
Ellastone and Wootton to Lord Bathurst, by whom they
were resold about the year 1728, to Richard Davenport,
Esq. of Calveley, Cheshire, who built Wootton Hall.
The manorial rights are now vested in Davenport Bromley,
Esq.

The church is very pleasantly seated on the summit of a
rising-ground, and with the parsonage-house immediately

*Hume.   †Erdeswick's Staffordshire.
32

contiguous, has an extremely picturesque appearance from
the road beneath. The tower is of the sixteenth century,
but the nave and other portions of the structure were
rebuilt in 1830. On the south side of the chancel is a
large altar-tomb of alabaster, bearing the recumbent effigies
of a knight in armour, and his lady in a flowing figured
robe, both greatly mutilated. The sides of the tomb are
sculptured with shields of arms, but no inscription can now
be discovered. It belongs most probably to one of the early
members of the Fleetwood family. A tablet affixed to the
opposite wall of the chancel is inscribed to the memory of
Richard Fleetwood, of Calwich, who died in 1721.

Beneath a decorated niche in the same wall, is a monument of black marble, with an inscription to Abel John
Ran, a lineal descendant of Thomas Ran, Bishop of Ferns
in the reign of Elizabeth. He died at Calwich Abbey in
1822. There are also other monuments of the Fleetwood
and Granville families.

The living is in the gift of Davenport Bromley, Esq.
The Rev. George Hake is the present incumbent.

The parish of Ellastone, including the townships of Calwich, Prestwood, Ramsor, Stanton, and Wootton, contains
1344 inhabitants, and the annual value of the real property
therein is assessed at £9,161.

A short distance north of Ellastone Church, stands
WOOTTON HALL, the seat of Davenport Bromley, Esq.
There is perhaps scarcely a spot within or bordering on
the entire range of the Vale of Dove that is more fitly
adapted for a noble mansion. Its situation is a lofty
sloping bank, rising from a forest-like seclusion, and commanding an almost unbounded landscape of mountain,
meadow, and sylvan scenery, whilst the demesne itself, and
the contiguous districts are hardly less varied in character.

Mr. Gisborne, whose lines, "The Vales of Wever," were
written for the most part during a residence here, sketches
it with a poet's fervour :—

" From my bold terrace bursts the scene,
Rob'd in a waving vest of green ;
Swift slopes my foreground's velvet lawn,
Late glistening with the tears of morn ;
Bends o'er the shelving cliffs, or shrinks,
And tufts with fern the giddy brinks ;
While mingling oaks in rude arcades
Chequer the green expanse with shades.
Fronting, a sister lawn displays
Umbrageous promont'ries and bays;
With grace superior swells sublime,
And marks the mouldering wrecks of time;
Sees the disjointed crags dissolve,
Or down the echoing banks revolve;
Sees the wild torrent's maddening tide
Her grass-enamell'd lap divide,
Grow with the storm, disclose huge caves,
Scoop out an empire for his waves :
Or marks, as now, with happier smile,
Nor tempest rave, nor torrent boil,
But sunshine clothe her birchen crest,
The white rill gleaming down her breast.
Then o'er the dark embowering trees
Wind the green slopes with graceful ease;
Culture each sidelong bank inlays,
And 'mid the scatter'd umbrage plays.
High on those undulating lands
Half lost in leaves the village stands,*
Lifts her gray tower with age o'erspread,
And light reposes on its head :
Then branches wide the vale below,
And all the opening landscapes glow;
In reaches bold, in grand removes,
Sweep hamlets, lawns, and cluster'd groves,
Till the sky-tinctur'd distance fades
Beyond those dim retiring glades,
Where, floating wide, cerulean haze
Empurples EATON's leafy maze."†

In this mansion the historian Hume procured a retreat
for his gifted, but capricious friend, Jean Jacques Rousseau.
A victim to imaginary terrors, Rousseau fled from his native country and his friends to take refuge in England.

---

*Ellastone.   †Eaton Woods.

He at first intended taking up his residence in Wales, but
in April, 1766, he settled at Wootton. "Here" he says,
"I have arrived at last, at an agreeable and sequestered
asylum, where I hope to breathe freely and at peace."
This retreat might indeed have been supposed every way
in consonance with his romantic and melancholy disposition. But who can 'minister to a mind diseased?' In the
month of April following he abruptly quitted his "sequestered asylum," and returned to the continent, after a violent
quarrel with Hume and others, his most disinterested
friends. To allure him into this country, the rent of
Wootton Hall had been reduced, and his wounded pride on
the discovery of this circumstance, was probably the cause
of his sudden departure. On one occasion, whilst here,
he received a present of some bottles of choice foreign wine,
but being a gift, his pride would not permit him to taste
it, and he left it in the house untouched for the next
comer. For some unknown reason, he had formed a determination not to see Dr. Darwin. Aware of his prejudice,
the Doctor placed himself on a terrace which Rousseau had
to pass, and occupied himself seemingly in the examination of a plant. "Rousseau," said he, "Are you a botanist?" They entered into conversation, and were intimate
at once. But Rousseau, on reflection, imagined that this
meeting was the result of design, and he discontinued the
intimacy.* Botany was Rousseau's favourite pursuit, and
amidst the sylvan groves and forest glades of Wootton he
had ample space to prosecute the study. A circular cluster
of oaks, termed locally, "The Twenty Oaks," beneath
whose shade a glimpse of some beautiful scenery was obtained, was formerly shown as one of his chosen retreats:

> "Lo! where those oaks encircling meet,
> There genius formed his rural seat.
> Oft in calm solitude the sage
> Compos'd his fascinating page;
> Or bending on the turf survey'd
> With nice regard, each flower and blade."—*Vales of Wever.*

*Rhodes's Tourists' Guide.

The Vales of Wever are an extension, as it may be called, of that beautiful series of wild romantic dells, which mark the course of the Dove, the Hamps, and the Manifold. Let the reader picture to himself another of those winding rocky chasms, where silence and solitude reign supreme, save when dispelled by the feeble bleat of the mountain sheep, the hoarse cawing of the raven, or the warblings of the innumerable tribe of feathered songsters, which here revel in gladness and security; at whose base flows a purling rivulet, or mayhap, at certain seasons, an impetuous foaming torrent; whose sides are screened by broad masses of shady wood, the prospect opening at intervals, through rich glades, or from rocky summits, into a more extended and cultivated vale beyond; he will then realise to his mind's eye one of the many beautiful spots over which dark Wever rears his towering outline.* These dells are verdant and fertile, but the surface of the steeps and high lands by which they are environed, being exposed alike to the chill blast of winter and the withering sun of summer, are sterile and unprofitable. An ancient distich, expressive of their barrenness, quoted by Dr. Plot, and other topographers, is yet prevalent:

"Wootton under Wever,
Where God came never."

"It is high time," says the shrewd Dr. Fuller, in his ' Worthies of England,' " this old prophane proverb should die in men's mouths for ever. I confess, in common discourse, God is said to come to what he doth *approve; to send* to what he only *permits;* and neither to *go* nor *send,* to what he doth *dislike* and *forbid.* But this distinction, if admitted, will help nothing to the defending of this prophane proverb, which, it seems, took its wicked original

---

*Wever Hills are a very elevated situation, overlooking, or at least as high as any of the Moorland or Derbyshire Peak hills, which may be seen from their summits. I believe them to be from one to two hundred yards higher than any of the hills in the south of the county. The fall even from the foot of those hills to the highest part of the Dove or the Churnet, is very great, and those rivers are very rapid.—*Pitt's Survey of Staffordshire.*

from the situation of Wotton, so covered with hills from
the light of the sun, a dismal place, as report representeth
it. But were there a place indeed where " *God came never*,"
how many years' purchase would guilty consciences give
for a small abode therein, thereby to escape divine justice
for their offences."

For a few passages illustrative of the scenery around
Wootton, viewed under the varied aspects of the revolving
seasons, by a close and accurate observer, we again quote
" The Vales of Wever :"—

> " When bleak December's arctic breath
> Urges the giant " work of death,"
> Prone from these crags, high-roofed with snow,
> Pellucid piles *incessant* grow :*
> Vast columns deck'd with fret-work nice,
> Glimmer on pedestals of ice,
> The sun, the whelming whirlwind brave,
> And seem to prop the pensile cave.

> *   *   *   *

*" The incessant droppings from many of the cliffs in the vicinity of Woot-
ton produce in the course of a severe winter some of the most singular and beautiful pillars of ice that imagination can devise. In the month of January,
1795, I measured many of them that were from four to eleven feet in altitude,
and from six inches to four feet in circumference. Some of these columns
were of unequal periphery, and jagged and fluted in a fantastic manner. Those
that were of uniform thickness appeared as elegant supporters to the impending shelves and canopies of rock. The surfaces of the adjacent crags are
beautifully glazed and decorated with a bright coating of ice, through which
the *marchantia polymorpha* and several species of moss and fern displayed the
luxuriancy of spring. From the ceiling of the celebrated cavern in Dovedale
(well known by the name of Reynard's Hall) vast pendants of ice were clustered together, many of which, I believe, were full four yards in length; and
these were tapered down to so fine a periphery, that their extremities were as
sharp as the point of a sword. Others were twisted in a singular mode, and
variegated with white incrustations of ice and snow, and the sides of the cavern were partially embossed with crystal nodules. The floor of this spacious
cavern appeared decorated by the hand of magic. Wherever the droppings
fell upon it they became congealed, and hence one drop freezing upon
another produced eccentric pillars of ice. These were of various dimensions,
and of different colour. Had the frost continued a month longer, it is probable
that these pillars would have come into contact with the growing pendants
from the roof.—*Mr. Gisborne's Notes.*

"O Wootton! oft I love to hear
Thy wintry whirlwinds loud and clear;
With dreadful pleasure bid them fill
My listening ears, my bosom chill.
As the sonorous North assails
Wever's bleak wilds and leafless vales,
With awful majesty of might
He bursts the billowy clouds of night,
Booms the resounding glens among,
And roaring rolls his snows along.
In clouds against my groaning sash
Broad feathery flakes incessant dash,
Or wheel below, and mingling form
The frolic pageants of the storm.
Hark! with what aggravated roar
Echo repeats her midnight lore;
Rends her dark solitudes and caves,
And bellowing shakes the mighty graves,*
Appals with horror Fancy's mind,
While ghosts disturb'd shrill-shriek upon the wind.
Couch'd on her seat the timid hare
Listens each boisterous sweep of air,
Or peeps yon blasted furze between,
And eyes the snow-bewildered scene;
Instant retracts her shudd'ring head,
And closer nestles to her bed.
All sad and ruffled in the grove,
The fieldfare wakes from dreams of love;
Hears the loud north and beating snow,
Regards the drifted brakes below,
Swift to her wing returns her beak,
And shivers as the tempests break.
Up starts the village dog aloof,
And howls beneath his rifted roof:
Looks from his den, and blinking hears
The driving tumult at his ears,
Instant withdraws his fear-froze breast,
Shrinks from the storm, and steals to rest.
So shrinks the pining fold and sleeps
Beneath the valley's vaulted deeps;

*   *   *   *

*Alluding to the numerous barrows on Wever and the adjacent hills. One of them Mr. Gisborne saw opened, when several large urns of burnt clay were discovered. When removed they broke in pieces, and disclosed a quantity of ashes, bones, and teeth, and a piece of brass or copper, apparently the head of a spear.

Or crops the sescue's dewy blade,
And treads unseen the milky glade.

"Thus night rolls on, till orient dawn
Unbars the purple gates of morn,
Unfolds each vale, each snow-clad grove,
Mute founts and glossy banks above.
Thin streaky clouds unvex'd by storms
Slowly expand their tissued forms,
Long bars of gray and crimson bright
Divert the golden threads of light;
Till glory's nascent curve displays
One splendid orb, a world of rays!
Then lightens heaven's ethereal bound,
And all the spangled country twinkles round.

"But leaves the Muse her flowery plain
For surly Winter's drear domain,
Her babbling founts, her spacious shades,
For leafless groves and dumb cascades?
Come, let us range yon winding wood,
Where nature frowns with aspect rude;
Wild drapery hangs her craggy seat,
And silver chills her lone retreat.

　　*　　　　*　　　　*　　　　*

"Now as we climb our Alpine way,
Wide bursts around the vault of day.
Blaze not so fierce, ye torrid beams,
Assuage your scintillating streams;
Hither diffuse, ye summer clouds,
Your lucid veils, your fleecy shrouds;
Breathe cool, ye pausing airs, and sweep
Earth's thyme-wove hills and emerald deep:
So shall my flowers their gems unrol,
And stud with golden stars each knoll;
O'er these aerial heights disclose
A brighter blush when evening glows.

"See how majestic Wever's brow
Swells from each broken scene below!
O'er the wide vales he bends sublime,
And triumphs in his polar clime;
Basking and tann'd, the landscapes hail
His frown the shade, his sigh the gale.
Sunk on the cushion'd moss I view
Hills half-immers'd in vapours blue;

WOOTON LODGE

Drawn & Printed by Rayner, Derby.

Published by Dawson & Hobson, Ashbourn.

There his pale barrier Malvern rears,
And *here* ambitious Wrekin peers;*
Buoy'd on a sea of mist he soars,
And looks o'er Cambria's winding shores;
Lifts his tall crest with jealous fear,
And seems to prop the leaning sphere.
Stretch'd at my feet, what prospects glow!
A world of verdure smiles below.
Smooth'd in one vast expanse of green,
Hamlets, and hills, and woods are seen:
And where yon far-famed valley leads
Her velvet o'er a thousand meads,
Dove wanders with increasing force,
And threads of silver mark his course:
But north of these encircling graves,
Where Bunster's ridgy outline waves,
Fresh from his boiling source he guides
Round fringed isles his infant tides;
Or chill'd with awful shadows sweeps,
And murmuring rolls his glossy deeps:
Shoots o'er the shoals, and bounding steers
Long lines of foam from rock-built wears.
Then far beyond rude hills aspire,
Range above range, in blue attire;
Where the lost eye pursues in vain
Gigantic Grindon's bleak domain,†
Where yawning THOR the vale alarms,
And Beauty sleeps in Horror's arms."

Leaving Wootton Hall on the right, a turn westward
leads to the entrance-gates of Wootton Lodge, a fine old
castellated mansion, said to have been designed by Inigo
Jones. The principal entrance is by a broad and ample
flight of stone steps, through a curiously-ornamented door-
way, surmounted by the arms of Sir Richard Fleetwood,
who is believed to have built the mansion, and by whom
it was garrisoned for the royalists in the civil wars of
Charles I.‡ For the purposes of defence it is far better

---

* The Wrekin, in Shropshire, and the Malvern Hills, in Worcestershire,
may be seen from the summit of Wever, on a clear day.

†The village of Grindon is situated on a hill of remarkable elevation.

‡See page 18.

33

adapted than might, at a passing glance, appear, both from the natural advantages of its situation, and the massive strength of its walls. Tradition indeed, affirms, that despite of the facilities for cannonading afforded by the hills that nearly on all sides surround it, the parliamentarian artillery were never able to effect a breach in the front. The building extends from the level lawn to the very edge of a lofty and precipitous rock, on which its foundations are laid, and this side, at least, presents a bold front to an enemy. The structure retains, for the most part, its original character, though it appears to have been at one time of greater extent. The principal rooms have been modernised, and the whole is in excellent repair, large sums having been expended in restoring and improving it by the family of the proprietor, the Rev. Edward Unwin, of Derby. His son, James Wheeler Unwin, Esq. is the present occupier.

About the close of the seventeenth century, Sir Richard Fleetwood, a descendant of the former baronet of that name, sold Wootton Lodge to John Wheeler, Esq., of Stourbridge, in the county of Worcester, from whom it descended to the family of Unwin.

Part of the demesne belonging to Wootton Lodge was once inclosed as a deer-park, estimated to contain a thousand acres. It was stocked with deer till about the year 1750, and some vestiges of the wall are yet standing.

The Lodge was formerly approached by a remarkably fine avenue of trees, (an indispensable appendage to a building of note in ancient times) now unfortunately destroyed. The park-grounds, however, are uncommonly beautiful,—beautiful in the absence of art, for even now the 'monarch of the forest' and his stripling progeny flourish side by side, in all their native wildness and luxuriance, here forming open winding groves, and there arrayed in dark sombre masses; while, perhaps, surmounting all, a

pile of rugged cliffs, that has withstood the blast of
ages, starts boldly from the edge of the overhanging
acclivities:

> "Dark from these heights a wood impends,
> And round the dizzy bank extends,
> Shoots down the tangled vale beneath,
> Hangs o'er the brook a verdant wreath;
> Then forms each hill's continued screen,
> And paints with verdure all the scene.—
> Welcome, ye forest glens! ye bays!
> Ye crags that glimmer in the maze!
> Welcome, ye paths through winding shade!
> (Where oft your musing Rousseau stray'd;)
> High o'er your mix'd attractive powers
> Yon venerable mansion towers;
> Swells from the dusky depths between,
> And gloomy grandeur crowns the scene.
> Fix'd on a rock, the castled pile
> Hears unconcern'd the whirlwinds toil,
> Bids her embattled walls defy
> The vollied storms of Winter's sky."

—Vales of Wever.

CHAPTER XIII.

Alton Towers, Staffordshire, the seat of the Earl of Shrewsbury—The Gardens and Scenery—Loudon's Description of—The Abbey—Pictures and Works of Art—The Chapel—Village and Ancient Castle of Alveton.

PURSUING the road to the left of Wootton Lodge, in a westerly direction, the tourist approaches ALTON TOWERS, the magnificent domain of the Earl of Shrewsbury.* The

* "Alton Abbey, for effect, should always be approached by the Earl of Shrewsbury's private carriage road. Pass through Ellastone, and pursue the Uttoxeter road one mile farther, where a turn to the right leads to the park gates, the entrance into this privileged drive. Here the beautiful scenery of this noble demesne commences. On passing along, several openings occur amongst the trees on the left, that let in some delightful views of the scenery about Alton. Within about half a mile of the house, on the right, is a conservatory, ornamented with statues, busts, and vases; and on the left a lake of water. Visitors should here stop their carriage, and, for a short time, enjoy the scenery before them. A little farther on, there is a gothic temple, close to the road side. At this point, Alton Towers and the intervening gardens burst upon the eye in all their beauty and magnificence. It is a peep into a terrestrial paradise. Proceeding onwards another quarter of a mile, through a plantation of pines, this noble mansion stands before you in all the fulness of its splendour. The lake, the lawn, the arcade bridge, the embattled terrace, the towers, and the surrounding foliage, come broadly and instantaneously upon the view—a splendid and imposing picture—a place to be gazed on and wondered at. This approach to Alton Towers is decidedly the best; the house and grounds are seen increasing in effect at every step, until they open upon the spectator in one magnificent combination of architectural grandeur and sylvan beauty."

—*Rhodes's Tourists' Guide.*

Drawn & Printed by Rayner, Derby

ALTON TOWERS.

The Seat of the Earl of Shrewsbury.

Published by Dawson & Hobson, Ashbourn.

village of Farley, half a mile distant from the Abbey, is the usual rendezvous of visiters, and at the inn there (Orrell's Hotel) tickets to view the gardens are obtained.* The Abbey is a gothic castellated structure, of great extent and commanding exterior, occupying the rising ground of a lawn, that slopes with an easy declivity to the level of a lake, on the opposite side of which stands a large pile of farm-building or stabling, with a castellated front. The gardens are entered through one of the principal arches of a lofty gothic arcade, which separates them from the lawn and lake, and forms a highly ornamental feature of the scenery when viewed from below.

The site of these gardens is one of the numberless deep narrow valleys which we have before described as the distinguishing feature of the district. Here, in a spot originally romantic, but presenting few natural advantages, has been produced a combination of garden building and garden scenery, which is characterised as one of the most extraordinary in Europe.†

"The late Charles, Earl of Shrewsbury (writes Mr. Loudon)‡ began to ornament it with walks and garden buildings, about 1814, and continued employing in it hundreds of labourers, mechanics, and artizans, from that day to his death in 1827, consulting numbers of artists, and amongst others, ourselves. The architects employed were chiefly Thomas Allason and Thomas Abraham, Esqrs.

"We visited Alton Towers in 1826, and again in 1831. By the road leading from Uttoxeter we came unexpectedly close to the house, and near the head of the north side of the valley, which contains the chief wonders of the

---

*It should be observed that admission to this princely seat is restricted to parties coming in private carriages.

†Loudon's " Observations on Cottage and Villa Architecture."

‡ We quote this tolerably minute description (with slight abridgment,) from "The Enclyclopedia of Cottage, Farm, and Villa Architecture."

place.   The first objects that met our eye were the gothic
bridge, and the embankment leading to it, with a huge
imitation of Stonehenge beyond, and a pond above the
level of the bridge along side of it, backed by a mass of
castellated stabling.   Further along the side of the valley
to the left of the bridge, is a range of architectural conservatories, with seven elegant glass domes, designed by Mr.
Abraham, richly gilt.   Further on, still to the left, and
placed on a high and bold native rock, is a lofty gothic
tower or temple, also designed by Mr. Abraham, consisting of several tiers of balconies round a central staircase
and rooms, the exterior ornaments numerous, and resplen-
dent with gilding.   Near the base of the rock is a cork-
screw fountain of a peculiar description, which is amply
supplied from an adjoining pond.   Behind, above, and beyond the range of conservatories, are two lakes; and beyond
them is another conservatory, curiously ornamented; below
the main range of conservatories, are a paved terrace-
walk, with a Grecian temple at one end; and a second
terrace containing a second range of conservatories.   The
remainder of the valley to the bottom, and on the opposite
side, displays such a labyrinth of terraces, curious architectural walls, trellis-work arbours, vases, statues, stairs,
pavements, gravel and grass walks, ornamental buildings,
bridges, porticos, temples, pagodas, gates, iron railings,
parterres, jets, ponds, streams, fountains, seats, caves,
flower-baskets, waterfalls, rocks, cottages, trees, shrubs,
beds of flowers, ivied walls, moss-houses, rock, shell,
and root-work, old trunks of trees, &c., that it is utterly
impossible for words to give any idea of the effect.   There
is one stair of one hundred steps; a cottage for a blind
harper, as large as a farm-house; and an imitation cottage-
roof, formed by fixing dormar windows, and two chimneys, accompanied by patches of heath, to imitate thatch,
on the sloping surface of a large grey mass of solid rock.
This, seen from a distance, protruding from a steep bank

of wood, bore naturally some resemblance to the roof of a cottage, grey with lichens, and the chimney tops and windows were added to complete the idea. As the sandstone rock protrudes from the sides of the valley in immense masses, abundant use has been made of it to form caves, grottoes, caverns, and covered seats; it has even been carved into figures : in one place we have Indian temples excavated in it, covered with hieroglyphics ; and in another a projecting rock is formed into a huge serpent, with a spear-shaped iron tongue and glass eyes. There is a rustic prospect-tower over an Indian temple, cut out of solid rock, on the highest point of the north bank ; and in the lowest part of the valley there are the foundation and two stories (executed before the death of the late Earl,) of an octagon pagoda. This pagoda was intended to be 88 feet high. It is placed on an island in the centre of a small lake, and was to have been approached by a Chinese bridge, richly ornamented. The diameter of the base of the pagoda, is forty feet, and there were to have been six stories, the lower one of stone, and the others of cast-iron. From the angles were to have been suspended forty highly enriched Chinese lamps, and these were to be lighted by a gasometer in the lower story. Besides the lamps there were to have been grotesque figures of monsters projecting over the angles of the canopies, which were to spout water from their eyes, nostrils, fins, tail, &c., a column of water was also to have been projected perpendicularly from the terminating ornaments on the summit of the structure, which from the loftiness of the source of supply, would have risen to the height of seventy or eighty feet. This fountain was designed by Mr. Abraham, but only the lower story has been executed. The pagoda, the gothic temple, the range of gilt conservatories, and the imitation of Stonehenge, form the leading artificial features of the valley. The valley itself is upwards of a mile in length ; it gradually widens from its commencement at the stone bridge, with the pond above it, till it terminates by opening into the wide valley containing the Churnet, (there a considerable stream) and a navigable canal.   This immense valley, it is said, the late Earl intended to cover entirely with water ; and as it would have saved the canal company several miles of canal, they offered to form the dam or head at their own expense.   This lake of some thousands of acres would have been as easily produced as that of Blenheim was by Brown.   In approaching from Cheadle we arrive in front of the castellated stables, and see the Abbey across the pond, above the level of the bridge.   Proceeding a little further towards the dry bridge, Stonehenge appears in the foreground, and the tops of the seven gilt glass domes of the main range of conservatories below.   Raising the eyes, the lofty gothic temple appears on the left of the picture; and on the right, across the valley, the harper's cottage.   In the centre of the picture, over the domes in the fore-ground, the valley loses itself in a winding bank of wood, in a style of great grandeur and seclusion.   None of the details of the valley here obtrude themselves, and the effect, after passing through a wild country, exhibiting no marks of refinement, is singularly impressive.   It fills the mind with astonishment and delight to find so much of the magnificence of art and the appearance of refined enjoyment amidst so much of the wildness and solitary grandeur of nature.   The imitation of Stonehenge, too, is a feature in artificial landscape which we have not elsewhere seen ; and a stranger is puzzled and confounded by finding a stream and a small waterfall supplying a lake on what he conceives to be the highest point of ground."

The gothic temple, in the structure of which great taste is displayed, contains a fine marble bust of the late Earl Shrewsbury, from the chisel of Campbell.   A pedestal beneath bears the appropriate inscription,—" *He made the desert smile.*"

To the foregoing account of these famed gardens there is little to be added, though since it was written much has been done in the way of improvement. No effort of the pen can convey a satisfactory idea of the gorgeously magnificent scene here displayed. 'Detail and description' it is well observed, 'are useless in such a place.' The fastidious visiter, selecting particular objects or detached scenes, may cavil and criticise, but no one, we should think, be his ideas of taste and beauty ever so refined, can be insensible to the charms of this Elysian dell, when its floral beauties are fully developed. "Those who have read the 'Arabian Nights' Entertainments' (says Mr. Rhodes,) and been blinded with the splendour of the scenes in that popular romance, have only to imagine a series of gardens and grottos, and temples, almost equal in magnificence, and the visionary picture their fancy creates, may, perhaps, shadow forth a faint resemblance of the gardens at Alton."

After the gardens, visiters who are fortunate enough to obtain tickets of admission, are usually conducted to the Abbey. For the following description of the interior we are indebted to Mr. Rhodes:*

"A broad flight of steps leads through massy folding doors to the Hall of Entrance, a lofty but not very large apartment, hung round with swords, spears, helmets, shields, and various other implements of war. Here, seated in an ancient gothic chair, may generally be found an old Welch bard, the minstrel of the mansion, habited in a picturesque costume, striking his harp to songs of other days. This is a pleasing incident in the arrangements of the place, and prepares the mind for the scene that immediately follows.

* From his "Derbyshire Tourists' Guide," an excellent companion to the 'Wonders of the Peak,' as well as to Alton Towers. It abounds with information indispensable to the tourist. The illustrations to the quarto edition of Mr. Rhodes's "Peak Scenery," engraved by George Cooke, chiefly from drawings by Sir Francis Chantrey, are worthy of all praise for their graphic fidelity, —those of Dovedale in particular.

34

This Hall communicates with the Armoury. The numerous
and rare assemblage of objects which are here displayed,
in one continued range of about three hundred feet, (including the long perspective of the Saloon and Picture Gallery,)
is, perhaps, unrivalled in effect in any mansion in the
kingdom. The first compartment, the Armoury, is divided
from the Picture Gallery, by a pierced-work ornamental
bronze screen, which extends across the whole width of
the apartment, and is composed of halberds, spears, lances,
and other implements of war, so arranged as to form but
little obstruction to the view. The figures of fifty knights,
placed on pedestals, and armed cap-a-pie, in polished suits
of mail, are disposed along the walls, and on the floors;
and hung on the sides of the room are sundry specimens
of bows and arrows, ordnance, musketry, &c. of various
fashions, and belonging to different periods of time. The
broad battle-axe of ancient warfare, the richly ornamented
Turkish yhatagan, and polished stiletto,—

> " Helmet and hauberk, targe and spear,
> Cuirass, and sword, and culverin,
> In dread array are gleaming here."

"This apartment is perfect in its kind: seats of dark
carved oak are placed at intervals; and the roof, in style,
ornament, and colour, is in perfect consistency with all
below. The light, which is admitted through stained glass
windows only, is of that dubious kind which throws over
every object a half defined, unreal, and visionary effect.
Nothing is palpably and distinctly seen, but sufficient is
developed to fill the mind with images of days, and scenes,
and customs long since departed.

"The next apartment, the Picture Gallery, in form and
dimensions, is similar to the Armoury. The ceiling, which
is flat, is divided, by richly ornamented gothic tracery, into
different compartments of ground glass, so disposed as to
admit of an equal distribution of light; and, therefore, admirably calculated to give effect to an exhibition of pictures.
I should not envy the feelings of any man who could enter

such a place as this, and gaze upon the splendid works before him with indifference. They are not the emanations of common minds. An accurate knowledge of character, through all its varieties and inflexions—a nice perception of beauty of form and colour—a sovereign power of expression to excite and sway the sympathies of the heart—an entire mastery in the use of his materials, and much previous study—all these, and more than these, are requisite to form a painter in the higher classes of the art: and here these qualities are all combined. Sentiment, passion, pathos, grace, and beauty, speak from the living canvass that adorns these walls.

"The busy grouping and luxuriant colouring of the Venetian and Flemish style of painting, are here contrasted with the still, sober, and more dignified character of the schools of Rome, Florence, and Bologna. Some of the finest pictures here, however, are by Spanish masters, particularly those by Murillo and Velasquez. Others of the first note, belonging to the same high class of art, liberally contribute to the splendour of this collection. These schools have each their peculiar excellencies. The first, lively, bright, and sunny as a summer's day; the latter, quiet, unobtrusive, still and matronly as autumn. The works of art with which the Earl of Shrewsbury has enriched Alton Towers are now so numerous, that a mere catalogue of them, with brief notices only, would fill a volume. A selection of even a small portion of the best, would occupy more space than can be here afforded. A list, however, unaccompanied by critical observations, will be appended to this detail. In this rich depository of art, there are pictures of such rare excellence, as scarcely to admit of competition. The Adoration of the Shepherds, by Giacomo Bassano; and the Adoration of the Magi, by Garofalo, are wonderful productions. The Madonna and St. Francis, by Alonza Cano, is, if possible, of a still higher character of excellence: the figure of the Saint, in drawing, colouring, and expression, is the perfection of art. The Madonna is feminine and graceful; and the infant Jesus is the most beautiful, the most heavenly, and yet the most natural nude form that ever painter imagined. In this masterly production, the realities and sympathies of life are so successfully portrayed on canvas as to wear the very semblance of nature. Amongst the many other fine pictures that we particularly noticed, the following are, perhaps, the best:— A Madonna by Fra Bartolomeo, a lovely production; a Holy Family, by Giorgione; a Magdalen, by Guido Reni; a Magdalen, by Guercino, very fine; two pictures by Wouvermans, Hawking, and Hunting, the latter masterly; and the portrait of Philip the Fourth, by Velasquez. The number and value of this fine collection of works of art have lately been greatly increased by the Earl of Shrewsbury's purchase of nearly the whole of Madame Lætitia Buonaparte's picture gallery at Rome.

"To this splendid apartment the Saloon, or Sculpture Gallery, succeeds: it is a noble room, of an octagonal form, and in structure and ornament has altogether the character of a gothic Chapel, or Cathedral Chapter-house. A clustered column rises in the centre, from the foliaged capital of which the ribs that sustain the roof ramify, and form different compartments along the ceiling. It is lighted by tall lancet-shaped windows of painted glass, rich in colour, and beautiful in design and execution. The finest work in this apartment is a statue of Raffaelle, by Cecarini, a Roman sculptor, and pupil of Canova's. The countenance is intelligent, imaginative, and expressive; the position graceful, and the drapery is free, easy, and natural. The figure is seated, and the left hand supports a tablet, on which Raffaelle's famous picture of the Transfiguration is portrayed.

"The sculptures in this room are not numerous: there are, however, some busts in this collection which any one might be proud to to call his own. Two colossal heads, a Juno and a Jupiter, from the antique, are worthy a distinguished place in any gallery of art, however exalted its

reputation. In the countenance of Juno, dignity and grandeur are tempered with the milder and more fascinating
graces of feminine beauty. Jupiter seems formed to govern
and keep a world in awe:—

"The stamp of fate and fiat of a God"

seem enthroned upon his brow. Between these noble works
is placed a bust of the late Premier, William Pitt—a head
doubly colossal; a bad subject, certainly, for a bust, and
only worthy of notice on account of its size. Nearer the
entrance into the conservatory are two masterly busts, by
Campbell, of the present Earl and Countess of Shrewsbury:
they are eminently beautiful, and, in style and manner,
strongly resemble some of Sir F. Chantrey's most successful
efforts. Cardinal Gonsalvo, by the same admirable sculptor,
is a finely executed head, and so like Thorwaldsen's bust of
this amiable prelate, in the gallery at Chatsworth, as to be
mistaken for a copy. The style of this head is peculiarly
chaste and simple, and the expression of the countenance
bland and benevolent in the highest degree. It is a pleasure
to look on such a face, even in marble.

"The next room, the House Conservatory, is one of the
glories of the place. This apartment, one hundred and
fifteen feet in length, is, in general character, not unlike
the aisle of a Cathedral; it is lighted by tall ornamented
windows, with light and tasteful mullions on both sides;
and, midway, it is divided into two sections, by the inter-
vention of an octagonal compartment of greater altitude
and broader dimensions. In this elegant and delightful
retreat, the refinements of art are skilfully blended with the
loveliest productions of nature. The various shrubs and
plants; the tender germs of Spring, the flowers of Summer,
and the fruitage of Autumn, expand their beauties and
breathe their fragrance amongst some of the choicest and
finest works of art. Busts and statues, of the purest marble
and the most exquisite workmanship—urns and vases, elegant in form and rich in ornament, are associated with a
variety of other tasteful and beautiful objects: nothing,

indeed, seems to have been omitted which could add to the
splendour of the scene. Glass globes, with gold and silver
fish in continual motion—magnificent gilt cages, with birds
of the finest song and the richest plumage, hung amongst
the leaves and branches of the choicest exotics, all combine
to produce and perfect one of the most brilliant pictures
ever realized within the narrow confines of an earthly abode.
The chief attraction, however, of this splendid place is the
exquisite sculpture with which it is enriched: these productions are a lasting and invaluable treasure, which neither
" the churlish chidings of the wintry wind," nor the hot
suns of summer can affect for ages. A bust of Napoleon,
and another of Cicero, both masterly works, are the first
objects that present themselves on the right and left of the
entrance from the Saloon. Near these, a statue of Ceres,
a beautiful copy of the celebrated Greek original in the
Vatican, occupies a pedestal on one hand; and a figure of
Winter, finely draped and exquisitely sculptured, is placed
on the other. These are succeeded by two other statues of
decided excellence: the first is a figure of Plenty; the next,
Minerva Medica; and, a little farther, are the Flora of the
Capitol, and Mnemosyne, the mother of the Muses. These
four statues are copies from the celebrated Greek originals,
now in Rome. Nearer the drawing room transcept, placed
amongst flowers and foliage, are isolated statues of the
Nine Muses, and a fine copy of Canova's Flora.

" On the left of the Conservatory is a court or garden,
well stored with hardy shrubs and flowers, that seem
scarcely divided from the more favoured tribe within. The
right looks, almost uninterruptedly, upon what may be
termed the *pet* garden of the establishment, which contains
the rarest and most beautiful flowers, so arranged as to produce a singularly beautiful effect. These two gardens, connected with the Conservatory, form one continued and
united picture—each is a portion of the same design.

" Both the entrance and the exit from this delightful
spot is through folding doors, which have the semblance

of Cathedral windows; the frame-work is ornamented in the gothic style, and the panels are stained glass.

"From the Conservatory we entered the Transcept Gallery, a noble apartment, spacious, lofty, light, and cheerful. The furniture is uncommonly splendid; the pictures numerous, and of the first class of art: the Vandykes are admirable. There are in this gallery twelve ivory chairs, elaborately carved: they were a present from Warren Hastings, Governor General of India, to the late Queen Charlotte.

"From this "splendid gallery" we passed through Lady Shrewsbury's Library into the Music Room, the first of the new suite of apartments that form the western wing of Alton Abbey. The Northern Library succeeds, and at the further extremity, a door on the right opens into the Square Tower Library, a small, but very elegant apartment: it is lighted by stained glass windows, and the sides and ceilings are richly embellished. The ceiling is divided into numerous compartments; the ground is a delicate pale blue, the rosettes and mouldings are of burnished gold, and the extremities of the border of each division are relieved by what painters call *pickings out*, in bright crimson. The effect is peculiarly beautiful. Immediately on the left of this room are the Western Library, the principal Staircase, and the State Bed Room, with Dressing Rooms annexed, one of which occupies a lower story of the Octagonal Tower, at the South-west extremity of the house. The style and finish of this fine suite of apartments are not exactly uniform; the details are tastefully varied, especially in the ceilings, but the same general character, both in colour and ornament, prevails throughout the whole; and all are novel in design, and chaste and beautiful in decoration. The walls are coated over with a composition, to imitate richly variegated wood; and being covered with French polish, the figure or flower appears vividly beneath the varnish. These rooms were not entirely finished at the

time we passed through them : they have since been most
magnificently furnished.

"From a digression to this new part of Alton Abbey,
we returned into the Transcept Gallery, and from thence
passed into the Drawing Room, a long and beautiful
apartment, which extends to the northern extremity of the
building, and is so connected with the Transcept as to
appear to be a part of it, although distinguished by
another name. It is furnished in the same superb style,
and contains many choice and valuable pictures. The
porcelain scent-jars and vases, which are placed in these
apartments, are magnificent specimens of this beautiful
ware. England, France, Saxony, and China, have all contributed to enrich this collection; but in drawing, pencil-
ling, and artist-like execution, France may justly claim
the pre-eminence. We particularly noticed, in this room, a
tea service from the celebrated manufactory of Sevres, of
rare and exquisite beauty. The designs with which the
different pieces are embellished are by some of the first
artists in France; the gold ornaments are of the most
brilliant polish, and the paintings, to which they form a
kind of frame, are wrought to the highest perfection of the
art. They include a series of portraits of some of the most
distinguished personages in the records of French history,
and are so elaborately and exquisitely finished as almost to
rival some of Bone's finest enamels. As specimens of
miniature painting they are decided gems. This last
apartment is lighted by large stained glass windows, in
one of which is a whole length figure of Edward the Black
Prince, in armour, painted in a very masterly style.

"We were next conducted along a corridor, gay with
brilliant lights from variously coloured glass, to the Old
Dining Room, and from thence, down a singularly elegant
flight of stairs, into the new one—a spacious and lofty
apartment, upwards of forty feet high, lighted by a grand
cathedral-like window, of fine proportions and beautiful
workmanship. This magnificent room contains some

good pictures, one of which is remarkable for its dimensions, being above twenty-three feet by fourteen, exclusive
of the frame. The subject is, the Coronation of Barbar-
ossa, by Rippenhausen. It is a splendid composition, and
well painted; the figures, both men and horses, are as
large as life. A very clever picture, by Davis, occupies the
opposite side of the room. It represents the Earl and the
Countess of Shrewsbury, with their daughters, Lady
Mary Talbot, and the Princess Sulmona, receiving the
Papal benediction. The ceremony took place at Rome, and
all the personages introduced into the picture were present.
On the right are the Pope, Gregory XVI., Cardinal Con-
salvo, Gibson, the sculptor, and Canova, in the princely
costume which he wore on State occasions. The left of
the picture is occupied by the Shrewsbury family. The
likenesses are all considered excellent. There are several
other pictures in this apartment, of considerable merit, particularly the portraits of the Earl and Countess of Shrewsbury, by an artist of the name of Flore.

"Reascending the stairs, we passed through another
corridor, to Lady Shrewsbury's *Boudoir*, which is by far
the pleasantest apartment in the whole establishment, and
commands an uninterrupted view of the most beautiful
scenery about the place. The lawn, the lake, the arcade
bridge, the gardens, the conservatories, the gothic temple,
and the abundant foliage around, are all included in the
prospect.

"From Lady Shrewsbury's room we proceeded to the
Chapel, a fine Abbey-like structure of magnificent dimensions, and surmounted by a lofty square tower. It is
ninety feet long, thirty wide, and fifty-six feet high; well
pewed with carved oak below, and has a very handsome
gallery. This capacious Chapel is chiefly lighted by a
large stained window at the east end, under which is the
altar, surmounted by a sculptured image of our Saviour on
the Cross, and surrounded with the usual accompaniments
of Catholic worship. The pictures are not numerous.

The largest and most important is a copy, but a masterly one, by Durantini, of Raffaelle's Transfiguration. St. Jerome receiving the Sacrament, also a copy by Durantini, and nearly the same size as the Transfiguration, occupies another part of the walls. Among other good pictures, of less note, are—Christ Healing the Blind, a production of the Bolognese school; Monks receiving a Mantle; the Head of a Female Saint, surrounded by a wreath; and two subjects, the Fathers of the Church, from Pietro Perugino.

" At the back of the gallery, fronting the altar, we noticed a very extraordinary achievement of the pencil. The subject represents the interior of a Church, with Monks at devotion. The only light in this picture is from a window at the farther end; the figures on which it falls are so strongly relieved, that they absolutely appear to stand out from the canvass, and the effect is complete deception. The original of this picture is by Granet.

" From the gallery of the Chapel, a narrow corridor leads to a long and lofty terrace, with embattled parapets, at the East end of the building, along which, at short intervals, there are gothic towers or keeps, with their portals guarded by figures of armed men in complete suits of mail. I know not whether it is the custom of the place to admit casual visitors to this terrace; but unless this be allowed, it is scarcely possible fully to appreciate the surpassing beauty of the gardens at Alton Abbey. The floral richness of the view from this elevation, combined with the splendid architectural objects scattered about the grounds, present altogether a scene of enchantment. The Swiss cottage, the residence of the minstrel of the mansion, embosomed in foliage, is the nearest prominent object; a deep valley, with a bright lake, from which rises a sparkling fountain, lies below. The other side of the valley, from the very margin of the water to the topmost boundary line of the gardens, is covered with flowers of every variety and every hue. Terraces, temples, grottos, arbours, urns, vases, columns, busts, and statues—splendid conservatories, and bright parterres, constitute altogether an assemblage of objects, as cheerful, as brilliant, and as gay, as ever the eye beheld."

Concluding his description, Mr. Rhodes remarks,—" In hastily passing through such a place as Alton Towers, though much is seen, little comparatively can be remembered. Many objects worthy of notice will escape observation altogether : and others, perhaps, which ought to have fixed attention and excited admiration, be only briefly glanced at, or superficially observed. There is no compressing a year into a day, nor can all that is deserving of notice at this magnificent place be either fully seen or adequately estimated in the short space of four or five hours. Alton Abbey is, indeed, altogether one of the most splendid and interesting places in the kingdom. All the most important improvements in this noble mansion have been made by the present Earl; and yet there is an unity of design in the interior arrangements that might induce the supposition that the whole had been erected at one period of time. The same prevailing idea is evident throughout the whole ; and to carry this similarity of style and unity of design into effect, other considerations may, perhaps, in some instances have been sacrificed. The principal rooms are long and lofty, like the aisles of a gothic edifice, and succeed each other in a straight line ; the doors by which they are separated have generally more the character of open screens than doors ; they form mere stages, or resting-places for the eye, without materially interrupting the view. From East to West, one continued vista of apartments extends in long perspective, to the distance of more than three hundred feet ; and another division of one hundred and sixty feet is now in progress. In the direction from South to North, the line of apartments extends upwards of two hundred and sixty feet, the whole width of the present structure. Of this latter range, the House Conservatory forms a part."

The catalogue of pictures is here subjoined :—

Portrait of a Lady	*Paul Moreelze*	The Annunciation	*Lanfrancs*
St. Mary of Egypt	*Venetian School*	Our Saviour in the House of the Pha-	
Madonna	*Pontormo*	risee	*Paul Veronese*
Still Life	*Peter Boel*	A Martyr	*J. C Procaccin*
Madonna	*Raffaellino del Garbo*	Portrait	*Garofalo*
Annunciation	*Tintoretto*	Adoration of the Magi	*ditto*
Portrait of Raffaelle	*Paris Bordone*	Christina of Sweden	*Malo*
Holy Family	*ditto*	Flowers	*Rachel Ruisch*
Portrait	*Elliger*	A Pope	*Unknown*
St. Peter	*Spagnoletto*	Frank Hals	*Himself*
Portrait	*Amberger*	Annunciation	*Paul Veronese*
St. Jerome	*Albert Durer*	Madonna	*Sasso Ferato*
Portrait	*Gennari*	Portrait	*School of Bologna*
View in Holland	*Berkheyden*	Portrait	*ditto*
Descent from the Cross	*Le Sueun*	Portrait	*Paris Bordone*
St. Sebastian	*Loir*	Angels appearing to Shepherds	
Madonna	*Penni*		*Tintoretto*
Portrait	*School of Bologna*	Moonlight	*Vanderneer*
Portrait	*ditto*	The Prodigal Son	*T. Rombauts*
Belisarius	*David*	Family Group	*Palamedes*
Holy Family	*A. Caracci, after Garofalo*	Interior of a Church	*Steinwyck*
Magdalen	*Carlo Dolci*	Rembrandt's Daughter	*Rembrandt*
St. Catharine	*ditto*	A Lady	*Cranach*
Madonna	*Fra Bartolomeo*	Peasants, &c.	*Zucharelli*
St. Jerome	*N. Loir*	Tancred and Erminia	*Tiarini*
Portrait	*Unknown*	Guercini	*Himself*
Ditto	*Tinelli*	Flowers	*Mignon*
Erminia	*Il Prete Genovese*	A Duke of Burgundy	*Govaert Flink*
Ecce Homo	*School of Carlo Dolci*	Pope Paul Third	*Titian*
Madonna	*Carlo Maratta*	Child and Dog	*Gaspar Netscher*
Adoration of the Magi	*Seb. Ricci*	Adoration of the Magi	*Girol, da Carpi*
Portrait	*Gherardo della Notte*	A White Deer	*Flemish School*
A Doge	*Tintoretto*	Still Life	*J. Weeninx, younger*
Birth and Death of Adonis	*Giorgione*	Prodigal Son	*Franks*
Historical Group	*ditto*	Spagnoletto	*Himself*
Ditto	*Unknown*	Holy Family	*Vandyck*
Prodigal Son	*Bonifaccio*	Landscape	*Ruysdael*
A Bambochade	*Seb. Bourdon*	Landscape, with Cattle	*A. Cuyp*
The Eternal Father	*Guercino*	Landscape, with Figures, &c.	*ditto*
St. Agnes	*ditto*	Ditto	*ditto*
View of Rome	*Van Lint*	Family Group	*Quellinus*
View of Rome	*ditto*	Landscape	*J. B. Weeninx, elder*
Landscape	*ditto*	Fruit and Flowers	*David de Heem*
St. John the Baptist	*ditto*	Portrait	*Domenichino*
Lot and his Daughters	*ditto*	Ecce Homo	*Gherard della Notte*
Ecce Homo	*ditto*	Portrait	*Paul Veronese*

Abraham entertaining the Angels *Vandyck*

Judith with the head of Holofernes *Cristofaro Alloni*

Interior of the Church 11 Redentore, Venice *J. P. Pannini*

Exterior of ditto *ditto*

Finished Sketch of one of the Angels for the Dome of the Cathedral at Parma *Correggio*

Family Portraits *John Mabuse*

Madonna and Infant *Pietro Perugino*

Madonna *Raffaelle*

Madonna *Ber Butinone*

Holy Family, &c. *Beccafumi*

Madonna, &c. *Dion Calvert*

Romulus and Remus *Vandyck*

Madonna *Donnenichini*

Cupid *Eliz. Sirani*

Engagement at Sea *Joseph Vernet*

St. Joseph and Infant *ditto*

Original Sketch of the Martyrdom of St. Cecilia *Domenichino*

Portrait *Gonsala Coques*

Holy Family *D. Puligo*

Martyrdom of St. Sebastian *Lanfranco*

A Page with the Head of St. John the Baptist *Guido*

St. Augustine *ditto*

Artemisia *ditto*

Magdalen *ditto*

Hagar in the Desert *ditto*

Ecce Homo *ditto*

Portrait *ditto*

Landscape and Cupids *ditto*

Jacob's Dream *Domenica Feti*

Holy Family *Agostino Carracci*

Portrait *Slingelandt*

Madonna *Murillo*

Last Supper *C. Coello*

Madonna and St. Francis *Alonzo Cano*

Columbus *Pandits*

Holy Family *Annibal Carracci*

Ditto *Giacomo Francia*

Portrait of Mengs *Himself*

Old Man spinning *Annibal Carracci*

Portrait *Mayno*

Pius V. *L. Bassano*

Portrait *Giorgione*

Portrait *ditto*

Entombment of our Saviour *Ludovico Carracci*

Martyrdom of St. Stephen *ditto*

Madonna *John Mabuse*

Holy Family *Lagrini*

Card Players *Moya*

Madonna and Infant *Murillo*

Spagnoletto looking in a glass *Himself*

Death of Mary Magdalen *Schidone*

Philip the Fourth of Spain *Velasquez*

Birth of St. Catharine of Sienna *Ludovico Carracci*

Animals and Fruit *Snyders & D. de Heem*

Portrait of a Boy *Pessey*

Christ at the Pillar *Divino Morales*

A Caravan *Castiglione*

A Fox seized by Dogs *Snyders*

Dogs fighting *ditto*

Tigers, &c. *ditto*

Lion Hunt *ditto*

Magdalen *Luca Cambiaso*

Holy Family *Angelo Bron. Allori*

Portrait *ditto*

Descent from the Cross *Unknown*

Tintoretto *Himself*

Madonna *Innocenza d'Imola*

Archimedes *Spagnoletto*

St. John the Baptist *Vicenza Catena*

Passage of the Red Rea *Pilidore da Caravaggio*

Adoration of the Shepherds *Giacomo Bassano*

St. Mark *Schidone*

St. Mark *Vicenza Catena*

Peter Martyr *Titian*

St. George and Dragon *Razzi*

Children and Fruit *Gobbodei Frutti*

Pope Paul the Fifth *Alex. Bron Allori*

Pope Pius the Fourth *Titian*

Poultry *Hondecooter*

Ditto *ditto*

David with the Head of Goliah	*Tobar*	Landscape	*Herrlein de Fulda*
Madonna, &c.	*Andrea del Sarto*	Sea Piece	*Von Antem*
Eliazar presenting Jewels to Rebecca	*Mocyart*	Ditto	*ditto*
		Five Senses	*Lubienetski*
Portrait	*Lucini*	Ditto	*Peter Breughel*
Martyrdom of St. Erasmus	*Gasper Crayer*	Plundering a Convent	*Schellinks*
		Flight into Egypt	*Snellinks*
Vandyck's Marriage	*Legers*	Holy Family reposing	*ditto*
A Fruit Woman	*Spanish School*	Pasticcio	*Teniers*
Holy Family and Saints	*Seb. Bourdon*	Battle Piece	*Flugtenburg*
Fall of Simon Magus	*Subleyras*	Ditto	*ditto*
Sketch for Portrait of Pope Julius II.	*Giulio Romano*	Hunting Piece	*Wouvermans*
		Hawking ditto	*ditto*
Holy Family	*Titian*	Aman disgraced by Assuerus	
Sixtus Fifth			*Gerard Lairesse*
Madonna and Saints	*Vandergoes*	The disobedient Prophet	*Breemburg*
Sketch	*Salvator Rosa*	Cattle	*Ommaganck*
Sea Port	*ditto*	Grotto	*Hoock*
Landscape and Figures	*ditto*	Landscape	*Herman Swanfeld*
St. Francis	*ditto*	The Prodigal Son	*Luke of Leyden*
Sea Port	*Beerestraten*	Dutch Boors	*Teniers, younger*
Dead Game	*Biltius*	A Garden	*Van Artois*
Ditto	*ditto*	Pastoral scene	*Gaubau*
Ballad Singers	*Molenser*	Interior of a Cabin	*Dusart*
Triumph of Love	*Rottenhammer*	Boy and Owl	*Mieris*
Olindo and Sophronia	*Houbraken*	Siege by Moonlight	*Thielle*
Interior of a Church	*Morgenstern*	Flowers	*Trechsler*
Portrait	*Denner*	Boy and Girl	*Hoet*
Ditto	*ditto*	Landscape	*Claude Lorraine*
Madonna and Saints	*Van Eyck*	Cattle	*Teniers, father*
Crucifixion and Twelve Apostles		Sunset	*Both*
	Goltius	Landscape	*ditto*
Interior of Church, with Figures		Burning of Troy	*Breuzel d' Enfer*
	Neefs and Franks	Cattle	*P. Potter*
Ditto ditto	*ditto ditto*	Landscape	*Berghem*
Ditto ditto	*school of Neefs*	Head of St. Sebastian	*Razzi*
Ditto ditto	*ditto*	Winter Scene	*Vollerht*
Solomon adoring an Idol		Portrait of a Boy	*Titian*
	Franks, younger	St. Teresa	*Murillo*
Tailor's Shop	*Slingelandt*	Landscape	*Lint, (" studio")*
Gaming	*Janstein*	Children Playing with Cards	*Coypel*
Ditto	*ditto*	Landscape	*Lint, (" studio")*
Animals	*Rondhara*	St. Catherine	*Goltsius*
Ditto	*ditto*	Religion trampling on a Dragon	
Ditto	*ditto*		*ditto*
Hawking	*Singelbach*	The Virgin	*ditto*

Landscape and Cattle	*Koninck*	Landscape and Figures	*Michau*
Landscape *	*Mile*	Ditto ditto	*ditto*
Dead Birds	*Hamilton*	View in Venice	*Canaletti*
Shells	*Kobell*	Ditto	*ditto*
Flowers, with Medallion	*Segers*	Interior of a Stable	*Wouvermans*
View of the Rhine	*Shultz*	Ditto	*Peter de Laar*
Dead Game	*Biltius*	Landscape and Cattle	*Ruysdael*
Ditto	*ditto*	Madonna	*Buroccis*
Moonlight	*Dorfmeister*	Sunset	*Hue*
Sea Port	*J. Vernet*	Landscape	*Domenichino*
Sea Coast in a Mist	*ditto*	Ditto	*Swanfeld*
Sea Storm	*ditto*	Ditto	*Peter Breughel, father*
Landscape	*ditto*	Ecce Homo	*A. Durer*
Ditto	*ditto*	Portrait	*Ferburg*
Landscape and Figures		St. Jerome	*Schalcken*
	Glauber and Lairesse	Portrait of one of the Medici Family
Ruins	*P. Brill*		*Allori*
Landscape	*Brinkmann*	Circumcision	*J. Bellini*
The Angel releasing Peter	*Pereda*	Cattle	*P. Potter*
Sea Piece	*J. Vandervelde*	Children of Charles the First
Ferry over the Rhine	*Van Goyen*		*Vandyek*

*The pictures in the Transcept Gallery, the Dining Room, and the Chapel, and a number of others, are not included in this catalogue.

West of the Abbey, is a lofty prospect tower, of massive proportions, formerly the receptacle of a museum of rarities, comprehending ancient armoury, coins, minerals, and curious natural productions of almost every nation. This tower, now dismantled of its contents, was an object of great attraction to visiters.

The manor of ALTON, written anciently *Alveton*, (the *Elveton* of Domesday,) was a demesne of the crown in the time of the Conqueror. In the reign of Henry II. it came into the possession of the Norman family of Verdon, by the marriage of Bertram de Verdon, (whose first wife, Maud, daughter of Robert de Ferrers, Earl of Derby, died,) with Rohais or Rosia, to whom, as heiress of a former possessor, it appears to have descended. Bertram de Verdon was the founder of Croxden Abbey. He resided at the Castle of Alveton, originally a place of great strength and extent, the ruins of which are yet standing on the summit of a

bold and lofty rock, on the banks of the Churnet, overlooking the village and vale.   He served in the wars of the
Crusades, and, dying at Joppa, in 4 Richard I. 1192, was
buried at Acre.   His son, Thomas de Verdon, married
Eustachia, daughter of Gilbert Bassett, and died in Ireland (without issue) in the year 1199.   The manor and
castle of Alveton descended to Nicholas, his brother, and
from him to his only daughter and sole heir, Rosia, who
retained the name of De Verdon, and was the founder of the
Cistercian Abbey of Grace Dieu, Leicestershire. She married Theobald de Buttiler, of the noble Irish family of Buttiler, and died in 1347. Theobald de Verdon was Constable
of Ireland ; he died without issue at Alveton Castle in 1309,
and was buried at Croxden Abbey. A Theobald de Verdon,
who also died at Alveton, (10 Edward II.) was Lieutenant
of Ireland. His daughter and heiress, Joan, who married
Thomas Lord Furnival, inherited the castle of Alveton,
with its members, Wootton, Stanton, Farley, Ramsor, Cotton, Bradley, Spon, Denston, Stramshall, and Whiston. She
died in 8 Edward III. and was buried before the high
altar at Croxden.   Alveton afterwards passed to Thomas
Neville, who married Joan, the daughter and heiress, (it is
supposed,) of William, Lord Furnival.   The famous Lord
John Talbot, Earl of Shrewsbury, married Maud, eldest
daughter and coheir of Thomas Neville. To her descended
the manor and castle of Alveton, and their dependencies,
with all Verdon's and Furnival's lands in other counties.*
Alveton has ever since formed part of the inheritance of the
noble house of Talbot.

John Talbot, surnamed for his bravery, " the English
Achilles," was the second son of Richard, Lord Talbot, of
Blechmere, in Shropshire.   He served in France in the
reign of Henry V. and distinguished himself at the sieges
of Caen, Rouen, Mans, and Pontoroso.   At the ever me-

---

* From a M.S. Pedigree of the Verdons, in the possession of the Rev. J. P.
Jones, Vicar of Alton.

morable siege of Orleans, Talbot displayed such resistless
valour, that his courage became proverbial even with the
enemy.   On the surrender of the Earl of Suffolk, he was
invested with the command of the English forces.   Being
closely pressed by the enemy, on his march to Paris, he
was advised to make an expeditious retreat; but he refused
to show his back to his foes, and was in consequence taken
prisoner after a sharp conflict, with the loss of twelve hundred men.   After a captivity of three years and a half, he
was exchanged for a French officer of great reputation.
He now again hastened to the field, and exerted his accustomed skill and bravery in the taking of several fortified
places.   The capture of Pontoise was effected by him in a
singular manner.   In the beginning of 1437, the weather
was so extremely cold that the generals on both sides suspended military operations.   But Talbot having collected
a body of troops, and caused them to put white clothes or
shirts over their uniforms, in order that they might not
easily be distinguished from the snow with which the
ground was then covered, brought them by a night march
up to the walls of Pontoise, and making an unexpected
attack upon the garrison, made himself master of that important place.   For this and other important services during the campaign, he was advanced to the dignity of Earl
of Shrewsbury, in May, 1442.   He was afterwards appointed to the command in Ireland, with the title of Earl
of Wexford.   But his presence was soon found indispensable for carrying on the war in France.   His promptitude
and valour protracted the fall of Rouen a brief space.   Perceiving that the French had gained a rampart which had
been entrusted to the charge of the citizens, he rushed to
the spot, precipitated himself upon the assailants, hurling
the foremost of them into the ditch beneath, and having
repelled the enemy, put the treacherous sentinels to the
sword.   In 1452, the veteran warrior, now in his eightieth
year, again took the field, performing his usual wonders.
Landing with four thousand men, and supported by the

36

good-will of the Gascons, he advanced upon Bourdeaux, whereupon the French garrison, frightened, as Fuller quaintly observes, by the bare fame of his approach, fled from the spot. Chatillon having surrendered soon afterwards to his arms, Charles despatched a formidable force to recover it, and Talbot hastened to sustain his capture. By the celerity of his movements, he surprised and cut to pieces a French detachment; but on approaching the body of the enemy, he found it advantageously posted and well prepared to sustain his attack, being strongly entrenched, and provided with a field of artillery. Undismayed, however, by the fearful odds, and flushed by his recent success, the veteran hazarded an assault, and was so gallantly supported by his men, that for a time the balance of victory hung in suspense. But a shot having struck down their general, and fresh troops coming up at the critical moment, the English gave way and retreated on all sides. Talbot was first buried at Rouen, but his body was afterwards removed to Whitchurch, in Shropshire.*

Charles Talbot, twelfth Earl Shrewsbury, (created also Marquis of Alton and Duke of Shrewsbury) filled several important offices of state under James II., William and Mary, and Queen Anne.

Alveton Castle was garrisoned during the civil wars, with a force of about forty or fifty men. In February, 1645, a Mr. Thomas Salt was Governor, apparently for the Parliamentarians; and a tradition is current in the village, that the castle was destroyed by the firing of their artillery from the opposite hills.

The parish-church, near the castle, is a plain structure, with a square tower. Those portions of the original fabric that remain, are in the later Norman style. It was repewed in 1831, and is now in excellent repair. The living is a vicarage, in the gift of Earl Shrewsbury; the Rev. J. P. Jones is the present incumbent.

---

* Cunningham's Lives of Eminent and Illustrious Englishmen.

The parish is a large one, containing about 8,000 acres, and extending nearly ten miles from north-east to south-west. The manor is co-extensive with the parish. The Earl of Shrewsbury holds a court-leet annually in the moot-hall.

In the population returns, Cotton, Denston, and Farley, are included with Alveton; the number of inhabitants is stated to be 2,391, and the annual value of the real property is assessed at £8,726.

The ancient custom of presenting garlands of flowers to newly-married couples on leaving the church, is prevalent among the villagers of Alton.

CHAPTER XIV.

The Ancient Abbey of Croxden—Its Foundation and Endowments—Extracts from the Charter and Chronicle.—Barrow Hill.—Rocester—Ancient Abbey —Extracts from the Charter, &c.—The Church and Village.

THE ruins of the once extensive Abbey of Croxden are situated in a narrow valley watered by a small rivulet, in the hamlet of Croxden, about two miles south of Alton, and seven miles south-west of Ashbourn. In the year 1176, Bertram de Verdun gave to the Cistercian monks of Aulney, in Normandy, a piece of ground at Chotes whereon to build an Abbey of that order, which was in three years removed to Crokesden or Croxden. Chotes or Chotene, Bishop Tanner supposes to have been Cotton or Cawton, a member of the lordship of Alveton, the seat of the Verdons. From De Verdun's charter,* a translation of which is annexed, it appears that the monastery was dedicated to the Blessed Virgin, and styled, 'Abbatia de Valli Beatæ Mariæ de Croxden':—†

---

*The original (Latin) in "Dugdale's Monasticon Anglicanum".

†The circumstances of its foundation are curiously set forth in the following ancient rhymes :—

"Bertram son of the noble Norman Verdon
Founded the famous Abbey of Croxden
When Henry the Second was England's King
He did perform this very great thing

"Bertram de Verdun to all his men and friends, clerks or laics, present and future, greeting. Know ye that I have given and consigned, and by this my present charter confirmed to God, and St. Mary, and to the Abbey of the Valley of St. Mary at Crokesden, which I have founded, and to the Monks there serving God, in pure and perpetual alms, for the souls of Norman de Verdun my father, and Lucelina my mother, and of Richard de Humez who educated me, and of my predecessors; and for my own salvation, and that of Rochais my wife, and of my successors, all my land of Crokesden, with all its appurtenances, to found an Abbey there, with the exception of the out-assarts which my men [tenants] of Uldehure have made; and except that the monks of the aforesaid Abbey shall take no multure from my men for grinding at their mill of Crokesden; and except that I have retained for myself and my heirs the right to have as many fisheries and preserves as we think proper, in the rivulet that divides the land of Crokesden and the land of Bretlee; and also the right of taking earth or ground to make causeways from any part of the Abbey land near those causeways.

"This my land of Crokesden, and whatever I have in the same village, and all the fee of Alveton, and the fee of Madelie, and the fee of Crakemerse, I have given to the monks of the aforesaid Abbey, in alms, on the condition that the Abbey shall remain in the same village of Crokesden, founded in the territory of my patrimony. Besides I have given to the same Abbey all my land of Moseden, with all its appurtenances; and all my land of Aka, with

---

In the year one thousand one hundred and seventy-six
Upon this great work his mind he did fix
He dedicated it unto St. Mary
Of the order of Bernardine monks to be
One hundred pounds six shillings and seven pence
In lands he gave for its defence
Besides many other great gifts given
By persons devout for to gain heaven."

the wood or grove belonging to it, and all its other appurtenances; and my salt-work at Middilwich; and all the
service that Achard de Stanfort and his heirs owe to me for
the tenement which he holds of me in the village of Stanfort, and in the village of Castretone; and my mill of
Stanfort, which is between the bridge and the castle, with
all its appurtenances; and all the land which I have in the
same village of Stanfort; and the service of Ralph de Nor-
manvile and his heirs for the land which he holds of me in
the village of Burtone: viz. seven shillings a year, half to
be paid at Easter, and half to be paid at Michaelmas; and
all my demesne of Tokebi, in the village and without the
village, wood and plain, meadows and pastures, waters and
ways, and foot-paths, and the whole of the herbage belonging to the demesne; except that I have retained for me
and my heirs all the villanage, and all the farms of the village, and all the customs and services which the men of that
village have been used to do for me, and the rights which
those men have in the woods of that village, and all the aisia-
ments and common lands which I have been accustomed
to have in it. I have also given to the monks of the aforesaid Abbey the half of my grove of Greth, nearest to the
Abbey, with all its appurtenances; except that I have
reserved for myself and my heirs the site of the preserve
which is between Greth and Bretlee, and as much ground
as that preserve with all its appendages may require; and
I retain the right for me and my heirs to raise the causeway
of that preserve, as we may think proper. The monks,
however, shall not inclose the moiety of the grove of
Greth, on account of the common of pasture which my men
of Bretlee and of Alveton ought to have in that grove of
Greth. Besides I have given to those monks the moiety of
my grove of Crakemerse, nearest to the Abbey, with all its
appurtenances; and one carucate of land in the village of
Herteshorne, with all its appurtenances, which is called
Lees; and the church of Alveton, with all its appurtenances; and the church of Tokebi, with all its appurtenances.

" Wherefore, I will and firmly ordain, that the aforesaid Abbey and the monks in it serving God, have and hold all these my donations and alms, well and peaceably, freely and quietly, in integrity, abundantly and honourably, in wood and in plain, in meadows and pastures, and commons, in high-ways and by-ways, in passages and waters, within village and without village, and in all things, and places and liberties to them pertaining,—free, discharged, and quiet, from every service and custom, and secular exaction, to me and my heirs pertaining: and I prohibit on the part of God, and on my own part, any of my heirs from presuming to contravene or otherwise disturb this my donation." Witnesses, Robert, Prior of Kenilworth, Robert de Verdun, W. de Canville, &c.

The charter of Henry II. confirms the above-mentioned donations of Bertram de Verdun; also a grant of forty acres of land in Troseli, by Robert de Beausay.

The following are Extracts from the Chronicle of Croxden, by William de Shepsheved, one of the monks of that monastery:— *

A.D. 1176. Bertram de Verdun, by the grace 'of God, for the welfare of his soul, in redemption of all his sins, gave to the Monks of Alney the land of Chotes, to found an Abbey in the Vale of St. Mary; but he, who agreeably [sweetly] disposes all things, pre-ordained that they should elsewhere praise the name of the Lord.

1178. Thomas, the first Abbot of this monastery, by nation an Englishman, while yet a Deacon, on the day of Pentecost, about the third hour, as a pure receptacle of the Holy Spirit, was chosen Abbot. And for fifty-one years and a half he is supposed to have sustained many labours [laboured much] in the house of the Lord. And besides many works of building, he wrote with his own hand, as a perpetual memorial of his name, two excellent volumes,

---

*Dugdale's Monasticon. Cotton MS. British Museum.

forming a commentary on the greater part of the Bible.

1179. The convent removed from Chotene to Croxden.

1181. Dedication of the place of Croxden.

1192. Bertram de Verdun of pious memory, the founder of the monastery, died, and was buried at Acre in Palestine, on St. Bartholomew's Day.

1199. Thomas de Verdun died in Ireland, and his brother Nicholas succeeded him as heir.

1210. King John extorted presents, at his pleasure, from all his subjects, both clerics and seculars, except from certain poor monasteries. He despoiled the Cistercian monks.

1229. Thomas the first Abbot of this monastery rested in the Lord on the 2nd nones of December, and he was interred in the chapter-house, where he lies between two other Abbots, Walter de Shalcumbe, and John de Billesdon.

1230. Walter de Chaucumbe or Shalcumbe chosen Abbot of this house.

1237. William de Esseburne, the third Abbot of this house, on the 10th of the kalends of October died here, and was interred abroad. And to him succeeded John de Tilton, who resigned his office in 1242.

1242. Walter London, Prior of ——, by divine permission was chosen Abbot of this house, and on Sunday after the Ascension Day he assumed the government. To him we owe the special blessing of God on this place, for on his coming he wonderfully improved the Convent of Croxden; many very fair houses there, namely, the middle gates of the Monastery, the Church, the Chapter-house, and Refectory, the Kitchen, the Dormitory, the Infirmary, the Cloister, and the Muniment-house, and various other houses, [buildings] in his time he artificially erected; and for his successors and the rest of the officials of the Convent, he laudably prepared. Also in his last days he encircled half the cemetery of the Abbey with a stone wall, the remainder of which Henry de Measham, the seventh Abbot sufficiently completed.

1248. Lády Roysia de Verdun, foundress of the Abbey of Croxden, died on the 4th ides of February; and was succeeded by her son, Lord John de Verdun.

1267. Humfrey de Verdun born, on the eve of Pentecost.

1268. Walter London, fifth Abbot of this house, in whose days the Abbey was fully perfected, departed this life.

William de Howton was the next Abbot, who, among the memorable things he performed, finely built an upper and lower chamber, for the cutting and laying the polished stones for which he gave £100 sterling; and he purchased of Master Solomon, Archdeacon of Leicester, the whole Bible, with glossarial notes, in nine volumes, for fifty marks sterling.

1274. W. de Howton, sixth Abbot of this Monastery, went the way of all flesh, on the 16th of the kalends of October, at Dijon, in France, and was interred at Cisteaux, and at his exequies and funeral more than four hundred Abbots were present. He was succeeded in the government of the Abbey, on the day of St. Lucia next ensuing, by Henry de Meysham, who presided over this house ten years.

1284. Henry de Meysham, the seventh Abbot of this house, gave up the office on account of weakness, on St. Barnabas-day; when John de Billesdon was elected Abbot.

1293. John de Billesdon, Abbot of this Monastery, died on the eighth ides of July. The office remained vacant nearly a year, after which Richard de Twyford was chosen Abbot.

1297. Richard de Twyford, of pious memory, Abbot of this house, died on the day of the Holy Trinity; and the office was vacant six months.

William de Evera was elected Abbot on the 3rd of the kalends of January.

1308. William de Evera died, and was succeeded by Richard de Esseby, as Abbot of the house.

1309. Theobald de Verdun, patron of this Abbey died; and was buried at Crokesden, on the 3rd ides of October.

1313. R. de Esseby, Abbot of this house, resigned his office; and Thomas de Casterton, Prior of the Monastery, was chosen in his place.

1320. R. de Esseby was again made Abbot of this house, on St. Barnabas-day.

1329. Richard de Esseby, the eleventh Abbot of this Monastery, freely resigned his office on account of weakness. On the morrow Richard Schepesheved was raised to the honour, in his room.

1335. Richard de Schepesheved, the thirteenth Abbot of Crokysden, began to construct a new chamber for himself between the Kitchen, the Infirmary, and the Dormitory; and the next year, at great cost, he completed it.

Among the subsequent Abbots of Croxden, whose names are recorded, are Alexander de Cowley, Philip Ludlow, John Bromefield, Ralph Layland, Stephen Cadde, William Gunslow, Roger Prestone, William Burton, John de Chekewalton, John Shipton, and lastly, Thomas Chawner, who was Abbot at the Dissolution. Tanner says that besides the Abbot, the foundation consisted of twelve Monks.*

Of the seal attached to the surrender, being the Common Seal of the Abbey, there is a neat impression on red wax remaining in the Augmentation Office. The subject is the Blessed Virgin and her Infant; she is seated under an or-

---

*The temporalities of the Abbey were thus recorded in the taxation of 1291: *Dioces. Lincoln.* In Huntingdon, 8s.; in Decanat. Roteland, £6 9s. 6d.; in Decanat. Staunford, Goscote, Gudlakton, et Roteland, £46 13s. 4d. *Dioces. Coventr. et Lichf.* In archdiac Stafford, £36 19s.; in Decanat de Ripendon, £20; apud Hertescot. in Decanat. de Scarvesdale, 18s.

In the 26th of Henry VIII. the yearly revenues amounted in the gross to £103 6s. 7d.: in the clear income to £90 5s. 11d. They were derived chiefly from the tithes of grain and hay of the churches of Alveton, (co. Stafford) and Tokebi, (co. Leicester); from lands in Alveton, Chetill, Leke, Uttoxeter, Okyer, Glaston, Musden Grange, Calton, Onecote, and other places in the county of Stafford; Assheburn, Longford, &c. in the county of Derby; and from property in London, Chester, and the counties of Leicester and Northampton.

namented canopy, having on her right side a shield with
the arms of Bertram de Verdun, the founder; *Or, fretty
gules.* Within an arch underneath the Virgin, is an Abbot
standing with his crosier. Legend: s. ABBATIS. ET. CON-
VENTVS. ECCLIE. BEATE. MARIE. DE. CROKESDEN.

The site of the Abbey was granted in the 36th of Henry
VIII. to Geoffery Foljambe, of Walton, in Derbyshire.

The west end of the church, the south wall of the transept, part of the cloister, the outer walls of the chapter-
house, and some parts of the offices may still be traced.
The style of architecture corresponding with the date of the
foundation, the windows being lancet-shaped, and the
capitals of the columns foliated.

The parish church or chapel of Croxden is a small
building, of a date coeval with the Abbey.

Stow, in his annals, has recorded an anecdote relating to
Croxden Abbey, in the time of Edward III. Under the
year 1331, he says, " Such a wet summer, with exceeding
rain, was this year, that the corne in the field could not
ripe, so that in many places they began not harvest till
Michaelmas. The House of Croxton got not in their wheat
till Hallontide, and their pease not before St. Andrew's-
tide. The Monks, on Allhallown-day and Martlemas,
were served with pease green in the cods, instead of peares
and apples."*

King John was a benefactor to the Abbey of Croxden in
lands to the amount of £10 a year. The historical reader
will recollect, that when this monarch's opposing barons, as
a last and desperate effort for the preservation of their rights
and liberties, had invited over as their sovereign, Louis,
the eldest son of Philip of France, John assembled a powerful army to resist this intended usurpation of his throne;
and that on the passage of his forces across the Wash, on
the eastern coast, the returning tide overwhelmed and
swept away the whole of his baggage, carriages, and trea-

*Monasticon Anglicanum.

sure. In an agony of disappointment John retired to the Cistercian Abbey of Swineshead, where he took up his abode for the night. Here he was seized with a violent fever, the effect, perhaps, of gluttony and excess on a frame already inflamed and enervated, though the common belief was, that he received poison at the hands of a monk. He was conveyed the next day to the castle of Sleaford, and thence to that of Newark-upon-Trent. The Abbot of Croxden, who appears to have united in himself the functions of both physician and divine, was summoned to administer to the declining monarch. He, it is said, arrived in time to witness John's repentance, but his medical skill availed nothing, for on the 18th of October, 1216, the tyrant-king expired. His last words were, "I commit my soul to God, and my body to St. Wulstan. His heart was buried at Croxden, and his body in the Cathedral of Worcester, of which St. Wulstan was the patron saint.

In connexion with the foregoing notice of the ancient religious house of Croxden, we subjoin some particulars, from the best authorities, relative to monastic manners, customs, and discipline.

Monastic institutions, it is well known, were originally designed as retreats for those who, being devoutly inclined, wished to retire from the cares, troubles, and anxieties of the world. They were founded chiefly by the gifts and bequests of wealthy individuals, who believed, (as their charters of endowment seem to imply,) that by such an appropriation of their substance, they would secure to themselves, their friends, and sometimes their ancestors and successors, an immunity from punishment in a future state. At an early period in the history of this country, when the Roman Catholic religion was in its supremacy, we find the monastic houses numerous, wealthy, and powerful, and exercising no inconsiderable share of influence over the character and destinies of the nation. In the midst of much debasing ignorance, and consequent vice—perhaps the inevitable result of a system, which locked up the affections of its followers, entailing upon them seclusion from the world, a painfully rigid discipline, and a perpetual round of superstitious ceremonies—the monks attained to no ordinary proficiency in the chief arts that minister to the luxuries and necessities of life. As conservators of those arts, and to some extent of the literature of our country, in periods when her prosperity and improvement were threatened or disturbed by internal broil or foreign contention, they have obvious claims to our notice. To the monks we are indebted for the compilation and preservation of several valuable historical records. They were the registrars of public events, and it was their duty to record the succession of the king, and the births of the royal family. The writing of books was a monastic employment in the very earliest eras. The Anglo-Saxon monks were eminently skilful in the execution of their books, and the character they used gave rise to the beautiful modern small Roman. letter. A class of monks termed *Antiquarii*, were principally employed in transcribing the fathers and classics, either for the use of the monasteries, for their own emolument, or for presents. The illuminations of their beautifully-written missals, and other books of devotion, are splendid specimens of their skill in colouring and blazonry, though at the same time they bespeak an ignorance of the first principles of drawing. The binding of their most valuable books (also the work of their own hands,) often in wrought velvet, with gold and silver ornaments, was exceedingly sumptuous; but the most common binding was a rough white sheep-skin, pasted on a wooden board, sometimes with immense clasps and bosses of brass; and occasionally the covers were of plain wood, carved in scroll and similar work. The study of architecture, however, was the pursuit of all others, that produced the most splendid results. In the numerous remains of the ancient abbatial structures, in our cathedrals and parish-churches, we have palpable evidence of a purity of taste, a loftiness of conception, and a magnificence of design, which could only follow from a knowledge the most profound of the intricacies, harmonies, and sublimities of the art. If, on a survey of one of those ancient temples, the pride and boast of our land, we take into reflection, what varied acquirements were necessary (not in the mechanical arts merely) to plan and to mature them, we shall at least confess, that the accusation of unbounded ignorance and indolence preferred against their founders, cannot, in justice, be sustained. The monks probably cultivated a taste for the study of the arts before that of letters, for their original works in the latter department are few and unimportant. To their various employments they added the important one of educating youth. In accordance with the prevalent superstition of the age, their pupils, the novices, were first instructed in the rule and observances of their respective orders; and were required to commit to memory the entire psalter. A knowledge of the Latin language was indispensable, as was also French, which had been introduced at the Norman Conquest. They were, besides, as the monastic discipline relaxed, allowed to join in hunting, and other popular pastimes of the day, which were deemed conducive to health.

In this brief sketch of the avocations and attainments of the monks, we have examined, for the most part, the bright side of the picture. "Monachism" says the learned Fosbrooke, "was an institution founded upon the first principles of religious virtue, wrongly understood and wrongly directed. Superstition has its basis in the will, and therefore monachism never succeeded but when it was an act of volition. As soon as its duties became mechanical operations, the work was performed, and the principle disregarded, while the heart left open to the world, was constantly prompting those aberrations which naturally result from the opposition of sentiment to duty. Shame is of no avail, where security is to be gained from coparceny, evasion, or secresy. Hence the vices of the monks: gluttony, their grand crime, is the natural pleasure of those who are debarred from other enjoyments, whether by physical or moral causes. Who does not know the noble institution of monks? says an old poet; the fame of them has pervaded the whole world; they consume all things, and yet they are not satisfied with the birds of heaven, and the fishes of the sea; they seek many dishes, and a long time in eating them; another adds, 'Feed them but well, they care for nothing else.' Nigel de Wireker charges them with hiding many things, and pocketing provisions to eat on fast-days; and one of their own body says, 'All fowlowe our own sensyalitie and pleser, and thys religyon, as I suppose, ys alle in vayne glory.' Avarice, accompanied with villainy, sometimes characterized them. A certain knight had left 100 marks by will to a certain house, and lay there sick; upon getting well, the monks, that they might not lose the money, plotted his death by poison or suffocation. Barclay reproaches their avarice for begging alms over the country, though wealthy; and Nigel Wireker says of the Cistercians, who are elsewhere censured for singularity, avarice, and little communication with the world, that "they wished their neighbours to have landmarks, and none themselves.' Nor from this avarice can it excite wonder, that, as says an antient poet, 'they neither loved, nor were beloved by any one.' They were detractors, disobedient, proud, dissatisfied, rebellious, and otherwise criminal. Alas! says Alfred of Rievesby, I am ashamed to say how they get together, and abound in detractions and contentions. For, to be silent of lovers of the world, whose whole discourse is of gain or baseness; what shall I say of them, who, having professed to renounce the world, only dispute and converse of the belly, I will not say the delight of it, but burden.' When they were at leisure they were always revolving temporal matters. 'Sometimes,' says an ancient sermon, addressed to them, 'when a monk goes out under pretence of serving the convent, he becomes an importunate suitor to great persons, calling profit, however made, piety; and, when

he returns, he carefully enquires the hour of the day, lest
he should be obliged to go to the common table and
church; and though he professes to do all this from public
good, the true cause is, he does not like the half boiled ve-
getables of the convent, and wine mixed with water, and
thinks silence and sitting in the cloister a prison.   He
wants to eat better, drink more savorily, speak more freely,
lye more softly, watch more seldom, pray less.'   They were
ambitious and intriguing.   ' An ass is introduced into the
church,' says Nigell Wireker, ' a silly animal, that wishes
to have a different and larger tail than nature has given
him.   Thus a religious not content with his condition, no
more than the ass with his tail, scorns the claustral life, in
which he ought to continue to the end, seeking by every
method to be plucked away and transplanted from it; that
he may be able to increase himself with a new and long
tail, lay hold of a priory or abbacy, and insert nearer him a
long suite of relatives; who, afterwards, wherever he goes,
may rejoice in dragging his tail for him.'   They were fond
of law.   Peter of Blois says, "There is not a seat of justice
in which religious men have not a concern, and eagerly obtrude themselves; for deceiving the world with a specious
appearance of religion, they are wretchedly deceived; and
while dead to the world, barter for and hunt after what belongs to it.'   It seems they were in the habit of attending
to law concerns for parents and friends, and being bail for
seculars.   Their neighbourhood was dreaded much on account of this litigious spirit, since they took the property of
others away.   Pawning was not an uncommon thing among
them.   From the levity of indolence they indulged themselves in writing lampoons, or hunting after news; and, to
conclude this catalogue of vices, that they might go on with
impunity, persecuted those who led better lives than themselves."*

---

*British Monachism; or, Manners and Customs of the Monks and Nuns
of England.   By Thomas Dudley Fosbrooke, M.A., F.A.S.

"The duties of Monks were these. 'To pray, groan and weep for their faults; to subdue their flesh; to watch and abstain from pleasures; to bridle their tongues, and shut their ears from vanities; to guard their eyes, and keep their feet from wandering; to labour with their hands, exult with their lips, and rejoice at heart in the praises of God; to bare the head, bow down, and bend the knees at the feet of the crucifix; to obey readily, never to contradict their superiors; to serve willingly, and assist speedily, the sick brethren; to throw off cares of the world, and attend to celestial concerns with their utmost endeavours; not to be overcome by the arts of Satan, and to do everything with prudence.' To *monastic perfection* it seems eight things were requisite; keeping the cloister, silence, no property, obedience, no detraction or murmuring, mutual love, performance of the appointed duties, and confession. Besides, the monks were to be imitators of Christ, love an abject and lowly habit, be cloathed in vile garments, walk simply in discipline, upon rising to mattins meditate upon their actions; to bear patiently the injuries of others; to him that struck upon one cheek, to turn the other, so that such a change of character would be produced, 'that they who were prone to quarrels, and passionate, would now bravely endure the curses of others; nor be broken by contempt or injury, but bear all things with a resolute heart, and preserve their peace of mind and rest amidst reproaches;' to converse of and meditate the last judgment, wait for the Lord, and dread the anger of the judge; never to laugh, because being charged with the sins of the people as their own, constant lamentation was their duty; to have no private friendships, because prejudicing the concord of the community, by generating parties, and causing detraction; to be silent and solitary, because dead to the world; to use private prayer, when under a vitious impulse, and, because such prayer reminded them of their crimes, and made them think themselves more guilty; to have respect for their habit in act, speech, and thought: not to be querulous,

angry, slanderous; not to regard rashly the lives of their
superiors, nor to become rebellious, by beholding their
faults; and to walk with their heads down, a custom borrowed from the Pharisees."*

The Dove, whose course we have previously followed as
far as the village of Ellastone, rolls on to Rocester, without
presenting in its vicinity any object particularly worthy of
notice, if we except—

Dove-Leys, a pleasant mansion, seated on the right or
Staffordshire side of the river, and formerly the residence
of Colonel Riddlesden, now of Benjamin Heywood, Esq.;
and, half a mile lower down,

Barrow-Hill, the seat of Mrs. Whyte, occupying an
eminence on the same side the river. In this mansion
there are some valuable pictures. Among those most
worthy of observation, is a subject by *Raffaelle*, (from
the Orleans Gallery)—The Dead Body of the Saviour
reposing on the Virgin's lap. Also a very beautiful landscape, in the tints of evening, by *Van der Neer*.

Rocester, anciently *Rocetter* or *Roucestre*, is a considerable manufacturing village, situated about seven miles
and a half distant from Ashbourn, and four miles from
Uttoxeter. In the reign of the Conqueror (says Erdeswicke)
Hervey held it of Robert de Stafford. "And some of the
Staffords of Sandon, either founded there (as I take it) the
Priory, or were thereunto great benefactors. For in that
part of the Church which yet standeth for the parish
church, there are monuments yet remaining of them, and
very few of any others. The sight [site] of the House with
the demeans being both pleasant and very profitable, for
that it stands between Dove and Churnet, a good pretty
water. Where it enters into Dove, is now the seat of
Francis the son of Thomas Trentham, which Thomas his
father, being in Henry the Eighth's time a favourite, ob-

*Fosbrooke's British Monachism.

tained it of the King. The Trenthams derive themselves from a house of the Trenthams in Shropshire, which in Henry the Sixth's time were of good account, but now quite decayed or gone, for I know none of the house remaining, this of Rowcester excepted, which it pleaseth God to advance in good sort."

The monuments of the Stafford family, mentioned by Erdeswicke, as well as the ancient parish-church, have disappeared. The present structure is of modern erection, and the only traces of antiquity are a few fragments of stained glass in the south windows.

It is rather singular, that the name of Stafford does not once occur in the notice of Rocester Abbey given in "Dugdale's Monasticon Anglicanum." The charters inserted in that work, translations of some of which are annexed, show that the Abbey was founded by Richard Bacon, for Black Canons, (Canons of the order of St. Augustine); and the date of its foundation is fixed by Bishop Tanner, in the year 1146:—

Charter of Richard Bacun, concerning the Foundation and Endowment of the Priory.—" To Will. by the grace of God, Archbishop of York, R. Bishop of Chester, R. Earl of Chester, and to all the faithful of the Holy Church of God, as well laics as clerks, Richard Bacun wisheth health in the Lord. Know all ye, that for the salvation of my soul, and also for the salvation of my uncle Ranulf Earl of Chester, and of my predecessors and successors, I have given and granted, and by this my present charter confirmed to God and the church of the Blessed Mary, and to the Canons Regular of Roucestre of the order of St Augustine, all the village of Roucestre, and of Combrigge, with all my villanes [villagers] and their families, and all their chattels; with all my demesnes in Roucestre, Combrigg, and Wotton, with all appurtenances and liberties in Northulle, Denstone, Quickesulle, Rosintone; and together with an oxgang of land in Bredley, with its appurtenances; and with four oxgangs of land in Waterfall, with the appurtenances; together with the advowson of the church of

St. Michael in Roucestre, and the dependent chapels of
Bredley and Waterfal: and with all and all kinds of their
appurtenances, in Roucestre, Combrigge, Northulle, Wotton, Denston, Quickisull, Rossington, Bredley, Waterfall,
Calton; together with eight carucates and two oxgangs of
land, and the third part of two mills in Bruggeford, with all
their appurtenances—to have and to hold, for themselves
and their successors, in free, pure, and perpetual alms, for
ever, as well and freely as any alms whatever can be given
or granted.   I also give and grant to the said Canons and
their successors that all the men of Roucestre, of Combrigge,
and of Northull, and Wotton, and of Rossintone, and Waterfall and Bredley, and all who hold of the custom of Roucestre, shall perform at Roucestre all those customary
duties, usages, and works, which they have done for me in
my time, and likewise for Ranulf, Earl of Chester, in his
time; who for my service, gave to me the said lands of
Roucestre, and of Combrigge, and of Wotton, with all their
appurtenances, and all the customary dues, usages, and
works, to be done by the men of the aforesaid other
villages: namely, that they shall frequent the court of
pleas and halimot, for all and all kinds of disputes and
complaints, and for grindings of grain, and rade and lade, &c.
and for all other liberties and free customs.   Also that this
my donation and confirmation of my pure and perpetual
alms may obtain strength in perpetuity, I have corroborated
the present writing by the impression of my seal: and I
have asked the guarantee of my uncle R. Earl of Chester,
to the said Canons and their successors, in confirmation of
this grant."   Witnesses, Hugh Wac, &c. &c.

Charter of Ranulf, Earl of Chester, reciting and confirming the above-specified donation of Richard Bacun.—" To
all the Sons of Holy Mother Church to whom the present
page shall come, R. Earl of Chester wisheth health in the
Lord: Know all ye that I have granted, and by this my
charter confirmed the donation made by Richard Bacoun
to God and the Blessed Mary, and to the Canons of St. Mary

of Roucestre: [Here follows the list of lands, &c., as given in the foregoing charter.] After promising to guarantee and defend the donations, in perpetuity, the charter thus proceeds:—"Wherefore I will and firmly ordain that the Canons shall hold the aforesaid gifts, as well and peaceably, freely and quietly, as any other alms ever were held: and that they shall have all their customs, and liberties, and rights, and quittances, in all things, in city and without, in borough and without, in village and without, in market and without; in fields and pastures, in meadows, and ways, and places, and passages; in wood and plain, in waters and mills, in lakes and fisheries; in sok and sak, in tol and theme, and infange-thef, and waif and wreck, and other customs and liberties." Witnesses, Roger, Constable of Chester; Roger de Montealt, Seneschal of Chester; Thomas the Clerk, the writer of the deed, and many others: at Nottingham.

Charter of Foulque Fitz Foulque [Fulcher fil. Fulcheri,] relative to the Church of Edneshoure.—"To all the faithful, &c. Foulque Fitz F. greeting: Know all ye that I have given, and by this charter confirmed to God and St. Mary, and St. Michael the Archangel, and to the Abbot of Roucester, and the Canons of Leyes, their dependents, for the soul of Jordan my brother, and for the souls of my father and my mother, and for the soul of my spouse [spousa] Margaret; and for me and my wife, and for my sons and and my brothers, the church of St. Peter of Edneshoure, with all its appurtenances, in perpetual alms. Wherefore I ordain that they shall have and hold the church freely and peaceably, &c. under the jurisdiction of the Bishop of Lichfield, and the archdeacon of Derby." Witnesses, William Avenel, with many others.

Charter of William Basset, relative to the Church of Wodeford.—"William Bassett, to all the faithful, &c. greeting: Know all ye that for the salvation of my own soul, and that of my wife, and for the soul of William Bassett, my father; and for the souls of all my predecessors and

successors, I have given, and by this charter confirmed, in
pure and perpetual alms, to the church of St. Mary of Roucester, and the Canons Regular there, the church of Wodeford, with all its appurtenances and liberties; thus ratifying
the gift of the same church to the Canons of Roucester, by
my father Will. Bassett, and Osmund Bassett." Witnesses,
Thomas, Abbot of Crokesdene, &c.

Three other charters of the Abbey are inserted in the
Monasticon: one of William de Greselei, relative to his
gift of certain lands in Kingston, and the advowson of the
church in that village; another, of Patrick de Modberley,
concerning the moiety of the church of Mobberly, in Cheshire, and certain lands there, with which he endowed the
Abbey; and lastly, the charter of Henry III. confirming
the donation of Richard Bacun.

In the 16th Richard II. Sir Rob. Belknap, Knight,
defunct, gave the manor of Sharstede, near Roucester, a
moiety of Lydesinge, and other lands to this Convent, to
find a priest to sing for his soul.

There were two Cells belonging to this House, Lees, in
Staffordshire; and Halywell, in Warwickshire.

The names of the Abbots in succession from July 31st,
1255, to the Dissolution, are—Richard, Walter, Walter de
Dodelle, Robert Prior of Greseley, Roger de Lughteburgh,
Walter de Aston, Gilbert de Bosco, Henry de Hopton,
William, Thomas de Roucestre, John de Chesewardin,
Robert de Bawkewelle, Henry Smith, John Hanbury,
Robert Twys, and William Grafton.

No remains of the Abbey are now in existence.

An impression of the seal of this Priory is yet remaining
in the Augmentation Office. The subject is a prior holding a crosier in his right hand and a book in his left; on
each side of him are monks praying, and over his head a
representation of the Virgin Mary, with the divine infant,
having an angel on each side of them; legend imperfect.

The site of Roucester was granted, in the 31st Henry
VIII. to Richard Trentham, Esq. The reversion of it had

been previously granted to Robert Southwell and Margery his wife.*

Near Rocester is Woodseat, formerly a demesne of the ancient family of Bainbrigge.

In the population returns of 1831, the number of inhabitants in the parish of Rocester is stated to be 1,040. They are employed chiefly in the cotton-spinning factory belonging to Thomas Houldsworth, Esq.

The annual value of the real property in the parish is assessed at £6,374.

A branch of the Grand Junction Canal passes by the village.

The living is a perpetual curacy, in the patronage of the devisees of the late Thomas Bainbrigge, Esq., in whom also the manorial rights of the parish are vested. The Rev. George Hake is the present incumbent.

---

*The revenues of the Abbey at the Dissolution amounted in the gross to £129 12s. 2d.—derived from property in Rocester, Waterfall, Cambrigg, Elastone, Quykesell, Denston, Stanton, Swynscoo, (co. Stafford); Clowmans, Hognaston, Sedsall, Kynston, Somersall, Scropton, Edynsor, (co. Derby); and Woodford, (co. Northampton.)—*Monasticon Anglicanum.*

CHAPTER XV.

LEAVING Rocester, the course of the Dove leads to Crakemarsh Hall, the seat of Sir Thomas Cotton Sheppard, Bart.,
an elegant and commodious modern structure, very agreeably situated in the centre of a wide domain of fertile
meadow land. " Crakemerse" says Erdeswicke, is a goodly
and profitable lordship, lying in a very good soil between
Tene water and Dove, at their meeting." Before the Conquest, it was a demesne of Algar, Earl of Mercia. In the
20th year of the Conqueror's reign it was in the hands of
the crown, and was granted to Henry de Ferrers. Robert
de Ferrers gave Crakemarsh to his daughter Maud, on her
marriage with Bertram de Verdon. The estate afterwards
passed to Lord Burghersh, then to the family of Delves, and
from them to Lord Sheffield, whose descendant sold it to
his brother Christopher Sheffield. It was then purchased
by a Mr. Gilbert Collier, and by his son sold to Sir Gilbert
Gerard, Master of the Rolls, in whose family it remained

CRAKEMARSH HALL.

The Seat of Sir Thomas Cotton Sheppard.

Printed by I.W. & C. Foxfoord, London.

Published by Dawson & Hobson, Ashbourn.

many years. It passed afterwards to the Cottons, the heiress of whom (Elizabeth daughter of William Cotton, Fsq. of Crakemarsh) married in 1774, Thomas Sheppard, Esq. of an ancient Bedfordshire family. He was created a baronet in 1809, and on his death in 1821, was succeeded in his title and estates, by his son, the present Sir Thomas Cotton Sheppard, Bart.*

The market-town of UTTOXETER, formerly *Uttoxeshather*, and *Utcestre*, is finely situated near the west bank of the Dove, locally within the Hundred of Totmonslow South, in the Northern Division of the county of Stafford, fourteen miles distant from the county-town, nearly twelve miles from Ashbourn, eighteen from Derby, and 138 north-west of London. This town is of great antiquity, and from the fertility of its site was doubtless known to the ancient Britons, but the earliest existing records that have reference to it are those connected with the Honor of Tutbury, of which it formed a part, and was consequently included in the extensive grant of lands made by the Conqueror to Henry de Ferrers. Under this nobleman's son and successor, Robert de Ferrers, Uttoxeter was greatly improved, and we find there were at that time (the twelfth century,) one hundred and twenty-seven burgages in the town, the inhabitants of which were employed chiefly in the manufacture of iron. William de Ferrers, in the year 1251, granted to the town a charter of privileges, of which the following is a translated copy:—*

" To all men that shall see or hear this present deed, William de Ferrers Earl of Derby, sendeth greeting in the Lord : Know ye, that we have granted and by this present deed confirmed for us and our heirs, to all our burgesses of Uttoxeshather, that they hold from henceforth freely their burgage and burgages, with the appurtenances in the same town of Uttoxeshather, as some of them have formerly been assessed, and others hereafter shall happen to be, with free ingress and egress, to be held of us and our heirs to them and their heirs or assigns and their heirs for ever, as freely and as decently they shall and may hold the same as free burgesses, with all liberties, free common, and easements,

---

*Debrett's Baronetage.

to a free borough belonging. Yielding to us yearly and to our heirs for every burgage separately twelvepence sterling at two terms of the year, viz. : one half at the Annunciation of our Lady, and the other half at the feast of St. Michael, for all secular service, custom, and exactions to us and our heirs belonging. We have granted also to the said burgesses and to their heirs as abovesaid, that they may take within themselves upon their burgages aforesaid, chapmen and other freemen whom they will, enfeoffing them or granting them other easements within the said borough without injury to the same, and without hindrance of us and our heirs, saving our service in all. And further we will, that none carry on any trading within the said free common or liberty without reasonable and accustomed toll. We have granted also to the said burgesses and their heirs as aforesaid, and to all being within their commonalty, that they shall be within all our own lands and liberties free from toll wheresoever they shall pass for ever, saving other men's charters and liberties made and used before this deed. All these things aforesaid we have granted within the said commonalty of the aforesaid burgesses for ever, saving to us and to our heirs a reasonable toll of all our said burgesses and their heirs or assigns, and of all within their commonalty being, when as our lord the king that for the time shall be shall tax all his boroughs throughout England, so as the said tax be gathered by the hands of two burgesses to the use of us and our heirs, and also saving to us and our heirs the ovens and market, with their profits, and the site of the borough and market and of the court-leet also from them with pannage and all other liberties without our said borough, but so as the said burgesses and all within their commonalty being, have common and herbage within the ward of Uttox-eshather, where the men of the said town have been wont formerly to outcommon without our hindrance, so as it may be lawful for us and our heirs to make our profit of all other lands and tenements, meadows, pastures, woods, marshes, moors, and in all other places within the aforesaid town and ward, without contradiction of the said burgesses or their heirs. And if it happen that any burgage belonging to us or our heirs, by any means or by fire shall be in lack of occupation or service by the space of one year, then for want of a tenant the whole commonalty of the burgesses of the said town's street after the year shall take the said burgage into their hands, and make the best profit thereof, and answer to us and our heirs for the farm and service thereof, without any claim of him or his, who first held the said burgage : wherefore we will and grant for us and our heirs, that all things aforesaid be observed and kept to the said burgesses and their heirs for ever. In witness whereof this my present writing with the strength of my seal for me and my heirs I have fortified. These being witnesses, Hugh de Meynell, Robert de Essebourn, Robert de Punchardun, Richard de Mortimer, Jeffrey de Caudrey, Robert de Merinton, Thomas, (then rector of the church of Uttoxeter) Robert de Stretton, clerk, Jordan de Grindon, John de Twyford, clerk, and William de Rolleston. Dated at Uttoxeter on the day of the Assumption of the Virgin Mary, in the year of the reign of king Henry, son of king John, the six-and-thirtieth."*

*History of Tutbury, appendix, p. 384, 5, 6.

About the year 1255, Robert de Ferrers, the last Earl of
Derby, gave to John de Sulney, and his heirs and assigns,
120 acres of land upon the Brends, in the wood of Uttoxeter, with the timber growing thereon, to be held of him
and his heirs, unless they should be religious men or Jews,
freely with house-boote and hay-boote, throughout the
Ward of Uttoxeter, and rights of common in his forest of
Needwood. In the same year he granted letters patent to
Sir Walter Raleigh, of Uttoxeter, (a direct ancestor of the
celebrated statesman and soldier), and his heirs, empowering them 'to hunt and course the fox and hare within the
precincts of his forest of Needwood, with eight braches and
four greyhounds.'

The town and manor of Uttoxeter passed with the rest
of the Honor of Tutbury, from the Earls of Derby to
Edmund, Earl of Lancaster, who in 21 Edward I., (1292)
claimed free warren in Uttoxeter, a market on Wednesday
in each week, and a fair annually on the eve and nativity
of the Blessed Virgin. These liberties appear to have been
confirmed by grant from the crown to Thomas, second Earl
of Lancaster. In this reign the number of burgages had
increased to 140, and there were in the town two forges.
The free fishery of the Dove, with another fishery in the
pool of Uttoxhather, was estimated at £1 5s. annually.
There was a payment of 12s. by ancient custom at the two
great courts; and at the feast of St. Martin another payment of 5s. as a poll-tax upon young men; the sum total
payable from the town to the Lords of the Honor, including
the rents of assize of free tenants, and other customary
dues, was £61 5s. 5d. The advowson of the church was
valued at £66 13s. 4d.

Henry IV., on whose accession the Honor of Tutbury
was annexed to the crown, granted to Sir John Bagot,
ancestor of the present Lord Bagot, an annuity of forty
marks, payable from Uttoxeter. Others received similar
grants, it being the policy of Henry thus to attach his
most powerful nobles, by giving them an interest in the

maintenance of his possessions against the aggressions of the disaffected. On the rising of the Earl of Northumberland, however, a body of that nobleman's partisans, at the head of whom were three brothers of the names of Mynors, of an ancient family residing in Uttoxeter, committed various outrages on the persons and property of the King's tenants at Uttoxeter and other parts of the Honor, and for a time put a stop to the collection of the rents. These commotions after continuing about twelve months, were at length suppressed by the parliament.

From this period down to the reign of Charles I. there is little to be recorded of the town of Uttoxeter. On the 24th of May, 1625, Charles sold the manor to William, Lord Craven; Sir George Whitmore, Sir William Whitmore, and Mr. Gibson, who resold it again to several of the inhabitants, for £3,120; and these inhabitants conveyed to the various occupiers their interest in the same.*

The Ward of Uttoxeter, one of the five divisions of Needwood Forest) on which the inhabitants enjoyed rights of common, was about this time inclosed by the crown, not, however, without a strenuous opposition on the part of the freeholders. One-half the Ward was at length apportioned to them in lieu of their rights of common; and the King's moiety was granted in 1639, to Mr. Nevil, one of the officers of the royal household.†

This town appears to have shared to some extent in the alarm and privation consequent upon the civil dissensions in the reign of Charles. The first notice we have of the

---

*Sir O. Mosley's History of Tutbury.

†" For several years" continues Sir Oswald, " Mr. Nevil received rent for his portion without interruption; but a few years before the commencement of the civil wars, a party of soldiers, who had been impressed against their will, burnt the rails, destroyed the fences, and laid the ground waste: yet for this trespass several of the townspeople were prosecuted in the Star-chamber, and had not the political convulsion which followed put a stop to the proceedings, the greatest part of the inhabitants would have been subjected to a continuance of vexatious law-suits respecting it."

occupation of the town by the forces of either party, is when, early in the war, the royalists had possessed themselves of Stafford. From the parliamentarian narrative* of these transactions, it appears that the Moorlanders applied to Sir John Gell, (then at Derby,) for his assistance to dislodge the enemy from the position they had taken up: " Sir John asked them what assistance they would have; they said two hundred musquetiers and one saccer, not doubting but that they had men enough with that assistance to regayne the towne, and to save themselves. Hee commanded his Major Mollanus immediately with two hundred ffoot and one saccer to march towards their appointed rendezvous att Uttoxeter. His Major being there two or three dayes, and nobody coming to assist him, and hearing that the enemy increased, was forced to retreat in the night to Derby." Sir John Gell himself, joining his force with that of Sir William Brereton, soon afterwards marched upon Stafford. At Hopton Heath, near that town, he came up with the enemy, " whereupon hee sett his ffoot in order of battalis, and Sir William his horse, the enemy advancing in a full body with above one thousand, two hundred horse, whereof the Earl of Northampton was general, and soe setting upon their horse, Sir William's horse presently ran away, and left Sir John Gell alone with the ffoot. The enemy drew his horse into a body againe, and charged his ffoot, but hee gave them such a salute, that the enemy, in a disordered manner, drew off and marched away towards Stafford, but left many dead bodies behind them, whereof my lord of Northampton was one, Captayne Middleton and many other brave commanders of horse, and at least one hundred dragoones; and of our side three carters and two souldyers were slayne; wee lost two casks of drakes, which the dragoones had drawne a greate distance from the ffoot, under the hedges to save themselves,

---

*Narrative of the Services of Sir John Gell. See Glover's Derbyshire, vol. i. appendix, p. 62, 3. This narrative, it must be remembered, was written *for* the parliamentarians.

and soe Colonell Gell retreated with my Lord's dead body towards Uttoxeter, with his fforces, and Sir William Brereton with his forces towards Cheshire. And att Uttoxeter Colonell Gell remayned three dayes, and set Staffordshire in as good posture as hee could; within the said three dayes their came a trumpetter to him from my younge Lord of Northampton, for his father's dead body, whereupon hee answered, if hee would send him the drakes which they had gotten from their dragones and pay the chirurgeons for embalming it, hee should have it: but hee [the Earl of Northampton] returned him an answer, that hee would do nither th' one nor th' other, and soe Colonell Gell caused him to be carried in his company to Derby, and buried him in the Earle of Devonshire's sepulcher in All Hallowes Church."

The accounts of the churchwardens and constables of the parish present some very curious memoranda in reference to the events that took place in the town, at this and subsequent periods. The following are extracts:—

1642. Paid to them that swept Mr. Ward's hall for King Charles the First, 1s.

Trained soldiers' pay here, and to Stafford to wait on the King, £34 6s.

Charges when the country went against Stafford the first time, 3s. 4d.

Doveridge men's charges when they came to guard the town, 1s.

Paid for match, powder, and coals, for some of the town-ends, in February, £1 5s. 1d.

John Sherratt, for leading clods five days to the bulwarks, 16s.

Bestowed on the countrymen when they came to guard the town, when the soldiers went to Lichfield, 2s. 3d.

Paid to carpenters and labourers at the bulwarks, £5 13s. 2d.

For watching Lord Stanhope and his son at the Crown, 11s.

To a prisoner who came from Hopton battle, 4d. N.B. Fought near Stafford.

Paid for match, powder, candles, bullets, and coals, for some of the town-ends, in March, £2 10s. 9d.

For removing one of the bulwarks, and for entrenching, 12s. 4d.

Bestowed on Loxley men when they came to trench, 4d.

November. Paid for drink bestowed on Loxley and Tean men when they came to help the town against Worthley, 2s.

Paid for drink for Marchington, and Crakemarsh, and Creighton men, 2s.

1642. Paid to Johnson for prisoners which were Worthley's men, 6s. 7d.

1643. Fire and candle for the watch, being Derby men, 1s. 5d.

Paid for butter, cheese, five quarters of pease, and oats, to Tutbury and Lichfield, £19 2s. 8d.

Paid two men for going to Tutbury with provisions, 1s. 4d.

Paid William Ferrall and others who watched the ordnance at the Crown door, 1s. 6d.

Paid Richard Cartridge for watching on the church, 8d.

February. Charges when the country went against Stafford twice, £5 11s 4d.

Paid to the ringers when king Charles the First was here, 5s.

June. Paid to a townsman when he went to guard a field-piece to Tutbury, 8d.

Charges to Wooton-Lodge with a horse-load of bread, 1s.

July. Paid to workmen for pulling down the bulwarks and taking them away, 10s.

October. Paid down when Colonel Hastings was in the town, £5.

December. Ale for the Captain and his men, who brought a warrant from Lord Loughborough for fifty pounds,—3s.

For 25 strikes of oats, which were sent for by warrant to Tutbury, £2 4s. 10d.

Provisions sent to Ashburn by warrant from Colonel Dudley, in the king's army, £3.

For ale, tobacco, wood, coals, and hay for guards and centinels, £2 10s. 4d.

1644. January. Paid Captain Vernon what he laid upon the township, £11.

February 26. Paid to the Committee's Treasurer at Stafford, for weekly pay in money and returns, £100.

March 11. Paid to Tutbury Castle in money and returns, £50.

April. For a rope to hang the man who killed John Scott, and for a cord to pinion the prisoner, 1s.

May 7. For 8 cwt. 2 qrs. 7 lbs. cheese to Tutbury, £7 15s. 10d.

September. Levies upon the town of Uttoxeter, £608 13s. 2d.

1645. January 1. The parishioners of Uttoxeter paid £6 2s. 4d. weekly, besides extraordinary expenses to a considerable amount.

Paid to Prince Rupert's cook for his fee, 5s.

Hay, oats, beer, tobacco, wood, and coals for the guard three nights, when the Parliament forces went against Tutbury Castle, £1 19s. 8d.

For guides to go a scouting three nights, 9s.

October. For a sheet, making the grave, ringing, beer, and for burying the soldier that was slain in the street, 4s.

1646. February 5. The constables' accounts amounted to £975 7s. 1d.

October 6. Paid to two men for blocking up the town-ends with carts, 6d.

Beer for soldiers for barricading the town ends, 1s.

February 8. Paid Commissary Ward three weeks' contribution, £14 13s. 8d.

Paid General Egerton, at Tutbury, £30.

February 14. For two horses and a man to carry bread and cheese to Tutbury in the night, *being in great want*, 3s. 4d.

February 22. For carrying two soldiers to Caverswall, who were maimed in the High Wood beyond Uttoxeter, 2s. 6d.

Paid to Parson Langley's soldiers in bread and beer, 3s.

March 30. For provisions to the leaguers at Tutbury, £7 4s. 6d.

April 8. Ditto, £11 2s. 9d.

April 20. Paid Captain John Cloyd for pulling down the bulwarks at Tutbury, £3.

August 26. Paid to Ashburn by the Churchwardens of Uttoxeter when the town was infested with the plague, £3.

Paid to the inhabitants of Clifton when the plague was there, £5.

October. For quartering General Fairfax's soldiers, £20.

October 13. For quartering Colonel Cromwell's soldiers, £20.

December. Quartering Colonel Oakley's men, £13 2s. 6d.

1647. May 12th. To 15 men for pulling down Tutbury Castle, £2 10s. 4d.

October. To 46 travellers, or Egyptians, with a pass from Parliament, to travel by the space of six months together to get relief, 4s.

1648. May. For two men watching in the steeple when the town was fearful of an insurrection, 1s. 4d.

For quartering 15 of Colonel Monk's soldiers, 13s.

1651. For a warrant to fetch in and search for Papists' and delinquents' arms, 4d.

August 20. To ale, bread, and pottage, to relieve the Scotch prisoners, taken by Lieutenant-Colonel Downes, whilst in custody, £2 8s.

To another body of Scotch prisoners, £1 10s.

1658. Note.—£67 10s. was paid to the army yearly for seven years.

For proclaiming the Lord Protector, 1s.

1660. May. Paid the ringers when King Charles the Second was proclaimed, 5s.

1667. Royal aid at Christmas, £44 1s. At Midsummer, £44 1s.

1672. One month's pay to the Government, £14 13s. 6d.

April 8th. Two months' pay, £29 7s.

1672. July 30th. A *great fire* happened in the rear of Richard Cludd's house, which consumed most of the lower part of the town.

October 6. Repairing stocks and cuckstool, 10s.

The population of the parish, including the townships of Crakemarsh, Creighton, Stramshall, Woodlands, and the liberty of Loxley, according to the official returns for the respective periods, was in 1801, 2,779; in 1811, 3,155; in 1821, 4,658; in 1831, 4864;* exhibiting an increase of 2,085 inhabitants in thirty years. The parish contains about 10,000 acres of land, of which 2,440 are in the township of Uttoxeter; 1,066 in Crakemarsh; 1274 in Stramshall and Creighton; 1,735 in Loxley; and 2,419 in

*Of this number about 3,500 reside in the town.

Woodlands. The annual value of the real property in the entire parish is assessed at £24,257.

Among the principal landowners, are Thomas Sneyd Kynnersley, Esq., Sir Thomas Cotton Sheppard, Bart., (who is lord of the manors of Crakemarsh, Creighton, and Stramshall); Thomas Hart, Esq., Lord Bagot, James Henry Clough, Esq., Thomas Bladon, Esq., and others; who also possess the manorial rights.

Much of the opulence of this town is derived from the rich and beautiful agricultural district of which it forms the central point. A fine open plain of many thousand acres, chiefly pasture-land, extends eastwards for a mile in width, from the town to the banks of the Dove, and opens north and south-east with the course of the stream into a continuous winding vale of boundless fertility; and scarcely less fertile is the district sweeping round from the reclaimed forest-lands on the south, to the bleak northern ridge, the hills of Wever.

Uttoxeter seems to have been remarkable for the longevity of its inhabitants, attributable, no doubt, to the salubrity of its situation.

The markets are in great repute, being well attended, and plentifully supplied with corn, cattle, and provisions. A cattle-market is held every fortnight, and there are annually eight fairs, (including three for the sale of cheese.)*

The canal north of the town, opens an advantageous communication with the coal and limestone districts, and with the Trent and Mersey navigation.

The town is lighted with gas, and is supplied with water by conduits from Bramshall Park, a distance of two miles.†

*Cattle fairs, May 6, Sept. 19, Nov. 11 and 27; a colt fair, Sept. 1; cheese fairs, Thursday after the second Tuesday in March, the first Thursday in September, and the second Thursday in November. The market-day is Wednesday.

†These water-works were established and are repaired out of the yearly profits of the aftermath of Nether Wood and Broad Meadows (about 120 acres,) which are applied to the repairs of bridges, causeways, and other public uses of the town and its vicinity, and now yield about £50 a year.

40

The church is a neat and very convenient edifice, with a square tower surmounted by a spire, of early date. The nave, chancel, and aisles were entirely rebuilt in 1828, at the cost of £6,061 1s. 11d.—the style of architecture being the Decorated English. The interior is extremely well arranged, and is pewed with substantial British oak. It now affords 1,414 sittings, of which 422 are free.

Mr. Pitt, who described this church in its former state, mentions several ancient monuments, and an altar-tomb, with a mutilated effigy in alabaster. A chapel of the Mynors family was then (1817) used as a vestry-room.

There are several monuments of the Kynnersley family, and others; a mural tablet is inscribed to

" Thomas Oldfield, Esq., Major in the Marines, who fell during the memorable defence of St. Jean d'Acre, in Syria, by Sir Sydney Smith, against General Bonaparte and the army of Egypt, while leading a sortie made by the garrison on the 7th April, 1792, for the purpose of destroying the enemy's approaches. Ætat. 43."

A tomb-stone in the church-yard, over the cemetery of the Gardner family, bears the following epitaph :—

" In memory of Lieutenant-Colonel Gardner, late of his Majesty's eleventh regiment of Dragoons, in which he served with honour from a cornet, and died lamented, Aug. 1. 1762, aged 91 years. His widow, for the sincere affection she had for him, caused this stone to be erected."

The living is a vicarage, in the patronage of the Dean and Canons of Windsor. The Rev. C. F. Broughton is the incumbent, and the Rev. H. W. G. Armstrong is curate.

Joseph Bladon, Esq. is the present lay-improprietor of the tithes, which produce annually about £725.

The Wesleyans, the Society of Friends, the Independents, Baptists, and Primitive Methodists have their respective places of worship in the town; and a chapel is now being erected for the use of the Roman Catholics.

There is here a free-school, founded and endowed in 1558, by Thomas Allen, a priest, and celebrated mathematician; an Infant-School, a National School, built by subscription in 1829; and there are Sunday-Schools in connexion with most of the places of worship.

Printed by T. W. & C. Fearson, London.

UTTOXETER CHURCH, STAFFORDSHIRE.

Published by Dawson & Hobson, Ashbourn.

CHARITIES.—The gifts and bequests to the poor of this town, produce, according to the Commissioners' Report, a yearly sum amounting to about £309, which (deducting expenses) is applied to the support of the almshouses, and to other public purposes, in accordance with the intentions of the respective donors. The trusts are generally executed by the churchwardens and overseers.*

The Mynors family, already mentioned, were anciently seated at Hollingbury Hall, near this town. " At Utcestre" says Erdeswicke, "is a house of the Myneres, very ancient gentlemen they are." They were distinguished for their attachment to the naval service. Captain Richard Mynors, who flourished in the seventeenth century, served with great bravery in the Dutch wars, and also against the rebels at Colchester. His relative, William Mynors, sailed eleven times to the East Indies.

Loxley Park, between two and three miles south-west of Uttoxeter, is the inheritance and chief seat of the Kynnersley family, who, according to Erdeswicke, were established here at least as early as the 18th of Edward III. Thomas Kynnersley, Esq. of Loxley, was High Sheriff for the county of Stafford in the reign of Charles I.; and C. Kynnersley, Esq. served the same office in the reign of George III. Thomas Sneyd Kynnersley, Esq. is the present representative of the family.

*The Almshouses are *Mastergent's*, *Wright's* and *Lathropp's*, in Carter-Street. Among the charity estates are, the Talbot public-house, a small house adjoining, and Botham's croft, producing together, £68 per annum; Dynes Lane farm, near Marchington, (about 20 acres) now let for £40 per annum; the Parks, let for £18; Thorney Field and Russell's Spring, £25; Red Hill Field, £10; Wilgs Croft, £5; Swetholme Close, £14; Mansholme, £14; and others of smaller rents; together with several rent-charges.

Uttoxeter is the centre of a Union under the New Poor Law, comprising the parishes of Uttoxeter, Rocester, Croxden, Leigh, Bromshall, Marchington Marchington Woodlands, Draycott, Newborough, Abbot's Bromley, Blithfield, Kingstone, Gratwich, and Field, (co, Stafford); and Doveridge, Somersall, Sudbury, and Boylston, (co. Derby.) The Union Workhouse is a commodious and extensive building, occupying a site nearly three roods in extent.

Bramshall, two miles west of Uttoxeter, was formerly a lordship of the Staffords, and it passed afterwards to the families of Erdeswicke, Willoughby Lord Brooke, and Sir Fulke Greville. T. S. Kynnersley, is now the chief proprietor.

A short distance south-west of the town is Blount's Hall, "whereof" in Erdeswicke's time, "Blount, of Osbaston, in Leicestershire, was owner. A man would think, (continues this topographer,) that it should by the name, be the ancient seat of the Blounts, but that is not so. For this is a house of no great account, and but lately built by one that being a little glorious, would have it called by his name."

Thomas Allen, the mathematician, (whom we have before mentioned as the founder of a free-school,) was a native of Uttoxeter, and was born on the 21st of December, 1542. He was admitted scholar of Trinity College, Oxford, in June, 1561, and in 1567, took his degree of master of arts. In 1580 he quitted his college and fellowship, and retired to Gloucester Hall, where he studied very closely, and became famous for his knowledge in antiquity, philosophy, and mathematics. Upon the invitation of Henry Earl of Northumberland, he resided for some time at that nobleman's house, where he became acquainted with some of the most celebrated mathematicians of the age, among whom were, Thomas Harriot, John Dee, Walter Warner, and Nathaniel Torporley. Robert, Earl of Leicester, had a particular esteem for Allen, and would have conferred a bishopric upon him, but his love of ease and retirement caused him to decline the offer. His great skill in the mathematics made the ignorant and vulgar look upon him as a magician or conjuror; the author of a book called "Leicester's Commonwealth" has accordingly accused him of using the art of figuring, to procure the Earl of Leicester's unlawful designs, and endeavouring by the black art to bring about a match between him and Queen Elizabeth.

The absurdity of this accusation is manifest; but it is certain that the Earl placed such confidence in Allen, that nothing material was transacted in the state without his knowledge; and the Earl had constant information by letter from Allen, of what passed in the university. Allen was very curious and indefatigable in collecting scattered manuscripts relating to history, antiquity, astronomy, philosophy, and mathematics; these collections have been quoted by several learned authors, and are mentioned as having been deposited in the Bibliotheca Alleniana. That the character of Allen for talents and erudition stood very high, is clear, from the testimony of contemporary and succeeding writers. Selden says, "He was a man of the most extensive learning and consummate judgment, the brightest ornament of the University of Oxford." Camden affirms that he was "skilled in most of the best arts and sciences;" and Mr. Burton, who wrote his funeral sermon, styles him "not only the Coryphæus, but the very soul and sun of all the mathematicians of his time." Having lived to a great age, he died at Gloucester Hall, on the 30th of September, 1632.*

Uttoxeter gave birth to Sir Simon Degge, the antiquary. He is principally known for his topographical notes, and the curious paper on the possessors of Staffordshire abbey-lands, appended to Erdeswicke's survey of this county. He lived to the age of 92. The family sunk into obscurity, and finally became extinct, by the death of the last male descendant, about the year 1812.

That distinguished naval officer, Admiral Lord Gardner, was born at Uttoxeter, on the 12th April, 1742. He was the eighth son of Lieutenant-Colonel Gardner, of the 11th Dragoons. Having early expressed an ardent wish to enter the naval service, he was rated, when fourteen years old, as a midshipman on board the Medway of sixty guns, then under the immediate orders of Captain Peter Denis. In

*Chalmers's Biographical Dictionary.

this vessel he remained two years, during which time he was present in an action, when the Duc d'Aquitaine French ship of the line was taken. After several years' service, he was appointed Lieutenant on board the Bellona. In this station he distinguished himself at the capture of the Courageux, whereupon he was raised to the rank of commander, and appointed to the Raven of sixteen guns. He was afterwards made post in the Preston of fifty guns, and on the breaking out of the American war, he was nominated to the command of the Maidstone frigate, in which he sailed for the West Indies early in 1778, and in the course of that year was so fortunate as to make a rich capture on the coast of America. On the 4th November he fell in with the Lion, a French man of war, having on board fifteen hundred hogsheads of tobacco, and after a severe action, compelled the enemy to surrender. With this prize he sailed for Antigua, where he was promoted by Admiral Byron to the command of the Sultan of seventy-four guns. In the drawn battle which was fought some time after with the French fleet under Count de Estaing, off the island of Grenada, Captain Gardner led the van, and greatly distinguished himself. His ship, however, suffered so much, that he was ordered to Jamaica, whence he sailed for England. The Sultan having been discharged, Captain Gardner was appointed to the Duke, with which ship he sailed to join the fleet in the West Indies, then under the orders of Sir George Rodney, and arrived in time to participate in the glorious victory of the 12th April, 1782. On that memorable day, his ship was the first to break through the enemy's line of battle, according to the new plan of attack, then for the first time, put in practice. At one period of this action the Duke, in conjunction with the Formidable and Namur, had to sustain the fire of eleven of the enemy's ships. At the termination of the war, Captain Gardner acted as commodore on the Jamaica station, and in 1790 was appointed a lord of the Admiralty, when he likewise obtained a seat in Parliament. In the

year 1793, having been raised to the rank of Rear-Admiral
of the Blue, he hoisted his flag on board the Queen, of
ninety-eight guns, in which he sailed as commander-in-
chief to the Leeward Islands.   He then returned to England, and the following year, bore a part in the action of the
1st June, under the gallant Earl Howe.   On this occasion
his bravery was conspicuous in the extreme, and, in consequence, he not only received the thanks of the commander-
in-chief, but was appointed major-general of marines, and
created a baronet of Great Britain.   On the 22nd June,
1795, Sir Alan Gardner was present at the action off Port
l'Orient.   Two years after this event, when a dangerous
mutiny had broken out at Portsmouth, he manifested a
degree of firmness and resolution during that trying period.
worthy of his high character as a British naval officer,
From this time he continued to serve in the Channel fleet,
till the close of the year 1792, when he was sent with sixteen sail of the line, to reinforce the fleet off Cadiz.   He
was afterwards appointed to succeed Admiral Kingsmill,
the naval commander in Ireland, being previously raised to
the dignity of an Irish peer.   This post he continued
to hold till the year 1807, when he was appointed Admiral
of the Channel fleet, a command which ill health soon
compelled him to relinquish.   He died in 1810, and was
buried in the abbey church of Bath, with the grandeur
and solemnity due to his rank and merit.—He sat in three
successive parliaments.   In 1790 he was returned for the
town of Plymouth ; and in 1796, he was colleague to Mr.
Fox, in the representation of Westminster, on which occasion he was opposed by the celebrated John Horne
Tooke, whose wit, satire, and eloquence, were more alarming to the Admiral than a shower of cannon-balls from an
enemy's fleet.   Notwithstanding, he once more offered himself for the same city, and was again successful.   At this
time, Mr. Fox, in addressing the electors said, " A noble
Admiral has been proposed to you. I certainly cannot
boast of agreeing with him in political opinions ; but whom

could the electors pitch upon more worth of their choice, than the noble lord, in his private character universally respected, and a man who has served his country with a zeal, a gallantry, a spirit, and a splendour, that will reflect upon him immortal honour." Admiral Gardner married early in life, Susannah Hyde, only daughter of Francis Oale, Esq., a planter in Liguania.*

Mr. Samuel Bentley, of Uttoxeter, published in 1774, a volume of poems, one of which is entitled, "The River Dove: a Lyric Pastoral,"—a kind of rhyming description of the river and its scenery.†

Mary Howitt, the delightful poetess, whose writings, especially those for the young, are so favourably known to the world, is a native of Uttoxeter, and the greater part of her early life was spent here. Her maiden name was Botham,‡ and her parents were members of the Society of

---

*Imperial and County Annual Register, for 1810.

†The following is a specimen of Mr. Bentley's style:—

"Uttoxeter, sweet are thy views!
    Each scene of my past boyish days,
Past pleasure in fancy renews,
    While gratitude sings in thy praise;
Here Plenty with copious horn,
    Dispenses her bounties around,
And rosy thy sons, like the morn,
    In health, and in spirits abound.

"Thy buildings, what tho' they are plain,
    And boast no magnificent dome,
Enough for the wise may contain,
    Enjoying true pleasure at home;
How happy the poor who enjoy!
    Possessions o'er want to prevail;
Whose hills daily bread can supply,
    And sweet milky tribute the vale."

‡"She is, by her mother's side, directly descended from Mr. William Wood, the Irish patentee, about whose halfpence, minted under a contract from the government of George II., Dean Swift raised such a disturbance with his 'Drapier's Letters,' preventing the issue of the coinage, and saddling Mr. Wood with a loss of £600,000. Sir Robert Walpole, the minister, resisted all recom-

Friends. She first became known to the public as an authoress, shortly after her marriage, about the year 1822, when in conjunction, with her partner, William Howitt, himself a poet of congenial taste and disposition, and of the same religious persuasion, she published a volume of poetry, under the title of "The Forest Minstrel, and other Poems." This production is characteristic of both its writers in the particular walks of poetry in which they were hereafter to excel, the one in delineating natural scenery and rural life, the other in reviving the tradition and the legend of ancient times.

A singular circumstance is related of Dr Johnson, as having occurred in this town. His father, Michael Johnson, who was a bookseller at Lichfield, was accustomed to attend the weekly market at Uttoxeter, with a stall for the sale of books. Samuel sometimes accompanied him, but on one occasion, from motives of pride, he positively refused to do so. This act of disobedience afterwards preyed so acutely on his conscience, that he could not rest satisfied until, by a kind of self-imposed penance, he had endeavoured to expiate it. He accordingly proceeded to Uttoxeter, in very inclement weather, and stood for an hour, bare-headed and in the rain, upon the very spot which his father's stall used to occupy, the boys all the while hooting him in the street.

The village of DOVERIDGE, (co. Derby,) in Domesday-Book called *Dubrigge*, is situated on the banks of the Dove, one mile and a half east of Uttoxeter. The parish comprises also the hamlets of Eaton Dovedale and West Broughton. The manor of Doveridge, which had belonged to Edwin, Earl of Mercia, was held by the Prior of Tutbury under Henry de Ferrers. It appears to have been given to the Priory by Bertha, the wife of that nobleman.

---

pense for his loss, although Sir Isaac Newton, who was appointed to assay the coinage, pronounced it better than the contract required, and Mr. Wood, of course, justly entitled to remuneration. His son, Mr. Charles Wood, the grand-father of Mrs. Howitt, and who became assay-master at Jamaica, was the first who introduced platina into Europe.—*The Naturalist*, 1839.

The monks not long afterwards became possessed of an estate in this parish, called Holt Park, to which Sir William de Eyton and Henry Deneston quitted claim. In 1552, the manors of Doveridge and Doveridge Holt were granted to Sir William Cavendish, then Treasurer of the Chamber. Henry Cavendish, Esq., his descendant, held some important offices in the revenue department in Ireland, and was created a baronet in 1755. Sarah, the lady of his son, Sir Henry Cavendish, was in 1792 created Baroness Waterpark, of the kingdom of Ireland. The Doveridge estate was inherited by her eldest son, Richard, Baron Waterpark, on whose decease the title and estates devolved to Henry, his eldest son, the present Baron. His Lordship is descended from a branch of the same family as the Dukes of Devonshire.

A market on Thursday, at Dovebrugge, was granted in in 1275, to the Prior of Tutbury, but it has long been discontinued.

Doveridge House, the seat of Lord Waterpark, is a spacious and substantial edifice, chiefly remarkable for its fine situation,—the crowning point of a rising ground which overlooks the river, and commands a fine open view of the vale and town of Uttoxeter, bounded by a distant range of hills. The building was commenced in 1769, by the Right Hon. Sir Henry Cavendish, Bart. The basement story is of stone, and from it rise six pilasters, also of stone, which support a pediment; the rest of the front is brick.

Doveridge had a priest and a church at the time of the Norman survey. The present ancient structure is in the Early English style of the thirteenth century, with some alterations of a later date, and consists of a square embattled tower, surmounted by a spire; a nave, chancel, and aisles. The chancel has a fine perpendicular window; on the north wall is the gothic arched recess, termed in Roman Catholic times, *the holy sepulchre*; and on the opposite wall, the *piscina*, in good preservation. Affixed to this wall, is a very large monument, in two compartments, the uppermost of which exhibits two figures, male and female,

DOVERIDGE HALL,

The Seat of Lord Waterpark.

Printed by T.W. &c. Portland, London.

Published by Dawson & Hobson, Ashbourn.

clothed in black, in the attitude of prayer. In the lower compartment are the effigies of three females, in similar costume, also kneeling, and an infant, in repose. On a tablet below, are two inscriptions, one of which is scarcely legible; the other reads thus:—

"Gloria Deo in Excelsis. To the memory of William Davenport, of Henbury in the County of Chester, Esq., who by Mary his wife had issue, William, Grace, Isabel, and Thomazen, and died the 24th of June, 1640, in the 27th year of his age."

An alabaster floor-stone bears the effigies, partly defaced, of Ralph Okeover, Esq., who died A.D. 1495, and Agnes, his wife: he is represented in plate-armour, his head uncovered, resting on a helmet.

There is a monument to Sir Thomas Milward, Chief Justice of Chester, who died in 1658; also one in memory of the Rev. John Fitzherbert, formerly incumbent of the living, who died in July, 1785;* and several others to various members of the Cavendish family.

In 1392, a chantry was founded in this church, by Sir Robert Kniveton, the vicar, in honour of the Virgin Mary, and for the sustenance of poor people; the revenues were valued in 1547, at £6 per annum.

The church is dedicated to St. Cuthbert. The living is a vicarage, in the patronage of the Duke of Devonshire. The Hon. & Rev. Thomas Cavendish is the incumbent.

The manor of Eaton Dovedale belonged in the reign of Edward I. to the family of St. Pierre, whose heiress, about the year 1356, brought it to Sir Walter Cokesey, and Sir Hugh Cokesey, his grandson, died seised of it in 1445. One of the sisters and co-heirs of Sir Hugh, married John Greville, whose grandson, Sir Thomas Greville, otherwise Cokesey, died without issue about the year 1499. This estate, in consequence, devolved to the Russels, descended from the other sister and co-heir of Sir Hugh Cokesey. Sir John Russel died possessed of it in 1556. A few years

*He was the second son of William Fitzherbert, Esq. of Tissington.

afterwards it appears to have passed by sale to the Milwards, whose heiress brought it to the Clarkes of Somersall,
and it was in 1817 the property of their representative, the
Marchioness of Ormond.*

The old mansion in which Sir Thomas Milward is said
to have entertained Charles I. is now taken down.

The manor of West Broughton, which in the reign of
Queen Elizabeth belonged to the family of Palmer, is now
the property of Lord Vernon. In 1544, William Parr,
Earl of Essex, is said to have possessed an estate here.

The population of the parish in 1831, was 792, and the
annual value of the property therein is assessed at £10,412.

Passing the village of Marchington,† situated on the
south-east bank of the Dove, (county of Stafford) we next
approach

SUDBURY, a village, township, and parish in the hundred
of Appletree, and Southern Division of the county of
Derby, nine miles distant from Ashbourn, five from Uttoxeter, and thirteen from the county-town. The parish
includes the villages of Aston and Hill Somersall. The
manor formed part of the grant to Henry de Ferrers, who
had here a fine park. It was held at an early period under
the Earls Ferrers, by the Montgomery family. John
Montgomery, who in the reign of Henry II. gave part of
his demesne at Sudbury and Aston to the Priory of Tutbury,
is supposed to have been the immediate ancestor of this
family. In the reign of Henry VIII. a co-heiress of Sir
John Montgomery brought these manors to Sir John, son
of Sir Henry Vernon, of Haddon Hall. John Vernon,
grandson of Sir John, dying without issue, this branch of
the family beceme extinct, and the manors of Sudbury and

*Lyson's Magna Britannia—Derbyshire.

†Marchington formed part of the demesne of Henry de Ferrers, and was one
of the five Wards of the forest of Needwood. In the time of Henry III. William
Chamberlen, or Camden, held it of Ferrers, Earl of Derby. Earl Talbot is the
present lord of the Manor. Lord Bagot has an estate here, and within the
chapelry is Houndhill, a manor belonging to Lord Vernon.

Aston, with other estates, passed under his will to his widow, Mary, daughter of Sir Edward Littleton, with remainder successively to her sons by her first husband, Walter Vernon, of Houndhill, descended from one of the elder brothers of Sir John Vernon, who married the co-heiress of Montgomery. From Sir Edward Vernon,* the elder of these sons, Sudbury and Aston passed to his immediate descendant, George Venables Vernon, who in 1762, was created Lord Vernon. He was succeeded in 1780 by his eldest son, George Venables, on whose decease, without male issue, in 1813, the title and estates devolved to his half brother, Henry Venables, and from him to George Charles, his eldest son, the late Lord Vernon, who died in 1835, and was succeeded by his son, George John, the fifth and present Lord Vernon.

The family of Vernon has claims to great antiquity. William de Vernon assumed his name from the town and district of Vernon in Normandy, of which he was sole proprietor in 1052. Richard de Vernon, his eldest son, came over with the Conqueror, and was one of the seven barons, created by Hugh Lupus, the great Earl of Chester. The first connection of the family with the county of Derby, was by the marriage of Richard, a younger son of one of the Barons Vernon of Shipbrooke, in Cheshire, with a co-heiress of the Avenells, of Nether Haddon. This Richard died without male issue, leaving a daughter and heiress, married to Gilbert le Francis, whose son Richard took the name of Vernon, settled at Haddon Hall, and was common ancestor of the Vernons of Haddon, Sudbury, &c.

Sudbury Hall, the seat of Lord Vernon, is a very pleasing specimen of the domestic architecture of the seventeenth century.   It is built of red bricks, intermixed with others

*This Sir Edward Vernon married the heiress of a younger branch of the Vernons, who were of Hilton, in Staffordshire; Henry, his son, married the heiress of Sir George Vernon, of Haslington, in Cheshire, one of the Justices of Common Pleas, by which match his posterity became the representatives of the original elder male line of the Vernons, Barons of Shipbrooke. His grandson, Henry, married the heiress of Pigot, and representative of the ancient family of Venables, Barons of Kinderton, in Cheshire.—*Magna Brit. Derb.*

of a darker colour, and has two small wings. The centre has a handsome pediment, of elaborate construction, rising to the roof.   The original style is well preserved throughout, and the interior arrangements are tasteful and convenient.* Among the pictures in the gallery are portraits of the Lords Cromwell and Strafford, and Sir John Vernon, (three of the favourites of Charles I.,) with others of the Vernon family.

The front of the Hall shewn in our view, overlooks a fine deer-park of six hundred acres, stocked with nearly one thousand head of deer.   The opposite front commands an extensive prospect across the contiguous lake, over a country richly-wooded, and of great beauty and fertility.

In the immediate vicinity of the Hall, on the right, within the grounds, is the village-church, a venerable edifice, with a square tower, mantled over with ivy. It contains a number of monuments of the Vernon family.

A large monument of alabaster, within an arched recess, exhibiting the recumbent effigies of a male and female, bears an inscription in old English characters, as follows:

" Here lyeth the bodye of John Vernon, Esquier, the sonne of Henrye Vernon, sonne of Sir John Vernon, knight, and of Hellen, one of the Daughters and Co-heirs of Sir John Montgomery, by the which Hellen the manor of Sudbury and divers other lordships and lands lineallir descended unto the said John Vernon who deceased at ——— in the Countie of Essex, the 8th day of July, A.D. 1600, from whence his body was conveyed and here interred and this monument erected by Mary his Wife, Daughter of Sir Edward Little-ton, of Pillaton Hall, in the County of Stafford, knight."   [Underneath is an inscription to the lady.]

The other monuments are chiefly tablets of marble, and among the inscriptions are the following:—

" Near this place lyes buried the body of Sir Thomas Vernon, Knight, de-scended from the ancient family of the Vernons, of Haddon, for many years Representative in Parliament for the City of London.   He departed this life 10th February, 1709."

" In memory of the Honourable Ann Venables Vernon, surviving daughter of George Venables Lord Vernon, by his third wife, Martha, daughter of the Honourable Simon Harcourt.   Born March 2nd, 1754, died April 10th, 1837, aged 83 years.   This token of the most sincere affection was placed here by her brother, the Archbishop of York."

---

*It was built by Mrs. Mary Vernon, who died in 1622.

SUDBURY HALL

The Seat of Lord Vernon

Drawn & Printed by Rayner, Derby

Published by Dawson & Hobson, Ashbourn.

"Here lie the bodies of the Reverend Doctor Addenbrooke, Dean of Litch-field, and Rector of this parish, who died 25th February 1776, aged 84 years. Also of Dorothy his wife."

"The Honourable Anne Venables Vernon consecrated this tablet to the memory of her lamented sister, the Honourable Martha Venables Vernon, third daughter of George first Lord Vernon and Martha daughter of the Honourable Simon Harcourt. She was born Dec. 25, 1751, (O.S.) and died June 6, 1808. The following lines were written by her elder sister, the Honourable Elizabeth Venables Vernon, Countess Harcourt:—

> "Accept, lov'd shade, the tributary tear
> That fond affliction sheds upon thy bier.
> Ah, justly lov'd! thine was the noblest mind,
> Thine manly sense with female softness join'd;
> Thine warm benevolence, the generous heart,
> Anxious to all its blessings to impart;
> Bright beam'd in thee affection's purest rays,
> With modest diffidence that shrunk from praise.
> Oh! while we mourn thy loss, thy worth revere,
> May holy hope, faith, piety sincere,
> Teach us, like thee, our wishes to resign,
> In meek submission to the Will divine."

On a marble tablet to the memory of the Hon. Catharine Vernon, (second daughter of the first Lord Vernon,) who died in 1775, are inscribed some pleasing lines from the pen of William Whitehead, the Poet Laureat:—

> "Mild as the opening morn's serenest ray,
> Mild as the close of summer's softest day;
> Her form, her virtues, fram'd alike to please,
> With artless charms and unassuming ease.
> On every breast their mingling influence stole,
> And in sweet union breath'd one beauteous whole.
> This fair example to the world was lent
> As the short lesson of a life well spent:
> Alas! too short! but bounteous Heav'n best knows
> When to reclaim the blessings it bestows."

An elegant mural monument of white marble, with the busts of the late Lord and Lady Vernon, is thus inscribed:

"Under a yew tree in this church-yard, in a spot chosen by himself, are deposited the mortal remains of George Charles Lord Vernon, who died at Gibraltar, 18th November, 1835, aged 55 years. A man without guile or selfishness, a Christian in mind and action; following the steps of his Lord and Master, he humbly endeavoured to glorify his God by doing good unto all men.

" In the same place also are interred the remains of Frances Maria Warren Lady Vernon, relict of George Charles Lord Vernon, daughter of Sir John Borlase Warren, Bart. of Stapleford Hall, Notts.   Having sustained a long series of ill health and suffering, with truly Christian fortitude and resignation, she died at Poynton Hall, Cheshire, 17th September, 1837, aged 53 years, lamented and beloved by all."

Beneath the organ-gallery are two sculptured effigies, of stone, formerly in a recumbent position, but now placed upright, and belonging, it is probable, to some early members of the Montgomery family.

The church was re-pewed a few years ago, and is now in excellent repair. It is furnished with a handsome organ, the gift of the late Lady Vernon.

The living is a rectory, in the gift of Lord Vernon, and the Rev. Frederic Anson, Jun. is the present incumbent. The church is dedicated to All Saints.

By the munificence of the Vernon family two schools have been founded and are maintained for educating the children of the parish in the principles of the Established Church. The school-buildings are very neatly arranged, and the number of children now under instruction is about 130. A valuable parochial library is also established.

The number of inhabitants in the parish is about 642, and the estimated annual value of the property therein is £6,701.

CHAPTER XVI.

AMONG the objects of interest to the historian and antiquary connected with the town of Ashbourn and the valley of the Dove are the relics of the ancient and once famous Castle of Tutbury. When the feudal system prevailed in England, and the internal polity of the kingdom was regulated entirely according to the laws and usages of that social institution, Tutbury was a place of importance as the capital of an extensive territory called the Honor* of

---

*The term Honor, according to Spelman, was introduced into England by the Normans, to denote a barony, or the patrimony of a feudal baron ; deriving its specific appellation from its capital, (as in the case of Tutbury,) or sometimes from the family name of the baronial proprietor. As a manor might comprehend several knights' fees, tenements, customs, and services,—so an Honor comprised many manors, many knights' fees, many royalties, &c. It was likewise termed a royal fee, (feodum regale), because it was always held of the King in capite ; while a noble fee simply was more commonly held under a mesne Lord than immediately from the crown.—V. Glossar. Archailog. Ed. iii. 1687. p. 300.

Tutbury.   This Honor, it has been already observed,
comprised a great number of towns, hamlets, and places,
chiefly in the counties of Derby and Stafford, and including
all those described in this work; and hence some account
of Tutbury itself, and of the transactions of consequence,
civil or military, which took place in or near it, may be
deemed an appropriate addition.*

The site of the Castle is a commanding eminence on the
south bank of the river, within the township and parish of
Tutbury, in the Hundred of Offlow, and Northern Division
of the county of Stafford, about twelve miles south of
Ashbourn, and five miles north-west of Burton-on-Trent.

Some have conjectured that Tutbury was the site of a
town and castle in the time of the Saxon Heptarchy; and
that they were destroyed by the Danes in the ninth century:
but there is nothing of importance recorded concerning this
place till after the middle of the eleventh century, when a
castle was erected here by one of the dependents of William
I. usually styled the Conqueror.   Nearly the whole of
South Britain was by this Norman prince distributed into
feudal demesnes of various extent, many of which were
retained as the property of the Crown, forming one grand
source of the royal revenue; the others were granted under
various terms to the King's officers, civil and military, to
ecclesiastical bodies, and to divers individuals who had the
means of purchasing or otherwise obtaining the bounty of
the monarch.

From the ancient record of territorial property called
Domesday Book it appears that when the survey preparatory to that work was made (about 1080) Henry de Ferrers
had the Castle of *Toteberie* (Tutbury): and in the burgh
or town within the verge of the Castle there were forty-two
men who lived by merchandize; whose rents, with those

---

*Some of the following particulars relating to these events are derived from
Sir Oswald Mosley's " History of the Castle, Priory, and Town of Tutbury."
Octavo, London: 1832.

of the market yielded their lord £4 10s. a year.* Henry
de Ferrers was one of the commissioners appointed by the
King to superintend the Domesday Survey; and he was
himself one of the greatest landed proprietors in the kingdom, possessing a vast number of lordships in the counties
of Stafford, Derby, Leicester, Nottingham, and Warwick,
besides other estates in different parts of England. He was
not however the first Norman grantee of Tutbury, for King
William is said to have given the town and castle to Hugh
of Avranches, (Hugo de Abrincis,) who soon afterwards,
upon acquiring the more ample domains of the Earls of
Chester, surrendered this lordship to the royal donor, who
bestowed it on his favourite Henry de Ferrers. This great
Norman Baron was led by its central situation and other
local advantages to fix on Tutbury as the seat of his power
and the capital of his wide-spread territories. On one side
was an unreclaimed tract of forest and woodland, adapted
for the pleasures of the chase, constituting the all-absorbing
amusement of the princes and nobles of that period in a
time of peace; and in another direction stretched a fine
valley of fertile meadows, along the banks of the Dove, as
far as the eye could reach, affording abundant pasturage
for flocks and herds, and furnishing other produce for the
support of the household of the feudal lord, as well as for
that of his numerous tenants and retainers. We accordingly find that he founded, or rather rebuilt the Castle, on
the site of the ruinous fortress of Tutbury; but on a plan
much more capacious and magnificent than that of the
antecedent edifice. However there are no traces of the
work of Ferrers remaining, and the noble ruins that now
arrest the attention of the traveller formed portions of a
structure raised by a subsequent proprietor of the Honor of
Tutbury.

Terra Henrici de Ferrieres. In Pireholle Hund. Henr. de Ferrieres habet
Castellum de Toteberie. In Burgo circa Castellum sunt 42 Homines de mer-
cato suo tantum vivantes: et reddibant, cum Foro, 4 lib. et 10 sol."—*Domesd.
Staffordsh.*

The Castle, together with the princely domain to which it belonged, was held by the lineal descendants of Henry de Ferrers till the reign of Henry III. when Robert de Ferrers, Earl of Derby, and lord of the Honor of Tutbury, having repeatedly joined in the insurrections of the Barons against the reigning monarch, he was attainted of treason, and all his estates became forfeited to the crown. King Henry having thus acquired a legal right to the ample territories of the ancient Earls of Derby, took advantage of the circumstance to form an appanage for his younger son Prince Edmund, afterwards Earl of Lancaster, and titular King of Sicily, to whom the demesnes of the rebellious noble were transferred by royal charters. The Honor of Tutbury was now vested in the Lancastrian branch of the royal family of Plantaganet. After a few regular descents through male heirs, Tutbury came into the possession of John (Plantaganet) commonly styled John of Gaunt, the fourth son of King Edward III., in consequence of his marriage with Blanch, one of the daughters and co-heiresses of Henry Duke of Lancaster, the grandson of Prince Edmund. From this period, the reign of Edward III., the Honor and Castle of Tutbury became part and parcel of the Duchy of Lancaster; and Henry, the son and heir of John of Gaunt, by his consort Blanch, having ascended the throne, under the title of Henry IV. after the deposition of his cousin Richard II., the Duchy with all its appendages, and Tutbury among the rest, was annexed to the crown. Edward IV. in 1465 gave the Honor of Tutbury to his brother the Duke of Clarence; but in a very few years the grant was resumed; and ever since, except during the suspension of the regal government after the fall of Charles I. it has continued to form a part of the demesnes of the crown.

Notices of the early lords of Tutbury, the Earls Ferrers of Derby, and the Plantaganets, Earls and Dukes of Lancaster, have been given in a preceding part of this work;*

*See Chapter I. p. 6, &c.

most of those personages having been lords of the manor of Ashbourn: it is not necessary therefore to enter further into the general history of those princes and nobles: but there are some facts and statements especially pertaining to the Castle of Tutbury, and the feudal authority of its proprietors, which are of too much importance to be omitted.

An account of the rights and privileges enjoyed by Robert de Ferrers, the last Earl of Derby of his name and family, occurs in a tenure-roll of the Hundred of Offlow, of the reign of Henry III. about 1255. It states that the "Earl of Derby holds of the King, Tutbury, Rolveston, Marchington, and Barton [under Needwood.] He hath a free court at Tutbury, in which are pleaded all pleas but such as are specially excepted. And he hath a view of frank pledge independent of the Sheriff. And there are in the said liberty seven hydes and a half, besides the vill of Barton, where there is one hyde. And he hath there a market and a fair; but it is not known by what warrant, or from what time. And he hath the right of waif there."*

Edmund Earl of Lancaster, the successor of this nobleman as lord of the Honor of Tutbury, possessed the same feudal power, and the right of holding courts of judicature, within his demesne, at which his officers presided. The manner in which justice was administered, or rather the mal-administration of judicial proceedings in the feudal court of Tutbury, seems to have been by no means creditable to the presiding judges. This may be inferred from the following extract from the Hundred Rolls in the Tower of London, which also exhibits an example of the summary punishment of a culprit worsted, and thus convicted in the trial by battle, as it took place under the sanction of the baronial court of Tutbury, in the reign of Edward I.:—

"The Bailiffs of the Lord Edmund, amongst whom was Clement the Clerk, and others of the Castle of Tutbury,

*X. 10: Bibliot. Harleian.

in the second year of King Edward, immediately after the Feast of St. Michael, (1273,) took prisoner a certain robber, named William Knout, who became an approver, [or turned king's evidence]; and these Bailiffs kept the said approver in custody, and he charged Richard Astell as being one of his accomplices, which Richard having been apprehended, he gave the said Bailiffs ten shillings, that he might escape. The same approver also accused Ralph de Aunsedley of robbery; he was likewise arrested, and gave money to the said Bailiffs that he might be set free. John Walcepot also was indicted on his evidence, and after being apprehended by the said Bailiffs, was acquitted in the court of the Lord Edmund. There moreover came one Ralph le Young of Rolleston, and charged the said approver with robbery in having stolen a cow, which the approver then had in his possession; and the accuser and the accused fought together at Tutbury, and the said Ralph having vanquished the said William, the latter was hanged. Also Gilbert Brende being accused by the aforesaid approver, gave four shillings to the said Bailiffs on that account."*

It may fairly be concluded that the officers belonging to the Court of the Honor of Tutbury were not more corrupt than those of many (perhaps most) other feudal courts throughout the kingdom. It was doubtless in consequence of a knowledge of the abuses that existed in these courts, that King Edward I. to a certain extent superseded their authority by the appointment of Justices of Assize, or judges sanctioned by the King himself, and empowered to make circuits through the realm twice a year, and hold sessions for the trial of causes civil or criminal, such as had been heretofore decided in the feudal courts, or those of municipal establishments, or else prosecuted with great trouble and expense before the royal judges at Westminster or other places where the King kept his court. To this

---

*Rotul. Hundred. An. 4. Edw. I.

prince, who has been styled the English Justinian, we owe
in a great measure not only this valuable improvement in our
legal polity, but also the regular institution of a popular
legislature; for it was in his reign and under his auspices
that the parliament took its present form, as consisting of
a House of Peers or Nobles, and a House of Commons, or
Delegates from the People at large; for though Knights
of Shires, Citizens, and Burgesses had occasionally assisted
in national councils in the reign of Henry III. and perhaps
at an earlier period, it was not till that of Edward I. that
they permanently constituted any integral part of the legislature.

Thomas, who succeeded his father Edmund Plantaganet,
as the second Earl of Lancaster, paid homage to the King,
and had livery of his estates in the twenty-sixth year of
Edward I.; and he afterwards obtained licenses for holding
markets and fairs at different places within the Honor of
Tutbury. He repaired and embellished the Castle, and
made it his principal residence; and finding that the
people around had been impoverished and distressed
through the interference of their former lord, the Earl of
Derby, in the civil wars which had convulsed the kingdom,
he turned his early attention to a redress of their grievances,
and the promotion of their prosperity, and thus contributed
to the improvement of his own revenues. These were so
abundant that his great wealth must have added considerably to the influence he possessed as a prince of the blood
royal, and he seems to have lived in a style of magnificence
suited to his exalted station. The splendour and costliness
of his establishment may be estimated from the ensuing
statement of his domestic expenditure for one year (1313)
as furnished by Henry Leicester, his treasurer :— *

The charge of the pantry, buttery, and kitchen	3495	0	0
To 184 tuns and 1 pipe of red or claret wine, and 2 tuns of white wine	104	17	6
To grocery	180	17	0

*History of Tutbury, p. 39, &c.

To 6 barrels of sturgeon	19	0	0
To 6,800 stock-fish (so called), and for dried fish of all sorts, such as lings, haberdines, &c.	41	6	7
To 1714 lbs. of wax, vermilion, and turpentine	314	7	4½
To 2319 lbs of tallow candles, for the household, and 1870 of lights for Paris candles, called perchers	31	14	3
To charge of the Earl's great horses, which were generally more than 1500, and servants' wages.........................	486	4	3½
To linen, for the Earl and his chaplains, and for the pantry..	43	17	0
To 129 dozen of parchment and ink	4	8	3½
To 2 cloths of scarlet, for the Earl's use; 1 of russet, for the Bishop of Anjou; 70 of blue, for the knights; 28 for the esquires; 15 of medley, for the clerks; 15 for the officers; 19 for the grooms; 5 for the archers; 4 for the minstrels and carpenters; with the sharing and carriage of the Earl's liveries at Christmas	460	15	0
To 7 furs of valuable miniver, or powdered ermine, 7 hoods of purple, 395 furs of budge, [the dressed furs of lambs] for the liveries of barons, knights, and clerks; 123 furs of lambs, bought at Christmas, for the esquires	147	17	8
To 65 saffron-coloured cloths, for the barons and knights in summer; 12 red cloths, for the clerks; 26 ray cloths, for the esquires; 1 for the officers; and 4 ray cloths, for carpets in the hall	345	13	8
To 100 pieces of green silk, for the knights; 14 budge 'furs, for surcoats; 13 hoods of budge, for clerks; 75 furs of lambs, in summer, with canvass and cords to truss them	72	19	0
To saddles for the Lord's summer liveries	51	6	8
To 1 saddle, for the Earl, of the Prince's arms	2	0	0
To several items (unknown)	241	14	1½
To horses lost in the Earl's service	8	6	8
To fees paid to earls, barons, knights, and esquires	623	15	5
To gifts to Knights of France, the Queen of England, nurses to the Countess of Warren, esquires, minstrels, messengers, and riders	92	14	0
To 168 yards of russet cloth, and 24 coats, for poor men, with money given to the poor on Maundy Thursday............	8	16	7
To 24 silver dishes, 24 saucers, 24 cups, a pair of Pater-nosters, 1 silver coffer, all bought this year	103	5	6
To divers messengers about the Earl's business..............	34	19	8
To sundry things in the Earl's chamber....................	5	0	0
To several old debts paid this year	88	16	0½
The expenses of the Countess, at Pickering, in the pantry, buttery, kitchen, &c.	285	13	4½
In wine, wax, spices, cloths, furs, &c. for the Countess's wardrobe	154	7	4½
Total......	7449	13	0½

The sum of £7,500 a year would not be thought very extraordinary as the expenditure of a nobleman of the highest rank at the present time; but considering the difference in the price of silver, the above sum must be at least tripled to make it correspond in value with modern money.

This nobleman, who during the reign of his uncle, Edward I. saw the kingdom flourishing in wealth and power under the administration of that great and wise monarch, must have witnessed with mingled anger and contempt the profligate weakness and folly of his cousin, Edward II. and the unbounded extravagance and daring insolence of the King's favourite minister, Piers Gaveston, created Earl of Cornwall. With a mixture of patriotism and ambition often apparent in public characters, the Earl of Lancaster engaged in active opposition to the measures of the court, and became the chief of an association of the leading men in the kingdom, who resolved to displace the royal minion, and rectify the disorders in the government. The King was obliged to submit to the requisition of this powerful confederacy, and Gaveston was banished, but speedily recalled by his doting master; he was banished a second time and again recalled, but only to meet with his deserved fate; for the Barons, headed by Lancaster, again appeared in arms, and having taken Gaveston prisoner, they at once put him to death. For this irregular proceeding they with some difficulty extorted a formal pardon from the King. But he never really forgave these ministers of a nation's vengeance on a great criminal. The Earl of Lancaster, as having been the leader of Gaveston's foes, was marked as the principal object of the King's displeasure, which was manifested in various ways. Lancaster had married the heiress of the Earl of Lincoln, who was prompted to elope from her husband, and seek a divorce on the pretext of a previous contract with a retainer of the Earl Warren. King Edward had adopted a new favourite, Hugh le Despencer, who like Gaveston soon rendered him-

43

self obnoxious to the old nobility of the kingdom. He took forcible possession of some lands on the Welsh border, belonging to the Earl of Hereford; and this act of injustice, in which he was supported by the King, was the signal for a new confederacy of the Barons, under the Earl of Lancaster. They collected a body of forces, and having marched to London, where Parliament was then sitting, a charge of high crimes and misdemeanours was brought against Despenser and his father, who were sentenced to the forfeiture of their estates and banishment for life. A few months afterwards, however, the King procured a revocation of the sentence; and acting with more energy than usual, he raised an army, and seized the castles and estates of the Barons who had opposed him. The Earls of Lancaster, Hereford, and other nobles, on their part collected troops, and made preparations for resistance. They took their stand at Pontefract, where Lancaster waited for some time in the hope of receiving assistance from the King of Scotland, with whom he had made a secret alliance. Meanwhile the people flocked in great numbers to join the King, who was preparing to advance from his quarters at Coventry towards Tutbury, threatening to lay waste the feudal territories of the Earl of Lancaster. That chief, disappointed of the expected aid from Scotland, hastily abandoned the siege of Tickhill Castle, garrisoned by the royalists, and marching southward, with all his forces, amounting to thirty thousand men, he arrived at the Castle of Tutbury, in the beginning of March, 1320. Here he purposed to make a stand till the arrival of reinforcements from the north. But the royalists acted with unexpected promptitude, and having passed the Trent, and taken the town of Burton, they prepared to attack the Castle of Tutbury, whither their defeated antagonists had retired. The difficulties and misfortunes of Lancaster and his associates rapidly multiplied. Deprived of the hope of succour, and unprepared to sustain a regular siege at Tutbury, the Earl determined to return to Pontefract.

Previously to his defeat, Lancaster had caused a considerable quantity of Scottish coin to be forwarded to Tutbury, concluding that it would be wanted to pay the
soldiers whom his allies had promised to send him. Not
having had occasion to use it for such a purpose, he intrusted it, together with a large amount of English and
Flemish money, to the care of his treasurer, Henry Leicester, with directions for the transmission of it as speedily as
possible to Pontefract. The hasty approach of the royalists
obliged the Earl to flee from Tutbury, before the arrangements for the transport of the treasure were perfected. The
military-chest was sent off under the guard of a strong
detachment; and Lancaster with his troops left the Castle
but a very short time before the King's forces entered that
fortress. In the alarm and confusion which attended the
passage of the river Dove, (below the town of Tutbury,) by
the fugitives, the chest with the money it held was lost.
Leicester was obliged to abandon his charge; and the treasure, buried beneath a deep bed of sand and gravel, the
deposit of successive floods, remained concealed from
human eyes for more than five centuries, when it was once
more brought to light by accidental circumstances.

In the year 1831, Mr. Webb, the proprietor of cotton-
mills at Tutbury, being desirous to procure a greater fall
for what is technically termed the tail-water from the
wheel that works the machinery of his mill, he with that
view extended an embankment between the mill-stream
and the river much further below the bridge than it had
formerly reached; and for this purpose it became requisite
to take a considerable quantity of gravel out of the bed of
the river, from the end of the water-course, as far up as the
new bridge. While the workmen were engaged in this
operation, on the 1st of June, 1831, they met with several
pieces of small silver coin, about sixty yards below the
bridge: as they proceeded up the river, they continued to
find more lying about half a yard below the surface of the
gravel, apparently having been brought by the stream from

a higher situation. On the 7th of June the men suspended their work to seek for more coin, and they were not disappointed, for several thousand pieces of money were obtained on that day; as they advanced up the river they became more successful, and the next day they struck on the grand deposit of coins, whence those already found had been washed, about thirty yards below the bridge, and from four to five feet beneath the surface of the gravel. The coins were here so abundant that one hundred and fifty were turned up in a single shovel-full of gravel, and nearly five thousand of them were collected by two of the individuals who were thus employed on that day. They were sold to the by-standers at from six shillings to eight and sixpence a hundred; but on the day following, as the quantity found decreased, the prices advanced. The great bulk of the coins was found within an area of about three yards square, near the Derbyshire bank of the river. More than three hundred persons were engaged in this search at one time, and the idle and inquisitive were attracted from various quarters to the spot. Disputes, as might have been expected, took place, and the magistrates interfered; but the officers of the Crown having obtained intelligence of the discovery, set up a claim on the part of the King to all the coin which might in future be found in the bed of the river, as treasure-trove, appertaining to the Duchy of Lancaster. A commission was issued by the Chancellor of the Duchy, prohibiting all unauthorised persons from searching the river; and at the same time ordering a further search on behalf of the Crown; in consequence of which, between the 28th of June and the 1st of July, more than fifteen hundred additional coins were procured. The excavation whence the coins were chiefly taken was then filled up, and gravel spread over the bed of the river so as to impede any further examination. The following list of the coins discovered is furnished by Sir Oswald Mosley, Bart. (from whom the preceding statement is derived,) on the authority of Mr. Edwards, solicitor, of Burton-on-Trent:—

" The English coins were those of the first coinage of
Henry III. and of that in the thirty-second year of his
reign; those of the seventh and twenty-eighth of Edward I.
and those of Edward II., who does not appear to have had
any *great* coinage, although during the course of his reign
he coined largely. The series of coins of Edward I. is
quite complete at Tutbury, presenting those coined at London, Canterbury, York, Durham, Chester, Lincoln, Exeter,
Bristol, St. Edmunds, Berwick, Kyngeston, and Newcastle,
in England; and at Dublin, Waterford, and Cork, in Ireland. The prelatical coins of Durham are also complete
during the reigns of Edward I. and II.: namely, those of
Bishop Beck, Bishop Kellar, and Bishop Beaumont. Some
prelatical coins of York were also found, and others with
the name 'Rob. de Hadley' upon them, which Mr. Edwards conjectures to have been struck at the mint of the
Abbot of St. Edmunds. The Scotch coins are those of
Alexander III., John Baliol, and Robert Bruce, besides
which there are a number of foreign sterlings of Brabant,
Lorraine, Hainault and the [German] Empire.—The total
number of coins thus found is supposed to have been, on
the most moderate computation, one hundred thousand."*

On the flight of the Earl of Lancaster, the King entered
the Castle of Tutbury without opposition; and after having
rested there five days, he gave orders that it should be dismantled, and marched northwards, in pursuit of his opponents, whom he branded, by public proclamation, with the
guilt of treason and rebellion. They fell before him. The
Earl of Hereford was killed in battle; and Lancaster, being
taken prisoner, was executed as a traitor, with more than
the usual marks of ignominy and cruelty to which such
state criminals were exposed. The King determined to glut
his vengeance for the death of Gavestone, shewed no mercy
to the adherents of his fallen foe : several of the nobles
were beheaded, many knights were hanged in chains, and
great numbers confined to a prison.

*History of Tutbury, p. 325, &c.

On the execution of Earl Thomas, Tutbury with his other estates devolved to the crown; but Henry Plantaganet, the brother of the late Earl, in the reign of Edward III. procured a reversal of the attainder, and recovered his patrimony. Some account of this nobleman, and of his son and successor, Henry, the first Duke of Lancaster, may be found in a previous part of this work.

The Duke left no male issue; and his title, with the Honor of Tutbury, was inherited by his son-in-law, John of Gaunt, as elsewhere stated. This Prince rebuilt nearly the whole of the Castle, which had remained in ruins ever since the death of Thomas Earl of Lancaster, a period of more than forty years. The present gateway, and the northern front of the apartments afterwards occupied as a presence-chamber by Mary Queen of Scots, are the only subsisting portions of John of Gaunt's edifice. " We are now (says Sir Oswald Mosley) arrived at a period of uncommon splendour in the annals of Tutbury: the inhabitants of that town had suffered most severely from the effects of the rebellion of Thomas Earl of Lancaster; and the removal of the subsequent proprietors from the long-frequented residence of their predecessors, had tended much to increase the depression under which they languished; a new scene was now about to open, surpassing in gaiety and magnificence any thing which they had before witnessed. The mouldering turrets of their ancient castle arose, phœnix-like from their ashes, with redoubled glory; the rank weeds no longer flourished within the neglected area of its walls; the breeze no longer sighed sorrowfully through the shattered casement; crowds of attendants were now beheld bustling through the paved courts; knights and squires, in gorgeous apparel, were now seen passing and repassing from the gates on well trained steeds, whose trampling hoofs made the massive walls resound; mirth and festivity once more resumed their sway in the baronial hall, and a state of prosperity, greater than was ever before known, now exhilarated the happy tenants of John of Gaunt."

This prince possessed both talents and virtues, but his public career was by no means faultless, and his private character was in many respects obnoxious to censur. He was married to his first wife at the early age of twenty; and interest rather than affection may well be supposed to have been his inducement to wed the co-heiress of one of the richest and most powerful of the English nobility. Blanch of Lancaster was not distinguished either for personal attractions or mental acquirements: her health was indifferent, and her retiring disposition but ill accorded with the aspiring views of her ambitious partner. She lived with him ten years, and the latter part of her life was embittered by the knowledge of an intrigue that subsisted between her husband and one of her attendants, named Catharine Roet. This young lady was the daughter of Sir Payne Roet, a native of Hainault; and having when young, together with her sister Philippa, been taken into the family of the Duchess, she was through the interest of her patroness married to Sir Otes Swinford, while Philippa became the wife of the celebrated poet Chaucer.

The fair but frail Catharine Swinford, preferred her lover to her husband, and attended the Duke of Lancaster in his foreign campaigns for three successive years, in the course of which she became the mother of several children, who received the surname of Beaufort, from the place in which they were born, a castle in Normandy. Upon the return of the Duke to England, in November, 1369, he found that his consort Blanch had died of the plague in the preceding September, and had been interred in St. Paul's Cathedral, London, where he caused a splendid monument to be erected for her, the chief material of which was alabaster procured from Tutbury; and the expense of the structure, including the carriage of the stone, amounted to £486. By this Duchess he had a son, who afterwards reigned under the title of Henry IV., and two daughters, whom the Duke, with little regard for decency, placed under the tuition of Catharine Swinford. His attachment to this favourite concubine did not however prevent him from contracting a new and splendid matrimonial alliance. For in 1372, while residing at Bourdeaux, where he kept a court in almost regal magnificence, as Governor of Gascony, John of Gaunt heard that Don Pedro, King of Castile and Leon, had died, leaving two daughters, who resided at Aire, a city about sixty-five miles from Bourdeaux. By the persuasion of the Gascon barons he was induced to espouse the eldest of the royal sisters, and endeavour to wrest the crown to which she was heiress from Henry de Trastamere, the illegitimate brother of Don Pedro, who had taken possession of the kingdom. The nuptials were celebrated by splendid feasts and entertainments at the Duke's castle at Bourdeaux. The knights and nobles of Gascony presented to the royal pair many rich jewels, and medals were struck in honour of the union.* But how much soever the pride of the prince might be gratified by this alliance, in consequence of which he assumed the title of King of Castile, he found his ambitious views disappointed; and after some attempts to vindicate his claims to the crown by force of arms, he was obliged to submit to the superior fortune of his rival.

John of Gaunt on his return from Gascony to England, with his Queen-Duchess, gave her the choice among his various castles that she might select one for her future abode, and she gave the preference to Tutbury, which was accordingly fitted up for her reception. On the 23d of

---

*One of these medals is now in the possession of Godfrey Meynell, Esq. of Meynell Langley. An engraving of it is given in " The History of Tutbury." p. 74. The front exhibits a representation of the Duke of Lancaster, with a wreath of roses upon his head, his left hand resting on the Bible, while his right hand clasps that of his royal bride; she wears a crown upon her head, to which, as Queen of Castile and Leon, she was justly entitled. Above them is a radiated sun, and around the margin a legend in Latin, which, translated, reads, " We join our right hands with mutual desire under a friendly compact;" on the reverse, within a circle of roses, " A chaste wife is a sweet rose;" and round the margin, " As the sun of God when it arises, so is a good woman the ornament of his house."

April, in the 47th year of the reign of Edward III. Sir
Robert Attemore, the receiver of Tutbury, had orders to
repair the Castle there, and make the building fit for the
residence of the Queen, and the children of John of Gaunt,
by his first wife, before the next Whitsuntide, as also to
lay in two tons of good wine, sixty quarters of wheat, and
a sufficient quantity of wood and coal for the use of the
household.   Additional repairs were also made to the
Castle, in the autumn of the following year; a garden and
a vineyard were planted for the use of the Queen, and a
new park formed under the Castle walls, called Tutbury
Park, which was stocked with ten bucks and twenty does,
from the park of Castle Hay.

Tutbury Castle was now at its highest prosperity, enlivened and adorned by the Queen's court, the number of
strangers who daily resorted thither, and the magnificent
liberality of the princely proprietor.   The town of Tutbury
was enlarged beyond its ancient dimensions ; the agricul-
turist here found a ready market for the produce of his
land, the merchant for his goods, and everything contributed to enrich the inhabitants, and augment the value of
property in their vicinity.

Among the amusements of the rich and great in the
fourteenth century, music held a distinguished place ; and
though it was not of so refined or complicated a character
as modern taste approves, it seems to have afforded equal
if not greater delight to less fastidious ears.   The reward
assigned to the minstrel in those days was circumscribed,
but the attention and respect he obtained shewed the high
estimation in which the art he cultivated was held by those
who patronised him.   A chair was set for him at the upper
end of the hall, which he never failed to occupy on all festal
occasions; and hence he excited the feelings of the guests,
by the recital of mysterious legends, tales of the battle-
field, or simple ballads presenting interesting pictures of
domestic life.   Many such bards had from time to time
found a hospitable asylum beneath the roof of the lords of

44

Tutbury; but now when a regal court was established at
the Castle, under the presidency of the Queen, who was
passionately fond of music, and had endeavoured to improve
the taste of the English by the introduction of singers from
her own romantic country, the number of minstrels who
flocked to Tutbury became so great, as to render requisite
some rules for the maintenance of peace and order among
them. With this view, John of Gaunt appointed a governor
over them, with the title of " King of the Minstrels." Subsequently to this appointment a court was established for
the decision of disputes which might arise between minstrels,
styled " The Minstrels' Court." It was held before the
Steward of the Honor of Tutbury, on the morrow of Ascension Day, when the jury, consisting of musicians, elected
four stewards, one of whom was to be King of the Minstrels
for the ensuing year. These officers had full power and
authority to enforce the payment of all such fines and
amerciaments as were inflicted by the jury of the court
upon any minstrels, for the infraction of such orders as were
made for the government of that society; and the amount
of such fines was returned at every audit, by the stewards,
one moiety of which went to the Duke of Lancaster, and
the other to the stewards, for their trouble. Among the
orders for the regulation of the minstrels are several
enacted as recently as the fifth year of the reign of Charles
I., to the effect, " that no person shall use or exercise the
art and science of music, within the said counties [of Derby
and Stafford] as a common musician or minstrel, for benefit
and gains, except he have served and been brought up in
the same art and science by the space of seven years, and
be allowed and admitted so to do at the said court by the
jury thereof, and by the consent of the steward of the said
court for the time being, on pain of forfeiting for every
month that he shall so offend, three shillings and fourpence.
And that no such musician or minstrel, shall take into his
service, to teach and instruct any one in the said art and
science for any shorter time than for the space of seven

years, under the pain of forfeiting for every such offence
forty shillings."*

The usages of feudal times afford some singular examples
of broad humour, which are curious as indications of the
character of the age. Such are the strange customs by
which manors were sometimes held in lieu of rents or beneficial services. Few of these have attracted more notice
than the tenure of the manor of Whichnor, in Staffordshire,
which required that a flitch of bacon should be kept by the
lord of the manor, until claimed by a wedded pair, who,
after having worn the chains of Hymen a year and a day,
had yet known no repentance. It has been supposed that
for the purpose of reconciling his Queen to a residence
so remote from court, John of Gaunt instituted at the
period of her abode at Tutbury Castle several whimsical
customs connected with feudal tenures within the Honor of
Tutbury ; and among them the premium for matrimonial
happiness.

Sir Philip de Somerville, whose vivacity and good humour had long rendered him a welcome guest at the Castle,
inherited the manors of Whichnor and Sirescote, which his
ancestors had held since the Conquest, as one knight's fee
and three parts of another: like other lands held by military service, these were subject to reliefs and aids paid to
the superior lord of the fee upon stated occasions ; but the
Duke of Lancaster was now pleased to remit, to his favourite and his heirs, one moiety of these claims for ever, upon
the following singular condition: namely, that he, Sir
Philip de Somerville, should "find, maintain, and sustain
one bacon flyke hanging in his hall at Whichnor, ready
arrayed all times of the year but in Lent, to be given to
every man or woman married, after the day and year of
their marriage be passed; and to be given to every man of
religion, archbishop, bishop, prior, or other religious, and
to every priest, after the year and day of their profession

---

finished, or of their dignity received, in form following:
Whensoever that any such before named will come for to
inquire for the bacon, in their own person, or by any other
for them, they shall come to the bailiff or to the porter of
the lordship of Whichnor, and shall say to them in the
manner as ensueth; "Bailiff, or Porter, I do you to know,
that I come for myself (or if he be come for any other, showing for whom he demands) to demand one bacon flyke,
hanging in the hall of the Lord of Whichnor, after the form
thereunto belonging." After which relation, the bailiff or
porter shall assign a day to him upon promise by his faith
to return, and with him to bring twain of his neighbours.
And in the meantime, the said bailiff shall take with him
twain of the freeholders of the lordship of Whichnor, and
they three shall go to the manor of Rudlow belonging to
Robert Knyghtley, and there shall summon the aforesaid
Knyghtley or his bailiff, commanding him to be ready at
Whichnor the day appointed, at prime of day, with his carriage, that is to say, a horse and a saddle, a sack and a
pryke, for to convey and carry the said bacon and corn a
journey out of the county of Stafford at his cost. And then
the said bailiff shall, with the said freeholders, summon all
the tenants of the said manor to be ready at the day
appointed at Whichnor, for to do and perform the services
which they owe to the bacon. And at the day assigned, all
such as owe services to the bacon, shall be ready at the
gate of the manor of Whichnor, from the rising of the sun
to noon, attending and awaiting for the coming of him
that fetcheth the bacon. And when he is come, there
shall be delivered to him and his fellows, chaplets, and to
all those who shall be there to do their services due to the
bacon. And they shall lead the said demandant, with
trumpets and tabours and other manner of minstrelsy, to
the hall door, where he shall find the lord of Whichnor, or
his steward, ready to deliver the bacon in this manner:

He shall inquire of him who demandeth the bacon, if he
has brought twain of his neighbours with him; and he

must answer, "They be here ready." And then the steward shall cause these two neighbours to swear, if the said demandant be a wedded man, or hath been a wedded man; and if since his marriage one year and a day be passed; and if he be a freeman or a villain. And if his neighbours make oath, that he hath for him all these three points rehearsed, then shall the bacon be taken down, and brought to the hall door, and shall there be laid upon half a quarter of wheat, and upon one other of rye. And he that demandeth the bacon, shall kneel upon his knee, and shall hold his right hand upon a book, which book shall be laid above the bacon and the corn, and shall make oath in this manner: "Hear ye, Sir Philip de Somerville, Lord of Whichnor, maintainer and giver of this bacon, that I (A) since I wedded (B) my wife, and since I had her in my keeping and at my will, by a year and a day after our marriage, I would not have changed for any other, fairer or fouler, richer or poorer, nor for any other descended of greater lineage, sleeping or waking, at any time. And if the said (B) were sole and I sole, I would take her to be my wife before all the women in the world, of what condition soever they be, good or evil, as help me God and his saints, and this flesh and all fleshes."

And his neighbours shall make oath, that they trust verily he hath said truly. And if it be found by his neighbours before named, that he be a freeman, there shall be delivered to him half a quarter of wheat, and a cheese; and if he be a villain, he shall have half a quarter of rye without cheese. And then shall Knyghtley, the Lord of Rudlow, be called, for to carry all these things afore rehearsed: and the said corn shall be laid upon horse, and the bacon above it; and he to whom the bacon appertaineth, shall ascend upon his horse, and shall take the cheese before him, if he have a horse, and if he have none, the Lord of Whichnor shall cause him to have one and a saddle, until such time as he has passed his lordship; and so shall they depart the manor of Whichnor, with the corn and the bacon, before him that hath won it, with trumpets, tabrets, and other manner of minstrelsy; and all the free tenants of Whichnor shall conduct him past the lordship of Whichnor; and then all shall return, except him to whom appertaineth to make the carriage and journey out of the county of Stafford, at the costs of his lord of Whichnor. And if the said Robert Knyghtley do not cause the bacon and corn to be conveyed as is rehearsed, the Lord of Whichnor shall cause it to be carried, and shall distrain the said Robert Knyghtley for his default, for one hundred shillings, in his manor of Rudlow, and shall keep the distress so taken irrepleviable."

Whether any claimants ever appeared for the Whichnor bacon we are not informed, but we find that Sir Philip duly performed the singular service thus imposed upon him. In the 16th of Edward I. he granted to Hugh de Newbold several small pieces of land in Dunstall, upon condition that he should render him and his heirs eight hens annually at Christmas, and one chaplet or nosegay of white and red roses, to decorate the bacon at Whichnor, on the feast of St. John the Baptist; also that the bacon should be dressed in a similar manner, with flowers or evergreens, at ten other stated times in the year.*

Another feudal custom which prevailed in the Honor of Tutbury, was that of "Bull Running," a popular amusement, which connected as it was with the Minstrels' Court, long remained as a memorial of the olden time. This ancient usage, like the preceding, may be traced to the period when John of Gaunt was lord of Tutbury, and to him, we presume, it owed its origin. But this practice, more honoured in the breach than the observance, has been already described, and therefore requires no further notice.†

---

*History of Tutbury, p. 79, &c. John of Gaunt is said to have borrowed this curious tenure from Dunmow, in Essex, where a similar custom was instituted in the reign of Henry III. The Spectator, No. 608, contains a humorous account of supposed candidates for the Whichnor bacon.

†See page 92, 95.

After the death of his brother, Edward the Black Prince, and during the minority of his nephew, Richard II., the Duke of Lancaster took an active part in the affairs of government. Very little of his time was devoted to the society of his Queen Constance, who continued to hold her secluded court at Tutbury Castle. The visits of the Duke to that place were few and transient. He was there from the 10th to the 21st of August, in 1374; and again from the 10th to the 20th of the same month in 1380; but the attractions of Catharine Swynford had such influence over him as to prevent him from paying even a decent attention to his royal consort, who was in every respect worthy of a happier fate: for she has been justly characterized as "a lady, above ladies innocent and zealous."* Her whole establishment was regulated with the utmost propriety: the expense of her private chamber and her wardrobe did not exceed five hundred marks annually; and the stipends of the few friends and attendants who formed her court were no more than sufficient to enable them to keep up a respectable appearance. She passed her time at Tutbury amidst the quiet amusements and avocations of domestic life, happier, probably, notwithstanding the desertion of her husband, than if she had been burthened with the splendid cares of royalty.

When he visited Tutbury in 1380, the Duke was suddenly called away to march against the Scots, who had invaded England, and wasted the counties of Westmoreland and Cumberland with fire and sword. This expedition led to a truce between the two nations; and when it was nearly expired, the Duke of Lancaster went as ambassador to the Scottish court, to make further arrangements for the preservation of peace. It was while he was absent on this mission that the memorable insurrection under Wat Tyler took place. John of Gaunt at that time was by no means popular; and the destruction of his noble palace of the

---

*Mills's Catalogue of Honour.

Savoy in the Strand, between London and Westminster, was one of the prominent atchievements of the infuriated mob.

The alarm arising from the outrageous proceedings of the rabble extended even to the solitary Castle of Tutbury, and the Queen of Castile sought refuge in the fortress of Pontefract. Such however was the cowardice or treachery of those who held that place, that though they were in the service of the Duke of Lancaster, the Queen, his consort, was refused admission; and she was consequently obliged to advance seven miles further, in the midst of a dark and cheerless night, by torch-light, to the castle of Knaresborough, where she fortunately remained unmolested till the re-establishment of the public peace enabled her to return to Tutbury.

During the reign of so weak and tyrannical a sovereign as Richard II. and amidst the frequent and serious commotions that consequently occurred among the people, it was almost impossible for a prince so nearly connected with the crown as John of Gaunt to remain a passive observer of the state of public affairs. His rank and station as first prince of the blood royal rendered him an object of suspicion to the King and his favourites; and at length a direct accusation of disloyalty was brought against him. The Duke was at that time at his Castle of Tutbury, in consultation with the Queen about a plan which he had formed for the invasion of Spain, and the vindication of their joint claim to the crown of Castile. On receipt of intelligence warning him of the King's hostile intentions, he prudently resolved to leave Tutbury, and summoned a band of well-armed followers to protect him in his retreat to Pontefract, which fortress, he could in case of necessity render secure against any sudden assault from his adversaries. Here he remained till the storm passed over; and through the active interference of the Princess Joan of Kent, (widow of the Black Prince, and mother of Richard II.) a reconciliation between the King and his uncle was effected. The Scots having again invaded the northern part of England, the Duke of Lancaster was sent against them. King Richard also himself at the head of a large army, marched across the Tweed, and captured and burnt the city of Edinburgh. It is a favourable trait in the character of John of Gaunt, that in gratitude for the hospitality with which he had been treated by the Abbot of the monastery of Holyrood, when on his embassy to Scotland, he persuaded the King to preserve that establishment from the fate of the surrounding buildings.

Not long after a circumstance occurred which revived the long-cherished purpose of the royal Duke to make a new attempt to obtain possession of the throne of Castile. John King of Portugal, having derived important assistance from a body of English troops in his wars with the French and Spaniards, was induced to apply to King Richard for further aid. The Duke of Lancaster exerted all his influence in support of the application of the Portuguese monarch, and the King, anxious to divert the attention of his powerful and ambitious uncle from objects nearer home, was ready to yield to his advice. A large armament was collected at Bristol in the following spring; and on Easter Sunday the Duke and Queen Constance took leave of the royal family; when his Majesty presented the Duke with a crown of gold, and the Queen Anne of Bohemia gave another to Constance. This expedition proved ultimately unsuccessful. The King of Castile yielding to the impetuosity of the invaders, abandoned the open country, and directed his chief attention to the preservation of the walled cities and fortresses, leaving the enemy exposed to all the inconveniences of protracted warfare in a foreign and hostile land. The result was fatal to the English army, which suffered so much from the heat of the climate and the scarcity and badness of provisions, as to render the prosecution of the undertaking hopeless. A negociation was opened between the contending powers, and the war was terminated by a treaty of marriage between Henry, son and

heir of the King of Castile, and Catharine, the only child
of the Duke of Lancaster by the daughter of Don Pedro of
Castile.   The treaty being concluded, in November, 1390,
the Duke of Lancaster returned to England, and attended
King Richard at Reading, where he held a council of state.
The same year John of Gaunt was created Duke of Aquitaine; and soon after he held a grand hunting party at
Leicester, where he entertained the royal family, with a
great number of the nobility of both sexes.   After these
amusements were over, the Duke appears to have passed
a short time at Tutbury Castle, then again become the
abode of his Castilian consort.   Her health had suffered
from fatigue and disappointment during the recent visit to
the land of her nativity; and her illness was aggravated by
the severity of her devotional exercises.   The scene which
presented itself at Tutbury was much too solemn to be
pleasing to the Duke, whose opinions as to religion were
tinctured by the doctrines of Wycliffe, of whom he had
been at one time the active partizan and protector, though
probably by no means aware of the tendency of the notions
propagated by that divine.   Little interested therefore, in
the pursuits of his consort, for whom he had never entertained a very tender affection, he soon afterwards took his
final leave of her.   She died within an interval of two
years, while he was absent in France: and it does not appear that he ever after visited the place of her long abode.

John of Gaunt was succeeded in the possession of his
Lancastrian estates, including the Castle and Honor of
Tutbury, by his son Henry, surnamed of Bolingbroke, who
on the deposition of Richard III. in 1390, was chosen
King of England, under the title of Henry IV.   Upon this
event Tutbury, with the other estates and feudal possessions of the new proprietor, became annexed to the
crown, as appertaining to the Duchy of Lancaster.   During
a few years in the reign of Edward IV. the Honor of Tutbury was held by the Duke of Clarence, the King's
brother, but the grant made to that prince was recalled in

1374; and it has ever since been vested in the crown, except during the interregnum.

After the termination of the long and sanguinary contest for the English sceptre, between the rival houses of York and Lancaster, Henry Tudor, called Henry VII. into whose hands it fell, had the good fortune to enjoy a comparatively peaceful reign. His leisure was devoted to the amusement of hunting; and the Castle of Tutbury was sometimes the resort of the King and his court, when he pursued this diversion in the adjacent forest of Needwood. The connexion by blood of Henry of Richmond with the House of Lancaster, must have endeared to him this seat of their former residence, whilst the woods and lands surrounding it presented him with ample facilities for indulgence in the pleasures of the chase. Hence he seldom visited his mother the Countess of Derby, who resided at Lathom House, in Lancashire, without enjoying on his way thither, a short respite from the cares of state at the seat of his forefathers. On one occasion a somewhat singular adventure occurred to him, which is thus related by Sir Oswald Mosley:—

"One day during the ardour of the chase, he was separated from all his companions, and having in vain sought to join them again through the thick masses of wood with which the forest abounded, he determined at length to extricate himself from his difficulties by proceeding to the nearest village, and inquiring his way from thence to Tutbury: it so happened, that for this purpose he stopped at the house of a poor man named Taylor, in the village of Barton-under-Needwood, whose wife had not long before presented him with three sons at a birth; the father volunteered his services to conduct the King, who did not disclose his rank, to the place of his inquiry, and whilst he was making himself ready for that purpose, the mother introduced her three little babes to the stranger at the cottage door: the King was much pleased with the adventure, and in reward for the poor man's services, undertook to pay for the education of the three children, if they should live long

enough to be put to school. Taylor expressed his grateful
thanks, and the King did not forget his promise. When
the three children attained man's estate, they had made
such good use of the learning thus afforded them, that they
all became doctors of divinity, and obtained good preferment. John Taylor, the eldest of them, became archdeacon
of Derby, rector of Sutton Coldfield, and clerk of the parliament that sat in the seventh year of the reign of Henry the
Eighth. He was made Master of the Rolls in 1528, and
died in 1534; but not before he had proved his gratitude to
the Almighty disposer of events for the singular mercies
extended to himself and his brothers, by erecting the present church of Barton near the site of the cottage where
they first saw the light."*

Since the time of Henry VII. Tutbury seems to have
occupied but little of the attention of the proprietors; and
in the reign of Henry VIII. partly in consequence of
alterations in the state of society, and partly from other
causes, the feudal rights and privileges of the lords of
Tutbury were sometimes but little respected by their
tenants and retainers. A system of license was introduced,
which was continued under succeeding reigns; and from a
survey of Tutbury in the reign of Philip and Mary, we find
that the keepers of the various wards and parks had been
for many years committing sad devastation of the property.
As wood at that time formed the only kind of fuel which
the inhabitants of this part of the kingdom could obtain,
the temptation to commit excesses of this nature were great,
and it is supposed that young timber-trees were often cut
down without restraint, to be used for fire-wood.

"A number of encroachments had from time to time
been made at the edge of the forest, upon which cottages
had been erected; and these were inhabited by a race of
men not very delicate in committing further trespasses:
they were in general indolent and poor in the extreme, and

---

*History of Tutbury, p. 133, 4.

as they depended entirely upon the produce of the forest for subsistence, they were often regardless of the manner in which they obtained it. Not only the timber, but the deer and game suffered much from their lawless plunder; and when the use of fire-arms had been introduced, these depredations were carried on with greater ease. In deer-stealing many of them were particularly expert; and every kind of stratagem was resorted to in evading the vigilance of the keepers. Under the pretence of driving his cow or swine home at the decline of day, the forest peasant would frequently watch the deer browsing in their accustomed haunts, and when a well-fed buck could be singled out with the least risk of detection, the loaded barrel was soon withdrawn from its concealment beneath his frock, and applied to the rude stock which had often served a similar purpose. In the event of a successful shot, the stricken deer was quickly despatched, and carefully deposited amongst the gorse or brambles near the spot where he had fallen; but during the night, or in any case before the middle of the following day, the prize was conveyed to the larder of some opulent neighbour, whose power could awe, or liberality avert, the dreaded vengeance of the keepers. Reward was the sure attendant of such a capture, and his innate propensity to plunder was willingly indulged, whenever any of his wealthy protectors required an addition to the luxury of his table. Besides, exploits like these were a theme of praise amongst the forest peasantry; that man who could perform them with the most cunning and dexterity, was looked upon in the adjacent villages as a sort of hero; the fear of disgrace, which is generally the most powerful preventive of crime, attached itself not to him. His equals gave him credit for sagacity and valour; his superiors protected him from future harm; and the daring acts of his life were not confined to the simple annals of his native village, for they often formed one of the most enlivening topics of conversation at the hospitable table of his patron. But these marauding expeditions were not unattended with danger; the pride of the keepers was occasionally offended at being so frequently foiled in detecting the stealers of their deer, and bloody encounters between these rival parties occasionally ensued; the offender was sometimes apprehended, fined, and imprisoned; nay, perhaps, even forfeited his life to his temerity.

"A fatal instance of this kind will appear in the following traditional account of the death of a deer-stealer, which was related to me [Sir Oswald Mosley] by one of his descendants about twenty-five years since; [1807] and the truth of his story is corroborated by the circumstance of two places at the time of the inclosure of the forest being distinguished by his name, which was in each instance coupled with an allusion to the particular occurrence that there took place.*   Upon the verge of the forest, near Tatenhill Gate, there stood within memory a small cottage, the owners of which had for several generations borne the name of Wilmore, and more recently Witmore.   The latter designation was that by which my informant was known; and he stated that one of his ancestors, to whom the same property formerly belonged, supported himself and his family for many years upon the fruits of the spoils which he obtained from the forest.   He had two small cows depastured there in the summer, for which he provided a little hay from the land around his cottage; his fuel he obtained from the neighbouring woods; and his food was in a great measure supplied by his successful attacks upon the deer and game with which they also abounded.   His strength and activity were more than a match for any single keeper; and his company so agreeable, that the under-keepers themselves found it irresistible, whenever they chanced to meet with him in an ale-house. Often would he engage them in drinking at such places, and when he saw a convenient opportunity, he would steal away from his unsuspecting companions, to kill a buck or doe in the

---

*"The spot where he engaged the keepers is called 'Wilmore Fought,' and the bog where he was lost was called 'Wilmore Drowning.'"

recesses of the forest. A screw-barrelled gun was always his companion upon these occasions, the greater part of which was concealed within the lining of his coat; a dog was also taken with him, the diminutive size of which was supposed to render it harmless, but this little creature had been so well trained by its master, that upon it in a great measure depended the success of his expedition. Thus attended, he used to ascend a tree on the border of one of the small plains with which the forest abounded; and by a well-known signal, his dog would ramble about until it met with a herd of deer; the instant it had attracted their attention, this cunning animal would run away, apparently in great alarm, and the finest bucks, together with a principal part of the herd, soon joined in the chase after so insignificant an intruder. When it had thus amused them for a short time, it would skulk off to the tree in which it knew its master to be fixed, and would take its stand just below it, whilst the deer stood at a short distance from it, gazing with unsuspecting curiosity. This was the moment that Wilmore seized upon to mark the fattest buck; his aim was certain, the devoted prize was soon secured; his faithful dog immediately ran home, and he then ascended the tree again, in which he staid till dusk, watching his prey; at night he would take it home, and conceal it in a part of his cottage which he had formed on purpose, and with such skill, that whenever his house was searched, this secret chamber was always overlooked. The next day a ready customer was sure to be found amongst the richer yeomen, with whom he was acquainted. He had carried on a lucrative trade of this kind for some years, when one evening, in the month of September, he was detected in the act of killing a deer, almost within view of Byrkley Lodge, where the woodmote courts were then held, and the chief forester occasionally resided; four under-keepers suddenly rushed upon him; he sprang from their grasp and dashed through Lint Brook, which was then swollen from the effects of a thunder-storm; but the treacherous bank on

the opposite side gave way beneath his weight; he fell,
and before he could recover himself two of his assailants
had reached the spot; one of them he laid senseless by a
blow from the stock of his gun; with the other he had a
long and severe struggle; but after receiving and returning
some dangerous blows, he succeeded in escaping up the
steep woody bank which rose to a considerable height
above the brook in this place, and directed his steps home-
wards as expeditiously as his wounds would permit him.
In the direction he went there was a deep bog, over which
he was obliged to pass, unless he had taken a more circui-
tous route, which might have exposed him to the other
keepers who were still in pursuit; and he therefore ventured
to cross over the quaking ground, an attempt he had often
succeeded in before. The windows of his cottage were full
in sight; his thoughts were already fixed upon his secret
chamber, as a proper place in which to conceal himself
from the vigilance of his pursuers; although bruised and
dispirited he was still anxiously anticipating an escape
from present danger, and greater success upon future occasions, when suddenly he missed his footing, fell headlong
into the liquid mass, and sank to rise no more."*

The survey above mentioned as having taken place in
the reign of Philip and Mary was followed by one pursuant
to a commission issued by Queen Elizabeth, in the first
year of her reign, in which it was intended that all the
castles, lordships, manors, and other territorial property
belonging to the Duchy of Lancaster should have been
included; but from some unknown cause the survey was
never completed. It affords, however, some interesting
information concerning Tutbury itself, at the time when it
was drawn up. It states that "The castle, sometime the
lord's habitation and capital mansion, is situated very
stately within a park, on the north side of the town of
Tutbury, upon the height of a round rock of alabaster, and

---

*History of Tutbury, p. 146, &c.

inclosed for the most part with a stone wall embattled, whereupon may be seen all the lordships and manors appertaining to the Honor in the counties of Stafford, Derby, and Leicester, very delightfully situated both for pleasure and profit; for as the river Dove from Uttoxeter to the river Trent divides the counties of Stafford and Derby, so did it also at the beginning divide Champain and Wood Land; that on the one side of the water, in the county of Derby, being all champain and very good and beneficial for meadows, pastures, and corn, extending from Tutbury to the Peak, in distance twenty miles; and all the Peak is high and moor lands, yet parcel of the said honor, good sheep pasture, and large wastes; and on the other side of the river, in the county of Stafford, for the most part it was all wood land, as appears probable from divers ancient grants, made from the Lords Ferrers, sometime Earls of Derby, in the reigns of Richard the First, King John, and the beginning of Henry the Third; but it is now by men's industry converted into tillage and pasture."*

The Castle though now deserted by its regal proprietors, and except in the case of James and Charles I. not honoured even by a transitory visit, was twice for a brief and melancholy period the residence of a crowned head, fallen indeed from her high estate to the miserable condition of a captive in the power of a jealous and perhaps justly-offended rival. Mary Queen of Scots, the victim of her own imprudence, was forced to flee from the land in which she had exercised sovereign power, and become a suppliant for protection from her rebellious subjects, in the dominions of the English Queen, Elizabeth. On the 17th of May, 1568, she took refuge in England, with a few attendants; and one of her first measures was to address a letter to Elizabeth, requesting an interview, apparently with a confident expectation of obtaining her friendship and support. But she was accused of heinous crimes by her own subjects, and

*History of Tutbury, p. 149, 150.

was the object of both political and personal jealousy in the opinion of Elizabeth. That princess and her ministers therefore soon after the arrival of Mary in England, appear to have decided on treating her as a dangerous prisoner of state. Thus woefully disappointed in her hopes of assistance, without friends or advisers who could yield her effectual service, the tedious remnant of her life and captivity was employed in brooding over misfortunes which she doubtless believed to be undeserved, and in contriving schemes to secure her escape and safety by the destruction of her too-powerful rival.

The Scottish Queen resided for a while at Bolton Castle, in Yorkshire, which belonged to Lord Scrope; and while there she entertained the addresses of Thomas Duke of Norfolk, who through ambitious motives secretly solicited her hand; but the intrigue having been discovered by Elizabeth, it cost that nobleman his life. In January, 1569, Mary was removed from Bolton to Tutbury Castle, where she was in the custody of George Earl of Shrewsbury. An account has been preserved of the preparations made at Tutbury for the reception of the Scottish Queen:

" 20th January, 11th of Queen Elizabeth, wardrobe stuff sent to Tutbury Castell, by Rafe Rowlandson, groom of the removeing warderobe of balls, for service of the Scottish queen.

" From the Tower. Six peeces of tapistry hangings, of the history of the passion, lyned with canvas. Six peeces of tapistry hangings, of the story of ladyes, lyned with canvas. Seven peeces of hangings of tapistry, of the story of Hercules, lyned. Fowre great carpets, of Turky making. Fowre beds and bolsters of tyke, filled with fethers. Fowre counterpoints of verdure, lyned with canvas. Fowre payre of fustians. Three chaires, of crimsin clothe of gold. Eight cushins of clothe of gold. Towe stooles, the seats embroiderid with clothe of gold upon crimsin sattin. Three foote stooles covered with tissue. Towe bare hydes of oxe leather, to cover carts. One standard.

" From the Removing Warderobe. Twelve small carpets of Turky making. One fynare stoole covered with tissue.

" From the great Warderobe. Towe payre of sheetes, of fyne Holland clothe. Towe payre of pillow beeges of assay, of lyke Holland. Eight payre of pallet sheetes, of coarse Holland. Towe cart canvasses of seven bredthes of canvas. Towe thousand hookes, one thousand crockets, towe hammers, one bolt of cords to trusse beds, towe clothe sacks, and one ease of leather for a bedstead."

The period of Mary's first residence at Tutbury Castle, was by no means the most unpleasant part of her captivity. She appears to have had no reason to find fault with the accommodations provided for her; and though she could not help perceiving that her motions were closely watched by those placed around her, yet she was treated by her host and hostess with the respect and deference due to her exalted rank, and indulged with amusements which tended to relieve the tedium of existence in the peculiar situation in which she was placed.

Few subjects have afforded more scope for discussion than the life and character of the Queen of Scots; and those who are interested about them may derive amusement if not conviction from the researches of Goodhall, Robertson, Tytler, Whitaker, and other writers. All that is intended here is to present the reader with a few notices of the history of this unfortunate princess while she resided at Tutbury. To the restless intrigues of her partizans Mary owed much of the rigour of her confinement. Towards the end of November she was conveyed under a strong escort to Coventry, where she was kept for two months under the superintendence of the Earls of Shrewsbury and Huntingdon, after which she was brought back to Tutbury Castle. During her stay at Coventry no person except such as were employed by her attendants was permitted to have access to her, nor was she ever suffered to appear abroad. On the 22nd of January, 1570, we find her again at Tutbury, for there is extant a letter of hers, dated from that place. Soon afterwards she was at Wingfield; and thence during the summer of 1570 she was removed to Chatsworth. Here the rigour of her imprisonment was somewhat relaxed. She was permitted to ride out in company with the Earl of Shrewsbury, over the adjoining moors, and upon the whole it may be concluded that her visits to that place were attended with more real enjoyment than any other part of her long captivity. For the next fourteen years she resided principally at Sheffield,

occasionally visiting Chatsworth and Buxton. In the
year 1584 Mary was again at Wingfield, under the charge
of Sir Ralph Sadler, who had succeeded Lord Shrewsbury
as keeper of the royal captive.

After the death of the Duke of Norfolk, the machina-
tions of Mary's partizans were suspended for several years,
or were conducted with such caution and secresy as hardly
to attract the notice of the English ministry. At length
that princess worn out with anxiety and suspense, and become careless of consequences, gave her sanction to fresh
projects and conspiracies, the discovery of which involved
herself and her friends in utter ruin. While thus the crisis
of her fate was approaching, she was not deprived of
the indulgences to which she had been accustomed, and
though a captive was yet suffered to retain much of the
stately pomp of royalty. We learn from the papers of Sir
Ralph Sadler, that at this period her domestic establishment consisted of forty-seven persons : namely, five gentlemen, fourteen servitors, three cooks, four boys, three attend
ants of her gentlemen, six gentlewomen, two wives, ten
wenches and children. She had four coach-horses of her
own, and six horses for her attendants. There were at
Wingfield about two hundred and ten persons employed in
guarding her; but on her removal to Tutbury, the number
was reduced to one hundred and fifty. Her ordinary diet
consisted of sixteen dishes, at both courses. Her two
secretaries, the master of her household, her physician, and
Monsieur de Prean, had a mess of seven or eight dishes ;
and they always dined before the Queen. Her. female
attendants also had two messes of meat, each day, of nine
dishes at both courses, for those of high degree; and five
dishes for the others. There were about ten tons of wine
consumed in the year, besides what was used for the
Queen's bath, for bathing in wine was by no means an unusual luxury in those days.

Soon after her arrival at Tutbury, the Scottish Queen
transmitted to Elizabeth a most dismal account of the fur-

niture of the castle: she accused those who had the ordering of it of a base intent to annoy her, by rendering her
habitation uncomfortable; and she sent a long list of articles
requisite for her accommodation. Her complaint met with
attention; new furniture was procured; and the Queen
wrote a letter to Sir Ralph Sadler, which conveyed some
gentle reproaches for having entrusted the fitting up of the
castle to negligent persons, and at the same time communicated the welcome intelligence that his repeated solicita-
tions to be relieved from the burthensome charge confided
to him would be no longer disregarded.

While Queen Elizabeth appears to have been anxious
that her unhappy prisoner should be provided with all the
conveniencies and even luxuries due to her former rank
and station, the utmost jealousy was still manifested with
respect to her amusements, lest they should afford her
opportunities for the prosecution of new schemes for the
recovery of her liberty. Hence it was, that during this last
residence at Tutbury, Sir Ralph incurred the displeasure of
his sovereign by permitting the Scottish Queen to ride out
with five or six attendants, in the vicinity of the Castle,
that she might join in the amusement of hawking. This
levity procured for the old knight a sharp reprimand from
the Secretary of State, Sir Francis Walsingham. In his
reply, Sadler stated that he had sent for his hawks and fal-
coners for the purpose of amusing himself during the irk-
some period he was destined to remain at Tutbury, and
that the captive Queen had so earnestly intreated permission
to accompany him that he could not deny her, adding,
however, that on all such occasions he had been attended
by forty or fifty of his servants, retainers, and others, on
horseback, many of whom were armed with pistols.* In

*In a letter subsequently addressed to the treasurer, Lord Burleigh, he refers
again to the subject:—

"I am sorry her Majestye mislyketh of the lybertye permytted to this queen
of late in hawking upon the ryver not far from the castell, wherein I have
much exceeded my commission, having always ben well assured to answer the

April, 1585, Sir Ralph Sadler resigned his charge to Sir Amias Poulet and Sir Drewe Drury, under whose *surveillance* the Queen of Scots remained till death terminated her protracted misery. It was on the 21st of December that she took a final leave of Tutbury, whence she was removed to Chartley, a house belonging to the Earl of Essex.* During her residence there was concocted the conspiracy of Anthony Babington and others, her concurrence with which furnished abundant grounds for the trial to which she was shortly after exposed. The concluding scenes of the life of this princess, in which she appeared

---

charge comytted unto me, as indede, I see no maner cause of feare of her fourthcomying, so long as this countrey remayneth in so good quyetness, as it is now. And now for the tyme of my contynuance here, which I hope shall be very shorte, I will do what I can to kepe her more pryvately from intelligences, which I assure your Lordship is very harde to do, having so many about her as she hathe, both English, French, and Scottishe, as well men as women, which have so many errants and occasions to go aboute their necessary busynes, that all the souldiours here ar to few to attende upon them, which nevertheles shal be loked unto as well as Mr. Somer and I can desire, whereof both he and I have ben, and will be, most carefull according to my dueties."

*Mr. Edwards, in his " Tour of the Dove," alludes thus beautifully to Mary's residence at Tutbury :—

> " The palace prison once of Scotland's queen!—
> Ah, hapless Mary, hurried to the tomb
> By bloody hands, the tools of jealous spleen!
> Henceforth, whoever treads the shadowy gloom
> Of yon proud ruins, will bewail thy doom
> And long captivity:—Thou wast a gem
> Of royalty, in beauty's roseate bloom :
> Thy nobles would have kissed thy garments' hem;—
> Yet thou upon the block didst bow thy diadem!

> " The pilgrim's motto, "Earth is not our home,"
> On yonder walls is doubly written : Time
> In broken lines, and History from her tome
> Have scribed it. Like the exile's speech sublime
> Who sate on ruined Carthage, their deep chime
> Of meaning awes me.—Oh, within these walls,
> Roofless, defaced, and sullied now with slime,
> Is there no ghost doth rise to tell the thralls
> Of her that sate enthroned in Edin's regal halls ?"

perhaps to greater advantage than at any other period, took place at Fotheringhay Castle, in Northamptonshire, where she was beheaded, in February, 1587.

From this time to the reign of Charles I. there is little of importance to be recorded concerning Tutbury, if we except an occasional visit of James I. who came hither to enjoy the diversion of hunting in the adjoining forest of Needwood.

In 1634 Charles I. is said to have passed a fortnight at his Castle of Tutbury; and he made another visit to this place in the month of August, 1636. In the civil war which broke out a few years after, a royal garrison was stationed at this Castle, under the government of Lord Loughborough. The fortress was repeatedly assaulted or threatened by the parliamentarians, but its defenders successfully resisted their opponents till the declining state of the King's affairs rendered all further attempts to support his cause unavailing. One of the most active adherents of the parliament among the gentry of Staffordshire and Derbyshire was Sir John Gell, who, after the garrison of Tutbury had remained for some time unmolested, determined to station a party of his own men in the neighbourhood to watch the proceedings of the royalists. The further measures he adopted, and the contests that subsequently took place in this part of the country, have been already briefly noticed in former chapters of this work.

After Sir John Gell had placed a garrison at Barton Blount, many skirmishes took place from time to time between the soldiers of this fortress and the King's troops at Tutbury. The supplies of the garrison within the Castle were frequently intercepted, and more peremptory orders were issued by the officers in command there to the constables of the adjoining townships, who not unfrequently excused the disobedience of their orders, through the danger to which they were exposed. The following is a specimen of the warrants issued upon these occasions :—

" To the Constable or Headborough of Marchington cum membris.—These
are in his Majestie's name to charge and command you, immediately upon
sight hereof, to bring to Tedbury castle to me foure sufficient able horses, or
twenty pounds in money, to provide the same towards the recruitinge of my
troope.   And if any of your parishioners refuse to contribute to the same, you
are hereby required to bringe them to me, to answer their neglect.   Fayle not,
as you will answer the contrary att your utmost perills.   Given under my hand
the 6th of March, 1645."   "GILBERT GERARD."*

On the 24th of May, 1645, the King himself, at the
head of a large army, accompanied by Prince Rupert, came
to Tutbury.   Sir Andrew Kniveton, the Governor of the
Castle, afforded his majesty the best accommodation that
circumstances would permit; but the town being too small
for quartering any other than his body guard, the main
army proceeded to Burton.

The last visit of the unfortunate Charles to his garrison
of Tutbury, was on the 12th of August, 1645, when on
his way from Lichfield, and the following day he proceeded
to Ashbourn.   The defeat of the royalists at Naseby, which
occurred in the month of June preceding, was the prelude
to the ruin of the King's interest.   Protracted resistance
became useless, and Sir Andrew Kniveton, after having
witnessed the fall of the neighbouring fortresses of his
party, surrendered the Castle of Tutbury on honourable
terms, April 20th 1646, to the parliamentary general, Sir
William Brereton.   In the articles of surrender it was
agreed that the fortifications of the Castle should be
destroyed.

" The neighbouring peasants were engaged in crowds to
level this majestic pile.   Some, indeed, had so great a
reluctance to the task, that they rather submitted to be
fined, than to yield obedience to the hateful summons;
others, however, were found less scrupulous, and came fully
armed with pick-axes, mattocks, and bars of iron, to carry
on this work of spoliation; perhaps a few might even be
found, who, smarting under the recollection of recent

*History of Tutbury, p. 256, &c.

exactions, secretly rejoiced at the prospect of thus exone-
rating themselves and their posterity from similar demands.
The buildings within the area of the castle walls were
principally composed of wood-work, framed together and
filled up with plaster panels; these, since they could be
thrown down with the least difficulty, were the first to
suffer from this ruthless attack: the apartments formerly
occupied by Mr. Dorell, the Scotch and French Secretaries,
and the Queen of Scots herself, were speedily levelled to
the ground, and exhibited one indiscriminate heap of rubbish; but when these rude assailants attempted to disturb
the massive stones of the presence-chamber, high tower,
and other buildings situated near the walls, the compact-
ness of the masonry resisted their efforts to such an extent,
that they were glad to abandon their unprofitable employment, and fortunately for the gratification of the admirer of
picturesque beauty, left the present relics of their former
grandeur. Part of these ruins, about the middle of the last
century, were injudiciously converted into a farm-house.
Within the walls is an area of about three acres, on the
western side of which is an elevated mound, on which the
Juliet, or Julius' Tower, as Sir Ralph Sadler calls it, formerly stood, the site of which is now occupied by an
artificial ruin; on the lower and more level part of this
space is the castle well, forty-three yards deep, and bearing
marks of great antiquity. The remains of a broad and deep
foss still surround three sides of the castle, over which (at
the gateway I should imagine), Dr. Plott states, there had
been 'a large bridge standing within memory, that was
made of pieces of timber, none of them much above a yard
in length, and yet not supported underneath either by
pillars or arches, or any other prop whatever.'"*

Henry de Ferrers, ancestor of the Earls of Derby, about
the year 1080 founded a priory here for monks of the
order of St. Benedict. This religious house was amply

*History of Tutbury, p. 233, 235.

47

endowed by its founder, his wife Bertha, and his successors, and by the grants from time to time of various other individuals, all of which are recorded in the registers and foundation charters. At the Dissolution, the value of its revenues was estimated at £242 15s. 3d. Queen Elizabeth granted the site of the priory to Edward Earl of Lincoln, and William Raven, of Horsepool Grange in the county of Leicester, who sold it to Thomas Crompton and Edward Clement, from whom it passed to Sir William Cavendish, the direct ancestor of the Duke of Devonshire.

The only portion of the priory now existing is the church, a large edifice with a square embattled tower, (situated within three hundred yards south-east of the Castle,) on the north side of which, adjoining, stood the cloisters, dormitory, and other monastic offices, covering a site more than three acres in extent. The church exhibits some fine specimens of Norman architecture, the most remarkable of which is the grand western door-way. The southern aisle is of later date, the windows being in the pointed style, and the walls of less massive construction. Henry de Ferrers, the founder of the priory, who died about the year 1089, was buried in this church.

The great tithes of the parish passed a few years ago from the Cavendish family to John Spencer, Esq. of Rolleston Park, who devised them to Robert Stone, Esq. of Needwood-House. The advowson of the church was given by the Duke of Devonshire in exchange for the patronage of the new church at Buxton, to the vicar of Bakewell, who has the right of presentation. The present annual value of the vicarage is about £200.

There is here a free-school, founded in 1730, by Richard Wakefield, now educating about fifty scholars; and a large Sunday-School attached to the Establishment. The Independents, Wesleyans, and Primitive Methodists, have ther respective chapels in the town.

The ancient trade of the town, that of wool-stapling, is extinct; but there are on the Dove, a corn-mill, a cotton-

factory, and an establishment for cutting and working
glass. Three fairs for horned cattle are held annually, on
Feb. 14th, Aug. 15th, and Dec. 1st.; a statute-fair for
hiring servants on the second Monday after Michaelmas.
A weekly market, formerly held on Tuesday, has long been
discontinued.

At the census of 1831 the number of inhabitants in the
parish was 1,553, and the annual value of the real property
is assessed at £5,472.

The manorial rights and a fine estate of 2,000 acres, are
still vested in the crown, whose lessees are, Lord Vernon,
(of the Castle); John Spencer Stone, Esq. (of the demesne,
with Stockley Park); and Earl Dartmouth, (of the Castle-
Hay Park.

The Duke of Devonshire was appointed Steward of the
Honor of Tutbury by letters patent under the Duchy Seal,
in 1812. He appointed John Philip Dyott, Esq. to the
office of Steward of the Honor, who presides over the
Court of Record which is held at Tutbury every third
Tuesday throughout the year. All persons residing within
the Honor have a right to sue at this Court for the
recovery of debts and damages under forty shillings.
Robert Hinckley, Esq. of Lichfield, is Steward of the manor,
and holds a Court Leet for the Crown, annually.

The offices of Escheator and Coroner throughout the
Honor are still claimed by the singular tenure of a hunting-
horn, which is now (or was lately) in possession of the
Rev. Francis Foxlowe, of Staveley, whose father purchased
this horn and the grant attached thereto, from Charles
Stanhope, Esq., and the Coroners of the High Peak have
been ever since appointed by them.*

Among the *memorabilia* of Tutbury some notice may be
expected of the imposture of Anne Moore, called the

---

*The reader who wishes to derive further information respecting the feudal
government of the ancient lords of Tutbury, and the duties of the various
officers of the Honor, many of whose appointments have been long obsolete,
may consult Sir Oswald Mosley's History, the Appendix to which contains a
number of documents, amply sufficient to gratify his curiosity.

"Fasting Woman of Tutbury." In 1807, this female, whose appetite had been for some years declining in consequence of ill health, had the hardihood to assert that she was able to live without any sort of nourishment. Her motive doubtless was the hope of attracting the charitable compassion of the public, as a source of pecuniary emolument, and as a blind to her deceitful purpose, she made a great profession of religion. To put her veracity to the test, a surgeon, of Lane-End, subjected her to a strict watch for sixteen days; at the termination of which the medical men who watched her, and many inhabitants of the town firmly believed that she had not tasted solid food during the whole of that time, nor liquid of any kind for thirteen days. The story soon spread, and the Fasting Woman of Tutbury became an object of notoriety. She had crowds of visitors, whose liberality rendered the imposture sufficiently profitable to induce her to persevere; and for six years no further attempts were made to detect the fraud. But she overrated her powers of abstinence; and rashly agreed to submit to a second trial, for a period of four weeks. The watch commenced on the 21st April, 1813, and was conducted with such strictness that she found it impossible to elude the vigilance of the watchers. The signs of exhaustion became manifest, her countenance gradually grew paler and more sickly, her flesh wasted, and she appeared to be labouring under the usual symptoms of catarrhal fever, which increased to such an alarming degree, that her life was endangered, and on the 30th of April it was deemed advisable to discontinue the watch.* Her imposition was now soon brought to a close, though she still for some time persisted in her former statement. At length she signed a declaration before a magistrate of the county, acknowledging her guilt and falsehood; and shortly

---

*See "A Statement of Facts relative to the supposed Abstinence of Ann Moore, of Tutbury, Staffordshire," by the Rev. Legh Richmond; and an "Examination of the Imposture of Ann Moore, &c." by Alexander Henderson, M.D. 1813.

afterwards quitted the town amidst the jeers and execrations of the populace.

The river Dove, winding round the base of the hill on whose summit stand the proud ruins of Tutbury, passing, in her course over a wide and fertile plain, the village of Marston* on the one hand, and the demesne of Rolleston† on the other, unites her waters with the Trent at Newton Solney.

---

*Marston-on-Dove, in the hundred of Appletree and deanery of Castillar, about eight miles and a half from Derby. The parish comprises the townships of Marston, Hatton, Hilton, and Hoon.

The manor of Marston-on-Dove, which had been given to the priory of Tutbury by its founder, Henry de Ferrers, was granted, after the Reformation, to the Cavendish family, and is now the property of his Grace the Duke of Devonshire. In the parish church are some memorials of the family of Wolley.

The manor of Hatton is held on lease by Lord Vernon, whose ancestor, Henry Vernon, Esq. was lessee in 1660.

In 1712 the manor of Hilton belonged to the Earl of Chesterfield, and is now the property of William Eaton Mousley, Esq. There was formerly a chapel of ease at Hilton.

The manor of Hoon was held at the time of the Domesday Survey by Siwallis, ancestor of the Shirley family, who continued to possess it in the reign of Henry VIII. In the 17th century it was purchased by John Pye, Esq. (younger son of Sir Robert Pye, of Farringdon, Berks.) He settled at Hoon, and was created a baronet in 1664. His son Sir Charles Pye, was a great traveller. The two sons of Sir Charles, Richard and Robert, successively enjoyed the title and estate. The title became extinct on the death of Sir Robert, the younger, who was in holy orders, in 1734. The manor afterwards passed by inheritance to a family of the name of Watkins, and was purchased from them by Mr. W. J. Lockett, who sold it in severalties.—*Lysons, &c.*

†The seat of Sir Oswald Mosley, Bart., three miles and a half north-west of Burton-on-Trent, in the county of Stafford. The manor was anciently held by a family of its own name, from whom it passed to the knightly house of Mosley. On the failure of male issue of Sir Edward Mosley, Bart. who married Catharine, daughter of William Lord Grey, of Wark, the baronetcy became extinct; and his widow marrying Charles, son of Dudley Lord North, he became possessed of this manor, and in the 25th Charles II. was summoned to Parliament by the title of Lord North and Grey, of Rolleston. Oswald Mosley, Esq. a descendant of a second branch of the family, afterwards became possessed of Rolleston, and was created a baronet in the 6th of George I. The title and estates descended to Sir Oswald, the present baronet, who is also lord of the manor of Manchester. The Rev. J. P. Mosley is rector of the living, which is worth about £300 per annum, and is in the patronage of the family.—*White's Staffordshire, &c.*

ADDITIONS.

Page 27. John Hieron made some collections for a Parochial History of Derbyshire, which are now in the possession of Godfrey Meynell, Esq. of Langley.

Page 38. The present Sir William Boothby, Bart. married in 1805, Fanny only daughter of John Jenkinson, Esq. of Winchester, brother of Charles first Earl of Liverpool. She died on the 2nd of January, 1838.

Page 57. The Deanery of Ashbourn, one of the six ecclesiastical divisions of the county of Derby, includes Ashbourn, Edlaston, Norbury, Bradley, Mappleton, Thorpe, Fenny Bentley, Parwich, Kniveton, Hognaston, Tissington, Bradbourn, Kirk Ireton, Carsington, Wirksworth, Cromford, Matlock, Bonsall, Hartington, and their dependent chapelries.

Chap. VII. Beilby Porteus, afterwards Bishop of London, married (13th May, 1765) Margaret, eldest daughter of Brian Hodgson, Esq. of Ashbourn.

Chap. VII. Thomas Blore, Esq. a native of Ashbourn, made considerable collections for a topographical History of Derbyshire. In 1793, he published a History of the Manor and Manor House of South Wingfield, as a specimen of his intended work. He was also the author of several other topographical fragments.

Page 104. The church registers of Longford parish are preserved from the year 1538. Some of the entries are curious:

1599. "Elizabeth Stanford daughter of Robert registered 18th of April; she was [brought] to the Church of Langford, by

Ellen Baker daughter of Nicholas, & Elizabeth & Henry Lead-
beater, who gate down upon their knees at the churchdoor of
Langford, & begged Christendom for Jesus sake to that infant."
In August 1745, are registered the burials of several soldiers
slain in the civil wars; also of John Malley, who " had his house
broken in sundry places by souldiers, the first of November in
the night, and because they could not get in, and he would not
yield they fired at him with a slugge into the head. He died
and was buried the 2nd day of November, 1645."

Page 106. The Rev. A. Norman, curate of Brailsford, was
the author of a work on the Christian Evidences, entitled ' Literæ
Sacræ', and another ' On the Necessity of a Revelation,' both of
which display much critical acuteness and power of argument.

Page 108. At the Domesday survey, the manor of Yeldersley, (Geldeslei) was held under Henry de Ferrers, by Cole,
whose son Robert conveyed it to Sewal de Monjoy. This family
possessed it for several generations, and from them (temp. Ed.
III.) it passed to the Irelands, who held it in the reign of Henry
VII. The Montgomerys soon afterwards possessed the manor,
from whom it passed to the Vernons, and then to the Meynells.
The Shirleys at a remote period held this as a mesne manor,
under its early lords.—Lysons.

Page 110. The supposition that the Meynells of Bradley are
descended from the family of the same name seated at North
Kilvington, Yorkshire, is incorrect. Authentic documents prove
them to be of Derbyshire from the time of Henry I.; and this
proof is confirmed by the difference in the heraldic bearings of
the two families.

Page 114. The living of Kniveton is a perpetual curacy.

Page 198. Charles Haughton Okeover, Esq. is present owner
of the Okeover estates. His mother, (the lady of Robert Plumer
Ward, Esq.) is daughter of General Sir George Anson, G.C.B.
M.P. for Lichfield, and brother to the late Viscount Anson.

INDEX.

48

ERRATA.

Page 38, line 9, for D.D. *read* LL.D.

   43, — 22, *for* now Lord St. Helens, *read* the late Lord St. Helens.

   60, — 7, *for* though, *read* thou.

   87, — 28, *for* Cheeshunt, *read* Cheshunt.

 102, — 6, (Longford) *for* fourth, *read* elder,

 107, — 19, *for* sepulchural, *read* sepulchral.

 114, — 2, (Atlow) *for* vicarage, *read* perpetual curacy.

 124, — 34, *for* the celebrated Charles Cotton, *read* Charles Cotton the elder.

 161, — 19, *for* from, *read* form.

 168, — 36, (note) *for* south, *read* north.

 224, — 2, for *(" Honorum suum re-emerret"),* read *("Honorem suum re-emeret.")*

 292, — 23, *(in part of the impression only) for* relgion *read* religion.

In the lettering of the plate facing page 229, *(part of the impression only) for* Norbury Church, Staffordshire, *read* Norbury Church, Derbyshire.